Centennial College
P.O. Box 631, Station A,
Scarborough, Ont.
M1K 5E9

CONTEMPORARY ISSUES IN CRIME AND JUSTICE SERIES

The Invisible Woman

Gender, Crime, and Justice

15G 914289

JOANNE BELKNAP
University of Cincinnati

WITHDRAWN

Wadsworth Publishing Company
I(T)P™ An International Thomson Publishing Company

Belmont • Albany • Bonn • Boston • Cincinnati • Detroit • London • Madrid
Melbourne • Mexico City • New York • Paris • San Francisco • Singapore
Tokyo • Toronto • Washington

Philosophy Editor: Sabra Horne
Assistant Editor: Claire Masson
Editorial Assistant: Louise Mendelson
Production Editor: Julie Davis
Managing Designer: Stephen Rapley
Print Buyer: Karen Hunt
Permissions Editor: Jeanne Bosschart
Copy Editor: Melissa Andrews
Compositor: Margarite Reynolds
Cover Design: Sandra Kelch/Third Space Design
Printer: Malloy Lithographing, Inc.

Printed in the United States of America
1 2 3 4 5 6 7 8 9 10—01 00 99 98 97 96

For more information, contact Wadsworth Publishing Company.

Wadsworth Publishing Company
10 Davis Drive
Belmont, California 94002
USA

International Thomson Editores
Campos Eliseos 385, Piso 7
Col. Polanco
11560 México D.F. México

International Thomson Publishing Europe
Berkshire House 168-173
High Holborn
London, WC1V 7AA
England

International Thomson Publishing GmbH
Königswinterer Strasse 418
53227 Bonn
Germany

Thomas Nelson Australia
102 Dodds Street
South Melbourne 3205
Victoria, Australia

International Thomson Publishing Asia
221 Henderson Road
#05-10 Henderson Building
Singapore 0315

Nelson Canada
1120 Birchmount Road
Scarborough, Ontario
Canada M1K 5G4

International Thomson Publishing Japan
Hirakawacho Kyowa Building, 3F
2-2-1 Hirakawacho
Chiyoda-ku, Tokyo 102, Japan

Library of Congress Cataloging-in-Publication Data

Belknap, Joanne.
    The invisible woman : gender, crime, and justice / Joanne Belknap.
        p.   cm.
    Includes bibliographical references and index.
    ISBN 0-534-15870-6
    1. Sex discrimination in criminal justice administration—United States.   2. Female offenders—United States.   3. Women—Crimes against—United States.   4. Policewomen—United States.
I. Title.
HV9950.B45 1995
364.973'082—dc20

95-8840

✠

This book is dedicated with the deepest admiration to

Jacqueline Gibson-Navin
The Light Center
Columbus, Ohio

for her work to help women in prison, women
coming out of prison, and girls society has forgotten
who are heading to prison.

Contents

II FEMALE OFFENDING

Preface

I was about nine years old when my mother brought my brothers, my sister, and me to a large toy store to buy one of my older brothers "The Visible Man" for his birthday. For weeks, he had been looking forward to owning the model, which was a clear plastic statue that stood about a foot high, came apart, and had removable internal organs as well as a skeleton. All of us were fascinated with this concept, but then a funny thing happened when we got to the store. "The Visible Woman" seemed infinitely more interesting than "The Visible Man." Not only did she seem more dimensional, but she had two different stomachs: a nonpregnant stomach and a pregnant stomach. There were more parts to play with, and there was also a little fetus that could be put inside of her large, round tummy. Apparently my brother also decided she was more interesting because he picked her instead of "The Visible Man." I certainly found her more fascinating than my stick-thin Barbie doll with conical breasts, whom I could never imagine looking like. "The Visible Woman" looked human, strong, *and* female.

When I decided to write a book on women and crime, I was struck by the recurring theme of women's and girls' everyday invisibility in society, in crime, and in the crime-processing system. If women are represented, it is often in stereotypical, passive, or sexual images. I remembered the model my brother had gotten for his birthday, and how the "visible" woman seemed strong, fascinating, and real. The title of this book reflects the focus on women's invisibility while the contents attempt to make them visible with descriptions of the lives, experiences, and strengths of real women.

I think of the many women I have met in prison who are forgotten in society and in the crime-processing system; sadly, these women often are forgotten by their young children as well. When I visit or interview women in prison, I am often struck with how normal these women seem, not scary and repulsive as represented in the media (if they are represented at all). These women face deplorable conditions and desperate situations. Who will look after their children? Can they get counseling to deal with the incest and battering in their pasts? Can they get decent dental care? Can they get mammograms for breast lumps? Are their lawyers really working on their appeals? Can they get tampons or sanitary pads when they are menstruating? The strength of many of these women under these conditions is humbling. As this book describes, women make up such a small proportion of prisoners that they are often invisible and their needs are ignored.

I think of the women police officers and jail and prison guards I have interviewed and met, who have reported intensely hostile working environments, created by some of their male coworkers and supervisors. Often, even in those cases where they felt sufficiently empowered to formally report their experiences to officials within the organization, nothing was done to the offending men. One ex-policewoman who spoke to one of my classes reported some of the worst sexual harassment experiences I had ever heard. She had considerable documentation of the numerous ways and times her male coworkers and supervisor had violated the sexual harassment laws, including displays of pornographic pictures with her face pasted on them and taped obscene phone calls to her home. Unfortunately, this woman was further victimized when she brought these offenders to court on sexual harassment charges. The male judge agreed with the defense attorney that the case should be a mistrial, since this 39-year-old woman also reported having been raped when she was 16. Apparently, she had already been allotted her one "credible" rape.

This book documents not only the high rates of sexual abuse of girls and women, but also the increased likelihood of women survivors of child sexual abuse being sexually victimized again as adults. This book also traces the unfair treatment that sexual abuse victims often experience in the crime-processing system. The original and revictimization rates of females have long been ignored or misunderstood; thus it is hardly surprising that official responses to these victims is often lacking at best and damaging at worst.

Regarding the invisibility of women victims, I think about my classes where women have regularly written in their journals about incest, stranger and date rapes, sexual harassment at jobs they needed to keep, and the battering and stalking by boyfriends, ex-boyfriends, husbands, and ex-husbands. These women, understandably, rarely feel comfortable discussing these victimizations in classes, yet often do.

When women are made visible, it is often in stereotypical and offensive ways. For instance, one of my students, whose batterer (her second husband) shot and killed her first husband (who had come to help her) in front of her children, was asked about her sexual history when her batterer went to trial for the murder. Not only is the rate of women battering unrecognized in society, but also the many useless responses to women's cases such as in my students case, is unknown. This book describes the high rates of woman battering, as well as a crime-processing system that has been reluctant to take action against batterers. Moreover, it presents the risks of battered women being murdered by their batterers, or killing their batterers in self defense and subsequently spending many years or life in prison, invisible to society at large.

Like my brother's toy model, women in society and the crime-processing system are often invisible, but they are also often strong and capable. The chapters ahead focus on the theme of women's invisibility, and the book concludes on a note of hope and optimism regarding changes that have advanced the visibility and status of women and girls in the crime-processing system.

ACKNOWLEDGMENTS

Many individuals and organizations have supported me and made the writing of this book possible. First, I would like to thank Roy Roberg. Not only did he encourage me to do this project just a few months after I received my Ph.D., but also he was extremely patient for this end result, which took far longer than I had ever imagined. I would like to thank many people who read various drafts of chapters and gave me feedback: Francis Cullen, Edna Erez, Donna Hale, Violet Hall, Christina Johns, Susan Miller, Lorry Swain, and Patricia Van Voorhis. Thanks also to Charles W. Dean, University of North Carolina at Charlotte; M. George Eichenberg, Sam Houston State University; Helen Eigenberg, Old Dominion University; Penelope J. Hanke, Auburn University; Barbara L. Hart, University of Texas at Tyler; Jacquelyn McClure, San Jose Sate University; Risalyn Muraskin, University of Cincinnati; Joycelyn Pollock, Southwest Texas State University; and Jill Rosenbaum, California State University at Fullerton. Clearly, however, any shortcomings are specifically my responsibility. I thank Kelly Brown, my graduate assistant in 1993–1994, for her diligent and expedient work tracking down sources, and the Interlibrary Loan Department personnel in the University of Cincinnati Langsam Library for the lengthy list of sources they acquired for me in a timely manner.

I am also grateful to the University of Cincinnati Friends of Women's Studies for partially funding the research for this book. Likewise, I thank the University of Cincinnati Chapter of the American Association of University Professors for working to keep our sabbaticals; it is difficult to imagine that I could have finished this book without a sabbatical. Thanks also goes to the Future Environments Day Care, particularly Lynn, Kristen, and Nicole, for allowing me the security of knowing my baby was in capable and caring hands.

Finally, I would like to thank my family and friends for sharing in my frustration and excitement over writing this book, as well as for shaping some of my views and thoughts over the years: Joanne, Pat, Lynette, Beverly, Brian, Steve, Patte, Sully, and Mike (not in any particular order). I thank my parents, Barbara and Jon Belknap, for always asking how the book was going. I am most grateful to R. S. Summers for providing unyielding support, encouragement, and faith that I would finish this project, as well as for helping me with my other project: Cast Belknap-Summers. It has been ironic and wonderful that these two dreams and labors, for a book and a baby, have come to fruition simultaneously.

PART I

Introduction

1

Emergence of Gender in Criminology

This book presents the current state of women and girls in *criminology* (the study of crime) and *criminal justice* (the processing of victims and offenders). Whereas criminology is concerned with developing theories on what causes crime, criminal justice focuses on workers in the criminal justice system and how decisions are made about victims and offenders. To understand the current state of women and girls and how gender relates to crime and criminal justice, it is first necessary to comprehend the historical evolution of the status of women and girls in the home, society, and the workplace. Therefore, this book includes relevant historical factors that have affected the status of women and girls in crime today. Finally, this book examines successes in effecting change for women and girls as victims, offenders, and professionals in the criminal justice system.

The term *criminal justice* is most often used to describe the practices of workers in the system (such as police, judges, and prison staff), as well as the processing and treatment of crime victims and offenders. This book will replace the term *criminal justice* with the term *crime processing,* given that there is little evidence that the criminal "justice" system is just or fair in its treatment of female victims, offenders, and workers. In fact, the lack of justice for women and girls is the focus of this book.

The purpose of this chapter is to expose readers to an overall view of the important concepts behind women and crime. These include a presentation of females' invisibility in criminology and crime-processing studies, relevant concepts and definitions, and an understanding of how the images of women and

girls in society have affected their experiences as victims, offenders, and professionals in society and in the crime-processing system.

INVISIBILITY OF
WOMEN AND GIRLS IN CRIME

The major areas covered in this book are (1) women and girls as offenders, (2)
women and girls as victims, and (3) women professionals working in the
crime-processing system. As stated previously, a common characteristic of
women and girls in these areas is their *invisibility*. This section briefly explains
how females' experiences have been denied or ignored. Moreover, this section
discusses how women and girls do not always fit neatly into the categories of
offenders, victims, and professionals in the crime-processing system. Rather,
there is a great deal of overlap. Given the prevalence of violence against women
and girls in society, it is not surprising that many women professionals and offenders are survivors of male violence.

Any discussion on the invisibility of women and girls in the study of crime
must address the current resistance to this topic in academic research as well as
in the classroom. It is apparent that research often neglects to include females.
In conducting the research for this book, the author found it frustrating to
search through mainstream journals (and some books) to find out if women
and/or girls were included in the research questions or samples. For example,
studies with male-only samples rarely identified this in the title, while studies
with female-only or female and male samples almost consistently reflected this
in their titles. If women were excluded from the study, then most authors perceived no need to include "male" in the title. Moreover, a recent feminist analysis of education in "criminal justice" departments noted that although feminism has had clear effects on the curriculum, pedagogy, and campus climate,
"it has not been enough to transform criminology/criminal justice education
so that gender is a central organizing theme. Feminist criminology/criminal
justice education seems to remain at the margins of the 'male-stream' [a reflection that 'mainstream' is really about males]" (Renzetti 1993, 219).

Women and Girls as Offenders

Most criminology theories are concerned with the etiology of crime and thus
focus on factors related to offending, primarily male juvenile offending. Until
the late 1970s, it was highly unusual for these studies to include girls (or
women) in their samples. Although gender is the strongest factor indicating a
person's likelihood to break the law, these (almost exclusively male) researchers
rarely thought it was necessary to include females in their samples. The irony is
that "sex, the most powerful variable regarding crime has been virtually ignored" (Leonard 1982, xi). Leonard goes on to say that criminology theories
were constructed "by men, about men," and explain male behavior rather than
human behavior. Furthermore, "[e]xploring why women commit fewer crimes

than men (if indeed they do) could arguably provide clues for dealing with men's criminality" (Morris 1987, 2).

When the researchers did include females in their samples, it was typically to see how girls fit into boys' equations. That is, rather than include in the study a means of assessing how girls' lives might be different from boys' lives, female delinquency has typically been viewed as peripheral and unnecessary to understanding juvenile offending and processing. Thus, these theories failed to address gender differences in criminal behavior (Leonard 1982; Morris 1987). While social class, access to opportunities to learn crime, and area of residence in a city have been used to explain in boys' likelihood of turning to crime, the causes of female criminality have rarely been addressed. Additionally, criminological theory has historically tended to view women as "driven" to crime because of biological influences, whereas men turn to crime because of economic or sociological forces. For instance, Shaw and McKay's (1969, 365) book *Juvenile Delinquency and Urban Areas* devotes only a few pages to female delinquency, and then implies it is mostly sexual—associated with the "hunting ground" these girls live in, which is composed of dance halls, massage and bath establishments, movie theaters, and so on. Chapter 2 in this book discusses how the early criminologists (such as Cesare Lombroso, Otto Pollack, W. I. Thomas, and even Sigmund Freud) emphasized biology to explain female criminality.

Female delinquency was seen as neither interesting nor important until the last couple of decades, and there still is a paucity of research on this topic. Similarly, theory has traditionally placed males in the center. Feminist theories not only attempt to focus females more centrally, but they include how the inequalities between the sexes can differentially affect male and female experiences and behaviors. Furthermore, feminist theory has been increasingly committed to examining how such factors as racism, classism, and heterosexism, in addition to sexism, are useful for understanding gender differences and discrimination dynamics. "It is one thing to say that women have been excluded from general theories of social phenomenon. It is another matter to wonder how theories would appear if they were fashioned from women's experiences and if women had a central place in them" (Daly and Chesney-Lind 1988, 504).

Another aspect of the invisibility of female offenders is the "correctional" institutions provided for women and girls. The prisons and delinquent institutions for women and girls, both historically and presently, vary drastically from those for boys and men, mostly to the disadvantage of females. Moreover, historically, treatment and punishment issues/opportunities differed vastly for women based on race (Freedman 1981; Rafter 1985). The excuse for the lack of research on institutions housing female offenders, as well as the lack of training, vocational, educational, and counseling programs available to incarcerated females, is that females make up a small percentage of offenders. This lack of interest in and opportunities for women and girls is particularly disturbing given that their incarceration rate is growing much faster than men's (Immarigeon and Chesney-Lind 1992).

Women and Girls as Victims

Current research on victimization rates and fear of crime often fails to account for the ways that victimization and fear of victimization differ between the sexes. Some scholars have noted that society and the legal system often fail to distinguish "normal" heterosexual sex from rape, with the assumption that male dominance, and even violence, is acceptable sexuality (Edwards 1987; McLean 1988; Smart 1989). The crimes that women and girls are most likely to experience—sexual victimization (rape) and woman battering (domestic violence)—not only are the most underreported, but also are violent, humiliating, and dangerous. Yet researchers still frequently inform us that females are "oddly" more afraid of crime while being less vulnerable to victimization (see Stanko 1990, 1992). Research, however, has established that the discrepancy between women's low rates of reported victimization and high levels of fear can be explained by disproportionately high rates of serious acquaintance victimizations (Stanko 1990; Young 1992). Moreover, most young women and girls grow up with strong messages about dangerous men lurking in alleys and behind bushes; thus, in a sense, females are trained to fear crime.

Women as Professionals in the Crime-Processing System

The final major area of women and crime covered in this book is women's employment in the crime-processing system. The three major types of employment opportunities in crime processing include prisons and jails, policing, and the law. Part IV of this book examines historical and current issues for women correctional officers, policewomen, and women lawyers and judges. All of these women have faced considerable resistance to employment in the crime-processing field. This resistance is based primarily on the attitude that women are unsuitable because working with male offenders requires "macho" men. The 1970s, particularly Title VII (a 1972 amendment to the 1964 Civil Rights Act), proved crucial for women's professional entrance to the crime-processing system. Unfortunately, women's advancement in both numbers and rank has been slow. Despite current efforts by law schools and police departments to hire more women, the rates of women in these occupations are still quite low, as is the employment of women in men's penal institutions, which make up the majority of "correctional" facilities. This persisting low representation of women in crime-processing jobs is due to the lack of adequate training and education necessary to support them and is further aggravated by the resistance they meet from male administrators and coworkers.

Blurring of Boundaries of
Women's Experiences in Crime

In addition to acknowledging the invisibility of female offenders, female victims, and women working in the crime-processing system, it is important to recognize the overlapping of these categories in many women's experiences. The author's research on women working as police officers and in jails included numerous disclosures by these workers of having survived incest, extrafamilial child sexual abuse, stranger rape, and woman battering in intimate relationships. (A number of the policewomen discussed battering perpetrated by their police officer husbands.) Moreover, given the high rates of women in general who experience male violence (some statistics suggest as many as half of all women in the United States; see Chapters 6 through 8), it would be difficult to have women working in the crime-processing system who *hadn't* been victimized. Although this hasn't been empirically studied, women's victimization experiences may be related to their desire to work in the crime-processing system.

Many incarcerated women have experienced victimizations similar to those described by women professionals (and women in general). Recent research has identified running away from home and drug use as women's and girls' means of coping with and surviving abuse in their homes. The "escape" options open to women and girls who are being sexually and/or physically victimized are often illegal. For example, girls who run away from abusive homes often become dependent on prostitution for economic survival and on drugs in order to numb the pain (see Gilfus 1992). These survival means, in turn, often lead to incarceration.

There is growing documentation that women prisoners have disproportionately high records of victimization, usually incest, rape, and battering, before their incarceration (American Correctional Association 1990; Arnold 1990; Carlen 1983; Chesney-Lind and Rodriguez 1983; Daly 1992; Fletcher and Moon 1993; Immarigeon 1987a, 1987b; Sargent et al. 1993). Many of these accounts confirm the likelihood that prior victimization, offending (especially prostitution, running away, and drug offenses), and subsequent incarceration are interrelated (Arnold 1990; Carlen 1983; Chesney-Lind and Rodriguez 1983; Daly 1992; Gilfus 1992).

U.S. prisons house many battered women survivors who killed their batterers as a last resort (see Browne 1987). Although the crime-processing system has failed to respond to battered women as victims, it has responded harshly to them as "offenders." However, these women rarely have any criminal record before the murder, they are almost always the ones who notify the police of the murder, and the murder almost always occurs during a battering incident where the victim is acting in self-defense (see Maguigan 1991). These women typically receive longer sentences than men who kill their wives (Schneider and Jordan 1981). In the past decade, governors from Ohio, Illinois, Maryland, and Texas received considerable press for commuting the sentences of women who had served time after killing their abusive partners in self-defense.

As discussed earlier, female victims, offenders, and professionals in the crime-processing system have historically remained invisible. Because of the shame associated with sexual abuse and battering, these crimes are not routinely reported to crime-processing authorities, research interviewers, or even family members and health care officials. Similarly, offending women have remained invisible because they have rarely made up more than 6 percent of the prison population. Finally, roles for women professionals were largely nonexistent until the 1970s. The goal of this book is to make issues surrounding women and crime more visible, to trace the changes in society and the crime-processing system that have occurred, and to propose changes that still need to occur. But first, to understand these issues, it is important to have an understanding of feminism and the difference between sex and gender.

SEX VERSUS GENDER

Differences between males and females have been divided into two categories: sex differences and gender differences. *Sex differences* are biological differences, including differences in reproductive organs, body size, muscle development, and hormones. *Gender differences,* on the other hand, are those that are ascribed through society and that relate to expected social roles. Examples of gender differences include clothing, wages, child-care responsibilities, and professions. Most differences between males and females are *gender* differences, which are determined by society; they are *not* biologically determined. Moreover, socially based differences are largely rooted in inequality (MacKinnon 1990). Because society creates these inequalities, society must also be the solution to restructuring the images and opportunities of women and men (and girls and boys), in order to achieve equality.

Women's and men's different roles historically have been viewed as "biologically based and unalterable." More recently, however, feminists assert that "women's roles are learned and socially determined" (Klein 1984, 3). Thus, it is important to examine and acknowledge how sex differences influence gender differences. For instance, when only boys are allowed to take part in sports programs, girls are prevented from exercising their bodies and becoming strong. It is necessary to acknowledge that even in the traditional sense, some women are stronger than some men. Also, the relative differences in men's and women's times for running marathons, shorter running events, and swimming have significantly decreased since the 1930s, possibly due to girls' and women's increased access to exercise and training for sports (Fausto-Sterling 1985). In fact, between 1964 and 1984 women's marathon times decreased by more than one-and-one-half hours, whereas men's times decreased by only a few minutes (Fausto-Sterling 1985). In addition to women holding the records in marathon swimming, the first woman ever "allowed" to swim the English Channel (in 1926) "not only astounded the world by succeeding at all, but she broke the men's record by two hours!" (Fausto-Sterling 1985, 218).

Court cases on sex discrimination have historically confused sex and gender differences, often ruling to the disadvantage of women on the basis that cultural/societal (or gender) differences are "immutable" (Rhode 1989, 3). That is, legal discourse rarely distinguishes sex from gender differences, viewing both as inherent and failing to realize the role society plays in perpetuating gender inequalities. In fact, some scholars believe that most societies, including the United States, are invested in perpetuating gender distinctions (Epstein 1988, 120). Daly and Chesney-Lind (1988, 504) clearly delineate the importance of gender and a feminist approach (see the following chart).

The Five Elements That Distinguish Feminist Thought
From Other Types of Social and Political Thought

- Gender is not a natural fact but a complex social, historical, and cultural product; it is related to, but not simply derived from, biological sex differences and reproductive capacities.
- Gender and gender relations order social life and social institutions in fundamental ways.
- Gender relations and constructs of masculinity and femininity are not symmetrical but are based on an organizing principle of men's superiority and social and political–economic dominance over women.
- Systems of knowledge reflect men's views of the natural and social world; the production of knowledge is gendered.
- Women should be at the center of intellectual inquiry, not peripheral, invisible, or appendages to men.

SOURCE: Kathleen Daly and Meda Chesney-Lind. 1988. "Feminism and Criminology." *Justice Quarterly* 5:504.

Inherent in this distinction between sex and gender are the concepts of sexism and patriarchy. *Sexism* refers to oppressive attitudes and behaviors directed at either sex; that is, sexism is discrimination or prejudice based on gender. In practice, the discrimination, prejudice, and negative attitudes and behaviors based on sex and gender are directed primarily at females (that is, females are not as "good" as males, females exist for the sexual pleasure of males, females are defined by their beauty, and so on).

Patriarchy, on the other hand, refers to a social, legal, and political climate that values male dominance and hierarchy. Central to the patriarchal ideology is the belief that female nature is biologically, not culturally, determined (Edwards 1987). What feminists identify as gender differences (for example, the ability to nurture children), therefore, are often defined as sex differences by the patriarchy. The patriarchal social structure of modern times is not as strong as it once was. Nevertheless, MacKinnon (1989) notes that the state operates from men's standpoint; the laws are consistent with men's experiences. Patriarchy and its privileges, then, remain as part of the defining quality of the culture, and thus of criminology and crime processing.

It is often assumed that changes made to advance gender equality will result in unfairness to men. This view not only is used to justify opposition toward equality, but also ignores the fact that changes may benefit men. For instance, Cincinnati Bell Telephone was brought to court for failure to hire women to work on telephone poles. The court upheld that such a practice was discriminatory, which resulted in Cincinnati Bell devising new and improved equipment so that women could more easily perform the job. Such innovations included making lighter ladders and tools with improved torque that required less muscle power. The male workers responded, "Why didn't you do this a long time ago?" Such changes made the job open to a wider range of male workers, as well as female workers.

As stated earlier, some women are physically stronger than some men. Even so, exceptionally strong women historically have been denied access to "men's" jobs that require physical strength. Unfortunately, such dedication to exclusively male occupations is not restricted to jobs associated with high use of physical strength. Traditionally, women have faced obstacles in their efforts to enter fields associated with high mental abilities such as science, engineering, law, and medicine. Ironically, women's so-called "tender susceptibility" has barred them from prestigious professions "but not from grueling and indelicate occupations like factory and field labor" (Rhode 1990, 200). Only recently has women's access to traditionally male jobs become more commonplace.

Understanding the distinction between sex and gender informs us that most differences between males and females are societally based (gender), not biologically determined (sex). Although this is encouraging in that it is more likely that we can change society than it is that we can alter biology, this book examines how gender differences are strongly entrenched in tradition and have negatively affected the lives of women and girls, including in the crime-processing system. Furthermore, sex differences, such as the ability to become pregnant, have also worked to women's disadvantage in many law cases.

WHAT IS FEMINISM?

Feminism and feminists recognize that gender inequalities exist in society, and they value change that enhances gender equality. While the perspectives of feminism are numerous, the approach has been to attempt to answer the "woman question(s)," where "partial and provisional answers intersect, joining together both to lament the ways in which women have been oppressed, repressed, and suppressed and to celebrate the ways in which so many women have 'beaten the system,' taken charge of their own destinies, and encouraged each other" (Tong 1989, 1–2). Although the first "unmistakably feminist voices were heard in England in the seventeenth century," feminist philosopher Alison Jaggar (1983, 1) states:

> In a sense, feminism has always existed. Certainly, as long as women have been subordinated, they have resisted that subordination. Sometimes the resistance has been collective and conscious; at other times it has been solitary and only half-conscious, as when women have sought escape from their socially prescribed roles through illness, drug and alcohol addiction, and even madness.

Black feminist bell hooks defines feminism simply as "the struggle to end sexist oppression" (1984, 26). She compares patriarchy to racism and other forms of oppression and points out that for sexism to end, racism and other forms of oppression cannot remain intact. Feminism, therefore, is part of the larger movement to end domination in all of its forms (hooks 1990). The aim of feminism

> … is not to benefit solely any specific group of women, any particular race or class of women. It [feminism] does not privilege women over men. It has the power to transform in a meaningful way all our lives.
>
> (hooks 1984, 26)

Unfortunately, a number of myths have damaged the concept of feminism as a legitimate issue and approach. Journalist Susan Faludi (1991) documents in her book *Backlash* how the media and politicians exaggerate or manipulate statistics and incidences in order to condemn feminism and keep women in gender-specified roles. Daly and Chesney-Lind (1988) identify three myths about feminism: (1) Feminism lacks objectivity, (2) feminist analysis narrowly focuses on women, and (3) there is only one feminist perspective. Regarding charges that feminism lacks objectivity, Daly and Chesney-Lind (1988) point out that men and nonfeminists are no more objective about gender issues than women and feminists. The problem is that too often "men's experiences are taken as the norm and are generalized to the population" (1988, 500). With regard to the criticism that feminism focuses too narrowly on women, in fact, feminist analysis does not ignore men and masculinity; rather, men are included in, but not the center of, the analysis. Obviously, it is necessary to examine masculinity and men's lives and viewpoints in order to fully understand women's lives (1988, 500). "The irony is that feminist scholarship is characterized as being only about women or as hopelessly biased toward women, when in fact the project is to describe and change both men's and women's lives" (1988, 501).

An examination of feminist analysis quickly establishes that there are many feminist perspectives. The five major strains of feminist theory are *liberal, Marxist, socialist, radical,* and *postmodernist* feminism. The origins of *liberal feminism* can be traced back to the late eighteenth century with Mary Wollstonecraft's publication *A Vindication of the Rights of Women* and later John Stuart Mill's article "The Subjection of Women." Fundamentally, liberal feminists argue that women's access to equality in education and employment, or the "public world" in general, is blocked by customary and legal constraints (Tong 1989). Gender justice, therefore, requires that the rules to the "game" are fair and that no one's civil rights and economic opportunities are disadvantaged in playing the "game" (Tong 1989).

Marxist feminists, on the other hand, are most concerned with inequalities set up in a capitalist society. They believe that abolition of a class society, where the means of production are shared and wealth is not owned by a few, will liberate women because they won't be economically dependent on men. Marxist feminists do not view women's oppression as a result of individuals' intentional actions, but rather as due to the political, economic, and social structures of capitalism (Tong 1989). Marxist feminism is most concerned with work-related inequities and has advanced understanding of the trivialization of women's work in the home (especially raising children) and the boring, poorly paid jobs women have predominantly occupied (Tong 1989).

The socialist and radical feminist theories are largely reactions to Marxist feminism. In particular, *socialist feminism* purports that class alone fails to explain women's subjugation; thus, both class and the patriarchy must be examined as dual systems of domination. Gender and class play equal roles in explaining women's oppression (Tong 1989). Socialist feminists criticize Marxist feminists for implying that the abuse women suffer from men is inconsequential compared with what the proletariat (worker) endures from the bourgeoisie (the production managers and owners) (Tong 1989).

Radical feminists, also disillusioned with Marxist feminism, first organized in the 1960s and 1970s. Radical feminism was also a result of women active in the "New Left" antiwar and civil rights movements being treated as "second-class" citizens within these movements (Donovan 1985). Unlike Marxist feminists, radical feminists believe that patriarchy is central to women's oppression. Radical feminism points out that Marxist feminism's focus on work-related concerns has left little room to address other feminist issues, particularly reproductive freedom and violence against women (Tong 1989). Radical feminism is also more apt than the other strains of feminism to hold individual men, rather than society, responsible for oppressing women (Tong 1989).

Finally, *postmodernist feminism* argues against socialist feminism's "unrealistic" goal to synthesize feminism and find one theory to explain women's oppression (Tong 1989). Rather, postmodernists propose that because women's experiences differ based on class, race, sexual, and cultural lines, feminist theory should reflect this (Gagnier 1990). Rosemarie Tong concludes her book on feminist thought by relating that although these various approaches to feminism are at times confusing and splintered, "feminist thought permits each woman to think her own thoughts. Apparently, not the truth but the truths are setting women free" (1989, 238).

EFFECT OF SOCIETAL IMAGES
ON WOMEN IN CRIME

It is difficult to understand how women victims, offenders, and professionals are viewed and treated in the crime-processing system without first understanding the images of females in society. Rafter and Stanko (1982) have identified six images of women that influence how they are perceived in the crime-processing system, and in society as a whole, when they offend, are victimized, or work in crime-processing jobs. The first image is *woman as the pawn of biology,* where women are viewed as "gripped by biological forces beyond [their] control" (1982, 3). For example, when Walter Mondale selected Geraldine Ferraro as his running mate during the 1984 presidential election, numerous journalists and others made such observations as "What if he dies and she becomes president? She might go through menopause and get us involved in a nuclear war." Similarly, women's menstruation and premenstrual syndrome have often been inappropriately used to explain women's behavior.

The second image of women offered by Rafter and Stanko (1982) is *woman as impulsive and nonanalytical,* where women are perceived to act illogically and intuitively. A person with these perceived characteristics is unlikely to be hired as a professional, particularly to deal with crime or important court cases. The third image, *women as passive and weak,* implies that women are easy prey for victimization, will blindly follow criminal men into a life of crime, and as professionals are incapable of assuming authority. Rafter and Stanko's (1982, 3) fourth image, *women as impressionable and in need of protection,* implies that women are "gullible and easily led astray." Again, this stereotype makes women appear inadequate for crime-processing jobs. The fifth image, *the active woman as masculine,* views any women who break from stereotypical passive roles as deviant and likely to be criminal. This woman is also likely to be viewed as lesbian (whether or not she is); thus, she is prey to the hostility and discrimination associated with homophobia in society. The final image, *the criminal woman as purely evil,* implies that it is worse for women than men to be criminal, since women not only are breaking out of law-abiding boundaries, but perhaps more important, are stepping out of stereotypical female role boundaries.

Criminology research has also helped to reinforce stereotypes of women and girls, which affects their assessment in society and the crime-processing system. For instance, the concept of "victim precipitation," used by Hans Von Hentig, Menachem Amir, and Marvin E. Wolfgang, has largely been used to see how women (and men) "attract" victimization. Whether it is to reinforce myths that women who wear certain clothes are "asking to be raped," or that women who stay in battering relationships are "masochistic," victim precipitation models have often been used to deny women's real risk of victimization while at the same time blaming them for this victimization.

Feminist research on other images includes acknowledgment that women's lives have been dichotomized into "madonnas" or "whores" (Feinman 1986). This model asserts that women are often assigned to either a madonna category, where they are sweet and passive and produce children, or to a whore category, which includes any women who don't follow the prescribed societal role defined by the madonna category (Feinman 1986). Young (1986) challenges the madonna/whore typology to the extent that it may apply only to Anglo women. She claims that where the madonna/whore dichotomy implies a good girl/bad girl dichotomy, categories for women of color include no "good girl" categories. Instead, she views African American women as falling into four categories, all of which are negative. The *amazon* is seen as inherently violent and capable of protecting herself; the *sinister sapphire* is vindictive, provocative, and not credible; the *mammy* is viewed as stupid, passive, and bothersome; and the *seductress* is sexually driven and noncredible as a victim or professional (Young 1986). These limited categories are damaging for women of color. The categories also fail to account for the diversity among women and how identical behaviors (such as engaging in sexual activity or committing crimes) can be viewed quite differently based on whether a male or female is "acting out" the behavior.

DIVERSITY AMONG WOMEN

One of the many challenges for feminism in general, and feminist criminology in particular, is the paradox of acknowledging diversity among women while claiming women's unity in experiences of oppression and sexism (Daly and Chesney-Lind 1988, 502). Historically, feminist scholarship has focused too strongly on the lives and experiences of European American (Anglo or white), largely middle-class, women. This focus has failed to account for the diversity in women's experiences and backgrounds and the importance of race and class, in particular, in discussing women's and girls' experiences. "Experience of racial prejudice, for example, is an integral part of 'being Black' and Black women's experiences of crime and in the criminal justice system obviously differ from white women's because of this" (Morris 1987, 15).

Feminist legal theorists have proposed the concept of *multiple consciousness:* that we are often born with more than one identity (Harris 1990; Matsuda 1989). Multiple consciousness is a "process in which propositions are constantly put forth, challenged, and subverted" (Harris 1990). Harris (1990, 585) criticizes Anglo feminists for a tendency toward "gender essentialism," where women's experiences are "isolated and described independently of race, class, sexual orientation, and other realities of experience." This can be evidenced from the suffrage movement in the United States, in which the Anglo feminist leaders failed to seriously address racial oppression or the experience of African American women (1990, 586).

Similarly, Asian American legal scholar Mari J. Matsuda (1989, 7) describes how legal training in most law schools includes "training the students out of the muddle-headed world where everything is relevant and into the lawyer's world where the few critical facts prevail." Matsuda describes how this training results in *bifurcated thinking,* separating what a person believes is relevant from what the legal training has taught is relevant. This involves "shifting back and forth between consciousness as a Third World person and the white consciousness required for survival in elite educational institutions" (1989, 8). Further, a woman of color may feel more able to bring up issues of male violence in a law or criminal justice class where the professor is an Anglo woman instead of an Anglo man, but she may not feel that she can "safely" bring up issues of racism as well as male violence. Or, a woman of color attorney may feel able to bring up her client's racism experiences before a man of color judge, but less comfortable discussing her client's sexism experiences relevant to the case. Hence, multiple consciousness is the result. However, multiple consciousness as a method "encompasses more than consciousness-shifting as skilled advocacy. It encompasses as well the search for the pathway to a just world" (1989, 9). Matsuda (1989, 10) closes with this information:

> I cannot pretend that I, as a Japanese American, truly know the pain of, say, my Native American sister. But I can pledge to educate myself so that I do not receive her pain in ignorance. And I can say as an American, I am choosing as my heritage the 200 years of struggle by poor and working people, by Native Americans, by women, by people of color, for dignified lives in this nation. I can claim as my own the Constitution my father fought for at Anzio, the Constitution that I swore to uphold and defend when I was admitted to the bar. It was not written for me, but I can make it my own, using my chosen consciousness as a woman and person of color to give substance to those tantalizing words "equality" and "liberty."

In the same vein, this book hopes to make women's and girls' lives visible as victims, as offenders, and as professionals in the crime-processing system, while acknowledging that women's and girls' experiences may differ based on their race, class, sexual preference, and other personal characteristics.

SUMMARY

This chapter presented the numerous ways that women's and girls' experiences as victims, offenders, and professionals in the crime-processing system have been made invisible. The concepts of sex, gender, feminism, and patriarchy were explored. Finally, this chapter included discussion on the importance of not assuming a monolithic experience for women and girls, and discussed why race, class, sexual preference, and other variables must be considered when discussing and researching female experiences and behaviors.

REFERENCES

American Correctional Association. 1990. *The Female Offender: What Does the Future Hold?* Arlington, VA: Kirby Lithographic Company.

Amir, Menachem. 1971. *Patterns in Forcible Rape*. Chicago: University of Chicago Press.

Arnold, Regina. 1990. "Processes of Victimization and Criminalization of Black Women." *Social Justice* 17:153–166.

Browne, Angela. 1987. *When Battered Women Kill*. New York: Free Press.

Carlen, Pat. 1983. *Women's Imprisonment: A Study in Social Control*. London: Routledge & Kegan Paul.

Chesney-Lind, Meda, and Noelie Rodriguez. 1983. "Women Under Lock and Key." *Prison Journal* 53:47–65.

Daly, Kathleen. 1992. "Women's Pathways to Felony Court." *Review of Law and Women's Studies* 2:11–52.

Daly, Kathleen, and Meda Chesney-Lind. 1988. "Feminism and Criminology." *Justice Quarterly* 5:497–538.

Donovan, Josephine. 1985. *Feminist Theory*. New York: Frederick Ungar.

Edwards, Anne. 1987. "Male Violence in Feminist Theory: An Analysis of the Changing Conception of Sex/Gender Violence and Male Dominance." Pp. 13–29 in *Women, Violence, and Social Control*, edited by J. Hanmer and M. Maynard. Atlantic Highlands, NJ: Humanities Press International.

Epstein, Cynthia F. 1988. *Deceptive Distinctions: Sex, Gender, and Social Order*. New Haven, CT: Yale University Press.

Faludi, Susan. 1991. *Backlash: The Undeclared War Against Women*. New York: Doubleday.

Fausto-Sterling, Anne. 1985. *Myths of Gender: Biological Theories About Women and Men*, 2nd ed. New York: Basic Books.

Feinman, Clarice. 1986. *Women in the Criminal Justice System*, 2nd ed. New York: Praeger.

Fletcher, Beverly R. and, Dreama G. Moon. 1993. "Introduction." Pp. 5–14 in *Women Prisoners: A Forgotten Population*, edited by B. R. Fletcher, L. D. Shaver, and D. G. Moon. Westport, CT: Praeger.

Freedman, Estelle. 1981. *Their Sisters' Keepers: Women's Prison Reform in America, 1830–1930*. Ann Arbor: University of Michigan Press.

Gagnier, Regenia. 1990. "Feminist Post-modernism: The End of Feminism or the Ends of Theory?" Pp. 21–32 in *Theoretical Perspectives on Sexual Difference,* edited by D. L. Rhode. New Haven, CT: Yale University Press.

Gilfus, Mary E. 1992. "From Victims to Survivors to Offenders: Women's Routes of Entry and Immersion into Street Crime." *Women and Criminal Justice* 4:63–90.

Harris, Angela. 1990. "Race and Essentialism in Feminist Legal Theory." *Stanford Law Review* 42:581–615.

hooks, bell. 1984. *Feminist Theory: From Margin to Center.* Boston: South End Press.

—————. 1990. "Feminism: A Transformational Politic." Pp. 185–196 in *Theoretical Perspectives on Sexual Difference,* edited by D. L. Rhode. New Haven, CT: Yale University Press.

Immarigeon, Russ. 1987a. "Women in Prison." *Journal of the National Prison Project* 11:1–5.

—————. 1987b. "Few Diversion Programs Are Offered Female Offenders." *Journal of the National Prison Project* 12:9–11.

Immarigeon, Russ, and Meda Chesney-Lind. 1992. *Women's Prisons: Overcrowded and Overused.* San Francisco. National Council on Crime and Delinquency.

Jaggar, Alison M. 1983. *Feminist Politics and Human Nature.* Totowa, NJ: Rowman & Allanheld.

Klein, Ethel. 1984. *Gender Politics.* Cambridge, MA: Harvard University Press.

Leonard, Eileen B. 1982. *Women, Crime, and Society.* New York: Longman.

MacKinnon, Catherine. 1989. *Toward a Feminist Theory of State.* Cambridge: Harvard University Press.

—————. 1990. "Legal Perspectives on Sexual Difference." Pp. 213–225 in *Theoretical Perspectives on Sexual Difference,* edited by D. L. Rhode. New Haven, CT: Yale University Press.

Maguigan, Holly. 1991. "Battered Women and Self-Defense: Myths and Misconceptions in Current Reform Proposals." *University of Pennsylvania Law Review* 140:379–486.

Matsuda, Mari J. 1989. "When the First Quail Calls: Multiple Consciousness as Jurisprudential Method." *Women's Rights Law Reporter* 2:7-10.

McLean, Sheila A. M. 1988. "Female Victims in the Criminal Laws." Pp. 195–215 in *The Legal Relevance of Gender,* edited by S. McLean and N. Burrows. Atlantic Highlands, NJ: Humanities Press International.

Morris, Allison. 1987. *Women, Crime, and Criminal Justice.* Oxford, Basil Blackwell.

Rafter, Nicole H. 1985. *Partial Justice: Women in State Prisons 1800–1935.* Boston: Northeaster Press.

Rafter, Nicole H., and Elizabeth A. Stanko. 1982. "Introduction." Pp. 1–28 in *Judge, Lawyer, Victim, Thief: Women, Gender Roles and Criminal Justice,* edited by N. H. Rafter and E. A. Stanko. Stoughton, MA: Northeastern University Press.

Renzetti, Claire M. 1993. "On the Margins of the Mainstream (Or, They *Still* Don't Get It, Do They?): Feminist Analyses in Criminal Justice Education." *Journal of Criminal Justice Education* 4:219-249.

Rhode, Deborah L. 1989. *Justice and Gender: Sex Discrimination and the Law.* Cambridge, MA: Harvard University Press.

—————. 1990. "Definitions of Difference." Pp. 197–212 in *Theoretical Perspectives on Sexual Difference,* edited by D. L. Rhode. New Haven, CT: Yale University Press.

Sargent, Elizabeth, Susan Marcus-Mendoza, and Chong Ho Yu. 1993. "Abuse and the Woman Prisoner." Pp. 55–64 in *Woman Prisoners: A Forgotten Population,* edited by B. R. Fletcher, L. D. Shaver, and D. B. Moon. Westport, CT: Praeger.

Schneider, E. M., and S. B. Jordon. 1981. "Representation of Women Who

Defend Themselves in Response to Physical or Sexual Assault." In *Women's Self-Defense Cases: Theory and Practice,* edited by E. Bochnak. Charlottesville, VA: Michie Company Law Publishers.

Shaw, C., and H. McKay. 1969. *Juvenile Delinquency and Urban Areas.* Chicago: University of Chicago Press.

Smart, Carol. 1989. *Feminism and the Power of Law.* London: Routledge & Kegan Paul.

Stanko, Elizabeth A. 1990. *Everyday Violence: How Women and Men Experience Sexual and Physical Danger.* London: Pandora.

_____. 1992. "The Case of Fearful Women: Gender, Personal Safety and Fear of Crime." *Women and Criminal Justice* 4:117–136.

Tong, Rosemarie. 1989. *Feminist Thought.* Boulder, CO: Westview Press.

Von Hentig, Hans. 1948. *The Criminal and His Victim.* New Haven, CT: Yale University Press.

Wolfgang, Marvin E. 1958. *Patterns in Criminal Homicide.* Philadelphia, University of Pennsylvania Press.

Young, Vernetta D. 1986. "Gender Expectations and Their Impact on Black Female Offenders and Victims." *Justice Quarterly* 3:305–327.

_____. 1992. "Fear of Victimization and Victimization Rates Among Women: A Paradox?" *Justice Quarterly* 9:419–442.

PART II

Female Offending

2

Critiquing Criminological Theories

> Despite the public's obsession with crime, despite the morbid fear it arouses, despite the endless volumes written to account for it, sex, the most powerful variable regarding crime, has been virtually ignored.
>
> (LEONARD 1982, XI)

Criminology is not unique from other academic disciplines in its historical exclusion of females from most research questions (see Fausto-Sterling 1985; Morris 1987; Smart 1976; Spender 1981). Most criminological theories explain why some males, but not females, break the law. Additionally, it has been pointed out that theoretical criminology has been constructed by men and about men (Leonard 1982; Messerschmidt 1993). There are two important implications of focusing solely on males' experiences: (1) The theories are really theories of male crime, and (2) we must question the validity of any "general" theory if it does not apply to women (Morris 1987, 2).

Rasche (1975) identifies three reasons or excuses why females have been consistently neglected in studies of criminal behavior. First, women make up a small percentage of prisoners (approximately 6 percent). Second, research on female offenders is more likely to be opposed by correctional authorities and by the women themselves than research on male prisoners. Third, women have generally been deemed insignificant as a topic of interest. In short, the lack of attention to female offenders is largely a result of not defining female offending as a social problem.

The neglect of female crime stands in stark contrast to the extensive amount of research that has been devoted to deviations more consistent with stereotypical aspects of women's lives: maternal deprivation, insanity, and mental breakdowns (Smart 1976). Further, female lawbreakers historically (and even today) have been viewed as "abnormal" and as "worse" than male lawbreakers—not only for breaking the law, but also for stepping outside of prescribed gender roles of femininity and passivity.

Recently the amount and nature of attention to female criminality have begun to change. One reason is that the number of women in prison has increased at an unprecedented rate—indeed, at a pace much greater than male imprisonment. Feminists and the women's movement also have helped at least some scholars redefine criminological research as pertaining to females as well as males. Although there still exists a tendency for studies on offenders to be conducted solely on males, grant-giving institutions and journal editors are more likely to request a legitimate explanation as to why a sample would be all male. In short, although there is a great deal of catching up to do in order to understand, respond to, and explain female criminality, important strides have been made in recent years.

This chapter discusses the various schools of criminological theories developed in this and the last century: classical, strain and subcultural, differential association, labeling, social control, Marxist/radical, and women's liberation/ emancipation. During the periods in which these theories developed, studies often either routinely ignored women or viewed them through a stereotypical lens.

CLASSICAL STUDIES

The classical, or original, studies of female criminality were conducted between the end of the last century and the middle of this century. The most prominent researchers included Cesare Lombroso and William Ferrero (1895), W. I. Thomas (1923, 1967), Sigmund Freud (1933), and Otto Pollak (1950, 1961). These studies were grounded in the belief that *biological determinism* accounts for female criminality: Whereas men are rational, women are driven by their biological constitutions. The classical studies were informed by four main assumptions: (1) Individual characteristics, not society, are responsible for criminal behavior; (2) there is an identifiable biological nature inherent in all women; (3) offending women are "masculine," which makes them incompetent as women and thus prone to break the law; and (4) the differences between male and female criminality are due to sex, not gender, differences. The classical theorists, not surprisingly, have been accused of viewing women as turning to crime because of their "perversion of or rebellion against their natural feminine roles" (Klein 1980, 72). In addition to the sexist nature of the classical studies, they have been classist, racist, and heterosexist, focusing on wealthy, Anglo, married women as the "feminine" standard. These theorists' works are reviewed in the following sections.

The Atavistic Female Offender

Cesare Lombroso, who studied male and female prisoners in nineteenth-century Italy, is often referred to as the "father" of criminology. In addition to moving the study of criminology from the domain of legal and social science experts to the domain of biologists, physicians, and psychologists who embraced his positivist approach, Lombroso has been influential in setting the stage for a sexist, racist, and classist view of female criminality. Lombroso dismissed the effects of socialization or social-structural constraints as important determinants of criminal behavior. Instead he focused exclusively on the physical and psychological makeup of the individual in determining criminal behavior. Inherent in his approach was the assumption that women are driven by their biological inferiorities, including a madonna/whore duality, where women are either good or bad:

> Implicit in the madonna/whore duality is women's subservience to men, who assumed the role of protectors of the madonna and punishers of the whore.... A good woman is a loyal, submissive wife who serves her husband, and for this she is honored and protected. The evil woman, on the other hand, destroys man and brings pain and ruin.
>
> *(Feinman 1986, 4)*

Lombroso and (his son-in-law) Ferrero's (1895) now-discredited book *The Female Offender* explains female criminality through atavism. *Atavism* is a concept that defines all deviant behavior as a "throwback" to an earlier evolutionary stage in human development. Thus, in his early theorizing, "Lombroso firmly maintained that deviants are less highly evolved than 'normal' law abiding citizens" (Smart 1976, 31). Lombroso and Ferrero concluded that women offenders showed less degeneration than men simply because women had not evolved as much as men. Despite their perceived slower evolution, however, women were viewed as less likely than men to be criminal.

In their search for degeneration and atavism, Lombroso and Ferrero measured and documented incarcerated women's craniums, heights, weights, hair color (and baldness), moles, and tattoos. Smart (1976) offers a critical analysis of Lombroso and Ferrero's work. "Significantly, although they found some signs of so-called degeneration, like misshapen skulls or very thick black hair," observes Smart (1976, 31), "the offenders in their study did not fit well into the theory of atavism." Lombroso and Ferrero also assumed that criminal behavior was a sex, not a gender, trait. This led to the tenuous assumption that a woman exhibiting criminal tendencies "is not only an abnormal woman, she is biologically like a man" (Smart 1976, 33). Finally, Smart (1976) has criticized Lombroso and Ferrero's analysis for assuming that middle-class women's inactive and dependent roles in nineteenth-century Europe were "natural." This view fails to acknowledge the varied roles of women in other places and times.

Given this context, it is hardly surprising that kleptomania, a biological "explanation" of middle-class, Anglo women's shoplifting, was identified in the late nineteenth century as a "uterine ailment" (Abelson 1989). More recently, in the 1970s and 1980s, PMS (premenstrual syndrome) was often characterized as a biological problem of *all* women. This reinforced cultural stereotypes and implications about women's "place," and even was used as a defense in trials of women accused of murder (see Rittenhouse 1991). Thus, the marks of biologism and women continue to linger.

The Unadjusted Girl

W. I. Thomas's work, published in the books *Sex and Society* (1907) and *The Unadjusted Girl* (1923, 1967), was heavily influenced by Lombroso, although Thomas was more liberal. Thomas advanced Lombroso's work to define criminality as "a socially induced pathology rather than a biological abnormality" (Smart 1976, 37). Similar to Lombroso and Ferrero, however, Thomas viewed differences in males' and females' likelihood to become "politicians, great artists, and intellectual giants" as a result of sex rather than gender, thus overlooking the strong societal restrictions of women during that era (Smart 1976). An example of a "sex" difference that Thomas attributed to women was the inclusion of more varieties of love in their nervous systems:

> [Thomas] argued that it was this additional and intense need to give and feel love that leads women into crime, particularly sexual offenses like prostitution. The prostitute, he argued, is merely looking for the love and tenderness which all women need, but the means by which she seeks satisfaction are not socially approved.
>
> *(Smart 1976, 39)*

Again, these assumptions completely deny the socialization of women and girls and the very real constraints on their opportunities.

Further, Thomas "equated female delinquency with sexual delinquency," confusing "promiscuity" with crime; notably, this kind of logic never occurs in studies of male crime (Heidensohn 1985, 117). The disadvantaged position of women and girls in society was of little importance to Thomas in his accounting of male and female differences. His later work, however, acknowledged that women were property of men, and he departed from social Darwinism to examine the complexity of the interaction between society and the individual (Klein 1980).

Thomas's analyses of class and sexuality are overly simplistic. He views class, sex, sexuality, and crime as related to each other. According to Thomas, middle-class women are invested in protecting their chastity and thus commit few crimes; poor women, on the other hand, long for crime in the manner of a new experience. In fact, he believed that delinquent girls manipulate males into sex as a means of achieving their own goals. Thus, Thomas favors psychological over economic motivations to explain female criminality. Given that Thomas was writing in an era of mass illness and starvation, the choice to ignore economic deprivation as a potential cause of female crime is rather remarkable (Klein 1980).

Anatomy as Destiny

Psychiatrist Sigmund Freud's attempts to explain female behavior center around the belief that women are anatomically inferior to men—hence, Freud's infamous "penis envy" approach to explaining female behavior. To

Freud, the healthy woman experiences heterosexual sex as a receptor, where sexual pleasure consists of pain, while the sexually healthy man is heterosexual, is aggressive, and inflicts pain (Klein 1980).

Thus, the deviant woman is a woman who wants to be a man, and she will only end up neurotic in her fruitless search for her own penis. "Women may be viewed," says Klein (1980, 72) of this psychological explanation, "as turning to crime as a perversion of or rebellion against their natural feminine roles." Included in this analysis is a glorification of women's duties as wives and mothers, and, in turn, the view that treatment involves "helping" deviant women to adjust to their "proper," traditional gender roles (Klein 1980). Again, in addition to the obvious sexism, Freud's theories are fraught with racism, classism, and heterosexism: "Only upper- and middle-class women could possibly enjoy lives as sheltered darlings. Freud sets hegemonic standards of femininity for poor and Third World women" (Klein 1980, 89).

Behind the Mask

Although Otto Pollak's (1950, 1961) study of female criminality, *The Criminality of Women,* was published more than a half century after Lombroso and Ferrero's work, it has been closely linked with their approach. Like Thomas, Pollak believed that sociological factors, in addition to biological factors, have some relevance in crime determination. To Pollak, however, the fundamental influences on female criminality are biology and physiology; he thus repeats many of the assumptions and prejudices encountered in Lombroso and Ferrero's and Thomas's works (Smart 1976).

The major thrust of Pollak's analysis is the "masked" nature of female criminality. He assumes that male and female crime rates are similar. In part, claims Pollak, female crime is "masked" by the supposedly chivalrous or lenient treatment of women in the crime-processing system. But Pollak's main point is that women are better at hiding their crimes.

He emphasizes the "deceitful" nature of women, using as supporting evidence females' ability to hide the fact that they are menstruating or having orgasms, and their inactive role during sexual intercourse. Pollak fails to consider, however, that women's inactive role during heterosexual sex may be culturally rather than biologically determined. Further, women's training in acquiescence to men, particularly during sex, could account for the fact that women were not hiding orgasms, but rather were not experiencing them. Smart (1976, 47) compares Pollak's analysis to Eve's deceit with Adam (in the Bible), where women are viewed as evil and cunning:

> It is Pollak's contention that women are the masterminds behind criminal organizations; that they are the instigators of crime rather than the perpetrators; that they can and in fact do manipulate men into committing offenses whilst remaining immune from arrest themselves.

Again, Pollak's analysis fails to account for the power imbalance between men and women. His discussion is based on speculation, with no empirical evidence. Rather, he is convinced that a great deal of female criminality is undetected and thus unreported.

Legacy of the Classical Theorists

The enduring effects of the classicalists can be viewed in the research on female criminality that was published in the 1960s and 1970s. Similar to Pollak, Gisela Konopka (1966) portrays women in her book *The Adolescent Girl in Conflict* as the instigators of crime. Her main point is that women and girls are driven to crime because of emotional problems, specifically loneliness and sexuality (Klein 1980). Economic and social explanations are ignored at the expense of explaining female criminality through physiology and psychology.

Similarly, Vedder and Somerville (1970) stress the importance of the female as criminal instigator in *The Delinquent Girl*. Not only do they claim that female delinquency is simply a result of maladjustment to the "normal" female role, but also they ignore the causal importance of social and economic factors. Most disquieting, they attribute high rates of delinquency among black girls to "their lack of 'healthy' feminine narcissism"—an explanation with racist overtones (Klein 1980, 99). Following this logic, they see therapy as the solution to female delinquency, and ignore the need to address the potentially criminogenic social and economic constraints in which many delinquent girls are enmeshed.

Finally, in their book *Delinquency in Girls,* Cowie, Cowie, and Slater (1968) use masculinity, femininity, and chromosomes to explain female criminality. "In this perspective, the female offender is *different* physiologically and psychologically from the 'normal' girl," in that she is too masculine; she is rebelling against her femininity (Klein 1980, 101).

Thus, in the classical school, since female behavior was believed to be largely biologically determined, the complexity of female criminal behavior was reduced to a challenge of the traditional gender role—a role that was not rooted in nature but societally specified. They assumed that the girl or woman who defied the prescribed gender role had a problem, and thus they were blind to the possibility that there was a problem with the prescribed role that women, regardless of resources or situation, are expected to fulfill. Indeed, it has been recognized recently that there is not one societally prescribed role for all women, but that "appropriate" gender roles vary depending on a woman's race and class, and that a dominant patriarchy does not affect all women the same (Rice 1990).

STRAIN AND SUBCULTURAL THEORIES

Drawing on Durkheim's *anomie* (state of normlessness) theory, Robert Merton (1938, 1949) has been credited with developing strain theory. A refreshing departure from biological determinism, Merton's premise is that strain and frustration occur when individuals are taught the same goals in their culture, but are denied equal access to legitimately attain these goals. For example, the values of educational success and upward mobility are ingrained in U.S. culture, but not all citizens have the means of achieving these shared values. There are a number of criticisms of strain theory, but the most important—and the one that applies most to females—is that this framework has examined strains primarily in terms of class inequalities, comparing the strains of the working class to the middle class, and then, only of males.

Delinquent Boys

In his book *Delinquent Boys,* Albert Cohen (1955) adapted Merton's strain theory to explain the development of delinquent gangs among working-class, U.S. boys. In Cohen's analysis, males have broad and varied goals and ambitions, whereas females' narrow ambitions center around males: dating, dancing, attractiveness, and, generally, acquiring a boyfriend or husband.

> The message from Cohen is manifest. Men are the rational doers and achievers. They represent all that is instrumental and productive in American Culture. Women's world is on the margins. Women exist to be the companions of men and that is their entire lot…. While men proceed with their Olympian task of running all aspects of the nation, women perform their role of helpmate.
>
> *(Naffine 1987, 11–12)*

Cohen thus believes that females have not adopted the competitive, spirited, successful goals depicted as the "American Dream."

Cohen also vividly depicts the masculinity of male delinquents. In contrast, he devotes only four pages of his book to female delinquents. He portrays them as boring and colorless, and as expressing their delinquency through sexual promiscuity (Mann 1984; Naffine 1987). Cohen thus joins the disturbing tendency in criminological theory to link inextricably females' criminality and sexuality, while ignoring or implicitly applauding the identical sexual conduct of males.

In short, Cohen believes that males have the "real" strains of employment and income in their lives, whereas females' only strain is to marry well. Cohen was so assured in the accuracy of this stance on female delinquents that he saw no need to confirm his hypothesis through data collection. Interestingly, it has been argued that Cohen's approach to explaining male delinquency has "fallen into disfavor" among criminologists, while in "the literature on women it has yet to be seriously contradicted" (Naffine 1987, 14). An exception to this is Campbell's (1987) study of Puerto Rican, female gang members. She rebuffs Cohen's belief that girls' delinquency is acted out through sexuality, instead claiming that gang membership for females, like males, is a means of fulfilling their identities in an environment plagued with classism, racism, and sexism.

Delinquency and Opportunity

Cohen's (mis)portrayal of female delinquents was reaffirmed in Cloward and Ohlin's (1960) *Delinquency and Opportunity.* In Cloward and Ohlin's opportunity theory, males were viewed as having legitimate struggles to gain the "American Dream," while females encounter only frivolous concerns, such as finding boyfriends. Cloward and Ohlin, however, took a different twist in their version of strain theory, which is known as opportunity theory. In this version, the focus was to explain that delinquent subcultural values and gangs served as a collective solution to the frustrations that lower class urban males experienced in schools and in terms of bleak job perspectives. Again, females were left out of the model.

The subculture, often represented by gangs, not only allowed juveniles a sense of belonging, but also provided them with opportunities to learn illegitimate means to achieve success. (Subcultural theories have been criticized for implying that crime occurs exclusively among the poor [Leonard 1982].) Cloward and Ohlin's approach is almost identical to Cohen's, concerning male versus female delinquency:

> The delinquent subculture is therefore a male solution to an exclusively male problem. Females are neither pressured to achieve the major success goals of their society nor offered a delinquent outlet for their frustrations. The horizons of the female are confined to the family. The limited nature of their offending, its predominantly sexual nature, reflects this narrow set of concerns with personal relationships.
>
> *(Naffine 1987, 15)*

Cloward and Ohlin, as well as other strain theorists, failed to recognize that females also experience unequal opportunities. "Indeed, logically, one might expect women to have a higher crime rate than men since their opportunities are more limited" (Morris 1987, 76). On the other hand, females may also have less access to illegitimate means than males (a less delinquent subculture than males, for example), which would account for their lower crime rates (Harris 1977).

Females and Strain

In 1964, Ruth Morris was the first scholar to focus strain theory on girls, as well as boys. She viewed girls as slightly more dimensional than did her predecessors: Girls were not just interested in husband hunting, but were also concerned with other affective relationships, such as with family members. Morris found that girls, delinquent and not, were faced with less subcultural support and more disapproval for delinquency than boys, and she believed this might explain girls' lower delinquency rates. Furthermore, delinquent girls were more likely than delinquent boys to describe their families as unhappy.

It is instructive that studies in the late 1960s and 1970s found that girls' efforts to find mates were not related to their delinquency rates (Sandhu and Allen 1969), and that the patterns of male and female delinquent behavior were quite similar, except that males' rates were higher (see Naffine 1987, 18). Research on gender differences in the role of youth subcultures (often measured as gangs) tends to confirm that males' subcultures are more prone to delinquency than females' subcultures (Esbensen and Huizinga 1993; Lerman 1966; Morash 1983, 1986; Morris 1964, 1965; Rahav 1984; Thompson et al. 1984). However, research addressing whether strain/blocked opportunity is more, less, or equally related to boys' and girls' delinquency rates has been inconsistent. Some studies have found that strain is more relevant in predicting female than male delinquency (Datesman et al. 1975; Segrave and Hastad 1983); another that strain is more influential in predicting male than female delinquency (Simons et al. 1980); others that strain was equally related to male and female delinquency rates (Cernkovich and Giordano 1979; Figueira-Mc-Donough and Selo 1980; Smith 1979); and yet another that strain variables were related in the opposite direction as expected for Anglo females, but in the expected direction for African American females (Hill and Crawford 1990). While the findings are inconsistent regarding the applicability of strain theory to females:

> [t]he weight of the evidence produced by researchers into strain has prob-ably tended more to contradict than to confirm Cohen's formulation. There is little here to justify the claim that the sexes react differently to impeded goals or indeed that their aims do not correspond. Theorists are therefore perverse in their belief that women's behavior is more uniform and conventional than men's because women are not subjected to the stresses of the male role.
>
> *(Naffine 1987, 23)*

DIFFERENTIAL ASSOCIATION THEORY

Edwin Sutherland, first alone and then in collaboration with Donald Cressey, developed the theory of differential association in the classic text *Principles of Criminology* (1939, 1966). Sutherland's attempt was to move away from poverty as the major explanation of crime; however, he also attacked Freud and other individual theorists. The basic tenet of differential association the-ory is that criminal behavior is learned, just as any other behavior is learned. Thus, one's group association is instrumental in determining whether one becomes delinquent.

While Sutherland and Cressey agree with Cohen's contention that there is unequal access to success in the United States, they depart from Cohen's belief that all classes have internalized the same goals (that is, the goals of middle-class males). Further, Sutherland and Cressey claim that criminal subcultures are not unique to frustrated working-class male youths; people of all classes, including white-collar workers, can and do partake in criminal behavior. Sim-ilarly, whereas Cohen defines a U.S. culture that excludes women and girls, Sutherland and Cressey's perspective is not as exclusively male *in theory,* and is presented as a general non-sex-specific theory (Naffine 1987).

Despite Sutherland and Cressey's promise of a non-sex-specific theory, they rarely address females. And where females are briefly mentioned, they are seen as uniform and homogeneous. Again, females are treated as periph-eral and insignificant to the mainstream culture. Thus, Sutherland and Cressey's gender-neutral approach exists only in words, not in content. What is additionally disturbing is how easily accepted Sutherland and Cressey's view of males as "free to engage in a range of behaviors" is contrasted with the view of females as belonging in the family (Naffine 1987). Further, females' perceived tendency toward abiding the law is portrayed as dull, rather than as positive and moral (Naffine 1987).

Despite this neglect, researchers have examined the relevance of differential association theory for an explanation of female criminality. One of the initial applications of differential association theory to male and female subjects found that girls were similar to boys in both their frequency of delinquent behaviors and their connections with delinquent companions (Clark 1964). In contrast, while finding support for differential association theory and a strong relationship between delinquent friends and delinquent behavior for both males and females, Hindelang (1971) found that females had fewer delinquent friends and less delinquent behavior than boys.

Another study of delinquent girls found that they were significantly influenced by their peers, and in fact were more influenced by their female than their male peers (Giordano 1978). "In other words, the more a girl thought her female friends approved of crime, the more likely she was to offend" (Naffine 1987, 37). A study of adult heroin users, on the other hand, found that Anglo males reported more benefits from both legal employment and illegal subcultures than African American males and females and Anglo females (Covington 1986). In conclusion, although Sutherland and Cressey ignored females in their research, their theory provides insight into gender differences and similarities in delinquent involvement.

Feminist criticisms of differential association theory have centered mainly on Sutherland and Cressey's decision to avoid discussing females in any meaningful way (see Leonard 1982; Naffine 1987). Some feminists have suggested, however, that differential association theory is a useful way of examining male and female delinquency rates and of explaining gender differences. Two points are important.

First, girls' relatively lower crime rates may largely be a result of the constraints that they experience compared to boys. For example, at least traditionally, girls have been expected to stay closer to home, are more likely to have curfews, are more likely to be disciplined (particularly for minor infractions and sexual experimentation), and are generally provided less freedom than their brothers and other boys. The differential *socialization,* then, of boys and girls is believed to significantly affect gender behavior differences (see Hoffman-Bustamante 1973; Morris 1987). The second point is that the increase in girls' delinquency rates in the last couple of decades might be explained by females' increased freedom. Even Cressey (1964) asserted that where there is greater equality between the sexes, the crime–sex ratio is likely to be lower.

LABELING THEORY

Labeling theory is concerned with the process by which deviant labels are applied and received. Specifically, labeling theory speculates about how people are "branded" with a deviant, delinquent, or criminal label, and the effect of the label on future behavior. It has been suggested that being treated as deviant may relate more to "the kind of person" one is than to her or his particular behavior (Schur 1984). For example, labeling theory proposes that some people are more likely to be labeled criminal because of their race, sex, class, and so on. Moreover, labeling theory posits that once someone is labeled delinquent or criminal, she or he may accept this label unquestioningly and continue on in crime because of this.

Numerous researchers helped advance the concepts behind labeling theory (see Erikson 1962; Kitsuse 1962; Lemert 1951), but perhaps the most famous is Howard Becker (1963) in his research on jazz and dance musicians in the book *Outsiders*. Consistent with the theorists discussed thus far, Becker devotes his analysis almost exclusively to *male* musicians. He collected his data through participant observation, playing the piano professionally with his subjects. When women are examined in Becker's work, it is most frequently as the wives of the male musicians, and in these instances they are portrayed as boring, laughable, and "square." They are depicted as nags who threaten the livelihood of the band by trying to convince their husbands to get "real" jobs. When women musicians are given any attention in Becker's analysis, it is only as sex objects, not as legitimate musicians—an all too familiar approach to studying nonconforming and criminal women (Naffine 1987). In the work of Becker and many others, conforming women are portrayed as boring and spineless, whereas criminal men are seen as creative and exciting.

When labeling theory analysis is applied to women and girls, a key issue is how males and females might be labeled differently. Thus, the possibility that girls may be less likely than boys to be labeled or viewed as delinquent might also help explain their lower rates. Or perhaps females will be labeled more harshly for some crimes, while males are discriminated against for other crimes.

Research on these issues has revealed inconsistent findings regarding police and court actions. Some studies found no gender differences, some found preferential treatment for males, others found preferential treatment for females, and still others found that females were treated more harshly for some crimes and males were treated more harshly for others. Controlling for the amount of delinquency, one study showed that children, especially girls from mother-only homes, were more likely to be officially labeled delinquent than those from two-parent homes (Johnson 1986). In addition to helping explain female criminality, labeling theory also may be helpful in explaining the current strong trend in increasing rates of women's imprisonment, despite their persistently low crime rates:

> [C]onditions that previously protected women from the pernicious effects of labeling have declined. With this, women are more likely to be subject to the stigma of official labeling. The result, according to labeling theory, is an increased likelihood that their criminal involvement will become deeper and more intractable.
>
> *(Leonard 1982, 84)*

Another interesting point in examining gender differences in labeling is Morris's (1987) contention that women are more likely to be labeled mentally ill than men, and men are more likely to be labeled criminal than women. Accordingly, "mental illness is presented as both an alternative to and an explanation of crime" (1987, 55). Similarly, whereas men may be more likely to be labeled "criminal," women are more likely to be labeled "deviant," or labeled in general (for example, they are called nags and bitches, and are described as promiscuous and hysterical).

> [W]omen do not really have to engage in specific *acts* in order to be defined and responded to as deviant. Physical appearance—and in a sense perhaps even the mere condition of "being" a woman—can lead to stigmatization.
> *(Schur 1984, 190)*

Anthony Harris (1977) questions this investment in stereotyping women into roles of inherently conforming. He views this stereotyping as functional in a patriarchal society; it is a means to keep women out of prison and where they "belong"—home cleaning the house and raising the children. Furthermore, stereotyping African American ghetto males as inherently criminal is functional in perpetuating the myth that they fail to contribute to society in any way (Harris 1977). Fox (1977) discusses how women are controlled by the relentless pressure to be labeled "nice." This informal societal control is so effective that females are less likely than males to need the formal criminal label (Hagan et al. 1979).

Naffine (1987) is concerned with how women are represented in the works of Harris, Fox, and Becker. All three authors, she observes, fail to view women with any sense of intention and purpose. She points out that Fox and Harris are more descriptive than explanatory. Naffine (1987, 88) is troubled that even Harris's and Fox's portrayals, albeit less sexist than Becker's, fail to allow

> for the sort of individualism and glamour described by Becker when the male was the subject of interpretation.... While labeling theorists may be right in claiming that men have more freedom than women to deviate, they have developed their arguments about the socialized woman to a point at which her humanity has been extinguished.

SOCIAL CONTROL THEORY

The theories discussed thus far have focused on what makes people break the law. Taking a different approach, the social control theories are more concerned with explaining what compels most of society to abide by the law. This section discusses such theories.

Social Bond Theory

Travis Hirschi (1969), in his book *Causes of Delinquency,* focuses on what motivates people to obey laws. His theory, social bond or control theory, examines four categories of "social bonds" that prevent people from acting on their criminal desires: attachment, commitment, involvement, and belief. A person's

likelihood to offend will be related to her or his ties to (1) conventional people, especially parents; (2) conventional institutions and behaviors in her or his
employment and recreation; and (3) the rules of society. Although the theory
was described as non-sex-specific, it changed in its application. Thus, to test his
hypotheses, Hirschi analyzed only the responses of Anglo school boys. He
found that, indeed, the boys with stronger conventional ties were less likely to
report delinquency.

Given that Hirschi switched the approach of studying crime from "Why
do people offend?" to "Why don't people offend?" it has been suggested that
studying females—or, at least, *including females* in the sample—would have
made more sense, since most research suggests that they are more law-abiding
than males (Naffine 1987). Interestingly, Hirschi began his study with males
and females.

> Indeed Hirschi explains, in some detail, his empirical method for eliminat-
> ing bias from his samples by referring to both male and female cases.
> Then, unaccountably and without comment, he discards his female re-
> spondents and the research project becomes a study of social control as it
> applies to the male. From this one can infer that professional criminolo-
> gists regard it as perfectly right not to cater for the female experience in
> the tests of their theory, even when that theory is presented as non-sex-
> specific.
>
> *(Naffine 1987, 66)*

Or, as Mann (1984, 263) points out:

> Travis Hirschi stratified his samples by race, sex, school, and grade. He
> included 1,076 black girls and 846 nonblack girls; but in the analysis of his
> data Hirschi admits "the girls disappear," and he adds, "Since girls have
> been neglected for too long by students of delinquency, the exclusion of
> them is difficult to justify. I hope I return to them soon." He didn't.

Additionally, where delinquent males were often celebrated and revered in
prior theory focusing on why some people (males) commit crimes, in Hirschi's
approach the conforming (law-abiding) male becomes ennobled. This is particularly noteworthy given the image of conforming females in research testing the other theories; they are depicted as lifeless, boring, and dependent. In
the prior studies asking "Why do people offend?" the criminal male was portrayed as exciting, instrumental, and masculine. In Hirschi's approach, the noncriminal male becomes lauded as responsible. In fact, it has been pointed out
that men who conform are labeled "successful," while there is little or no reward for conforming women (Schur 1984). "What all this seems to indicate is
a profound criminological tendency to devalue the female and value the male
even when they are doing precisely the same things" (Naffine 1987, 67).

Social control theory was advanced by Michael Gottfredson and Travis
Hirschi in *A General Theory of Crime* (1990). This "general" theory purports to
explain criminal behavior as a function of individual self-control; it predicts
that individuals with low self-control are more prone to criminal behavior. General theory has been criticized, however, for (1) ignoring gender as a significant

power relationship, (2) dismissing and misrepresenting male violence against women, and (3) ignoring feminist research on gender divisions within families (Miller and Burack 1993). Even in the 1990s, the visibility of females in criminological theories is vague and/or distorted.

Research on Social Control Theory

Research on social control theory has been fairly extensive. A study of African American and Anglo male and female youth in California found that although introducing social control variables (measuring attachment to conventional people) greatly decreased the gender differences in reported delinquency rates, these social ties did not completely eliminate or explain males' higher offending rates (Jensen and Eve 1976). Another test of social control theory found that while conventional ties predicted both male and female offending, this relationship was stronger for males (Hindelang 1973). A study of female delinquents measuring social bonding as attachment to school and education found that although these factors played a role in determining delinquency rates, their effect was minimal (Torstensson 1990). Another study of high school students found that similar "bond variables" influenced both males and females (Figueira-McDonough et al. 1981). A study of adult males and females, on the other hand, found that even women with weak conventional ties were more law-abiding than males, thus implying that conventional ties do not explain females' greater conformity (Smith 1979).

A number of studies attempted to determine social control within the family, such as the effects of parental and sibling interactions and behaviors. A study following female delinquents over time found strong evidence that dysfunctional families increase the likelihood that girls will proceed from committing status offenses as youth to committing criminal offenses as adults (Rosenbaum 1989). A study comparing parents' and their children's drug use found, for both daughters and sons, more support for social learning theory (that is, modeling and evaluating behaviors of significant others) than for social control theory (Dembo et al. 1986). Another family study found that social control theory better explained female delinquency than male delinquency. The study also found that some parental behaviors influenced daughters' delinquency, while other parental behaviors influenced sons' delinquency (Cernkovich and Giordano 1987). Notably, another study found that the number of sisters a girl or boy has exerts no impact on her or his delinquency rate; however, the more brothers a boy has, the greater the likelihood that he will become delinquent, and the more brothers a girl has, the less likely that she will become delinquent (Lauritsen 1993).

Power-Control Theory

Hagan and his colleagues (1985, 1987) built on social-control theory through the development of power-control theory. One of the few theories to explicitly include gender, this theory joins class theory with research on gender and family relationships:

> Central to our extension of power-control theory is a conceptualization
> of class and family that focuses on power relations in the workplace and
> the home. A key premise of our extended theory is that positions of
> power in the workplace are translated into power relations in the house-
> hold and that the latter, in turn, influence the gender-determined control
> of adolescents, their preferences for risk taking, and the patterning of gen-
> der and delinquency.
>
> *(Hagan 1987, 813)*

Hagan (1987) found a greater gender difference in delinquency rates in *patri-archal* homes, where the mother had a lower status than the father, than in *egalitarian* homes, where parents had equivalent status or the mother was the only parent. Thus, this approach asserts that the gender-power makeup in the parents' relationship influences their daughters' subsequent delinquent behavior. Or rather, in a home where there is less sexism in the parents' roles, there theoretically should be fewer gender differences between sons' and daughters' behaviors. An assumption of this theory is that daughters from egalitarian homes are socialized, like their brothers, to engage in risk-taking behaviors, and since risk-taking behavior is associated with delinquency, girls from the more egalitarian homes will be more delinquent than their "sisters" from traditional, patriarchal homes.

The research by Hagan and his colleagues confirmed this belief, as did the research in a similar study (Singer and Levine 1988). Another study found, however, that while both maternal and paternal support were effective in reducing delinquency, girls were more affected by maternal support and boys were more affected by paternal support (Hill and Atkinson 1988). A related study reported that although girls' delinquency rates were more influenced than boys' by family risk factors—such as marital discord, marital instability, and discipline—the gender stereotypes did not always fit (Dornfeld and Kruttschnitt 1992). Yet another study with a more detailed measure of parents' power structure did not find that parents' relative equality affected the sons' or daughters' delinquency rates; rather, these rates were related to the family's social class and the negative sanctions from the father (Morash and Chesney-Lind 1991). Finally, another replication found no class–gender variations, yet gender differences by race were consistent with the theory: Gender differences were greater for Anglos than for African Americans (Jensen and Thompson 1990). The explanation offered for this difference was that "white families may be more 'patriarchal' than black families" (1990, 1016).

Still other studies have tried to integrate sex, social bonds (conventional ties), and masculinity/femininity. Generally, "masculine" girls did not have weakened conventional ties (Norland et al. 1981; Thornton and James 1979). While one study found that males reported more delinquency than females in four types of crimes (violent, property, drugs, and status), controlling for "masculinity" reduced the effect of sex on delinquency rates. Further, although scoring high on "masculinity" was related to both sexes' increased reported delinquency, this was particularly true for males (Cullen et al. 1979). Notably, another study found that girls who were neither "masculine" nor "feminine" had the weakest conventional ties and the highest delinquency rates (Loy and Norland 1981).

In summary, social control theory applied to females has inconsistent findings. Although females tend to have stronger conventional ties and lower offending rates than males, the social ties are generally insufficient to explain the gender differences in criminal behavior. Furthermore, females' increased attachment to conventional ties and decreased delinquency rates cannot be explained simply by their "femininity" or "masculinity."

MARXIST/RADICAL THEORIES

In the 1970s, a more radical perspective entered the ring of criminological theories. "Conflict theory" is grounded in Marxism. Although Marx himself wrote very little about crime, his perspective on class struggle and on social relations under capitalism are the basis for conflict or Marxist criminology.

Conflict theory proposes that rather than looking at the offender, we should focus on society, particularly lawmakers and powerful interests. This criminology begins with the assumption that laws are biased, reflecting the needs of the upper class, and thus enforcement of these laws is inevitably unjust. Crime itself is politicized and defined by the powerful elite. The key to solving the crime problem, then, is changing the economic system (Bonger 1969), and this is highly political in nature.

The Marxist or radical perspective on criminology was crystallized and even renamed the "new criminology" and "critical criminology" with the publication of Ian Taylor, Paul Walton, and Jock Young's books of the same names (*The New Criminology* [1973] and *Critical Criminology* [1975]). Other criminologists have also helped develop this perspective (see Gordon 1973; Platt 1975; Quinney 1972, 1975; Schwendinger and Schwendinger 1970). The most common criticism of the new criminology, which may be due in part to its newness, is that it is overly simplified and generalized (Leonard 1982, 161).

Marx and his early followers rarely addressed the topics of crime and women, and the "new criminologists" have been soundly criticized for continuing to ignore women (Heidensohn 1985; Klein and Kress 1976; Leonard 1982; Morris 1987). The same charge has been made regarding Marxist legal scholars (Rhode 1990). Indeed, in her book on the construction of women in criminology, Naffine (1987, 134–135) does not discuss the Marxist approach except in a footnote:

> A Marxist approach is not included in this volume for the simple reason that the Left has shown little specific interest in the female offender. In the mid-1970s, there were rallying calls about the need to revitalize the study of female crime within a radical critique of society.... Unfortunately they have yet to generate a recognizably Marxist account of the subject.

Similarly, Morris (1987, 11) states:

> Taylor, Walton and Young (1973), for example, argue that only the acceptance of Marxist methods can fill the "blank spots" left by other attempts to construct social theories of deviance. They are unaware of their own "blank spot": women. There is not one word on women in their text and, despite a sharp critique of criminology, they do not notice the relevance or applicability to women of the theories reviewed.

Leonard (1982) is kinder in her critique, allowing that it may be simply that the "new criminology" is so new that it has not had a chance to address women, although she expresses concern that even this radical approach will continue to overlook women. In fact, a 1980 edited book on radical issues in criminology devoted only one chapter to "women," which was written by a man and openly hostile to feminism.[1] An even more recent text on radical criminology devoted only five pages to women and gender (Lynch and Groves 1989).

The new criminologists also often fail to recognize that economic factors alone cannot explain gender differences in criminal behavior; they require a political analysis as well (Leonard 1982). In a refreshing departure from the numerous accounts of critical criminology that fail to address the "woman question," Dorie Klein and June Kress (1976) wrote an insightful article discussing how the status of women and sexist oppression were relevant to radical criminology. Other Marxist–feminist accounts declare that sexism is directly tied to capitalism, governing economic, social, and legal aspects of our lives (Messerschmidt 1988; Rafter and Natalizia 1981).

In summary, consistent with less liberal approaches, the new criminologists have been equally guilty of omitting women and girls from their theories and analyses, despite the powerful potential of gender and sexual stratification in society to explain criminal behavior and processing. It is hoped the more recent influx of feminists into the radical organizations within criminology will help change this.

WOMEN'S LIBERATION/ EMANCIPATION HYPOTHESIS

As we have seen, traditionally, criminological theory showed only a passing interest in explaining the offending and the system's crime processing of females. All changed in 1975, however, with the publication of Freda Adler's *Sisters in Crime* and Rita Simon's *Women and Crime*. These books, particularly Adler's, received a great deal of attention regarding their hypothesis that the women's "liberation" movement is linked to the female crime rate.

Also called the "emancipation hypothesis," this approach suggests that the feminist movement, while working toward equality for women, increased the female crime rate. Although similar overall, Adler and Simon parted ways concerning the types of crime the women's movement was expected to affect. Adler proposed that the *violent* crime rate would increase because of women's "liberation." In contrast, Simon proposed that only the *property* crime rate would increase with women's "liberation." Simon suggested further that women's violent crime would decrease because women's frustrations with life would diminish as they had access to new work and educational opportunities.

Naffine (1987) summarizes some of the assumptions present in the women's "liberation" theory: (1) Feminism brings out women's competitiveness; (2) the women's movement has opened up structural opportunities to increase places where women can offend; (3) women have fought and won the battle of equality; (4) feminism makes women want to behave like men; and (5) crime itself is inherently masculine. There are obvious problems with these assumptions. Even the most plausible assumption—that feminism has opened up women's structural opportunities—loses credibility when faced with statistics showing that women have not achieved equality in high-paying and managerial professions (see Chapter 9). These assumptions, and liberation theory in general, have been soundly criticized for being wrong, and also for misusing and manipulating statistics and their interpretations in efforts to prove that gender equality breeds female crime (see Crites 1976; Feinman 1986; Leonard 1982; Morris 1987; Naffine 1987; Smart 1976, 1982).

Another problem with the "emancipation" or "liberation" hypothesis is that it predicts the opposite of previous strain and class theories: that crime will *increase* with an improvement of opportunities. This implies an underlying fundamental difference between male and female criminality. The theories discussed thus far, when they accounted for class—as they often did—hypothesized that crime would increase with blocked or worsened economic opportunities (see Steffensmeier and Streifel 1992).

Most important, however, the hypothesis that women's violent crime rates are catching up with men's is questionable. (This topic, comparing men's and women's criminality, will be addressed more fully in the following chapter.) Besides Adler, most research on the relationship between women's violent crime rate and the women's movement has found that females' violent crime rate has remained relatively stable since the 1970s (see Feinman 1986; Steffensmeier 1980). On the other hand, research on property crimes, particularly larceny and petty property crimes, has shown that women's rates have increased since the feminist movement of the 1970s (for example, Box and Hale 1983, 1984; Chilton and Datesman 1987; Smith and Visher 1980; Steffensmeier and Streifel 1992).

The increase in women's property crime rates, however, is more likely a result of the changing economic situation than the strength of the feminist movement. "The absence, rather than the availability, of employment opportunity for women," observes Naffine (1987, 88) "seems to lead to increases in female crime, for when times are good, the offending of women stabilizes rather than escalates." Thus, the "feminization of poverty," the increased number of women (with and without dependents) living in poverty, is a better predictor of women's criminality—and then, of property crimes—than is the strength or weakness of the feminist movement. The "liberation" hypothesis is particularly ironic because the feminist movement has probably had a greater effect on middle-class, Anglo women than those women most vulnerable to arrest: poor and unemployed women of color (Smart 1982). In fact, the types of crime for which women were increasingly arrested after the women's movement of the 1970s, prostitution and offenses against the family (such as desertion, neglect, and nonsupport), are crimes not "altogether compatible with the view of the emancipated female" (Steffensmeier and Allan 1988).

It has also been found that general sentencing patterns of men and women alike (for example, "get tough on crime" eras) have done more than the feminist movement to increase females' official crime rate reported by the police (Box and Hale 1984). Furthermore, if the women's movement has had any negative effect on women's criminality, it is that women now appear to be more likely to have their behaviors defined as criminal or delinquent by judges and police officers (Curran 1984; Morris 1987). Notably, researchers specifically examining the effect of young women's adherence to feminist ideals (for example, regarding women and work and gender roles in the family) report that profeminist women and girls are no more likely to report aggression and criminal or delinquent behavior than their more traditional sisters (Figueira-McDonough 1984; McCord and Otten 1983).

SUMMARY

Theories attempting to explain the etiology of criminal behaviors (and reactions by the crime-processing system) have proposed biological, psychological, social, political, and economic causes. The earliest theories focused on biology and the individual, whereas more recent theories have focused on the societal, economic, and political sources of crime. Most of these theories were developed to explain male criminality. Until Adler's women's "liberation" theory, most theorists made little attempt to account for female criminality. When they did, their hypotheses were fraught with sexist stereotypes, often defining female crime in terms of sexuality. The findings of this research are inconsistent; it is still unclear how males' and females' socialization and responses by the criminal processing system differ, and how these may affect their crime and delinquency rates.

In 1975, for the first time, a theory was developed to explain women's criminal behavior: women's "liberation" theory (Adler 1975; Simon 1975). Unfortunately, this theory was based on erroneous assumptions about the feminist movement, and statistics and their interpretations were often misleading. Feminists and others have been laying the groundwork, however, to reassess existing theories and to develop feminist theories. These attempts will be discussed in Chapter 11. In the meantime, it is vital that future theory building and theory testing examine sexuality, family factors, social and economic status, same-sex friendships, and mixed-sex friendships as equally relevant (or in the case of sexuality, perhaps irrelevant) for studies of both males and females (Campbell

1990). Future theory building cannot assume, moreover, that women or girls as a group behave similarly to each other. For example, recent research applying various theories to Anglo and African American women found that social–psychological variables were more related to Anglo than African American women's involvement in crime, while African American women's crime rates were more affected by structural forces (Hill and Crawford 1990).

NOTE

1. The chapter by Mark Cousins (1980) was entitled "Men's Rea: A Note on Sexual Difference, Criminology and the Law," in a book entitled *Radical Issues in Criminology,* edited by P. Carlen and M. Collison.

REFERENCES

Abelson, Elaine S. 1989. "The Invention of Kleptomania." *Signs* 15:123–143.

Adler, Freda. 1975. *Sisters in Crime: The Rise of the New Female Criminal.* New York: McGraw-Hill.

Becker, Howard S. 1963. *Outsiders: Studies in the Sociology of Deviance.* New York: Free Press.

Bonger, Willem. 1969. *Criminality and Economic Conditions.* Bloomington: Indiana University Press.

Box, Steven, and Chris Hale. 1983. "Liberation and Female Criminality in England and Wales." *British Journal of Criminology* 23:35.

——————. 1984. "Liberation/Emancipation, Economic Marginalization, or Less Chivalry: The Relevance of Three Arguments to Female Crime Patterns in England and Wales, 1951–1980." *Criminology* 22:473–498.

Brown, Beverly. 1990. "Reassessing the Critique of Biologism." Pp. 41–56 in *Feminist Perspectives in Criminology,* edited by L. Gelsthorpe and A. Morris. Buckingham, England: Open University Press.

Campbell, Anne. 1987. "Self Definition by Rejection: The Case of Gang Girls." *Social Problems* 34:451–466.

——————. 1990. "On the Invisibility of the Female Delinquent Peer Group." *Women and Criminal Justice* 2:41–62.

Cernkovich, Stephen, and Peggy Giordano. 1979. "A Comparative Analysis of Male and Female Delinquency." *The Sociological Quarterly* 20:131–145.

——————. 1987. "Family Relationships and Delinquency." *Criminology* 25:295–321.

Chilton, Ronald, and Susan K. Datesman. 1987. "Gender, Race, and Crime: An Analysis of Urban Trends, 1960–1980." *Gender and Society* 1:152–171.

Clark, S. M. 1964. "Similarities in Components of Female and Male Delinquency: Implications for Sex-Role Theory." P. 217 in *Interdisciplinary Problems in Criminology,* edited by W. C. Reckless and C. L. Newman. Columbus: Ohio State University.

Cloward, R. A., and L. E. Ohlin. 1960. *Delinquency and Opportunity: A Theory of Delinquent Gangs.* New York: Free Press.

Cohen, Albert K. 1955. *Delinquent Boys: The Culture of the Gang.* New York: Free Press.

Cousins, Mark. 1980. "Men's Rea: A Note on Sexual Difference, Criminology and the Law." Pp. 109–122 in *Radical Issues in Criminology,* edited by P. Carlen and M. Collison. Oxford: Martin Robertson.

Covington, Jeanette. 1986. "Self-Esteem and Deviance: The Effects of Race and Gender." *Criminology* 24:105–138.

Cowie, John, Valerie Cowie, and Eliot Slater. 1964. *Delinquency in Girls.* London: Heinemann.

Cressey, Donald. 1964. *Delinquency, Crime, and Differential Association.* The Hague: Martinus Nijhoff.

Crites, Laura. 1976. *The Female Offender.* Lexington, MA: D. C. Heath.

Cullen, Francis T., Kathryn M. Golden, and John B. Cullen. 1979. "Sex and Delinquency." *Criminology* 17:301–310.

Curran, Daniel J. 1984. "The Myth of the 'New' Female Delinquent." *Crime and Delinquency* 30:386–399.

Datesman, Susan, Frank Scarpitti, and Richard Stephenson. 1975. "Female Delinquency: An Application of Self and Opportunity Theories." *Journal of Research in Crime and Delinquency* 12:107–123.

Dembo, Richard, Gary Grandon, Lawrence La Voie, and William Burgos. 1986. "Parents and Drugs Revisited: Some Further Evidence in Support of Social Learning Theory." *Criminology* 24:85–103.

Dornfeld, Maude, and Candace Kruttschnitt. 1992. "Do the Stereotypes Fit? Mapping Gender-Specific Outcomes and Risk Factors." *Criminology* 30:397–420.

Erikson, Kai T. 1962. "Notes on the Sociology of Deviance." *Social Problems* 9:309–314.

Esbensen, Finn-Aage, and David Huizinga. 1993. "Gangs, Drugs, and Delinquency in a Survey of Urban Youth." *Criminology* 31:565–590.

Fausto-Sterling, Anne. 1985. *Myths of Gender: Biological Theory About Women and Men.* New York: Basic Books.

Feinman, Clarice. 1986. *Women in the Criminal Justice System,* 2nd ed. New York: Praeger.

Figueira-McDonough, Josephine. 1984. "Feminism and Delinquency: In Search of an Elusive Link." *British Journal of Criminology* 24:325–342.

Figueira-McDonough, Josephine, and E. Selo. 1980. "A Reformulation of the 'Equal Opportunity' Explanation of Female Delinquency." *Crime and Delinquency* July: 333–343.

Figueira-McDonough, Josephine, William H. Barton, and Rosemary C. Sarri. 1981. "Normal Deviance: Gender Similarities in Adolescent Subcultures." Pp. 17–45 in *Comparing Female and Male Offenders,* edited by M. Q. Warren. Beverly Hills, CA: Sage.

Fox, G. L. 1977. "'Nice Girl': Social Control of Women Through a Value Construct." *Signs* 2:805.

Freud, Sigmund. 1933. *New Introductory Lectures on Psychoanalysis.* New York: W. W. Norton.

Giordano, Peggy C. 1978. "Girls, Guys, and Gangs: The Changing Social Context of Female Delinquency." *Journal of Criminal Law and Criminology* 69:126–132.

Gordon, David. 1973. "Capitalism, Class, and Crime in America." *Crime and Delinquency* 19:163–186.

Gottfredson, Michael R., and Travis Hirschi. 1990. *A General Theory of Crime.* Stanford, CA: Stanford University Press.

Hagan, John, A. R. Gillis, and John H. Simpson. 1985. "The Class Structure of Gender and Delinquency." *American Journal of Sociology* 90:1151–1178.

Hagan, John, John H. Simpson, and A. R. Gillis. 1979. "The Sexual Stratification of Social Control: A Gender-Based Perspective on Crime and Delinquency." *British Journal of Sociology* 30:25.

————. 1987. "Class in the Household: A Power-Control Theory of Gender and Delinquency." *American Journal of Sociology* 92:788–816.

Harris, Anthony. 1977. "Sex and Theories of Deviance: Toward a Functional Theory of Deviant Type-Scripts." *American Sociological Review* 42:3–16.

Heidensohn, Frances M. 1985. *Women and Crime: The Life of the Female Offender.* New York: New York University Press.

Hill, Gary D., and Maxine P. Atkinson. 1988. "Gender, Familial Control, and Delinquency." *Criminology* 26:127–149.

Hill, Gary D., and Elizabeth M. Crawford. 1990. "Women, Race, and Crime." *Criminology* 28:601–626.

Hindelang, M. 1971. "Age, Sex and Versatility of Delinquent Involvement." *Social Problems* 21:471.

——————. 1973. "Cases of Delinquency: A Partial Replication and Extension." *Social Problems* 21:471.

Hirschi, Travis. 1969. *Cases of Delinquency.* Berkeley: University of California Press.

Hoffman-Bustamante, Dale. 1973. "The Nature of Female Criminality." *Issues in Criminology* 8:117–136.

Jensen, Gary J., and Raymond Eve. 1976. "Sex Differences in Delinquency." *Criminology* 13:427–448.

Jensen, Gary J., and K. Thompson. 1990. "What's Class Got to Do with It? A Further Examination of Power-Control Theory." *American Journal of Sociology* 95:1009–1023.

Johnson, Richard E. 1986. "Family Structure and Delinquency: General Patterns and Gender Differences." *Criminology* 24:65–84.

Kitsuse, John I. 1962. "Societal Reaction to Deviant Behavior: Problems of Theory and Method." *Social Problems* 9:247–256.

Klein, Dorie. 1980. "The Etiology of Female Crime: A Review of the Literature." Pp. 70–105 in *Women, Crime, and Justice,* edited by S. K. Datesman and F. R. Scarpitti. New York: Oxford University Press.

Klein, Dorie, and June Kress. 1976. "Any Woman's Blues: A Critical Overview of Women, Crime, and the Criminal Justice System." *Crime and Social Justice* 5:34–49.

Konopka, Gisela. 1966. *The Adolescent Girl in Conflict.* Englewood Cliffs, NJ: Prentice-Hall.

Lauritsen, Janet L. 1993. "Sibling Resemblance in Juvenile Delinquency." *Criminology* 31:387–410.

Lemert, Edwin M. 1951. *Social Pathology: A Systematic Approach to the Theory of Sociopathic Behavior.* New York: Mc-Graw-Hill.

Leonard, Eileen B. 1982. *Women, Crime, and Society: A Critique of Criminology Theory.* New York: Longman.

Lerman, Paul. 1966. "Individual Values, Peer Values and Subcultural Delinquency." *American Sociological Review* 33:219–235.

Lombroso, Cesare, and William Ferrero. 1895. *The Female Offender.* London: Fisher Unwin.

Loy, P., and S. Norland. 1981. "Gender Convergence and Delinquency." *Sociological Quarterly* 22:525.

Lynch, Michael J., and W. Byron Groves. 1989. *A Primer in Radical Criminology,* 2nd ed. New York: Harrow and Heston.

Mann, Coramae Richey. 1984. *Female Crime and Delinquency.* Montgomery: University of Alabama Press.

McCord, Joan, and L. Otten. 1983. "A Consideration of Sex Roles and Motivations for Crime." *Criminal Justice and Behavior* 10:3–12.

Merton, Robert K. 1938. "Social Structure and Anomie." *American Sociological Review* 3:672–682.

——————. 1949. *Social Theory and Social Structure.* Glencoe, IL: Free Press.

Messerschmidt, James W. 1988. "From Marx to Bonger: Socialist Writings on Women, Gender, and Crime." *Sociological Inquiry* 58:378–392.

——————. 1993. *Masculinities and Crime.* Lanham, MD: Rowman & Littlefield.

Miller, Susan L., and Cynthia Burack. 1993. "A Critique of Gottfredson and Hirschi's General Theory of Crime: Selective (In)Attention to Gender and Power Positions." *Women and Criminal Justice* 4:115–134.

Morash, Merry. 1983. "Gangs, Groups, and Delinquency." *British Journal of Criminology* 23:309–335.

_____. 1986. "Gender, Peer Group Experiences, and Seriousness of Delinquency." *Journal of Research in Crime and Delinquency* 23:43–67.

Morash, Merry, and Meda Chesney-Lind. 1991. "A Re-Formulation and Patriarchal Test of the Power Control Theory of Delinquency." *Justice Quarterly* 8:347–378.

Morris, Allison. 1987. *Women, Crime and Criminal Justice.* Oxford: Basil Blackwell.

Morris, Ruth R. 1964. "Female Delinquency and Relational Problems." *Social Forces* 43:82–88.

_____. 1965. "Attitudes Toward Delinquency by Delinquents, Non-Delinquents and Their Friends." *British Journal of Criminology* 5:249–265.

Naffine, Ngaire. 1987. *Female Crime: The Construction of Women in Criminology.* Sydney, Australia: Allen & Unwin.

Norland, Stephen, Randall C. Wessel, and Neal Shover. 1981. "Masculinity and Delinquency." *Criminology* 19:421–433.

Platt, Anthony. 1975. "Prospects for a Radical Criminology in the U.S." Pp. 95–112 in *Critical Criminology,* edited by I. Taylor, P. Walton, and J. Young. London: Routledge and Kegan Paul.

Pollak, Otto. 1950. *The Criminality of Women.* Philadelphia: University of Pennsylvania Press.

Pollak, Otto. 1961. *The Criminality of Women.* New York: A. S. Barnes.

Quinney, Richard. 1972. "The Ideology of Law: Notes for a Radical Alternative to Repression." *Issues in Criminology* 7:1–35.

_____. 1975. *Criminology: Analysis and Critique of Crime in America.* Boston: Little, Brown.

Rafter, Nicole H., and E. M. Natalizia. 1981. "Marxist Feminism: Implications for Criminal Justice." *Crime and Delinquency* 81–98.

Rahav, Michael. 1984. "Norm Set and Deviant Behavior: The Case of Age-Sex Norms." *Deviant Behavior* 5:151–179.

Rasche, Christine. 1975. "The Female Offender as an Object of Criminological Research." Pp. 9–28 in *The Female Offender,* edited by A. M. Brodsky. Beverly Hills: Sage.

Rhode, Deborah L. 1990. "Feminist Critical Theories." *Stanford Law Review* 42:617–638.

Rice, Marcia. 1990. Challenging Orthodoxies in Feminist Theory: A Black Feminist Critique." Pp. 57–69 in *Feminist Perspectives in Criminology,* edited by L. Gelsthorpe and A. Morris. Buckingham, England: Open University Press.

Rittenhouse, C. Amanda. 1991. "The Emergence of Premenstrual Syndrome as a Social Problem." *Social Problems* 38:412–425.

Rosenbaum, Jill L. 1989. "Family Dysfunction and Female Delinquency." *Crime and Delinquency* 35:31–44.

Sandhu, Harjit S., and Donald E. Allen. 1969. "Female Delinquency: Goal Obstruction and Anomie." *Canadian Review of Sociology and Anthropology* 5:107–110.

Schur, Edwin M. 1984. *Labeling Women Deviant: Gender, Stigma, and Social Control.* New York: McGraw-Hill.

Schwendinger, Herman, and Julia Schwendinger. 1970. "Defenders of Order or Guardians of Human Rights?" *Issues in Criminology* 5:123–157.

Segrave, Jeffrey O., and Douglas N. Hastad. 1983. "Evaluating Structural and Control Models of Delinquency Causation." *Youth and Society* 14:437–456.

Shover, N., S. Norland, J. James, and W. Thornton. 1979. "Gender Roles and Delinquency." *Social Forces* 58:162.

Simon, Rita. 1975. *Women and Crime.* Lexington, MA: D. C. Heath.

Simons, R. L., M. G. Miller, and S. M. Aigner. 1980. "Contemporary Theories of Deviance and Female Delinquency: An Empirical Test." *Journal of Research in Crime and Delinquency* 17:42.

Singer, Susan J., and Murray Levine. 1988. "A Power-Control Theory, Gender, and Delinquency." *Criminology* 26:527–547.

Smart, Carol. 1976. *Women, Crime and Criminology: A Feminist Critique.* London: Routledge & Kegan Paul.

_____. 1981. "Criminological Theory: Its Ideology and Implications Concerning Women." Pp. 6–17 in *Women and Crime in America,* edited by L. H. Bowker. New York: Macmillan.

_____. 1982. "The New Female Offender: Reality or Myth?" Pp. 105–116 in *The Criminal Justice System and Women,* edited by B. R. Price and N. J. Sokoloff. New York: Clark Boardman.

Smith, Douglas A. 1979. "Sex and Deviance: An Assessment of Major Sociological Variables." *Sociological Quarterly* 20:183.

Smith, Douglas A., and Christy A. Visher. 1980. "Sex and Involvement in Deviance/Crime: A Quantitative Review of the Empirical Literature." *American Sociological Review* 45:691–701.

Spender, Dale. 1981. *Men's Studies Modified.* Oxford: Pergamon Press.

Steffensmeier, Darrell J. 1980. "Sex Differences in Patterns of Adult Crime, 1965–77: A Review and Assessment." *Social Forces* 58:1080–1108.

Steffensmeier, Darrell J., and Emilie A. Allan. 1988. "Sex Disparities in Arrests by Residence, Race, and Age: An Assessment of the Gender Convergence/Crime Hypothesis." *Justice Quarterly* 5:53–80.

Steffensmeier, Darrell J., and Cathy Streifel. 1992. "Time-Series Analysis of the Female Percentage of Arrests for Property Crimes, 1960–1985: A Test of Alternative Explanation." *Justice Quarterly* 9:77–104.

Sutherland, Edwin. 1939. *Principles of Criminology,* 3rd ed. Philadelphia: J. B. Lippincott.

Sutherland, Edwin, and Donald Cressey. 1966. Principles of Criminology. Philadelphia: J. B. Lippincott.

Taylor, Ian, Paul Walton, and Jock Young (Eds.). 1973. *The New Criminology: For a Social Theory of Deviance.* New York: Harper & Row.

_____. (Eds.). 1975. *Critical Criminology.* London: Routledge & Kegan Paul.

Thomas, W. I. 1907. *Sex and Society.* Boston: Little, Brown.

_____. 1923. *The Unadjusted Girl.* Boston: Little, Brown.

_____. 1967. *The Unadjusted Girl.* New York: Harper & Row.

Thompson, William E., Jim Mitchell, and Richard A. Dodder. 1984. "An Empirical Test of Hirschi's Control Theory of Delinquency." *Deviant Behavior* 5:11–22.

Thornton, W. E., and J. James. 1979. "Masculinity and Delinquency Revisited." *British Journal of Criminology* 19:225.

Torstensson, Marie. 1990. "Female Delinquents in a Birth Cohort: Some Aspects of Control Theory." *Journal of Quantitative Criminology* 6:101–115.

Vedder, Clyde, and Dora Somerville. 1970. *The Delinquent Girl.* Springfield, IL: Charles C. Thomas.

3

The Frequency and Nature of Female Offending

> Perhaps the least contentious proposition one can advance within the discipline of criminology is that women are more law-abiding than men.
>
> (NAFFINE 1987, 1)

As stated in Chapter 2, female crime has not historically been defined as a social problem. This is one reason criminologists and others have consistently left females out of their research models and study samples. Male crime, on the other hand, has been taken far more seriously, and male offenders are often seen as the "real" offenders. There is some truth to this: Studies consistently show not only that females generally commit fewer crimes than males, but also that their offenses tend to be less serious and violent in nature.

This chapter draws on prior and current research and data in order to assess female offending. However, for a complete understanding of the studies and data, female offending must be examined and understood in a number of contexts:

1. *The nature of female offending:* the types of crimes women and girls commit
2. *The extent of female offending:* the frequency with which women and girls commit crimes
3. *Gender comparisons in offending:* how the nature and frequency of female and male offending compare
4. *Changes over time* in the extent, nature, and gender differences in offending

DESCRIPTION OF OFFENDING

The *nature* of offending, for the purposes of this book, addresses the type and seriousness of the offense. The *extent* of offending, on the other hand, is the frequency with which various offenses are committed. The term *offending* rather than *crime* is used, given that many of the studies are of youth and status offenses, behaviors that are not considered crimes when adults commit them (for example, truancy, drinking alcohol, and running away).

Offending rates are measured a number of ways. Typically, the rate is the number of offenses per 100,000 people in the population. Other measures of offending rates include giving high school students self-report surveys asking them how often (if ever) they participate in various offenses, or conducting interviews with sample participants. Whatever the structure for collecting offending rates, these rates are used to examine the extent and nature of offending at one point in time, or over a period of time (if conducted repeatedly). Furthermore, males' and females' offense rates can be compared to determine whether there are gender differences in the extent and nature of offending, and if these differences have changed over time. This chapter addresses these issues.

The *patterns* of offending rates over time (especially of females) received increased attention with the advent of Adler's (1975) and Simon's (1975) "liberation" hypothesis. This hypothesis suggests that rather than stable differences between the sexes (Option A), or gender-divergence (increasing differences) between the sexes (Option B), gender-convergence (Option C) is likely to occur over time (see figure below). *Gender-stability* is any pattern over time where the differences between male and female rates are relatively stable. They co-vary: Male and female rates rise and fall together. Thus we would expect that in an era of "get tough on crime" policies or in times of economic depression, men's and women's crime rates would be equally affected. With *gender-divergence* the disparity in offending rates between the sexes increases over time, with gender differences growing. *Gender-convergence,* consistent with the "liberation" hypothesis, occurs any time that the distance between males' and females' rates is decreasing and their offending rates are becoming similar.

Examples of Comparing Gender-Offending Patterns Over Time

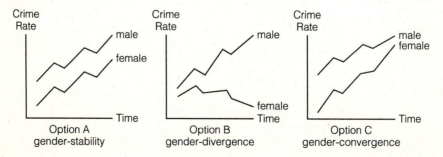

IMPORTANCE OF AGE,
RACE, CLASS, AND DATA TYPE

The typical adult female offender is young (usually under age 30), of color, undereducated, a single mother, poor, and a social service client (Sarri 1987; Wolfe et al. 1984). Chapter 2 pointed out how criminological theories have tended to be sex-blind, either completely ignoring females or viewing them through a stereotypical lens which usually distorts women's and girls' real-life experiences. Any analysis of gender must avoid a similarly restricted view by accounting for differences among females based on their age, race, and social class (see Simpson 1991). First, *age* is important because it has been well documented that there are relatively few "career criminals." Most people who break the law do so roughly between the ages of 15 and 24. Second, *race* is vital to understanding offending rates because of limited legitimate opportunities available to many people of color, as well as their increased risk of being labeled "criminal." Third, it is important to recognize that one's *social class* affects one's opportunities and treatment in our society. Class also affects the likelihood that one will turn to crime for survival, and similarly limits one's abilities to pay bond and to pay for a good attorney. Finally, the *type of data used*—official reports, victimization surveys, or self-reported offending—may influence the representation of offending rates. This is partially because most offending goes undetected by the juvenile and adult crime-processing systems, but also because official reports are apt to reflect bias, particularly in the forms of racism, classism, and sexism.

One of the most popular data sets used to assess crime rates in the United States is the Uniform Crime Reports (UCR). These reports summarize the yearly arrests from police departments in the entire country. Unfortunately, the reports do not control for social class. Nor do they control for race *and* sex at the same time, making it impossible to track African American women, Anglo women, African American men, and so on. Official statistics such as the UCR, court convictions, and imprisonment rates rely on the crime-processing system actors' *perceptions* of whether a crime occurred. Theoretically, police only arrest and judges and juries only convict when they believe that there is a strong likelihood that a person committed a crime. Thus, a major threat to the validity of using official statistics of crime rates is that discrimination may distort the statistics. For example, if Hispanic women are more likely than Anglo women to be arrested for the same offense, the official statistics would exaggerate Hispanic women's offending relative to Anglo women. Thus, it is not clear whether race, class, sex, and age differences represented by official statistics reflect different rates of offending or, rather, differential (discriminatory) processing of offenders.

Lewis's (1981) review of the research found that although African American women have been disproportionately incarcerated, analyses have failed to control systematically for sex *and* race, thus making it impossible, until recently, to determine how African American women compare to Anglo women, African American men, and so on. This problem has historically been even worse regarding people of color other than African Americans, particularly non–African American women of color. In fact, it was common until quite recently to combine Latinos and Native Americans with whites/Anglos in crime-processing statistics. Additionally, research on racial differences has focused almost exclusively on white and black offenders, ignoring other racial and ethnic groups. At any rate, Lewis's (1981, 93) review of research found that "correctional" statistics suggest that black women "display somewhat greater involvement with violent and other personal crimes than white women." However, she also cautions that when examining arrest records or other data to compare various races' offending patterns, it is important to control for age, since the higher rate of African American to Anglo females' violent crime rates might partially be explained by the fact that the African American population as a whole is younger (and thus in a higher risk age group) than the Anglo population (Lewis 1981). On the other hand, the age difference between African Americans and Anglos cannot by itself, according to Lewis, explain the offending differences between white and black women; these analyses must also consider economic deprivation, gender status inequality, socialization, gender role expectations, and racism.

> Black women, then, display gender role behavior, a social status and a crime pattern, all of which contradict acceptable feminine behavior, as defined by the dominant society. They tend to be assertive, function as unmarried heads of household and be convicted for violent person crimes. In short, they epitomize the type of deviant women the criminal justice system is committed to punish.
>
> *(Lewis 1981, 102)*

The importance of controlling for factors such as race and age, as well as the type of crime, can be seen in various studies. A study using national self-report data of women 18 to 23 years old found that while there were no significant differences between black and white women in the *composite* crime rate, when the types of crime were broken down, white women reported significantly more drug use than black women, and black women reported more involvement in major property and assault crimes than white women. Furthermore, that black women were more likely to report acquiring income from illegal activities suggested their increased economic vulnerability relative to white women (Hill and Crawford 1990). Another study of female arrests found few racial differences overall, but white women were more likely than black women to be arrested for serious property crimes, and black women were more likely than white women to be arrested for gambling, assault, family offenses, and violent crimes (Steffensmeier and Allan 1988).

Turning to the importance of age, a study of arrested females in a southern U.S. city found that women under 18 were involved mostly in petty property offenses and rarely were arrested for drugs/alcohol or prostitution; women 18 to 30 had high property and violent crime offense rates and the highest prostitution rates; and women over 30 were minimally involved in prostitution but had high rates of drug/alcohol arrests (Wolfe et al. 1984). A study of England and Wales found that while 3 percent of offenses committed by girls 10 to 14 years old were violent crimes against the person, this rose to 8 percent for girls 14 to 17 years old (Morris 1987).

Unfortunately, data gatherers in both official statistics and many self-report studies are either unwilling or unable to account for class differences, so little is known about this seemingly powerful variable. However, those studies that have controlled for race, gender, class, and age often find that these are important predictors of offending *behavior,* as well as *treatment* by the crime-processing system. Research has shown that making simple racial *or* gender comparisons is less useful than controlling for both race and sex to see how the experiences of women from different races compare, and how men and women of the same race compare. Finally, there is a danger in relying solely on official crime-processing statistics in that they may be a better reflection of bias than offending. Researchers should also use self-report surveys and interviews to present a more valid measure of offending.

FEMALE OFFENDING IN CONTEXT

This section discusses the findings from various studies regarding the extent and nature of female offending, and how it compares to male offending. Some studies were conducted solely on females, while others included females and males in their samples. First, some important concepts related to gender differences in crime are presented. Then, descriptions of female offenders and a comparison of male and female offenders are presented for various types of offenses. The following section will discuss gender patterns over time.

Concerning the extent of female crime, in both the United States and Canada, women constitute about 15 percent of people arrested by the police (G. Campbell 1990; Mann 1984). Regarding the nature of women's offending, the crimes for which females are most strongly represented are prostitution, running away, larceny/theft, fraud, and forgery/counterfeiting (Leonard 1982). While the concepts of the extent and nature of female crimes are relatively straightforward, making gender comparisons and examining changes over time are more complicated. Gender comparisons in offending are commonly evaluated by determining which offenses are *gender-related* and which are *gender-neutral* (see Smart 1976). Whereas gender-related crimes are more likely to be committed by one sex than the other, gender-neutral crimes are equally likely to be committed by either sex. Given males' higher propensity to offend, the majority of crimes are male gender-related, but especially rape and other violent crimes. The most common example of a female gender-related crime is prostitution.

Even if the legal *code* has progressed to define crimes as gender-neutral (not specifying "penis," "female," and so on), which makes either sex equally culpable of committing the same offense, the *enforcement* of the law may continue to be gender-specific (see Morris 1987). For example, the prostitution law may be changed to include male prostitutes or to go after clients as well as prostitutes, but the police and judges may continue to disregard these male offenders because they do not fit their stereotypes of offenders. In fact, it is likely that the police are even less likely to detect the male offenders because they do not picture them in these roles. Stereotypical assumptions about women, then, affect assumptions about the crimes they commit. For example, since the stereotype is that women shop and women use marriage to exchange sex for security, shoplifting and prostitution are viewed as extensions of women's "normal" roles (Morris 1987, 29–30).

Historically, legal codes have often not allowed that males could be prostitutes (similar to rape laws that did not allow that males could be victims). Additionally, both in law and in practice, the sanctioning of prostitutes (who are typically female) is much more rigorous than the sanctioning of prostitutes' clients (who are typically male, regardless of the prostitute's sex).

Finally, before addressing gender representation in specific offenses, a more recently recognized phenomenon is that of battered women who commit crimes with their batterers, often under duress and extreme pressure (see Walker 1993, 239). In some of these cases, if the male codefendant (batterer) is unknown to the legal system, the woman may take the entire blame. Similarly, there are cases of women sentenced to prison for unknowingly perpetrating a crime designed by their intimate male partners, or helping them in order to avoid risking their own or their children's well-being. The majority of these offenses involve selling drugs (see Tyson 1993).

Sexuality

There has been a concerted effort to control females' sexuality, both socially and legally, which has resulted in a double standard. For example, terms like *promiscuous, loose,* and *nymphomaniac* rarely are applied to males. In fact, males are often expected to be sexually active, regardless of their marital status. Females, on the other hand, are often expected to be chaste, or at least to limit themselves to one male partner. "A 'good' girl is never sexual, although she must be sexually appealing, while a healthy boy must prove his masculinity by experimenting sexually" (Chesney-Lind 1974). Given the homophobia in our culture, it is unclear with whom the "healthy" boys are supposed to have sex. Although female sexuality has received increased latitude since the 1970s, women and girls still experience more social constraints on their sexuality than boys and men do.

One female gender-related "offense" can best be labeled "promiscuity." This is a useful example of how official statistics fail to reflect the actual behavioral representations in society. That is, both males and females engage in voluntary sex. Although males engage in more voluntary sex than females, female juveniles are more often labeled with promiscuity "sex offenses" than males are. Many of the status offenses are directly or indirectly tied to both voluntary and abusive sexuality such as being sexually active (directly tied) or running away from home (indirectly tied). The status offenses of "running away" in the United States and "being in moral danger" in the United Kingdom are strongly related to sexual "promiscuity" (Smart 1976). Many girls (and boys) who run away from home are running away from sexual victimization, or incest. In fact, 20 percent of girls and 7 percent of boys seeking help from runaway and homeless centers report sexual abuse as a reason for their predicament; 9 percent of girls and 2 percent of boys who are runaways report sexual abuse by a parent (U.S. Department of Health and Human Services 1991).

Many runaways experience sexual victimization and/or are coerced or forced into prostitution after leaving home. One study of runaways found that 38 percent of boys and 73 percent of girls reported sexual abuse (McCormack et al. 1986). Moreover, although sexually abused runaway boys are no more delinquent/criminal than nonsexually abused runaway boys, sexually abused girl runaways are more likely than nonsexually abused girl runaways to be arrested, to be placed in jail, and to participate in a violent act (McCormack et al. 1986). Thus, not only are males and females labeled differently for consensual sexual activity, but sexual abuse appears to have a more detrimental effect on the subsequent delinquency of runaway females than of runaway males.

The crime-processing system, which has historically failed to respond to incest victims in the home, has diligently responded to girls who have run away from home. Girls have been labeled and severely punished for running away, regardless of the circumstances motivating their flight. The system's processing of these "offenders" will be covered in more detail in Chapter 4.

Child Abuse

Other female gender-related offenses are the nonsexual offenses against children and infants (Smart 1976), such as neglect, cruelty, and abandonment. Whether these crimes are actually committed more by women than men is debatable, especially if the amount of contact a parent has with her or his child is taken into consideration. Women probably abuse children much less often per hour spent with them than men do. If women are indeed more likely than men to be reported for cruelty to children, it is likely due to the fact that they shoulder most of the responsibility for child care (Smart, 1976). However, Dougherty (1993) is concerned that existing analyses of mothers who abuse their children ignore the influence of patriarchy within the family and how females' own past and present experiences of victimization, especially of male violence, may be related to the abuse they perpetrate. She suggests that future analysis should consider how both women's *power* (over their children) and *powerlessness* (in regard to their husbands) might influence the likelihood that they will abuse their children. Specifically, she notes research that states parents' stress is positively related to their likelihood to abuse their children, commenting on the high stress women battered by their husbands experience and how this might increase the chances that they will abuse their children.

Theft

Property offenses of a minor nature have often been attributed as female gender-related. Although larceny and thefts (for example, forgery, counterfeiting, fraud, and embezzlement) constitute a considerable amount of female arrests and convictions, males still account for the vast majority of these arrests and convictions (Eaton 1986; Leonard 1982). A study comparing changes in the imprisonment rates of women, however, indicated that while women's violent crime rates decreased by 8 percent between 1979 and 1986, the largest increase in women's imprisonment rate was due to an increase in larceny/theft convictions (Kline 1993). Similarly, a study of men's and women's arrests from 1960 to 1980 found overall gender-stability, except for larceny. While the majority of larceny arrests were still of men, women's arrests showed significant growth, particularly for black women (Chilton and Datesman 1987). Thus, it has been concluded that while men still dominate larceny crimes, women's rate is growing. This is likely due to women's deteriorating economic situation—the "feminization of poverty."

Shoplifting has frequently been assumed to be female gender-related. Stereotypes link women with shopping and portray them as being tempted by clothes, jewelry, and makeup. A closer examination suggests that shoplifting may be gender-neutral or *male* gender-related. Two studies found no significant differences between males' and females' shoplifting rates (Hudson 1989; Smart 1976). Other studies, however, report that males are more likely to shoplift than females (Buckle and Farrington 1984; Chesney-Lind and Shelden 1992; Mawby 1980), and steal more items and items of greater value than the food and clothing typically shoplifted by females (Buckle and Farrington 1984; Gibbens and Prince 1962; Hoffman-Bustamante 1973).

Juvenile Offending

It is important to recognize that both male and female offending, particularly of serious crimes, is relatively rare, and most juvenile offenses are minor, without a clear victim (Chesney-Lind and Shelden 1992). However, one study of over 15,000 Stockholm youth found that 30 percent of males and 16 percent of females had a conviction by the time they were 30 (Andersson 1990). Additionally, females were less likely to have a large number of convictions. For both males and females, prior convictions influenced the likelihood of future criminal involvement.

A study that followed females committed to the California Youth Authority in the 1960s found that the average age of offending onset was 14, and that two-thirds of the girls entered the system via a status offense arrest (Warren and Rosenbaum 1986). A majority of those women arrested as youth had a number of arrests, and they continued to be arrested into adulthood. The primary offense for half of the sample was a property offense, prostitution was the primary offense for 20 percent, and drugs were the primary offense for 13 percent (Warren and Rosenbaum 1986). Another study of women found that legal intervention as a juvenile was predictive of becoming an alcoholic (Miller et al. 1989). Of utmost importance is the potentially powerful negative impact of the status offense labeling of girls. Do the labels help make criminals? While more research is needed in this area, this and the next chapter discuss the important role of status offenses in controlling and affecting girls' lives.

U.S. data from UCR statistics on youth found that while the overall male–female arrest ratio is 4:1, the biggest gender gap is in serious property crimes (11:1) and violent crimes (9:1) (Chesney-Lind and Shelden 1992). However, even larceny theft, often strongly associated with the "female" offense of shoplifting, is committed predominantly by males (3:1); one-fifth of boys' and one-fourth of girls' arrests are for shoplifting. Status offenses, particularly "running away," continue to play a much bigger role in girls' than boys' arrests: One-fifth of girls' arrests and one-twentieth of boys' arrests are for running away (Chesney-Lind and Shelden 1992). Larceny/theft and running away have constituted the bulk of girls' delinquency arrests, accounting for approximately half of all female arrests since 1965 (Chesney-Lind and Shelden 1992, 10). Boys, on the other hand, are more eclectic in the types of offenses they commit, and they have a greater rate of offending.

Uniformity in male and female juvenile offending is most apparent in (1) less serious offenses, (2) self-report studies, and (3) more recent studies. This suggests that official statistics are a better indication of crime-processing system labeling than actual offending rates, and that girls' and boys' offending is most likely to portray gender-convergence for minor offenses.

Older self-report studies found males significantly more involved in status offenses and less serious delinquent behaviors (Gold and Reimer 1975; Jensen and Eve 1976), with African American males reporting the most offenses, followed by Anglo males, African American females, and Anglo females, respectively (Jensen and Eve 1976). Another older self-report study, however, found that while boys were more likely than girls to report delinquent activity and to commit offenses more frequently, "the activities most frequently engaged in by the males, are, by and large, the activities most frequently engaged in by the females" (Hindelang 1971, 526). Moreover, although girls were less likely to report delinquency than boys, girl delinquents were "generalists," committing a variety of offenses (Hindelang 1971).

More recent self-report studies indicate a similarity in male and female offending rates for status, drug, and less serious offenses, although male offending remains considerably higher for more serious property and all violent offenses (Canter 1982; Feyerherm 1981; Figueira-McDonough et al. 1981; Richards 1981). Where race and sex were controlled, studies found no strong gender–racial differences (Canter 1982; Cernkovich and Giordano 1979; Datesman and Aickin 1984; Jensen and Thompson 1990), except occasionally black males tended to be more delinquent than the remaining gender–racial categories (black females, white females, and white males), which clustered together (Hindelang 1981; Laub and McDermott 1985; Young 1980).

When categorizing offending patterns by gender–racial differences, age should also be considered, as there is a likelihood that patterns may vary between junior high, high school, and older populations (Chilton and Datesman 1987; Hindelang 1981; Richards 1981). Also, future research needs to use a variety of means in addition to official statistics and self-report surveys to assess gender differences in delinquency. For example, interviews with teenage prostitutes in Miami found numerous and extreme gender differences. Five percent of males and 87 percent of females reported prostituting in the prior 12 months, with an average of 26 acts for the males and 431 for the females (both males and females had male clients) (Inciardi et al. 1991). For the females, there was a high correlation between drug use and prostitution. Intravenous drug use was least prevalent among Anglo males and most prevalent among African American females. Finally, while only 3 percent of the males reported exchanging sex for crack cocaine, 71 percent of the females reported this (Inciardi et al. 1991).

In conclusion, regarding juvenile delinquency, there is a strong indication that for less serious crimes there are few differences in the commission rates of boys and girls, even when controlling for race. It has been stated that "the adolescent subculture of minor delinquency appears to now include both boys and girls, whereas it used to be a predominantly male domain" (Figueira-McDonough et al. 1981, 23). However, for the more serious offenses, gender differences appear to persist.

Girl Gangs

Female participation in gangs has typically been viewed as an extension of male gang membership. Historically, the female gang member was viewed as a sidekick and a sex object for male gang members (see Campbell 1990). Although limited information exists on girl gang members, more recent research suggests that they are more dynamic, independent, and interesting than the criminologists from the 1950s and 1960s would have us believe (see Campbell 1990). When female gang members fight, it is often over threats to their personal integrity, such as attacks on their sexual reputations, whereas boys are more likely to fight over a gang than over an individual challenge (Campbell 1984). A recent study reported that males and females are equally likely to belong to a gang (Bjerregaard and Smith 1993). Although gang membership increases both males' and females' delinquent activities, male gang members report significantly more delinquent activity and substance use than female gang members (Bjerregaard and Smith 1993; Morash 1983).

White-Collar Crime

The "liberation" hypothesis implies that as women become more equal to men, their offending rates will converge with men's. Given that the slow movement toward gender equality has benefited middle-class women the most, we might expect to see a similarity in men's and women's offenses most clearly in white-collar jobs. The limited research on this topic, however, has found significant gender differences. A study of white-collar convictions in U.S. federal courts found major differences between convicted men and women: (1) Women were usually employed as clerical workers, and men were usually employed as managers and administrators; (2) 60 percent of convicted female embezzlers were bank tellers, whereas only 14 percent of male embezzlers were tellers; (3) men's financial gains were much larger than women's; (4) women tended to work alone in committing the crime, whereas men were more likely to work with others; (5) women were more likely than men to report "family need" as motivating their offense; (6) women's crimes were more petty than men's; (7) women's share of corporate crime was low; and (8) men were more likely than women to be influenced by other white-collar workers to commit the crime (Daly 1989). In fact, the gender differences in these white-collar offenders were so extreme and the nature of the differences were such to make one wonder whether the crimes of most of these women should really be classified under white-collar offenses.

Robbery and Burglary

One of the few studies on female robbers examined imprisoned women and found that one-third acted alone or with another woman, and the major motivators were financial (often to purchase drugs) or peer pressure (often from a boyfriend). Two-fifths were arrested as juveniles, many were from single-parent homes, and most used a firearm in committing the offense (Fortune et al. 1980). The sample was evenly divided between two typologies: *situational* and *career robbers.* Situational robbers were motivated by external sources such as peer pressure or economic crises and had no commitment to robbery, while career criminals incorporated robbing as part of a continuing pattern of criminal activities (Fortune et al. 1980).

Although little effort has been made to study gender differences in burglary, in a notable exception, numerous gender differences were found: (1) Males were more likely than females to admit to crimes in addition to the burglary; (2) females were more likely than males to work with others in committing the burglary; (3) females were more likely than males to report being drug addicts; (4) males started their burglary "careers" at an earlier age than the females; (5) males reported committing more burglaries than the females; (6) females reported less contact with the crime-processing system than the males; and (8) males and females were equally likely to use drugs (Decker et al. 1993).

Drug Use

A study of Anglo and Chicana women drug users found that, like male drug users, theft is the most popular crime they commit, and that using prostitution to support the drug habit was relatively rare, especially among the Chicana women. While the women were more likely to turn to crime after (rather than before) the drug addiction, Anglo women reported less crime than Chicana women (Anglin and Hser 1987). Another study examined two cohorts of women drug users in Miami, reporting that the first cohort (1977–1978) was more heavily involved with drugs in general, while the second cohort (1983–1984) was more heavily involved with cocaine and narcotics (Inciardi and Pottieger 1986). Although both cohorts reported committing their first crimes at age 15 or 16, and both were heavily involved in property crimes and rarely involved in violent crimes, the younger cohort was more involved in drug sales and prostitution. Finally, a study of female violent street criminals found differences between women who had become criminals as girls (about age 11) and those who had turned to crime as young adults. Females initiated into crime as girls were more involved with drugs than females who became violent offenders as young adults. Moreover, addiction to drugs appeared to be related to an increase in violent offending for the group that became offenders as young adults (Baskin and Sommers 1993).

A review of the research on gender comparisons in illicit drug use reported interesting differences (Inciardi et al. 1993). First, young women are more likely to be introduced to drugs by husbands and boyfriends than young men are to be introduced by intimate female companions. (In fact, women are more likely to be in a position to have to exchange sex and companionship for drugs from a dealer.) Second, while both males and females often *begin* using drugs out of curiosity and a desire to experiment, there are gender differences in the motivations for continued drug use. Women are less likely than men to use illegal drugs for pleasure or thrill seeking and from peer pressure, and are more likely than men to use drugs as "self-medication" to "treat" existing depression. Thus, women are more likely than men to continue drug use in responses to crises and psychological stresses (and may be more likely to have crises and psychological stresses), and are more likely than men to have been depressed before developing a drug problem (see Inciardi et al. 1993). The primary research on women and crack cocaine found extremely high regularity of women performing oral sex (in particular) on men in crack houses in exchange for occasional hits of crack during the sexual act, an obvious form of prostitution:

> [I]t is also not unusual for a man to approach a woman for the purpose of having a sex partner throughout a smoking encounter. Some men will enter a crack house, purchase enough rocks for two people for several hours, and then make it clear to every woman in the house what he has in mind.... [T]here seems to be an expectation [in the crack house] that if a man wants to have sex with a woman, she will not oppose the offer. The expectations are implicit. Everyone involved—the house owner, the male user/customer, and the female user/prostitute are all aware of what is expected. Because the rules and the roles are known to all parties, there is little negotiating.
>
> *(Inciardi et al. 1993, 74–75)*

Although studies have not agreed on the link between prostitution and drugs, there is, undoubtedly, an important connection.

Homicide

A number of studies have been conducted recently on female homicide offenders, many of whom killed men who battered them (which is discussed in more detail in Chapter 8). Three studies conducted to describe female homicide offenders found them to be mostly African American, acting alone, poorly educated, and unemployed. They were most likely to kill someone of their own race, in the home, with a gun, and the victim was usually an intimate male partner (and very rarely a stranger) (Goetting 1988; Mann 1987; Weisheit 1984). In 4 to 9 percent of the cases, the victim was a child (Goetting 1988; Weisheit 1984). One study that attempted to determine whether a "new breed" of female homicide offenders resulted from the women's movement (testing the "liberation" hypothesis) found no such evidence, although the newer female offenders are younger and less likely to be married, and "robbery" has replaced "revenge" as the primary motive for homicides (Weisheit 1984). Probably due at least in part to the increased attention and prejudice blacks receive from the police, black women homicide offenders are more likely to have experienced contact with the crime-processing system than their white counterparts (Mann 1987).

Researchers estimate that 15 to 20 percent of all homicides in the United States are committed by women. A recent study, however, reported that the percentage of female homicide arrests decreased from 17 percent in 1960 to 10 percent in 1990 (Steffensmeier 1993). Men commit the vast majority of homicides, including of intimate partners. However, a much higher percent of female- than male-perpetrated homicides involve intimate partners. That is, "Although women in the U.S. rarely kill, when they do kill a male partner is likely to be the victim" (Browne and Williams 1989, 90). Careful analysis of these homicides points out the importance of women's ability to protect themselves from male aggression. Women who kill their male intimates are often acting in self-defense after a long history of abuse (Browne and Williams 1989; Goetting 1988; Jurik and Winn 1990). Incidentally, the most popular murder weapon of female homicide offenders is a firearm (Goetting 1988; Jurik and Winn 1990; Weisheit 1984), which often is the firearm that the batterer used to threaten them with in the past.

Notably, one study showed that female homicides of male partners decreased between 1976 and 1984, and these crimes were significantly lower in states with more domestic violence legislation and more resources for battered women (Browne and Williams 1989). Also, when audiences were present during the offense, they were more likely to *encourage* the violence of male offenders and to *discourage* the violence of female offenders (Jurik and Winn 1990). These studies show that although women rarely kill, when they do it is often their abusive male partners that they kill; thus, the roles of domestic violence and self-defense are vital to understanding the majority of female-perpetrated homicides.

CHANGES IN FEMALE
OFFENDING OVER TIME

This section takes the gender comparisons discussed in the last section one step further. To address the existence of support for the "liberation" hypothesis, that the feminist movement has increased both gender equality and female offending, this section presents studies evaluating gender patterns in offending over time. Specifically, this section draws on the concepts of gender-stability, gender-divergence, and gender-convergence (described at the beginning of this chapter) in order to analyze offending patterns over time.

Despite the "liberation" hypothesis, most researchers have agreed that women's crime rates have basically stayed the same except in the areas of less serious property crimes (Leonard 1982; Naffine 1987; Steffensmeier 1981, 1993; Steffensmeier and Cobb 1981; Steffensmeier and Streifel 1992) and possibly drugs. It is acknowledged that there are cyclical patterns of policies against crime, where an abundance of "get tough on crime" policies often result in increases in arrests and imprisonment rates, although there may be no corresponding increase in actual offending behavior. Overall, there is very little evidence for gender-convergence in crime rates.

A study following arrest rates in Toronto from 1859 to 1955 showed *gender-stability* in offending; overall, the patterns of males' and females' arrests increased and decreased at the same times (Boritch and Hagan 1990). Although men had much higher violent crime arrests, the long-term pattern suggested that violent crimes were decreasing for both sexes, and that the drop in arrest rates was particularly acute for women. Crimes of public order, such as drunk and disorderly conduct and vagrancy, constituted the largest proportion of both male and female crime. Following these crime rates over time indicated gender-convergence. However, the researchers concluded that official statistics may be a better indicator of criminalization practices than of criminal behavior. Furthermore, females' arrest rates decreased with corresponding increases in their economic opportunities (Boritch and Hagan 1990).

Numerous studies conducting gender offense comparisons over time in the United States have found overall *gender-stability,* with the limited evidence of *gender-convergence* usually for less serious property crimes and alcohol and drug use (Canter 1982; Chilton and Datesman 1987; Giordano et al. 1981; Steffensmeier 1993; Steffensmeier and Cobb 1981; Steffensmeier and Steffensmeier 1980). A study of juvenile offending over time, however, found no evidence of gender-convergence (Ageton 1983). Thus, where *gender-convergence* appears to exist, it can be largely explained by (1) changes in law enforcement practices, (2) the worsening economic position of women (the feminization of poverty), (3) changes in data collection methods, and (4) inflation in the small base of women's crimes (Canter 1982; Chilton and Datesman 1987; Giordano et al. 1981; Steffensmeier 1993; Steffensmeier and Cobb 1981; Steffensmeier and Steffensmeier 1980). If the gender gap in offending is closing, it appears to be for less serious property crimes, and possibly for drug use.

A more recent analysis of UCR data shows that while girls' arrests increased dramatically (by 250 percent) during the 1960s and early 1970s, this was largely due to the "baby boomers" hitting the high-risk age group. Although the percentage of females committing larceny increased some, this was temporary (Chesney-Lind and Shelden 1992). Studies from other countries have provided more indication of gender-convergence. Statistics from Canada suggest that although the changes from the 1960s to 1989 are inconsistent and largely for nonviolent offenses, *gender-convergence* occurs in property crimes (G. Campbell 1990). A study using official statistics in England and Wales from 1965 to 1975 found large proportional increases in female criminality, particularly violent offenses, but pointed out that these findings were suspect because of a small base and fluctuations in women's crime rates in earlier periods (the 1930s and 1940s) (Smart 1982).

Some studies have made a concerted effort to account for racial as well as gender differences in offending rates over time. However, there is no pattern in these studies' findings. One reported gender-divergence among both African American and Anglo juvenile populations (Laub and McDermott 1985); another reported gender-stability in larceny rates, although Anglo men and women of color now have similar rates (Chilton and Datesman 1987). Another study claimed that gender-stability appeared to be the pattern for Anglos, but gender-convergence was apparent for some offense types for people of color (Smith and Visher 1980). Finally, another study reported overall gender-convergence, especially for Anglo misdemeanor offenses, but gender-divergence for felonies perpetrated by African Americans (Farnworth et al. 1988). Thus, although it appears to be important to account for race in assessing gender offending patterns over time, to date it is unclear how race and sex interact in the overall gender-convergence, gender-stability, and gender-divergence patterns.

SUMMARY

In the studies of female offending, particularly those examining gender differences and patterns over time, the findings are inconsistent; however, some patterns have emerged. First, if there is any support for *gender-convergence* in offending, it appears to be for less serious offenses and drug use. This is particularly apparent in self-report data. Second, the reliability of studies finding gender-convergence for more serious crimes often suffered because of fluctuations in offending patterns over time; many fluctuations could be attributed to changes in the economy and in law enforcement practices. Third, analyses controlling for race and age are essential to understanding the true nature of female criminality and criminality in general.

Women's offending rates appear to be "catching up" to men's in the area of larceny/theft. This is probably due more to the feminization of poverty than to any liberating effects of the women's movement. Furthermore, although there is evidence that women's involvement in larceny/theft is increasing relative to men's, women still commit far fewer of these offenses. Although more recent data need to be analyzed, the most recent research suggests *gender-convergence* between Anglo males and African American females for some crimes, especially larceny. What used to be a fairly stable offending hierarchy represented by research, with African American males at the top, followed by Anglo males, African American females, and Anglo females, respectively, is appearing to collapse, although some studies find African American males distinctly ahead of other gender–race groups' offending rates. This may, however, be at least partially due to increased police surveillance of these youth. Future research needs to continue to follow these patterns, and to study other races in addition to black and white (such as Hispanics, Native Americans, and Asian Americans). In the meantime, it appears that regarding most offenses, especially serious and violent crimes, it is still a "man's world."

REFERENCES

Adler, Freda. 1975. *Sisters in Crime: The Rise of the New Female Criminal.* New York: McGraw-Hill.

Ageton, Suzanne S. 1983. "The Dynamics of Female Delinquency, 1976–1980." *Criminology* 21:555–584.

Andersson, Jan. 1990. "Continuity in Crime: Sex and Age Differences." *Journal of Quantitative Criminology* 6:85–100.

Anglin, M. Douglas, and Yih-Ing Hser. 1987. "Addicted Women and Crime." *Criminology* 25:359–397.

Baskin, Deborah R., and Ira Sommers. 1993. "Females' Initiation into Violent Street Crime." *Justice Quarterly* 10:559–581.

Bjerregaard, Beth, and Carolyn Smith. 1993. "Gender Differences in Gang Participation, Delinquency, and Substance Use." *Journal of Quantitative Criminology* 9:329–355.

Boritch, Helen, and John Hagan. 1990. "A Century of Crime in Toronto: Gender, Class, and Patterns of Social Control, 1859 to 1955." *Criminology* 28:567–599.

Browne, Angela, and Kirk R. Williams. 1989. "Exploring the Effect of Resource Availability and the Likelihood of Female-Perpetrated Homicides." *Law and Society Review* 23:75–94.

Buckle, Abigail, and David P. Farrington. 1984. "An Observational Study of Shoplifting." *British Journal of Criminology* 24:63–73.

Cain, Maureen (Ed.). 1989. *Growing Up Good: Policing the Behavior of Girls in Europe.* London: Sage.

Campbell, Anne. 1984. "GIRLS' TALK: The Social Representation of Aggression by Female Gang Members." *Criminal Justice and Behavior* 11:139–156.

——————. 1990. "Female Participation in Gangs." Pp. 163–182 in *Gangs in America,* edited by G. R. Huff. Newbury Park, CA: Sage.

Campbell, Gayle. 1990. "Women and Crime." *Juristat* 10:1–8.

Canter, Rachelle J. 1982. "Sex Differences in Self-Report Delinquency." *Criminology* 20:373–393.

Cernkovich, Stephen, and Peggy Giordano. 1979. "A Comparative Analysis of Male and Female Delinquency." *The Sociological Quarterly* 20:131–145.

Chesney-Lind, Meda. 1974. "Juvenile Delinquency: The Sexualization of Female Crime." *Psychology Today* (July):43–46.

——————. 1986. "Women and Crime: The Female Offender." *Signs* 12:78–96.

——————. 1987. "Girls and Violence: An Exploration of the Gender Gap in Serious Delinquent Behavior." Pp. 207–230 in *Childhood Aggression and Violence,* edited by D. Crowell, I. Evans, and C. O'Donnell. New York: Plenum.

Chesney-Lind, Meda, and Randall G. Shelden. 1992. *Girls, Delinquency, and Juvenile Justice.* Pacific Grove, CA: Brooks/Cole.

Chilton, Ronald, and Susan K. Datesman. 1987. "Gender, Race, and Crime: An Analysis of Urban Trends, 1960–1980." *Gender and Society* 1:152–171.

Daly, Kathleen. 1989. "Gender and Varieties of White-Collar Crime." *Criminology* 27:769–794.

Datesman, Susan K., and Mikel Aickin. 1984. "Offense Specialization and Escalation Among Status Offenders." *Journal of Criminal Law and Criminology* 75:1246–1274.

Decker, Scott, Richard Wright, Allison Redfern, and Dietrich Smith. 1993. "A Woman's Place Is in the Home: Females and Residential Burglary." *Justice Quarterly* 10:143–162.

Dougherty, Joyce. 1993. "Women's Violence Against Their Children: A Feminist Perspective." *Women and Criminal Justice* 4:91–114.

Eaton, Mary. 1986. *Justice for Women? Family, Court and Social Control.* Philadelphia: Open University Press.

Erez, Edna. 1988. "The Myth of the New Female Offender: Some Evidence from Attitudes Toward Law and Justice." *Journal of Criminal Justice* 16:499–509.

Farnworth, Margaret. 1984. "Male–Female Differences in Delinquency in a Minority-Group Sample." *Research in Crime and Delinquency* 21:191–212.

Farnworth, Margaret, M. Joan McDermott, and Sherwood E. Zimmerman. 1988. "Aggregation Effects on Male-to-Female Arrest Rate Ratios in New York State, 1972 to 1984." *Journal of Quantitative Criminology* 4:121–135.

Feyerherm, William. 1981. "Gender Differences in Delinquency: Quantity and Quality." Pp. 82–93 in *Women and Crime in America,* edited by L. H. Bowker. New York: Macmillan.

Figueira-McDonough, Josephine, William H. Barton, and Rosemary C. Sarri. 1981. "Normal Deviance: Gender Similarities in Adolescent Subcultures." Pp. 17–45 in *Comparing Female and Male Offenders,* edited by M. Q. Warren. Beverly Hills, CA: Sage.

Fortune, E. P., M. Vega, and I. J. Silverman. 1980. "A Study of Female Robbers in a Southern Correctional Institution." *Journal of Criminal Justice* 8:317–326.

Gibbens, T. C. N., and J. Prince. 1962. *Shoplifting.* London: ISTD.

Giordano, Peggy C. 1978. "Girls, Guys, and Gangs: The Changing Social Context of Female Delinquency." *Journal of Criminal Law and Criminology* 69:126–132.

Giordano, Peggy C., Sandra Kerbel, and Sandra Dudley. 1981. "The Economics of Female Criminality: An Analysis of Police Blotters, 1890–1976." Pp. 65–82 in *Women and Crime in America,* edited by L. H. Bowker. New York: Macmillan.

Goetting, Ann. 1988. "Patterns of Homicide Among Women." *Journal of Interpersonal Violence* 3:3–19.

Gold, Martin, and David J. Reimer. 1975. "Changing Patterns of Delinquent Behavior Among Americans 13 Through 16 Years Old: 1967–72." *Crime and Delinquency Literature* 7:483–517.

Hill, Gary D., and Elizabeth M. Crawford. 1990. "Women, Race, and Crime." *Criminology* 28:601–626.

Hindelang, Michael J. 1971. "Age, Sex, and the Versatility of Delinquent Involvements." *Social Problems* 18:522–535.

_____. 1979. "Sex Differences in Criminal Activity." *Social Problems* 27:143–156.

_____. 1981. "Variations in Sex–Race–Age Specific Incidence Rates of Offending." *American Sociological Review* 46:461–474.

Hoffman-Bustamante, Dale. 1973. "The Nature of Female Criminality." *Issues in Criminology* 8:117–136.

Hudson, Barbara. 1989. "Justice or Welfare? English and French Systems." Pp. 96–113 in *Growing Up Good,* edited by M. Cain. London: Sage.

Inciardi, James, Dorothy Lockwood, and Anne E. Pottieger. 1993. *Women and Crack-Cocaine.* New York: Macmillan.

Inciardi, James, and Anne E. Pottieger. 1986. "Drug Use and Crime Among Two Cohorts of Women Narcotics Users: An Empirical Assessment." *Journal of Drug Issues* 16:91–106.

Inciardi, James, Anne E. Pottieger, Mary Ann Forney, Dale Chitwood, and Duane C. McBride. 1991. "Prostitution, IV Drug Use, and Sex-for-Crack Exchanges Among Serious Delinquents: Risks for HIV Infection." *Criminology* 29:221–235.

Jensen, Gary J., and Raymond Eve. 1976. "Sex Differences in Delinquency." *Criminology* 13:427–448.

Jensen, Gary F., and Kevin Thompson. 1990. "What's Class Got to Do with It: A Further Examination of Power Control Theory." *American Journal of Sociology* 95:1009–1023.

Jurik, Nancy C., and Russ Winn. 1990. "Gender and Homicide: A Comparison of Men and Women Who Kill." *Violence and Victims* 5:227–242.

Kline, Sue. 1993. "A Profile of Female Offenders in State and Federal Prisons." Pp. 1–6 in *Female Offenders: Meeting the Needs of a Neglected Population*. Laurel, MD: American Correctional Association.

Laub, John H., and Joan M. McDermott. 1985. "An Analysis of Serious Crime by Young Black Women." *Criminology* 23:81–98.

Leonard, Eileen B. 1982. *Women, Crime, and Society: A Critique of Criminology Theory*. New York: Longman.

Lewis, Diane K. 1981. "Black Women Offenders and Criminal Justice: Some Theoretical Considerations." Pp. 89–105 in *Comparing Female and Male Offenders*, edited by M. Q. Warren. Beverly Hills, CA: Sage.

Mann, Coramae Richey. 1984. *Female Crime and Delinquency*. Montgomery: University of Alabama Press.

_____. 1987. "Black Women Who Kill." Pp. 157–186 in *Violence in the Black Family*, edited by R. L. Hampton. Lexington, MA: Lexington Books.

Mawby, Rob. 1980. "Sex and Crime: The Results of a Self-Report Study." *British Journal of Sociology* 31:525–541.

McCormack, Arlene, Mark-David Janus, and Ann W. Burgess. 1986. "Runaway Youths and Sexual Victimization: Gender Differences in an Adolescent Runaway Population." *Child Abuse and Neglect* 10:387–395.

Miller, Brenda, William R. Downs, and Dawn M. Gondoli. 1989. "Delinquency, Childhood Violence, and the Development of Alcoholism in Women." *Crime and Delinquency* 35:94–108.

Moon, Dreama G., Ruby J. Thompson, and Regina Bennett. 1993. "Patterns of Substance Use Among Women in Prison." Pp. 45–54 in *Women Prisoners: A Forgotten Population*, edited by Beverly R. Fletcher, Lynda D. Shaver, and Dreama G. Moon. Westport, CT: Praeger.

Morash, Merry. 1983. "Gangs, Groups, and Delinquency." *British Journal of Criminology* 23:309–335.

Morris, Allison. 1987. *Women, Crime and Criminal Justice*. Oxford: Basil Blackwell.

Naffine, Ngaire. 1987. *Female Crime: The Construction of Women in Criminology*. Sydney, Australia: Allen & Unwin.

Nagel, Ilene, and John Hagan. 1983. "Gender and Crime: Offense Patterns and Criminal Court Sanctions." Pp. 91–144 in *Crime and Justice: An Annual Review of Research*, Vol. 4, edited by M. Tonry and N. Morris. Chicago: University of Chicago Press.

O'Brien, Robert M. 1988. "Exploring the Intersexual Nature of Violent Crimes." *Criminology* 26:151–170.

Richards, Pamela. 1981. "Quantitative and Qualitative Sex Differences in Middle-Class Delinquency." *Criminology* 18:453–470.

Sampson, Robert J. 1985. "Sex Differences in Self-Reported Delinquency and Official Records: A Multiple-Group Structural Modeling Approach." *Journal of Quantitative Criminology* 1:345–367.

Sarri, Rosemary C. 1987. "Unequal Protection Under the Law." Pp. 375–393 in *The Trapped Woman*, edited by J. Figueira-McDonough and R. Sarri. Newbury Park, CA: Sage.

Simon, Rita. (1975). *Women and Crime*. Lexington, MA: D. C. Heath.

Simpson, Sally S. 1991. "Caste, Class, and Violent Crime: Explaining Difference in Female Offending." *Criminology* 29:115–135

Smart, Carol. 1976. *Women, Crime and Criminology: A Feminist Critique*. London: Routledge & Kegan Paul.

_____. 1982. "The New Female Offender: Reality or Myth?" Pp. 105–116 in *The Criminal Justice System and Women*, edited by B. R. Price and N. J. Sokoloff. New York: Clark Boardman.

Smith, Douglas A., and Christy A. Visher. 1980. "Sex and Involvement in Deviance/Crime: A Quantitative Review of the Empirical Literature." *American Sociological Review* 45:691–701.

Steffensmeier, Darrell J. 1980. "Sex Differences in Patterns of Adult Crime, 1965–77: A Review and Assessment." *Social Forces* 58:1080–1108.

_____. 1981. "Crime and the Contemporary Woman: An Analysis of Changing Levels of Female Property Crime, 1960–1975. Pp. 39–59 in *Women and Crime in America,* edited by L. H. Bowker. New York: Macmillan.

_____. 1982. "Trends in Female Crime: It's Still a Man's World." Pp. 118–130 in *The Criminal Justice System and Women,* edited by B. R. Price and N. J. Sokoloff. New York: Clark Boardman.

_____. 1993. "National Trends in Female Arrests, 1960–1990: Assessment and Recommendations for Research." *Journal of Quantitative Criminology* 9:411–441.

Steffenmeier, Darrell J., and Emilie A. Allan. 1988. "Sex Disparities in Arrests by Residence, Race, and Age: An Assessment of the Gender Convergence/Crime Hypothesis." *Justice Quarterly* 5:53–80.

Steffensmeier, Darrell J., and Michael J. Cobb. 1981. "Sex Differences in Urban Arrest Patterns, 1934–79." *Social Problems* 29:37–50.

Steffensmeier, Darrell J., and R. H. Steffensmeier. 1980. "Trends in Female Delinquency." *Criminology* 18:62–85.

Steffensmeier, Darrell J., and Cathy Streifel. 1992. "Time-Series Analysis of the Female Percentage of Arrests for Property Crimes, 1960–1985: A Test of Alternative Explanation." *Justice Quarterly* 9:77–104.

Tyson, James L. 1993. "Mandatory Sentences Lead to Surge of Women in Prison." *The Christian Science Monitor* (November 19):1, 18.

U.S. Department of Health and Human Services. 1991. *Annual Report to the Congress on the Runaway and Homeless Youth Program, Fiscal Year 1990.* Washington, DC: Office of Human Development Services.

Walker, Lenore E. 1993. "Battered Women as Defendants." Pp. 233–257 in *Legal Responses to Wife Assault,* edited by N. Z. Hilton. Newbury Park, CA: Sage.

Warren, Margaurite Q., and Jill L. Rosenbaum. 1986. "Criminal Careers of Female Offenders." *Criminal Justice and Behavior* 13:393–418.

Weisheit, Ralph A. 1984. "Female Homicide Offenders: Trends over Time in an Institutionalized Population." *Justice Quarterly* 1:471–490.

Wolfe, Nancy T., Francis T. Cullen, and John B. Cullen. 1984. "Describing the Female Offender: A Note on the Demographics of Arrests." *Journal of Criminal Justice* 12:483–492.

Young, Vernetta D. 1980. "Women, Race, and Crime." *Criminology* 18:26–34.

4

Processing Female Offenders

But men have indeed molded our legal system, which echoes the contradictions felt toward women: at times regarding them as evil and deceptive, at times treating them as childlike and defenseless.

(LEONARD 1982, 44)

Until the 1970s, it was unusual for anyone to question whether males and females were differently treated and processed by the police, prosecutors, judges, jurors, probation officers, prison guards, and parole boards. Although mainstream criminologists have agreed for some time that a defendant's *race* is inappropriate as a classification for processing in the system, the question of whether a person's *sex* is an equally inappropriate consideration has been unresolved. This is likely because "unlike claims of racism in the application of laws and sanctions, there is no general presumption that women have historically been subjected to a consistent pattern of discrimination" in crime processing (Nagel and Hagan 1983, 92).

Regardless of the historical lack of documentation of sexism in the official decision making of alleged offenders, it has long been the case that the official agents at every level of the system are "overwhelmingly male" (Schur 1984, 224). Unfortunately, increased interest in female offenders since the 1970s has focused more on questioning whether the feminist movement increased female offending than on stimulating awareness of the paucity of scholarly attention and programmatic change directed at female offenders (Chesney-Lind 1987).

Crime processing refers to responses by the juvenile and crime-processing decision-makers, from the police to parole boards, regarding the handling of alleged offenders. (For simplicity, the term *crime processing* will include the processing of status offenses, although technically these are not crimes.) Research on crime processing has been conducted at many different stages of decision making in the system (such as arrest, pretrial, conviction versus acquittal, and sentencing) and in many jurisdictions. Since the 1970s, increased attention has been given to exploring whether sex discrimination in crime processing exists. Unfortunately, this endeavor is hampered by the fact that there are no routinely collected statistics for court decision making (for example, sentencing length and conviction rates) in various states and jurisdictions, comparable to the statistics the Uniform Crime Reports provide for police decision making (for example, arrest rates) (Schur 1984).

This chapter discusses how sex discrimination has surfaced in both criminal and sentencing *laws,* and also describes current gender differences in crime processing in various jurisdictions and stages of the system. In addition, the processing of juveniles is discussed as well as how age, race, and class have affected how females are handled by the crime-processing system. Finally, the adherence of females to gender stereotypes will be examined to see how this influences the likelihood of leniency or increased harshness toward female offenders.

CRIMINAL LAWS
AND SEX DISCRIMINATION

The drafters of criminal law have been accused of attempting to perpetuate women's dependency (Scutt 1981), and the criminal laws themselves have been described as a measure of the gender inequality in society (Leonard 1982). This section discusses how criminal laws and their applications are often gendered.

Gender-neutral laws are written so that no differentiation is made regarding applicability to females and males. *Gender-specific* laws, on the other hand, specify in writing that they apply only to one sex, or specify that they apply differently to the sexes. (*Gender-neutral* and *gender-specific* may also be used to describe noncriminal laws, which will be evaluated more closely in Chapter 9.) There are three general forms of sex discrimination in criminal laws: (1) implementing and applying gender-specific laws, (2) applying gender-neutral laws differently to female and male defendants, and (3) applying gender-neutral laws in a manner that values males' victimizations more seriously than females' victimizations.

Historically, most laws have been gender-neutral, and with the exception of affirmative action laws, gender-specific laws have increasingly become gender-neutral over time. For example, until recently, most rape laws defined the offender as male and most prostitution laws defined the offender as female. In addition, the infanticide law, even as recently as the 1970s in England and Australia, applied only to women (Scutt 1981; Smart 1976). A review of Australian criminal law by Scutt (1981, 17) is equally applicable to U.S. and English criminal laws, as well as to those of other countries:

> As with many of our other institutions of power, the law has functioned to maintain the status quo. Where women are concerned, the law has been drawn with reference to the way in which men define women—as dependent wives with no ability to make their own decisions; or as wretched whores responsible for their "ability" to lead men into committing offenses against them.

Over time, particularly during the 1970s and 1980s, many gender-specific laws were revised to make them gender-neutral, consistent with the majority of the laws. Writing laws as gender-neutral, however, does not ensure that their application will be gender-neutral. That is, some laws that were intended to be gender-neutral have treated males and females differently in their applications. Smart (1976) discusses gender-neutral British laws whose applications have been influenced by the defendant's sex and marital status; for example, women who commit crimes with their husbands may be viewed as less culpable.

Numerous authors cite prostitution as an example of institutionalized sex discrimination in criminal laws and crime processing (Edwards 1984; Leonard 1982; Schur 1984; Smart 1976). The Contagious Diseases Acts passed during the 1860s in England were designed to guarantee sailors and soldiers a "clean" supply of prostitutes by incarcerating prostitutes with venereal diseases. The police had free reign to arrest any "suspicious" women (Windschuttle 1981).

Even today, prostitutes are singled out for "routine and perfunctory harassment" while the customers usually go free (Schur 1984, 225). A 1966 court ruling in Australia concluded that a man soliciting a woman to act as a prostitute was not "engaged in a sexual purpose," but a woman prostitute soliciting a customer was engaged in such a purpose. The man—unlike the woman—was thus undeserving of arrest (Scutt 1981). The huge gender discrepancy between the sanctioning of female prostitutes and male customers is further compounded when one accounts for race and class: The customers are typically white, employed, middle-class, middle-aged men, living in the suburbs, while those penalized for this crime are usually poor women of color (Bernat 1984; Leonard 1982).

Prostitutes not only report being harassed by the police for their offenses, but they are rarely taken seriously by the police when they are victims, particularly when they are raped and murdered (Morris 1987). Ironically, the 1910 White Slave Traffic Act (also known as the Mann Act)

> … was to be directed at the elimination of the business of securing women and girls and selling them outright or exploiting them for immoral purposes. Instead, it was used to prosecute the voluntary and ordinary immoralities of people and to punish the women "victims" whom the law was designed to protect.
>
> (Beckman 1985, 86)

In 1978, the implementation of a gender-neutral New York state statute to make prostitution and patronization of a prostitute crimes of equal severity did not result in gender-neutral application. The police continued their nonenforcement of patrons, and women were still discriminated against (Bernat 1985).

The third manner in which criminal laws may result in sex discrimination is not concerned with how male and female *defendants* are differently treated, but rather how the laws' enactments may judge the harshness of the crime based on whether the *victim* was male or female. Chapters 6 through 8 discuss this in more detail regarding female victims of rape and battering. Another example of this, however, is in the enactment of the gender-neutral death penalty laws, where women's and children's lives are generally less valued than men's. An in-depth analysis found that killing strangers for gain is much more likely to result in receiving the death penalty than killing a spouse (usually a woman) or child in anger (Rapaport 1991). Thus, it is hardly surprising that the crimes most likely to receive the death penalty are committed by men against men, or by men who killed women and children in *another man's* family (Rapaport 1991). Moreover, the death penalty is given in such a manner that male and parental dominance is supported because crimes in the home, of which women and children are disproportionately victims, are seen as less deserving of the death penalty than violence against (usually male) strangers, such as the "luckless clerk on night duty at a convenience store" (Rapaport 1991, 379).

Rapaport (1991) does not aim either to weigh the moral grounds of the death penalty or to minimize the murder of night clerks. Rather, she shows how the murder of women and children by men they know is ranked far less seriously than the murder of men by strangers (usually for financial gain) when examining who receives the death penalty. Another study found that decisions to try a case (rather than plea bargain) are based on the strength of evidence and the credibility and blamelessness of the victim. This study also found that cases where the *victims* were *male* were more likely to go to trial than be plea bargained, suggesting gender differences in credibility and blamelessness of victims (Myers and Hagan 1979).

In conclusion, with the exception of rape and prostitution laws, most laws are gender-neutral, written to apply equally to both sexes. In the 1970s and 1980s, most of the few gender-specific laws were changed to gender-neutral laws. Unfortunately, the practice of *enforcing* laws does not always follow the gender-neutrality written in most law codes. The next section of this chapter discusses how gender-specific legislation on sentencing has worked to the disadvantage of female offenders. The final section of this chapter discusses empirical research findings on gender differences in crime processing at various stages of the system.

SENTENCING LAWS
AND SEX DISCRIMINATION

Many of the efforts to improve the lot of women in the crime-processing system have backfired, resulting in worse treatment or stricter guidelines for females. Examples of this include the first sex-segregated penal institutions and sex-specific sentencing laws. This section shows how the history of sex-segregated prisons is related to discriminatory sex-specific sentencing laws.

Chapter 5 discusses in more depth how sex-segregated prisons often increase incarcerated women's oppression.

The first women-only prisons in England and the United States were designed to help women. They were labeled "reformatories" and "industrial homes" in an effort to distinguish them from the harsher "penitentiaries" housing male offenders. Women's prisons were designed to *rehabilitate,* whereas men's penitentiaries had *punishment* as the primary goal (Temin 1980). The assumption was that women were more malleable and amenable to rehabilitation than men.

The result of this supposed better rehabilitative treatment of female offenders was that judges' sentences for women became *indeterminate* (uncertain) and longer than males' *determinate* (fixed) sentences for the same crimes. The justification was that women should stay in prison until they were rehabilitated. Although most states had a limit on the maximum sentence for each crime, women were actually serving more time than men for the same crimes.

This patronizing "helping" of women offenders is analogous to the effects of the juvenile and family courts created for children in the late 1800s. The supposed increased care of minors through *parens patriae* (where the court is assigned to act in a protective parental role toward children) did more to restrict than to liberate children (see Chesney-Lind 1982; Naffine 1989). This is consistent with the contention that "the deprivation of rights of women as a group has been historically justified by their definition as inferior human beings" (Figueira-McDonough and Sarri 1987, 13–14), including treating them as children. The fact that both women and children have been subjected to this denial of rights in the name of "help," should not be lost. (The "infantalization" of women offenders is discussed further in Chapter 5.)

The 1913 Muncy Act of Pennsylvania is the most famous example of sex discrimination in sentencing. The act required judges to sentence women age 17 and older who were convicted of an offense punishable by more than one year to an indeterminate sentence in the Muncy State Industrial Home for Women. The act gave judges much less discretion for sentencing female than male offenders, particularly with regard to shortening women's sentences. The effect of this act was that women were not eligible for parole as early as men convicted of the same offenses. As recently as the 1970s, Arkansas, Connecticut, Iowa, Kansas, Maine, Maryland, Massachusetts, New Jersey, and Ohio had laws similar to the Muncy Act, which permitted longer sentences for females than males convicted of the same offense (Temin 1980).

The first attack on the Muncy Act occurred in 1966. Jane Daniel, a convicted robber, was originally sentenced to one to four years. One month later, her sentence was extended to three and one-half to ten years, as stipulated by the Muncy Act. Had Jane Daniel been a male, the judge would have been allowed to give "him" the one- to four-year sentence. The Superior Court of Pennsylvania denied that this was an infringement of her rights, stating that men's and women's inherent physical and psychological differences justified differential treatment. Therefore, it was deemed reasonable for women to receive longer sentences, especially since they supposedly received more effective rehabilitation while incarcerated.

The one judge who dissented in this opinion was sufficiently convincing for the Supreme Court of Pennsylvania to hear the appeal. Daniel's appeal was joined by the case of Daisy Douglas, a woman convicted of aggravated robbery with a male codefendant. Douglas's record consisted only of prostitution *arrests*, while her paramour and codefendant had six prior *convictions* for burglary. Following the Muncy Act, Douglas received the maximum allowable sentence—twenty years—while her codefendant received a three- to ten-year sentence. The appeal centered on denial of the Fourteenth Amendment's equal protection clause. The Douglas case was crucial in overturning Muncy because it could actually show that a woman and a man were treated differently in the same case. The court could find no reason why women should receive longer sentences, and ruled in favor of Douglas and Daniel. Connecticut followed suit shortly afterward, striking down their equivalent of the Muncy Act.

Unfortunately, two weeks after the Daniel decision, the Pennsylvania legislature passed the Muncy Act Amendment, which ordered the court not to fix a *minimum* sentence for a woman convicted of a crime; only a maximum sentence not to exceed the maximum term specified in the law could be given. Thus, women were still denied equal treatment, making the Daniel decision practically moot. Sex discrimination was further institutionalized because a man was entitled to have a minimum sentence set by a judge in an open hearing with mandated counsel, whereas women's sentences were decided in closed sessions by parole boards. "Arguably, this constitutes as much a denial of equal protection as the imposition of mandatory maximum sentences" (Temin 1980, 267).

Feinman (1992) traced a similar sentencing practice in New Jersey (*State v. Costello*, 1971). A 1973 State Supreme Court ruling struck down indeterminate sentencing of women when men received minimum–maximum term sentences, on the grounds that such decision making violated the equal protection clause of the Fourteenth Amendment (*State v. Chambers*, 1973). However, this practice ended only when a state code was implemented in 1979 (Feinman 1992).

In summary, during the 1960s and 1970s, there was a concerted effort to challenge many of the gender-specific laws requiring different sentencing practices for women and men. Observers of the implementation of these laws recognized that they resulted in *de jure* discrimination against women, who were receiving significantly longer sentences than men convicted of the same crimes. Challenges to these laws were resisted, but eventually most sexist laws were overturned in favor of gender-neutral sentencing laws.

THREE HYPOTHESES OF SEX DISCRIMINATION IN CRIME PROCESSING

Three hypotheses can be tested to establish whether there is sex discrimination in crime processing, and if so, whether it is against females or males: the equal treatment hypothesis, the chivalry (or paternalism) hypothesis, and the "evil" woman hypothesis. The *equal treatment* (or the null) hypothesis states that there is no sex discrimination in crime processing: Males and females are treated identically. An example of equal treatment would be minor males and females receiving similar sentences if caught drinking beer by a police officer. The *chivalry* or *paternalism* thesis hypothesizes that there is sex discrimination against male offenders; that is, females are treated or processed more leniently than males. This belief was first suggested by Thomas (1907) and then by Pollak (1950), who were discussed in Chapter 2. For example, a girl caught drinking beer would be told to pour her beer out and go home, whereas a boy caught drinking beer would be arrested and brought before juvenile court. The third category, the *evil woman* hypothesis, purports that sex discrimination against females exists in crime processing: Females are treated more harshly than males for similar offenses. The reasoning behind this belief is that offending females have violated gender roles as well as laws; thus, "female defendants will be sanctioned not only for their offenses, but also for their inappropriate sex role behavior" (Nagel and Hagan 1983, 116). The evil woman hypothesis is often viewed as the counterthesis to the chivalry or paternalism thesis. In this case, the beer-drinking boy would be sent home with no record, while the beer-drinking girl would be sanctioned and sent to juvenile court.

CHIVALRY AND PATERNALISM

It has been noted that criminologists and lay people frequently assume that chivalry is the most common practice of the three options (Curran 1983; Leonard 1982; Morris 1987; Visher 1983). Therefore, much of the research on sex discrimination in crime processing has focused on the idea of *chivalrous treatment* as an example of "reverse discrimination." Where it exists, however, chivalrous treatment is far more complex than the simple preferential treatment of females. Rather, chivalrous treatment is usually a bartering system in which women in general are viewed as being less equal. This bartering system is extended only to certain kinds of females, according to their race, class, age, sexual orientation, demeanor, and adherence to "proper" gender roles. Chivalrous treatment may be viewed as an exchange or bargain, where the interaction between the usually male official and the female violator "is transformed into an exchange between a man and a woman" (Visher 1983, 6). The chivalrous treatment is likely only extended, then, to females who conform to traditional gender stereotypes (Visher 1983).

To understand the current costs and complexities of chivalrous treatment, it is necessary to be aware of the historical underpinnings of chivalry and paternalism.

The term chivalry emerged in Europe during the Middle Ages. It described an institution of service rendered by the crusading order to the feudal lords, to the divine sovereign, and to woman kind. "Ladies" were special beneficiaries of the practice of chivalry—knights were sworn to protect their female weakness against dragons and devils. After the disap-

pearance of chivalry as a formal institution, however, a number of chivalrous practices regarding women continued to exist in the world of social
convention.

(Moulds 1980, 279)

Some believe that it is important to distinguish between chivalry and paternalism (Moulds 1980; Nagel and Hagan 1983). Chivalry is associated with placing an individual on a pedestal and behaving gallantly toward that person,
whereas paternalism involves taking care of the powerless and dependent. Both
chivalry and paternalism, however, imply weakness and a need to protect another person or group, which can have dangerous repercussions when "protect" becomes "control." It is often difficult to tell whether preferential treatment of female defendants, when it occurs, is due to chivalry or paternalism,
some combination of the two, or other factors.

A cursory look at the chivalrous treatment of women and girls may indicate that females inevitably benefit, often at the expense of males. This form of
human interaction, however, is more in tune with "political paternalism," for
which there may be a cost. "If the gentle treatment women are said to enjoy is
based on this political inferiority, we should be aware of the high price paid
for the so-called benefits of chivalry" (Moulds 1980, 278). On the other hand,
some question whether equal treatment is necessarily the right objective, because it ignores that men and women have different access to power in society
and often experience different roles and responsibilities (such as in childrear-
ing) (Daly 1989a; Morris 1987). These issues resurface later in this chapter and
again in Chapter 9, when we examine laws that have been used to "protect"
women from "men's" employment, often restricting women to the unpaid and
devalued work in the home. In short, there is often a high price to pay for
chivalrous/paternalistic treatment: Women are viewed as children in "need" of
additional attention and control.

EMPIRICAL FINDINGS ON GENDER
DIFFERENCES IN CRIME PROCESSING

It is difficult to evaluate the validity of the equal treatment, chivalry, or evil
woman hypotheses without accounting for the type of offense, the stage in the
crime-processing system, the demographic characteristics of the alleged offender, and the degree to which defendants fit gender stereotypes. In their review of research that tests the chivalry and evil woman hypotheses, Nagel and
Hagan (1983, 135–136) suggest that the evil woman hypothesis is not the opposite of the chivalry hypothesis, but rather its corollary. Women may receive
chivalrous treatment as long as they commit less serious crimes, exhibit the
"appropriate" passive demeanor, and have little evidence against them.

> Thus it may be that women are preferentially treated, compared with men,
> until such time as the basis for that preferential treatment—chivalry or
> paternalism—is rendered inappropriate. Then, by virtue of the seriousness

of the offense charged, the lessening of the presumption of innocence, and the evidence of deviation from traditional female patterns of behavior, the woman is moved into the evil woman category, and preferential treatment ceases.

(Nagel and Hagan 1983, 135–136)

The earliest research on gender differences in crime processing found strong support for the chivalry hypothesis rather than the equal treatment or evil woman hypotheses. For the most part, however, these findings supporting the preferential treatment of females could be explained by the studies' failure to account or control for two important *legal variables*: the defendant's prior record and the type of offense the defendant was accused of committing. If the crime-processing system is indeed just, then we expect the decision making to be related to legal variables about the case, and not *extralegal variables,* such as the defendant's sex, race, and class.

Since the 1980s, studies evaluating gender bias in crime processing have been more likely to include the type of offense and prior record. Consequently, there is less support for the chivalry hypothesis and more for the equal treatment hypothesis. To understand how this works, consider a study that simply compares the raw percentages of males' and females' arrest, conviction, and sentencing severity and finds that males are far more likely than females to be arrested, convicted, and given lengthy sentences. These percentages imply chivalry, or the lenient treatment of females. Say, however, that after the analysis controls for the seriousness of the offense and the defendant's prior record, it finds that males and females with similarly serious offenses and similar prior records receive the same rates of arrest, conviction, and sentence length. Such findings (which are common) point to a more fundamental gender difference (already discussed in the last chapter) than how alleged offenders are processed: Males generally receive harsher sanctions than females in crime processing because they generally commit more serious crimes and have lengthier and more serious records.

Despite the increasing evidence that chivalrous treatment is less common than once thought, the picture of gender differences in crime processing is more complex than simple support for the equal treatment hypothesis. First, there is some evidence that chivalrous treatment still exists in some situations, even when controlling for the legal variables. Second, some studies have found support for the evil woman hypothesis when controlling for the legal variables. Most important, even when analyses find evidence for chivalrous treatment or equal treatment in crime-processing decisions, there is often additional evidence that different factors were used to determine males' and females' culpability and punishment. For example, one study found that what appeared on the surface to be chivalrous treatment was actually the result of extraordinarily harsh sanctioning of African American males relative to everyone else (all females and Anglo males), implying that the intersection of race and sex alone can have a huge impact (Spohn et al. 1985). Thus, regardless of which of the three hypotheses are supported by the overall findings, many studies find that different factors are used to make decisions about females' versus males' culpability.

The remainder of this chapter describes findings from empirical studies that tested the three hypotheses on gender discrimination in crime processing:

the equal treatment, chivalry, and evil woman hypotheses. The factors that need to be considered to determine whether gender bias occurs in crime processing include (1) the race, class, and age of the alleged offender; (2) the importance of reforms in the processing of juveniles; (3) the stage in the crime-processing system; (4) the type of offense; and (5) how gender-role stereotypes affect gender bias in crime processing.

Differences Among Females: Race, Class, and Age

The idea behind chivalry, that women are placed on a pedestal and need to be protected, is likely to be afforded more to Anglo women than to women of color. Crime-processing decisions are often based on stereotypes that Anglo women are more feminine, fragile, and deserving of protection than women of color (see Young 1986). Similarly, with regard to social class, poorer women may be less likely to be treated as "ladies" than their wealthier sisters, and thus be less likely to experience chivalrous crime-processing treatment. Regarding the age variable, there is evidence that the evil woman approach is more predominant for girls than for women (Nagel and Hagan 1983, 115).

Any evaluation of crime processing must first recognize that there are different life experiences among females, depending on such factors as their race, class, and age. For example, interviews with African American women prisoners confirmed that childhood incest was related to running away from home, which was related to the delinquent labeling of these young women and to their subsequent imprisonment (Arnold 1990). The powerlessness of these women as girls had been compounded by class and "structural dislocation." (Structural dislocation, in this study, referred to ways that girls were marginalized within or forced to leave three primary socializing institutions: the family, education, and occupation. Such dislocation often increased the likelihood of turning to crime.) Many of the young women had been good students, but being a good student did not buy clothes and food. "Although school was a refuge for many women, it was not a sufficient counterbalancing force for the significant damage to personhood and self-esteem that occurred within an impoverished environment, and within the institution of the family" (Arnold 1990, 157). Not surprisingly, incest and other childhood victimizations were related to subsequent drug addiction. A less intensive study in Canada found not only that Native Americans were imprisoned disproportionately compared to Anglos, but that this was particularly true for women (LaPrairie 1989).

A considerable amount of research confirms that chivalrous treatment may be reserved for "certain kinds" of females, based on their personal characteristics. A number of crime-processing studies have found that African American women and other women of color tend to receive more severe responses by the system than Anglo women (Krohn et al. 1983; Kruttschnitt 1981; Spohn et al. 1987; Visher 1983), poorer women receive more severe responses than wealthier women (Kruttschnitt 1981), and younger women are discriminated against compared to older women (Farrington and Morris 1983; Visher 1983). The influence of age interacting with sex is somewhat difficult to determine, but some studies have found that younger women receive harsher treatment than older women (see Chesney-Lind and Shelden 1992; Hiller and Hancock 1981; Krohn et al. 1983). Regarding class and economic issues, one study found that welfare status had a more detrimental impact on sentencing severity than either race or income (Kruttschnitt 1981). A study of British magistrates' (judges') processing of women offenders found clear class bias in the sentencing of women:

> Respectable, middle-class wives and mothers are assumed to be so sensitive that they will be reformed by a minimum of punishment (or no punishment at all). Working-class women are perceived to be tougher (more like men?) and therefore need to be treated more harshly if any impression is to be made on them, on the grounds that punishment is the only thing "people like that" understand.
>
> *(Worrall 1990, 88)*

These findings confirm that not all females are treated similarly in the crime-processing system. As a rule, women of color, poor women, and younger women are afforded less leniency than other females.

Reforms in the Processing of Juveniles

The juvenile court has been accused of punishing the noncriminal (status) offenses of girls the same as or more harshly than the criminal offenses of boys (or girls) (Chesney-Lind 1973, 1981, 1987; Conway and Bogdan 1977; Datesman and Scarpitti 1977; Schlossman and Wallach 1982). Also, girls charged with promiscuity have historically been treated more harshly than girls committing other nonsexual offenses (Terry 1970). Girls not only have been formally and informally punished for consensual sexual activities that boys are more likely to "commit," but girls additionally have had their sexual victimizations merged with their sexual "offenses":

> One of the most problematic aspects of the juvenile justice system is its failure to distinguish offenders from victims. Nowhere is this more true than in the case of sexual abuse and sexual behavior. Females are often identically handled for abuse and promiscuous behavior or prostitution.
>
> *(Sarri 1983, 382)*

Perhaps the most disturbing aspect of the processing of females has been the historically pervasive forced submissions of juveniles to gynecological exams. The excuses given for these exams were to determine if they had venereal diseases and whether they were virgins. (The courts were apparently unconcerned with venereal disease or virginity in boys.) The first study to document this practice was conducted on Honolulu juvenile court cases between 1929 and 1964 (Chesney-Lind 1973). Only one-quarter of boys' but three-quarters of girls' arrests were for status offenses, and 70 to 80 percent of the girls were forced to have "physical exams," even for nonsexual charges such as larceny. The girls were more likely than the boys to be sent to pretrial detention, and they spent three times as long there as their male counterparts.

Besides the jail-like atmosphere that confronts young people held in detention facilities, young women in the past underwent an extra and significant violation of their civil rights: pelvic examinations and, more recently, vaginal searches.... The accounts suggest that blanket administration of pelvic examinations occurred well into the 1970s in various parts of the United States.

(Chesney-Lind and Shelden 1992, 149-150)

Shelden's (1981) study of Memphis, Tennessee, court records between 1900 and 1917 found that nonconsensual sexual experiences (rape victimizations) as well as consensual sexual activity of girls resulted in harsh sanctions against them. Such sanctions were nonexistent for boys. Gynecological exams to determine whether girls were virgins (in order to assess their criminality) were commonplace. Even when controlling for race, class, and offense, girls were treated more harshly than boys. In a similar study of Honolulu juvenile court cases between 1929 and 1964, Chesney-Lind (1973) found not only that girls were more likely than boys to be referred to court and forced to have pelvic exams, but also that three times as many girls as boys were institutionalized.

A more recent British study found that girls' sexual activity is still monitored more closely and punished more severely than boys', and the harsh treatment of girl runaways is linked to their sexual "promiscuity" (Gelsthorpe 1989). A U.S. study of family court records found that boys received harsher dispositions than girls for criminal offenses (felonies and misdemeanors), but girls received harsher dispositions than boys for status offenses. Half of the girls, but only one-fifth of the boys, had been referred to family court for status offenses (Datesman and Scarpitti 1980). U.S. studies also report that the family courts are most likely to warrant official intervention of status offenders when they are Anglo girls, and least likely when they are African American boys; this is consistent with race–gender stereotypes (Datesman and Aickin 1984; Datesman and Scarpitti 1980). An Australian court study on juveniles found that girls are more likely to be given such "rehabilitative" sentences as probation, supervision, and institutionalization, while boys are "treated" with more legalistic measures such as bonds, fines, and adjournment (Hiller and Hancock 1981).

A study of France, England, and Wales found that girls were only one-sixth of the youth with criminal charges, yet they made up half of the juveniles removed from the home and placed in institutions (Hudson 1989). Moreover, girls received special scrutiny and discrimination. They were judged by their "femininity" and were sanctioned for typical adolescent behavior, including immaturity in judgment and acting "silly." Boys who exhibited these same behaviors were less likely to be sanctioned for them. A study of youth recommended for supervision (a court punishment that requires checking in with a supervisor for two to three years) in England and Wales reported discrimination against girls, in that they were far more likely than boys to be recommended for supervision for trivial offenses (Webb 1984). Similarly, a comparative analysis of ten European criminal courts found that girls are still more severely punished than boys for status offenses, especially for sexual activity, and are more likely to be incarcerated and for longer periods than boys (Cain 1989, 232).

The role of parents in the offense processing of youths is particularly important, especially when the goal is to examine gender differences. There is ample evidence that parents play a crucial role in many juveniles' first formal contact with the crime-processing system, and that girls are at much greater risk than boys of having their parents turn them into the police or juvenile courts (Chesney-Lind and Shelden 1992; Hiller and Hancock 1981; Sarri 1983; Teilmann and Landry 1981). Parents are often less tolerant of their daughters' than their sons' identical behaviors whether they are status offenses (for example, running away, breaking curfews, drinking alcohol, and being sexually active) or more traditional offenses (for example, larceny, and assaults). Moreover, parents are more likely to report problems with daughters than with sons, and they are more likely to physically and sexually abuse their daughters (Chesney-Lind and Shelden 1992). (This victimization often causes juveniles to run away, to drink alcohol and to engage in other "acting out" behaviors, as discussed in Chapter 3.) Finally, one study reported that almost one-third of families refused to take their children back after their release from court custody as "persons in need of supervision" (PINS) (Conway and Bogdan 1977).

The establishment of the juvenile court in 1899 was the culmination of the "child-savers'" efforts to control youths' lives. This was particularly apparent for girls who were the "losers in the reform movement," which resulted in girls' high referral rates to juvenile courts and subsequently high institutionalization rates for "immorality" and "waywardness" (Chesney-Lind and Shelden 1992, 120). The police and the juvenile courts have historically condoned more punitive reactions to female than male status offenders, reaffirming a double standard for male and female sexuality. Although this was more common in the early years of the juvenile court, "there is evidence that the pattern continues" (Chesney-Lind and Shelden 1992, 115).

The Juvenile Justice and Delinquency Prevention (JJDP) Act of 1974 was designed to divert and deinstitutionalize status offenders from secure facilities. For states to receive federal funding for delinquency prevention programs, they had to discontinue institutionalizing status offenders in "training schools," detention centers, and adult jails, and develop plans to treat status offenders in places other than juvenile detention or correctional facilities. Because girls have been disproportionately sanctioned as status offenders, it was predicted that this would have a huge impact on the processing of girls. As expected, there was a decline in the admission of girls to detention facilities and "training schools" following the 1974 JJDP Act (Chesney-Lind 1986, 1988; Sarri 1983). Between 1975 and 1979, males' detention rate decreased by 20 percent, and females' rate decreased by 44 percent. These gender differences were largely due to the overrepresentation of girls in status offenses and to the policy's goal to divert status offenders from detention (Krisberg and Schwartz 1983).

The initial optimism that accompanied the deinstitutionalization of status offenders is tempered by the findings from (1) monitoring deinstitutionalization rates over time and (2) examining the private juvenile "correctional" system that replaced the traditional secure facilities. Regarding the first point, there is some concern that the decline of institutionalized status offenders leveled off between 1979 and 1982, and "the gains made against judicial sexism are very much in jeopardy" (Chesney-Lind 1986, 90). In fact, between 1982 and 1986, arrests for both male and female runaways increased (Chesney-Lind 1988). Moreover, while female admissions to "training schools" decreased 37 percent in the five years after the JJDP Act, male admissions increased by 9 percent (Krisberg and Schwartz 1983).

Now turning to the second point, it is not clear that the diversionary programs have resulted in any less stigmatizing of juvenile offenders than the detention facilities before the JJDP Act (Datesman and Aickin 1984). More important, however, a study in Minnesota discovered that many of the status offenders who previously would have been institutionalized in the traditional secure facilities (such as "training schools") were institutionalized in increasing numbers in the "hidden" or private juvenile "correctional" system following the 1974 JJDP Act. This system includes mental health and chemical dependency programs (Schwartz et al. 1984). Although this study did not examine gender per se, case studies portray many of these youth as females whose parents disapproved of their (often sexual) behavior: "More often than not, these youth are referred by their parents … [and] many of the admissions are not as 'voluntary' as one might think" (Schwartz et al. 1984, 382). The authors describe one case of a 16-year-old girl with no history of serious delinquency or chronic status offending, whose parents had her repeatedly institutionalized in private mental hospitals for periods as long as nine months, simply because her father, a prominent university administrator, was embarrassed by her "punk" attire and "punk" friends. The authors question what rights parents should have to institutionalize their children against their will in psychiatric or chemical dependency programs. It is also important to examine how this "hidden" juvenile-processing system might be affecting girls differently than it affects boys.

Similarly, a study of girls institutionalized in delinquent "homes" in England found that many girls were not in these homes for delinquent offenses, but because of emotional and family problems, such as their parents' fighting (Gelsthorpe 1989). In comparison, South Australia implemented a policy in 1979 to abolish status offenses. This act has been far more successful than the JJDP Act in the United States and other countries' attempts to curb the criminalization of juveniles. South Australia's abolishment of status offenses appears to have resulted in equal treatment for boys and girls and a decreasing concern with girls' sexuality (Naffine 1989).

The Presence of Gender Bias
in Different Stages of Processing

Many studies examine gender bias in various crime-processing decision points in the system: arrest, detention versus pretrial release, prosecution, dismissal of charges, negotiations and the guilty plea, conviction versus acquittal, incarceration, sentence severity, parole, and reconviction. It is often difficult to compare these studies because they are conducted in numerous and varied jurisdictions, at various stages or decision points in the system, and in different time periods. It is necessary, however, to attempt to determine the overall findings from these studies.

As stated in Chapter 3, women are generally far less serious offenders than men and have less extensive prior records. Thus, they are less likely to have their cases reach the final stages of the crime-processing system. Therefore, analyses that focus only on the latter stages may not adequately represent the processing of female offenders.

The first evaluation of studies on gender bias in crime processing stated that chivalry was most likely in the beginning stages and least likely in the later stages (Nagel and Hagen 1983). A more recent review, however, found the opposite: Chivalry is least likely in the beginning and most prominent in the later stages of crime processing (Chesney-Lind 1987). These opposing findings are likely due to the fact that the more recent evaluation was able to include more studies on the original contact with the system (the police) and the more recent studies have been more likely to control for legal variables. The overall findings regarding studies evaluated for this section of the chapter are consistent with the more recent (Chesney-Lind 1987) review: Chivalry is least common in the beginning stages of crime processing and most common in the latter stages.

As explained in detail below, the most support for the evil woman hypothesis is at the earliest stages of decision making (the police); support for the equal treatment hypothesis is most evident in the middle decision-making stages (the decisions to prosecute, dismiss charges, and convict); and support for the chivalry hypothesis is most evident in the final decision-making stages (the decision to incarcerate, the severity of the sentence, and the likelihood of reconviction). Most studies did not find sex to be a strong predictor, as the legal variables usually are. Many researchers found that evidence for chivalry in the original analyses of their data disappeared (or gender differences became negligible) when they controlled for other, usually legal, variables (Farrington and Morris 1983; Fisher and Mawby 1982; Landau 1981; Landau and Nathan 1983; Spohn et al. 1985).

Police Decision Making   Decision making by police is the stage that has the most support for the evil woman hypothesis. Even here, however, this support is not consistent, and can be explained by the unusually harsh police treatment of female status offenders. Two studies found that women were discriminated against in police decision making (Ghali and Chesney-Lind 1986; Wilbanks 1986), two found lenient or chivalrous treatment by the police (De-Fleur 1975; Krohn et al. 1983), and one found equal treatment (Visher 1983). Notably, the strongest and most consistent support for the evil woman hypothesis in police decision making was found in research on police responses to status offenders (Chesney-Lind and Shelden 1992; Hiller and Hancock 1981; Sarri 1983; Teilmann and Landry 1981).

In the past it was common for the police, when looking into nonsexual offenses of juveniles, to question girls—but not boys—about their sexual experiences, and then add the sexual offense charges to the original offense (Chesney-Lind 1974). Most young women, then, enter the crime-processing system as status offenders, for running away from home, incorrigibility, waywardness, curfew violations, and so on. Although females constitute a small proportion of the system, when they are in the system, it is most often for status offenses (Chesney-Lind 1981).

Most empirical research dispels the notion that females are treated chivalrously at the beginning stages of the crime-processing system.

Pretrial Court Decisions Most of the research on sexism in courtroom decision making focuses on judge, jury, and trial decisions, although fewer than one in ten cases go to a full trial (Figueira-McDonough 1985). Not only are pretrial decisions more common, but much of the pretrial decision making is not subject to the due process requirements of formal trials, leaving more room for discrimination.

An important stage in crime processing is the *detention versus pretrial release* decision, which "refers to the terms under which a defendant may be allowed to remain free in the interim between arrest and case disposition" (Kruttschnitt and McCarthy 1985). This decision not only is important regarding a defendant's immediate freedom, but can have implications on the subsequent processing of the case: A defendant who has been detained may be more likely to be viewed as a confirmed offender or "inmate" (see Frazier and Cochran 1986). Research on gender bias at the detention/pretrial release decision suggests that chivalrous treatment may be reserved for adult women who are not prostitutes (Bernat 1985; Frazier and Cochran 1986; Kruttschnitt 1984; Kruttschnitt and Green 1984; Teilmann and Landry 1981). The treatment of juveniles and prostitutes at the detention/release stage, on the other hand, was more consistent with the evil woman hypothesis.

Research examining gender bias in the decision to *prosecute or dismiss charges* largely supports the equal treatment hypothesis (Curran 1983; Ghali and Chesney-Lind 1986; McCarthy 1987; Nagel et al. 1982; Steffensmeier et al. 1993; Teilmann and Landry 1981), although there is some support for chivalry (Gruhl et al. 1984; Spohn et al. 1987; Wilbanks 1986). A study examining the likelihood of *referring juveniles to juvenile court* found chivalry in court referrals for youth charged with delinquent acts, but support for the evil woman hypothesis for youth charged with status offenses (Datesman and Aickin 1984). One study on juveniles, however, found that the sex of the offender had a significant interaction with her or his race regarding charge dismissal: Anglo boys had the best chance for dismissal, Anglo girls for diversion, African American girls for probation, and African American boys for formal processing (Sarri 1983).

Regarding the likelihood of *pleading guilty or negotiating* a plea, two studies found equal treatment of the sexes (Curran 1983; Gruhl et al. 1984), while two found support for the evil woman hypothesis (Ghali and Chesney-Lind 1986; Figueira-McDonough 1985). Figueira-McDonough's (1985) is perhaps the most important of these studies because it was the most carefully conducted. She found that while women and men were equally likely to plead innocent, men were nearly twice as likely to plead guilty to a lesser charge. Furthermore, the use or possession of a gun added seriousness to women's but not men's offenses, and the presence of a witness was more likely to influence women than men to plead guilty. Women were less able to bargain and more willing to plead guilty, which may have been due to their limited access to attorneys, education, and experience (or power in general). Men were also more likely to receive both charge reductions and sentence reductions. Finally, only men were rewarded for their guilty pleas.

Trial and Posttrial Decision Making   Research on the *conviction* stage of decision making consistently supports the equal treatment hypothesis (Curran 1983; Ghali and Chesney-Lind 1986; Gruhl et al. 1984; Steffensmeier et al. 1993), except for one study that supported the chivalry hypothesis (Wilbanks 1986). The research on gender bias at the *incarceration* decision was evenly divided between supporting the chivalry hypothesis (Gruhl et al. 1984; Nagel et al. 1982; Steffensmeier et al. 1993) and the equal treatment hypothesis (Ghali and Chesney-Lind 1986; Kruttschnitt and Green 1984). An Urban Reform Era study in Ontario, Canada, supported the evil woman hypothesis (Boritch 1992). Research findings consistently support the chivalry hypothesis in the *sentencing severity* stage of decision making (Curran 1983; Farrington and Morris 1983; Kruttschnitt 1984; Nagel et al. 1982; Steffensmeier et al. 1993; Wilbanks 1986). One study that evaluated a determinate sentencing policy found equal treatment of the sexes (but not races) (Zatz 1984). (Again, the Urban Reform Era study in Ontario supported the evil woman hypothesis regarding sentence severity [Boritch 1992].) Similarly, studies on gender bias in *reconviction* (Farrington and Morris 1983) and *probation* (Ghali and Chesney-Lind 1986; Nagel et al. 1982) decision making consistently supported the chivalry hypothesis, except for one study that found equal treatment of the sexes in probation decisions (Kruttschnitt 1984).

A final area of gender differences in court processing, one that has received little attention, is *death penalty* sentencing. Between 1976 and 1987, 14 percent of those charged with murder or nonnegligent manslaughter were women; however, only 2 percent of the prisoners on death row are female (Rapaport 1991). This appears to be chivalrous treatment of female offenders, but a closer examination by Rapaport (1991) suggests otherwise. First, felony murders are rarely committed by women (4 to 6 percent), and women are more likely to kill intimates in anger or defense than to kill strangers for a predatory purpose (such as economic or sexual gain) (Rapaport 1991). Second, male murder defendants are four times more likely than female murder defendants to have a prior conviction for a violent felony. Third, females are far less likely than males to be accused of murdering multiple victims (Rapaport 1991). Given these gender differences in murders and murderers, it is "logical" that women constitute only 2 percent of death row prisoners.

Gender Differences in Crime Processing
Based on the Type of Offense

In addition to determining the validity of the equal treatment, chivalry, and evil woman hypotheses based on personal characteristics of the offender and the stage in the crime-processing system, it is important to control for the type of offense. It is likely that the direction of sex discrimination (whether it is against males or females) may be closely linked with the nature of the offense. In fact, Naffine (1987, 2) states: "The agents of the law are clearly inconsistent, even in their paternalism." Her review of gender and crime-processing studies concluded that chivalry is more likely when women commit less serious crimes, but that women are treated more harshly than men when they commit more serious crimes. The less serious and more serious offenses, however, are closely linked with gender-role stereotypes. It has been stated that women whose offenses more closely fit traditional gender stereotypes (for example, shoplifting), will fare better than their less traditional counterparts who commit robberies, assaults, and so on (Nagel and Hagan 1983, 116). Therefore, women who commit traditionally "masculine crimes" are expected to be treated more harshly than men (Chesney-Lind 1987).

Some studies, however, have found that women are treated more chivalrously for felony or violent crimes and less chivalrously for minor and property offenses (Hepburn 1978; Steffensmeier et al. 1993; Visher 1983). A study on juveniles found that girls were treated chivalrously for property crimes, but as "evil women" for status offenses (Hiller and Hancock 1981).

Sarri (1987) states that examining the interaction between the offense type and the gender likelihood of committing the offense is necessary to determine gender disparities in crime processing. For some crimes, females and males are equally likely to be involved, and yet females are sanctioned more harshly (for example, running away and prostitution); for other crimes, males and females are equally likely to be involved and are treated equally (for example, larceny); and for yet others, females are much less likely to commit the crimes but are more severely sanctioned when they do (for example, sexually abusing children) (Sarri 1983). Similarly, a study on the abduction and fondling of children found that women are treated more harshly than men throughout the crime-processing system, while for charges of fraud, men are treated more harshly than women (Wilbanks 1986).

In summary, there are no consistent findings regarding the relationship between the type of offense and the presence of chivalry. This investigation merits further inquiry.

Gender Stereotypes and Crime Processing

Early studies on sex discrimination in crime processing recognized that chivalrous treatment was often reserved for females who displayed "appropriate" feminine behavior. A study of drug arrests found that females were less likely than males to be arrested if they cried, expressed concern for their children, or claimed to have been "led" by men (DeFleur 1975). Similarly, another study found that women whose demeanors represented antagonism toward the police were often discriminated against (Visher 1983), and a study on sentencing concluded that women generally fare better than men unless they are nontraditional women (Nagel et al. 1982).

In the late 1980s, an important addition to the understanding of gender bias in crime processing was the recognition that chivalrous treatment in the processing of adult offenders may not be the direct result of sexist behavior on the decision-makers' parts alone, but could also be the indirect effects of sexism and the very real gender differences in the responsibilities of women's and men's lives. That is, the specified gender roles in society likely influence differences in the processing of female and male defendants. Moreover, "women are more likely than men to be processed according to an assessment of their personal circumstances, rather than their offense" (Worrall 1981, 90).

For example, rightly or wrongly, persons in charge of dependent children and with little access to legitimate means may be given special consideration by crime-processing decision-makers. In most cultures, such persons are usually women. Thus, evidence of chivalrous treatment in crime processing might in fact be a manifestation of institutionalized gender roles in society at large. If women are fulfilling their "natural" roles as mothers, and to some extent wives, they may be given more lenient sanctions. This important addition to understanding gender differences in crime processing is attributed to Kathleen Daly, Candace Kruttschnitt, and Mary Eaton. Daly (1989a) points out that "protecting" women in so-called chivalrous sentencing might actually be an attempt to protect children and families.

Eaton's (1986) analysis of court cases in a suburb of London found that while men and women were treated similarly when they were in similar circumstances, women and men were rarely in similar circumstances. Although the court did not overtly discriminate based on sex, it endorsed separate and unequal roles for men and women, particularly with respect to traditional families. Men were expected to provide financially for families, while women's roles included emotional support and child care. Thus, when a probation officer conducted a home visit, a description of the home was more common with a female defendant than with a male defendant (Eaton 1986, 67). Eaton's study found some evidence of surface chivalry, such as women being more likely to get probation and less likely to be given prison or jail sentences; however, women also tended to have less serious crimes and records than men. Thus, chivalrous processing may be due more to an inherently unequal society than to an inherently biased crime-processing system. Moreover, the judges are not necessarily ignorant to women's status in the economic structure:

> Family circumstances and disposable income were rarely similar for men and women and this affected the sentences.... [M]any magistrates commented in interviews on the difficulty of fining a woman with no disposable income. The women before them were usually responsible for the care and maintenance of children, supported either by social security benefits or by such small housekeeping allowances that to deduct any amount to pay a fine would be to deprive the children.
>
> (Eaton 1986, 39)

Similarly, Daly's (1987) interviews with crime-processing court officials (judges, prosecutors, probation officers, and defense attorneys) found that they regularly described work and family roles to explain defendants' deserved leniency. Defendants described as "familied" provided care or economic support for others, and were provided more leniency than their "nonfamilied" counterparts, who had no such responsibilities. In a study of state criminal court judges, Daly (1989a) found the judges' primary motive in sentencing was to protect children (not women) and women's and men's economic support for families. The defendants' work–family relations influenced the sentencing of both men and women, but there were differences in sentencing of the sexes based on what they "did" for families. "Living with families, contributing to the support of families, or doing something for the welfare of others were positive qualities cited by these judges for men defendants" (Daly 1989a, 16). The "good family woman" cares for children or other dependents, and ideally, she works or obtains welfare to provide economic support; the "bad family woman," on the other hand, does not care or provide for young children (Daly 1989a, 17). Thus, judges found it harder to sentence "good family men" and "good family women"—those perceived as contributing to the well-being of their families in a manner consistent with gender stereotypes—to prison or jail.

"Family men" and "family women," however, are not evenly represented in either society or the offender population: More familied women than familied men exist in society at large and are processed in the courts, (Daly 1987, 1989a, 1989b). Therefore, women's chivalrous treatment may in fact be a result of a response to their increased likelihood to be "familied." "Even if a family woman provides economically for her family, the fact that she *cares* for dependents (almost always meaning children) while a family man usually does not explains why judges find it more difficult to jail the family woman than the family man" (Daly 1989a, 19). Notably, the judges ranked caring for children as more important than providing economic support; thus, familied women tended to fare better than familied men, especially among black defendants (Daly 1987, 1989a). Similarly, a study of British magistrates (judges) found that they favored giving women probation because it least disrupted their domestic duties (Worrall 1990). Conversely, another study found that men, *but not women,* who provided significant emotional support for dependents were less likely to receive prison sentences, and men who provided significant economic support for their children were *not* granted a break in sentencing (Bickle and Peterson 1991). This led the authors to conclude that taking care of familial dependents is rewarded "only when it is not a part of traditional gender-based role expectations" (Bickle and Peterson 1991, 385).

The *marital status* of a defendant appears in crime processing, similar to society at large, to be a more relevant factor for women than for men. Some studies found that being married helped women but not men in crime-processing outcomes (Erez 1982; Nagel et al. 1982). Similarly, being divorced or separated hurt women more than men in sentencing (Farrington and Morris 1983). While another study found that being married decreased the chances of both sexes being held in detention, this was only afforded to men when they had dependents as well as being married (Daly 1989b). Unexpectedly, another study found that marital status was unrelated to the sentencing of women, whereas men were treated more harshly if they were married than if they were not (Bickle and Peterson 1991).

Overall, the recent research on *dependent children* suggests that chivalrous sanctioning may be a result of women's increased likelihood (over men) to have dependent children (see Daly 1989a, 1989b; Eaton 1986; Steffensmeier et al. 1993; Worrall 1990). One of these studies found that pregnant women as well as women with children received more lenient sentencing from judges, but this was partly due to some judges' belief that the bad conditions in women's prisons resulted in extraharsh punishment for women (Steffensmeier et al. 1993). The advantages afforded to women with dependents in their sanctioning may be a more recent phenomenon. A study of the Urban Reform Era (1871 to 1920) in Ontario, Canada, concluded that "judges appeared to view women's criminality as prima facie evidence of their inadequacy as mothers and showed little hesitancy in removing them from their child-care roles" (Boritch 1992, 319).

Some research has focused on the influence of *employment status* and economic dependence on the crime processing of women (and men). Generally, women have been sanctioned more harshly for working outside of the home than for being homemakers (Boritch 1992; Kruttschnitt 1981, 1982). One study found that being employed decreased men's sentences, while being *unemployed* decreased women's sentences (Crew 1991). Another study found that unemployed women generally received harsher sentences than employed women, but unemployed *students* and full-time homemakers received more lenient sentences than women employed outside of the home (Kruttschnitt 1981). One study, however, found employment status related equally to women's and men's sentencing (Kruttschnitt 1984). Probation and parole officers in other studies were more concerned with men's than women's employment problems, although women reported equal or more severe employment problems (Erez 1989, 1992). Similarly, employment status affected men's more than women's pretrial release likelihood (Kruttschnitt and McCarthy 1985).

In addition to the variables typically associated with gender differences (such as marital and employment status, child dependents, and demeanor), studies have found other variables that differently affect male and female sanctioning. Some studies found that legal variables (for example, prior record and offense seriousness) tend to influence men's sanctions more than women's (Boritch 1992; Kruttschnitt and McCarthy 1985; Nagel et al. 1982; Steffensmeier et al. 1993). One of these studies of court outcomes in Ontario, Canada, from 1871 to 1920 concluded that "judges appeared to adopt the attitude that the form a woman's criminality took was secondary to the fact a woman appeared before the court on any charge" (Boritch 1992, 317). On the other hand, another study found that both being from a "broken home" and acting with another offender influenced women's sanctioning more than men's (Farrington and Morris 1983). There is some evidence, although this needs to be further explored, that characteristics about the *victim* may influence females' and males' sanctions differently (See Jamieson and Blowers 1993; Kruttschnitt 1992; Visher 1983). For example, in one study, the victim–offender relationship did not influence police decisions to arrest female suspects, but police were less likely to arrest male subjects who knew their victims (as friends or relatives) than those males who were unacquainted with their victims (Visher 1983).

In conclusion, despite which of the three sanctioning hypotheses is supported (equal treatment, chivalry, or evil woman), studies that have provided in-depth analysis find other variables often interact with sex in a manner that provides a different pattern for crime-processing male and female offenders. Most studies confirm that being married, caring for dependent children, and being a homemaker increase a woman's chance of chivalrous sanctioning. For men, having stable employment and providing for families appear to effect leniency in their sanctioning. Overall, since women are more likely than men to be "familied," and since "familied" women generally fare better than "familied" men, much of the chivalry in crime processing, at least at the sentencing stage, may be explained by these gender differences in responsibilities. Consistent with gender stereotypes, such factors as employment and legal variables appear to influence men's sentences more than women's. It should be noted that there is a built-in discrimination against lesbians and gays, people who are not married, and people who are childless, with regard to the above factors.

SUMMARY

This chapter covered the numerous factors likely to affect the crime processing of male and female offenders. Criminal laws and sentencing laws have historically included legal codes that specified different treatment of the sexes. Even when these laws are gender-neutral, however, this does not guarantee that male and female defendants will be treated equally. To determine support for the three sanctioning hypotheses on gender differences (equal treatment, chivalry, and evil woman), it is first necessary to acknowledge that the treatment of females may vary based on such characteristics as their race, class, and age, and that the treatment of female offenders may vary based on the types of offenses they commit. Moreover, the stage in the crime-processing system appears to influence gender patterns in crime processing: The evil woman hypothesis is supported most at the beginning stages, equal treatment at the middle stages, and chivalry during the latter stages. Finally, this chapter discussed the extraordinarily harsh treatment of female status offenders, as well as the impact of gender stereotyping in crime processing concerning the marital, dependent child, and employment status of women.

REFERENCES

Armstrong, Gail. 1982. "Females Under the Law: 'Protected' but Unequal." Pp. 61–76 in *The Criminal Justice System and Women*, edited by B. R. Price and N. J. Sokoloff. New York: Clark Boardman.

Arnold, Regina A. 1990. "Processes of Victimization and Criminalization of Black Women." *Social Justice* 17:153–166.

Beckman, Marlene D. 1985. "The White Slave Traffic Act: Historical Impact of a Federal Crime Policy on Women." Pp. 85–102 in *Criminal Justice Politics and Women*, edited by C. Schweber and C. Feinman. New York: Haworth Press.

Bernat, Frances P. 1984. "Gender Disparity in the Setting of Bail: Prostitution Offenses in Buffalo, NY, 1977–1979." Pp. 21–48 in *Gender Issues, Sex Offenses, and Criminal Justice: Current Trends*, edited by S. Chaneles. New York: Haworth Press.

——————. 1985. "New York State's Prostitution Statute: Case Study of the Discriminatory Application of a Gender Neutral Law. Pp. 103–120 in *Criminal Justice Politics and Women*, edited by C. Schweber and C. Feinman. New York: Haworth Press.

Bickle, Gayle S., and Ruth D. Peterson. 1991. "The Impact of Gender-Based Family Roles in Criminal Sentencing." *Social Problems* 38:372–394.

Boritch, Helen. 1992. "Gender and Criminal Court Outcomes: An Historical Analysis." *Criminology* 30:293–326.

Cain, Maureen (Ed.) 1989. *Growing up Good: Policing the Behavior of Girls in Europe*. London: Sage.

Chesney-Lind, Meda. 1973. "Judicial Enforcement of the Female Sex Role." *Issues in Criminology* 8:51–70.

——————. 1974. "Juvenile Delinquency: The Sexualization of Female Crime." *Psychology Today* (July): 43–46.

——————. 1981. "Judicial Paternalism and the Female Status Offender: Training Women to Know Their Place." Pp. 354–366 in *Women and Crime in America*, edited by L. H. Bowker. New York: Macmillan.

——————. 1982. "Guilty by Reason of Sex: Young Women and the Juvenile Justice System." Pp. 77–104 in *The Criminal Justice System and Women*, edited by B. R. Price and N. J. Sokoloff. New York: Clark Boardman.

——————. 1986. "Women and Crime: The Female Offender." *Signs* 12:78–96.

——————. 1987. "Female Offenders: Paternalism Reexamined." Pp. 114–140 in *Women, the Courts, and Equality*, edited by L. L. Crites and W. L. Hepperle. Newbury Park, CA: Sage.

——————. 1988. "Girls and Status Offenses: Is Juvenile Justice Still Sexist?" *Criminal Justice Abstracts* 20:145–165.

Chesney-Lind, Meda. and Randall G. Shelden. 1992. *Girls, Delinquency, and Juvenile Justice*. Pacific Grove, CA: Brooks/Cole.

Cohn, Y. 1970. "Criteria for the Probation Officer's Recommendation to the Juvenile Court." In *Becoming Delinquent*, edited by P. G. Garabedian and D. C. Gibbons. Chicago: Aldine.

Conway, Allan, and Carol Bogdan. 1977. "Sexual Delinquency: The Persistence of a Double Standard." *Crime and Delinquency* 23:131–135.

Crew, Keith B. 1991. "Sex Differences in Criminal Sentencing: Chivalry or Patriarchy?" *Justice Quarterly* 8:59–84.

Curran, Deborah. 1983. "Judicial Discretion and Defendant's Sex." *Criminology* 21:41–58.

Daly, Kathleen. 1987. "Structure and Practice of Familial-Based Justice in a Criminal Court." *Law and Society Review* 21:267–290.

——————. 1989a. "Rethinking Judicial Paternalism: Gender, Work-Family Relations, and Sentencing." *Gender and Society* 3:9–36.

_____. 1989b. "Neither Conflict Nor Labeling Nor Paternalism Will Suffice: Intersections of Race, Ethnicity, Gender, and Family in Criminal Court Decisions." *Crime and Delinquency* 35:136–168.

Datesman, Susan K., and Mikel Aickin. 1984. "Offense Specialization and Escalation Among Status Offenders." *Journal of Criminal Law and Criminology* 75:1246–1275.

Datesman, Susan K., and Frank R. Scarpitti. 1977. "Unequal Protection for Males and Females in the Juvenile Court." In *Juvenile Delinquency,* edited by T. N. Ferdinand. Newbury Park, CA: Sage.

_____. 1980. "Unequal Protection for Males and Females in the Juvenile Court." Pp. 300–319 in *Women, Crime, and Justice,* edited by S. K. Datesman and F. R. Scarpitti. New York: Oxford University Press.

DeFleur, Lois B. 1975. "Biasing Influences on Drug Arrest Records: Implications for Deviance Research." *American Sociological Review* 40:88–103.

Eaton, Mary. 1986. *Justice for Women? Family, Court and Social Control.* Milton Keynes: Open University Press.

Edwards, Susan. 1984. *Women on Trial: A Study of the Female Suspect, Defendant and Offender in the Criminal Law and Criminal Justice System.* Manchester, England: Manchester University Press.

Erez, Edna. 1989. "Gender, Rehabilitation, and Probation Decisions." *Criminology* 27:307–327.

_____. 1992. "Dangerous Men, Evil Women: Gender and Parole Decision-Making." *Justice Quarterly* 9:105–126.

Farrington, David P., and Allison M. Morris. 1983. "Sex, Sentencing and Reconviction." *British Journal of Criminology* 23:229–248.

Feinman, Clarice. 1992. "Criminal Codes, Criminal Justice and Female Offenders: New Jersey as a Case Study." Pp. 57–68 in *The Changing Roles of Women in the Criminal Justice System,* 2nd ed.,
edited by I. L. Moyer. Prospect Heights, IL: Waveland Press.

Figueira-McDonough, Josefina. 1985. "Gender Differences in Informal Processing: A Look at Charge Bargaining and Sentence Reduction in Washington, D.C." *Journal of Research in Crime and Delinquency* 22:101–133.

Figueira-McDonough, Josefina, and Rosemary C. Sarri. 1987. "Catch-22 Strategies of Control and the Deprivation of Women's Rights." Pp. 11–33 in *The Trapped Woman: Catch-22 in Deviance and Control,* edited by J. Figueira-McDonough and R. Sarri. Newbury Park, CA: Sage.

Fisher, C. J., and R. I. Mawby. 1982. "Juvenile Delinquency and Police Discretion in an Inner City Area." *British Journal of Criminology* 22:63–75.

Frazier, Charles E., Wilbur E. Block, and John C. Henretta. 1983. "The Role of Probation Officers in Determining Gender Differences in Sentencing Severity." *Sociological Quarterly* 24:305–318.

Frazier, Charles E., and John C. Cochran. 1986. "Detention of Juveniles: Its Effects on Subsequent Juvenile Court Processing Decisions." *Youth and Society* 17:286–305.

Gelsthorpe, Loraine. 1989. *Sexism and the Female Offender.* Aldershot, England: Gower.

Ghali, Moheb, and Meda Chesney-Lind. 1986. "Gender Bias and the Criminal Justice System: An Empirical Investigation." *Sociology and Social Research* 70:164–171.

Gruhl, John, Susan Welch, and Cassia Spohn. 1984. "Women as Criminal Defendants: A Test for Paternalism." *Western Political Quarterly* 37:456–467.

Hepburn, John R. 1978. "Race and the Decision to Arrest: An Analysis of Warrants Issued." *Journal of Research in Crime and Delinquency* 15:54–73.

Hiller, Anne Edwards, and Linda Hancock. 1981. "The Processing of Juveniles in Victoria." Pp. 92–126 in *Women and Crime,* edited by S. K. Mukherjee and J. A. Scutt. North Sydney, Australia: Allen & Unwin.

Hudson, Barbara. 1989. "Justice or Welfare? A Comparison of Recent Developments in the English and French Juvenile Justice System." Pp. 96–113 in *Growing up Good: Policing the Behavior of Girls in Europe,* edited by M. Cain. London: Sage.

Hutton, Chris, Frank Pommersheim, and Steve Feimer. 1989. "'I Fought the Law and the Law Won'": A Report on Women and Disparate Sentencing in South Dakota." *New England Journal On Criminal and Civil Confinement* 15:177–202.

Jamieson, Katherine M., and Anita Blowers. 1993. "A Structural Examination of Court Disposition Patterns." *Criminology* 31:243–262.

Kratcoski, P. 1974. "Delinquent Boys and Girls." *Child Welfare* 53:16–21.

Krisberg, Barry, and Ira Schwartz. 1983. "Rethinking Juvenile Justice." *Crime and Delinquency* 29:333–365.

Krohn, Marvin, James P. Curry, and Shirley Nelson-Kilger. 1983. "Is Chivalry Dead? An Analysis of Changes in Police Dispositions of Males and Females." *Criminology* 21:417–437.

Kruttschnitt, Candace. 1981. "Social Status and Sentences of Female Offenders." *Law and Society Review* 15:247–265.

_____. 1982. "Women, Crime, and Dependency." *Criminology* 19:495–513.

_____. 1984. "Sex and Criminal Court Dispositions: The Unresolved Controversy." *Research in Crime and Delinquency* 21:213–232.

_____. 1992. "'Female Crimes' or Legal Labels? Are Statistics About Women Offenders Representative of Their Crimes?" Pp. 81–98 in *The Changing Roles of Women in the Criminal Justice System,* edited by I. L. Moyer. Prospect Heights, IL: Waveland Press.

Kruttschnitt, Candace, and Donald E. Green. 1984. "The Sex-Sanctioning Issue: Is It History?" *American Sociological Review* 49:541–551.

Kruttschnitt, Candace, and Daniel McCarthy. 1985. "Familial Social Control and Pretrial Sanctions: Does Sex Really Matter?" *Journal of Criminal Law and Criminology* 76:151–175.

Landau, Simha. 1981. "Juveniles and the Police." *British Journal of Criminology* 21:27–46.

Landau, Simha, and Gad Nathan. 1983. "Selecting Delinquents for Cautioning in the London Metropolitan Area." *British Journal of Criminology* 23:128–149.

LaPrairie, Carol P. 1989. "Some Issues in Aboriginal Justice Research: The Case of Aboriginal Women in Canada." *Women and Criminal Justice* 1:81–92.

Leonard, Eileen B. 1982. *Women, Crime and Society.* New York: Longman.

Mann, Coramae R. 1990. "Female Homicide and Substance Use: Is There a Connection?" *Women and Criminal Justice* 1:87–110.

McCarthy, Belinda R. 1987. "Preventive Detention and Pretrial Custody in the Juvenile Court." *Journal of Criminal Justice* 15:185–200.

Morris, Allison. 1987. *Women, Crime and Criminal Justice.* Oxford: Basil Blackwell.

Moulds, Elizabeth F. 1980. "Chivalry and Paternalism: Disparities of Treatment in the Criminal Justice System." Pp. 277–299 in *Women, Crime, and Justice,* edited by S. K. Datesman and F. R. Scarpitti. New York: Oxford University Press.

Myers, Martha A., and John Hagan. 1979. "Private and Public Trouble: Prosecutors and the Allocation of Court Resources." *Social Problems* 26:439–451.

Naffine, Ngaire. 1987. *Female Crime.* Sydney, Australia: Allen & Unwin.

_____. 1989. "Towards Justice for Girls: Rhetoric and Practice in the Treatment of Status Offenders." *Women and Criminal Justice* 1:3–20.

Nagel, Ilene H., John Cardascia, and Catherine E. Ross. 1982. "Sex Differences in the Processing of Criminal Defendants." Pp. 259–282 in *Women and the Law,* Vol. I, edited by D. K. Weisberg. Cambridge, MA: Schenkman.

Nagel, Ilene H., and John Hagan. 1983. "Gender and Crime: Offense Patterns and Criminal Court Sanctions." Pp. 91–144 in *Crime and Justice,* Vol. 4, edited by M. Tonry and N. Morris. Chicago: University of Chicago Press.

Nagel, Stuart S., and Lenore J. Weitzman. 1971. "Women as Litigants." *Hastings Law Journal* 23:171–198.

Pollak, Otto. 1950. *The Criminality of Women.* Westport, CT: Greenwood Press.

Rapaport, Elizabeth. 1991. "The Death Penalty and Gender Discrimination." *Law and Society Review* 25:368–383.

Sarri, Rosemary C. 1983. "Gender Issues in Juvenile Justice." *Crime and Delinquency* 29:381–398.

_____. 1987. "Unequal Protection Under the Law: Women and the Criminal Justice System." Pp. 394–427 in *The Trapped Woman: Catch-22 in Deviance and Control,* edited by J. Figueira-McDonough and R. Sarri. Newbury Park, CA: Sage.

Schlossman, Steven, and Stephanie Wallach. 1982. "The Crime of Precocious Sexuality: Female Juvenile Delinquency in the Progressive Era." Pp. 45–84 in *Women and the Law,* Vol. I, edited by D. K. Weisberg. Cambridge, MA: Schenkman.

Schur, Edwin M. 1984. *Labeling Women Deviant.* New York: McGraw- Hill.

Schwartz, Ira, Marilyn Jackson-Beeck, and Roger Anderson. 1984. "The Hidden System of Juvenile Control." *Crime and Delinquency* 30:371–385.

Scutt, Jocelynne A. 1981. "Sexism in Criminal Law." Pp. 1–21 in *Women and Crime,* edited by S. K. Mukherjee and J. A. Scutt. Sydney, Australia: Allen & Unwin.

Shelden, Randall G. 1981. "Sex Discrimination in the Juvenile Justice System: Memphis, Tennessee, 1900–1917." Pp. 55–72 in *Comparing Female and Male Offenders,* edited by M. Q. Warren. Beverly Hills, CA: Sage.

Smart, Carol. 1976. *Women, Crime and Criminology.* London: Routledge & Kegan Paul.

Sokoloff, Natalie, and Barbara R. Price. 1982. "The Criminal Law and Women." Pp. 9–34 in *The Criminal Justice System and Women,* edited by B. R. Price and N. J. Sokoloff. New York: Clark Boardman.

Spohn, Cassia, John Gruhl, and Susan Welch. 1987. "The Impact of the Ethnicity and Gender of Defendants on the Decision to Reject or Dismiss Felony Charges." *Criminology* 25:175–191.

Spohn, Cassia, Susan Welch, and John Gruhl. 1985. "Women Defendants in Court: The Interaction Between Sex and Race in Convicting and Sentencing." *Social Science Quarterly* 66:178–185.

Steffensmeier, Darrell, John Kramer, and Cathy Streifel. 1993. "Gender and Imprisonment Decisions." *Criminology* 31:411–446.

Teilmann, Katherine S., and Pierre H. Landry. 1981. "Gender Bias in Juvenile Justice." *Journal of Research in Crime and Delinquency* 18:47–80.

Temin, Carolyn E. 1980. "Discriminatory Sentencing of Women Offenders: The Argument for ERA in a Nutshell." Pp. 255–276 in *Women, Crime, and Justice,* edited by S. K. Datesman and F. R. Scarpitti. New York: Oxford University Press.

Terry, Robert M. 1970. "Discrimination in the Handling of Juvenile Offenders by Social Control Agencies." In *Becoming Delinquent,* edited by P. G. Garabedian and D. C. Gibbons. Chicago: Aldine Press.

Thomas, W. I. 1907. *Sex and Society.* Boston: Little, Brown.

Tjaden, Patricia G., and Claus D. Tjaden. 1981. "Differential Treatment of the Female Felon: Myth or Reality?" Pp. 73–88 in *Comparing Female and Male Offenders,* edited by M. Q. Warren. Beverly Hills, CA: Sage.

Visher, Christy A. 1983. "Gender, Police Arrest Decisions, and Notions of Chivalry." *Criminology* 21:5–28.

Webb, David. 1984. "More on Gender and Justice: Girl Offenders on Supervision." *Sociology* 18:367–381.

Wilbanks, William. 1986. "Are Females Treated More Leniently by the Criminal Justice System?" *Justice Quarterly* 3:517–529.

Windschuttle, Elizabeth. 1981. "Women, Crime, and Punishment." Pp. 31–50 in *Women and Crime,* edited by S. K. Mukherjee and J. A. Scutt. North Sydney: Allen & Unwin.

Worrall, Anne. 1981. "Out of Place: Female Offenders in Court." *Probation Journal* 28:90–93.

——————. 1990. *Offending Women: Female Lawbreakers and the Criminal Justice System.* London: Routledge & Kegan Paul.

Young, Vernetta D. 1986. "Gender Expectations and Their Impact on Black Female Offenders and Victims." *Justice Quarterly* 3:305–328.

Zatz, Marjorie. 1984. "Race, Ethnicity, and Determinate Sentencing." *Criminology* 22:147–171.

5

✳

Punishing and Treating
Female Offenders

In sum, women's prisons increase women's dependency,
stress women's domestic rather than employment role, aggravate women's
emotional and physical isolation, can destroy family and other relationships,
[and] engender a sense of injustice (because they are denied many of
the opportunities available to male prisoners).

(MORRIS 1987, 126)

This chapter presents the many issues surrounding incarcerated females. Like males, females are incarcerated in juvenile institutions, such as "training" schools; in the short-term facilities known as jails; or in prisons, which are usually reserved for adults with sentences of a year or more. The first major studies on women prisoners were not conducted until the 1960s (Heidensohn 1985), and female offenders were not even mentioned in the huge 1967 report, a national study of crime, by the President's Commission on Law Enforcement and the Administration of Justice. In contrast to the vast and extensive research on men's prisons since the 1940s, little was known about the isolated and inaccessible women's prisons until the 1970s (Pollock-Byrne 1990; Sarri 1987). Furthermore, the earliest books on women's prisons have been noted more for their focus on the female prison subculture, especially homosexuality, than for their examination of the deplorable conditions of women's incarceration (see Giallombardo 1966; Ward and Kassebaum 1965). Like homeless and mentally ill women, women prisoners are among the most neglected and oppressed groups in society.

Three reasons have been offered for the invisibility of incarcerated women (relative to incarcerated men): (1) Women have constituted a small proportion (typically 5 percent) of the total prison and jail population, (2) generally women are incarcerated for less dangerous and serious crimes than men, and (3) incarcerated women are less likely than incarcerated men to "riot, destroy property and make reform demands" (Mann 1984, 190). Women prisoners, who have suffered the dual stigmas of "woman" and "prisoner," have been neglected even within the women's rights and prisoners' rights movements (Haft 1980). In fact, the first decade of U.S. federal court prisoners' rights cases, the 1960s, failed to benefit women prisoners (Leonard 1983). Even today, despite significantly worse prison conditions and opportunities, females are far less apt than males to file lawsuits against prisons and jails (Aylward and Thomas 1984; Barry 1991; Schupak 1986; Van Ochten 1993; Wheeler et al. 1989).

HISTORY OF
INSTITUTIONALIZING FEMALES

Women and men were subject to the same penalties in preindustrial societies, most of which were noncustodial and included burnings at the stake, whippings, hangings, and public ridicule (Dobash et al. 1986; Heidensohn 1985; Morris 1987). Although confinement in castles, monasteries, and nunneries existed during the Middle Ages, confining women and men for prolonged periods was unusual until the late sixteenth century, and was not accepted as the most appropriate response to criminals and deviants until the nineteenth century (Dobash et al. 1986).

Historians have noted that although the overall punishments of women and men were similar, the exceptions were largely to women's disadvantage and involved punishing them for crimes against their husbands, violating the standards for sexuality, or both. For example, during the Middle Ages, it was not uncommon for women to be burned to death for committing adultery or murdering a spouse, while male adulterers and wife killers were rarely considered offenders (Dobash et al. 1986). Similarly, during colonial times in the United States (1620 to the 1760s), women were punished far more harshly than men for adultery, and they could be punished by the church as well as the state (Feinman 1983). Public humiliation was also more common in the punishing of women than men, such as forcing female convicts to give confessions before they were hanged (Dobash et al. 1986; Feinman 1983). The strength of these antiwoman and antisex (for women) values carried over into this century. In 1923, half of the women in U.S. prisons were convicted of sex offenses (prostitution, fornication, and adultery) (Lekkerkerker 1931), and until 1950, women in Massachusetts convicted of having sex outside of marriage were charged with fornication and sentenced to prison (Janusz 1991).

In the early 1700s in England, a new alternative for a commuted death sentence was to transport convicts to the American colonies and Australia with various work sentences. Women were one in eight of those sent to Australia. They were usually young (in their teens or twenties), and typically were transported for a first offense such as a petty theft (Dobash et al. 1986). The conditions of the transported women were far worse than those of the transported men, and the women's "sentences" usually included being forced into prostitution in Australia (Dobash et al. 1986).

With the exception of a few private and often religious experiments, men and women prisoners were housed in the same institutions until the 1850s in England and the 1870s in the United States. Usually these prisons provided separate rooms for women and men, but both sexes were under the supervision of exclusively male wardens and guards. A similar regime was used for both male and female prisoners because the system was designed to respond to the majority of prisoners—the male prisoners (Heidensohn 1985; Morris 1987).

Although most historical accounts of imprisoning women and men together emphasize their similar treatment, the differences that existed were significant, particularly women's high risk of rape. Moreover, incarcerated women were often blamed for the "sexual disturbances"—their rapes (Rafter 1985, 12). There existed a policy of calculated neglect of women in the "men's" prisons, where the sexual abuse often resulted in pregnancy and the floggings sometimes caused death (Feinman 1981, 1983).

In addition to their high risk of rape, services for incarcerated women were substantially limited relative to incarcerated men, and the authorities were unwilling to hire female guards to supervise them because of their small numbers.

> These prisoners were thus often left entirely on their own, vulnerable to attacks by one another and male guards. Secluded from the main population, women had less access than men to the physician and chaplain. Unlike men, they were not marched to workshops, mess halls, or exercise yards. Food and needlework were brought to their quarters, where the women remained day in and day out, for the years of their sentences.
> *(Rafter 1985, xx).*

Thus, while women and men imprisoned in the same institutions were treated similarly overall, the few differences were largely to the gross disadvantage of women.

The movement for reform in women's prisons has occurred in fits and starts, without consistent progress. The most active reform in the imprisonment of women began in the last century and was conducted by wealthy Anglo women who often held stereotypical views of women's roles in society. On the one hand, they recognized that women offenders were often not deviant per se, but rather victims in a male economic and crime-processing system. On the other hand, these same women reformers generally strove to "purify" and control the "fallen women" whom they viewed as a threat to society (Feinman 1983). In both the United States and England, the women's prison reformers were particularly concerned with the sexual abuse of incarcerated women by male officials in institutions housing both sexes.

The reformers' solution was to help these women rather than to punish them. The first penal reformer to focus exclusively on women was Elizabeth Fry, who established the Ladies Society for Promoting the Reformation of Female Prisoners in England. A Quaker, Fry developed reforms based on the Society of Friends when she began her work in 1816. Her approach was to convince the authorities that women and men had different needs, women's specific needs being *"useful" labor,* which included needlework and personal hygiene, and *religious instruction,* requiring the hiring of "decidedly religious" female guards (Dobash et al. 1986, 52). Elizabeth Fry promoted the idea that female offenders were not dangerous criminals, but rather "fallen women" who needed a helping hand. Fry and her committee of "ladies" experimented on the women at London's Newgate Gaol in 1818, with their program of re-socializing the prisoners. The experiment was claimed a success by most (Windschuttle 1981).

Despite Fry's experimental success, only three of her requests in 1818 were passed by Parliament before 1948 (Morris 1987), and most of her ideas were quite unpopular by the time of her death (Windschuttle 1981). The three changes Fry was instrumental in effecting, however, were significant: (1) segregating prisons by sex; (2) hiring women to supervise women prisoners; and (3) decreasing the hard labor required of women prisoners (Morris 1987). With the exception of the sex of the employees and the requirement for hard labor, however, men's and women's institutions were still similar in their harsh regimens. Some reformers continued to believe after Fry's death that there should be more differences between men's and women's prisons, given that men were usually incarcerated for serious crimes, while women were typically imprisoned for drunkenness, prostitution, and petty thefts. Suffragists imprisoned between 1905 and 1914 in England provided the public with graphic descriptions of the deplorable conditions for these mostly petty offenders (Morris 1987).

The reform movement for incarcerated women in the United States began somewhat later than in England, and was also led by middle- and upper-class Anglo women. Similar to Fry's experiment, a group of these women established the Magdalen Home in 1830 to reform prostitutes through religious instruction and motivational instruction. The reform goal was to remold rather than punish women, by encouraging "proper" gender roles (Feinman 1981; Rafter 1985). The deaths of hundreds of thousands of soldier "breadwinners" in the Civil War resulted in a new class of poor women who filled the jails as prostitutes, vagrants, and thieves during the 1860s (Freedman 1974). After the Civil War, U.S. society was obsessed with controlling social disorder, and credited restoring "women's inherent purity" as one means of doing so. Therefore, female offenders were considered deserving of harsher punishment than male criminals, and thus experienced worse aspects of the prisons (Freedman 1974).

In the 1860s, U.S. women activists heightened public awareness of the significant increase in the rate of women's imprisonment, the horrendous conditions for incarcerated women, and the sexual abuse of women prisoners by male guards. The reformers of this time started questioning the "fallen woman" label and pointed out that "fallen men" were aiding and abetting women and girls into prostitution. Moreover, once confined in prison, it was not unusual for incarcerated women to be lashed until they would have sex with male prison officials. This is similar to the situation of the female offenders transported from England to Australia, who were forced into prostitution as part of their sentence. (Unfortunately, even today, high-ranking prison administrators solicit women prisoners for sexual "favors" [Aylward and Thomas 1984].) As in England, the U.S. reform movement called for single-sex prisons where women prisoners would be administered by women (Freedman 1982).

The reformers of the 1870s and 1880s in the United States were from the northern states, and they were Quakers, charity workers, and feminists. They viewed women prisoners as victims of male judges, wardens, and prison guards (Freedman 1982, 142). Rafter (1985) distinguishes between *custodial institutions* and *reformatories*. Custodial institutions were the traditional prisons that were usually designed for men but also housed women. Reformatories, as noted in Chapter 4, were designed specifically to house women offenders. Their structure reflects gender stereotypes, often entailing a cottage-style architectural design. To this day, many women's prisons are called reformatories. (Some facilities incarcerating juveniles are also referred to as reformatories.)

The first women's reformatory in England was constructed in London in 1853, and the first women's reformatory in the United States was opened in 1874 in Indiana. Shortly afterward, women's reformatories were built in Massachusetts and New York. The female staff in the first U.S. reformatories practiced Elizabeth Fry's correctional theories (Freedman 1974). Despite resistance and hostility from the male authorities who supervised the first sex-segregated and woman-managed reformatories, they were claimed a success. Thus, they were allowed to move from housing a small number of young, Anglo, and native-born female offenders, to a larger and more diverse group of convicted women.

The founders of the U.S. reformatories saw their goals as reform and refuge; their aim was to train the prisoners in the "important" female role of domesticity (Feinman 1981, 1983; Freedman 1982). Thus, an important part of the reform movement in women's prisons was to encourage and ingrain "appropriate" gender roles, such as vocational training in cooking, sewing, and cleaning. To accommodate these goals, the reformatory cottages were usually designed with kitchens, living rooms, and even some nurseries for prisoners with infants. Despite their relatively gentle appearances, these institutions were run with "firmness, authority, and strict discipline" (Freedman 1982, 145). Moreover, parole frequently involved being released to a "good" Christian home as a domestic servant (Feinman 1983; Rafter 1985). This indentured servant format was new in the United States, but not in Europe, and was supported by the middle class who could afford/exploit these inexpensive yet hard-working laborers (Janusz 1991).

The Progressive era, the first two decades of the 1900s, brought in a new generation of reformers. The two characteristics distinguishing this era's reformatories were the increased professionalism of the female prison administrators and the incorporation of a medical model (Rafter 1985). For the first time, the reformatories were managed by educated and experienced women professionals, who put more distance between themselves and the prisoners than their predecessors had. The Progressive era was also distinguished by the establishment of physicians', psychiatrists', and psychologists' roles in *classifying* offenders, and an obsession with identifying and responding to incarcerated women's venereal diseases.

Their approach was more feminist than that of the first wave of reformers. Although they continued to support a sex-segregated prison system, they questioned the treatment of women that encouraged them to stay in traditional roles, as these reformers had rejected such roles in their own lives (Freedman 1982). The second wave of reformers were less likely than their foremothers to base their beliefs on religious and biological underpinnings. They were less concerned with the "moral uplifting" valued by the first wave of reformers, and they targeted what they viewed as the cause of women's crime: low wages and limited opportunities for women in work and education (Freedman 1982). The reformers during the twentieth century were also invested in the suffrage movement, partly because they believed that the conditions for incarcerated women would improve with women's right to vote. But the success of the women's prisons soon resulted in their overcrowding, and legislators were unwilling to fund the needed expansion of vocational, recreational, and educational programs (Freedman 1982). Moreover, overcrowding resulted in disciplinary problems (Rafter 1985). Ironically, in 1915, just as the reformers started realizing that sex segregation meant reduced opportunities for incarcerated women (relative to incarcerated men), state officials were finally supporting the legitimacy of the sex-segregated facilities (Freedman 1982).

After 1915, the population of incarcerated women began to change, with a huge influx of incarcerated prostitutes and drug users and an increase in African American women prisoners due to the northern migration of southern blacks (Freedman 1982). African American women and drug users were perceived as dangerous and in need of being controlled, and racially segregated housing was used in the cottages (Freedman 1982). In the 1920s, the training of the women prisoners in "homemaking" became popular again. The women prisoners' "rights," therefore, were changed to include less rigid clothing rules and more freedom to decorate their walls. The vocational training, however, continued to support gender stereotypes (Freedman 1982).

Any vestiges of progressive features in women's reformatories were lost by 1930; sex segregation and the gender stratification of male and female institutional regimes had become standard throughout the United States (Freedman 1982). After the Great Depression, many custodial institutions were closed and most women were imprisoned in the reformatories, which lost many of the reformatory ideals and took on more of the custodial regimes (Rafter 1985). The 1940s and 1950s have been characterized as a time in which the reformatories switched the goal from turning women prisoners into good house*maids* to making them good house*wives* (Carlen 1983; Morris 1987; Windschuttle 1981). Either way, valuing women as domestic servants, in their own or others' homes, was commonplace in the women's penal reform movement. After this period, the reform movement for incarcerated women temporarily died down, and there was little change in women's imprisonment in the middle of the twentieth century (Heidensohn 1985).

Three occurrences in the 1960s and 1970s renewed interest in women's penal reform: (1) the rise of modern feminism and reappraisal of women's roles in society as deviants and as victims; (2) concern that women's crime rates were growing faster than men's; and (3) in England, a 1968 policy that claimed women offenders should be treated uniquely given their special physical and psychological problems (Heidensohn 1985). With the reemergence of feminism in the 1970s, U.S. reformers began to question the value of sex-segregated prisons. Although these segregated facilities had significantly decreased the (especially sexual) abuse of women prisoners, they had also served to promote damaging gender stereotypes and restricted incarcerated women's opportunities (Freedman 1982).

WOMEN'S PRISONS TODAY

Despite the discrimination and inequities that exist among police, judges, and prosecutors, the most serious problems for female offenders exist in residential facilities: jails, reformatories, lockups, and prisons.
(Sarri 1987, 415)

Among prison experts, there is agreement that women's prisons changed relatively little from the beginning of the twentieth century and into the 1980s (Feinman 1981; Sarri 1987). Unfortunately, the gender stereotypes that influenced the first women's reformatories continue to affect the treatment, conditions, and opportunities for the postprison success of incarcerated women today (Feinman 1981).

Currently, women's prisons are smaller, fewer in number, and different from men's prisons (Pollock-Byrne 1990). In both the United States and England, women make up a small proportion of prisoners (about 5 percent); thus, there are few women's prisons (usually one per state in the United States), and most jails simply throw all of the female offenders into one unit. This has resulted in a form of institutionalized sexism:

1. Women's prisons are generally a farther distance from friends and families because of their *sporadic and isolated locations,* making visits from children, other family, and friends more difficult, particularly for the poor.

2. The relatively small number of women in prison and jail is used to "justify" the *lack of diverse educational, vocational, and other programs* available to incarcerated women.

3. The relatively small number of women in prison and jail is used to "justify" *low levels of specialization* in treatment and failure to segregate the more serious and mentally ill offenders from the less serious offenders (as is done in male prisons and jails).

Structures built specifically to be used as women's reformatories in the United States usually have a cottage-style design and are often compared to college campuses. In addition to their "tamer" architectural appearance, these women's prisons are less likely to have gun towers, armed guards, high concrete walls, and other intimidating, prisonlike features. However, in the United States there has been a growing tendency to place high fences with rolls of barbed wire around these "campuses" in recent years. Despite the less threatening *appearance* of women's reformatories, the *conditions* for women prisoners are usually significantly worse than those for male prisoners (Morris 1987). For example, women prisoners have more restricted access to legal libraries, medical and dental care, and vocational and educational opportunities. This is discussed in more detail below.

Feminists who have worked toward establishing gender equality in the treatment of prisoners are mounting growing concerns about the response of prison administrators and policy-makers (Chesney-Lind 1991; Hannah-Moffat 1994; Wheeler et al. 1989). "Gender equality" has resulted in (1) a building "binge" to imprison more women (Chesney-Lind 1991), and (2) an assumption that female prisoners can simply "fit into" male prisoners' building structures and programs (Chesney-Lind 1991; Hannah-Moffat 1994).

The lack of adequate women's prisons concerned feminists in the 1970s, because women prisoners were often sent out of state if there were no institutions to house them in their own state (Chesney-Lind 1991). Since then, in both the United States and England, more women's prisons have been built and "holding tanks" for convicted women have been created by converting buildings designed for other purposes (for example, men's and juveniles' facilities) (Chesney-Lind 1991). In fact, two out of three facilities used as women's prisons in 1990 were not designed to house females (American Correctional Association 1990). Whether built or created to hold convicted women, women's prisons have appeared at exponential rates. Only two or three women's prisons were built or created per decade between 1930 and 1950, but there were an additional seven in the 1960s, seventeen in the 1970s, and thirty-four in the 1980s (Chesney-Lind 1991). Similarly, women's prison programs are designed along the same lines as those for men, with no consideration of the special needs of women, many of whom have survived rape and battering (Hannah-Moffat 1994). Thus, feminists have increasingly questioned why women's prisons should be expanded when they appear to harm more than help the women they so severely punish (Chesney-Lind 1991; Hannah-Moffat 1994).

The regime of women's prisons has been described as "discipline, infantalize, feminize, medicalize, and domesticize" (Carlen and Tchaikovsky 1985). *Discipline* for incarcerated women is overly harsh, especially relative to that for incarcerated men. A recent study of Texan prisoners found that women were far more likely to be cited for rule infractions, particularly minor ones, and far more severely punished for them (McClellan 1994). The women received citations for drying their underwear, talking while waiting in lines, displaying too many family photographs, and failing to eat all of the food on their plates.

"Contraband" included having an extra bra or pillowcase, a borrowed comb or hat, and candy. Sharing shampoo in the shower and lighting another prisoner's cigarette were classified as "trafficking." Such minor everyday occurrences never resulted in citations or punishment in men's prisons (McClellan 1994). Thus, in addition to reinforcing gender stereotypes such as domesticity and femininity, women's prison policies and supervision treat women like children (Carlen 1983; Fox 1975; Leonard 1983; Moyer 1984).

The *medicalization* of incarcerated women is also evident (Carlen and Tchaikovsky 1985; Dobash et al. 1986). For example, even women returning from such permitted leaves as court appearances, furloughs, and giving birth in hospitals are often subjected to vaginal searches for contraband (and the searches are typically by security, not medical, staff). These searches are not only humiliating, but often painful and dangerous, resulting in bleeding and infection (Holt 1982; Mann 1984; McHugh 1980). "What is ironic about this procedure is that these vaginal examinations are frequent, yet the preventive pap test for cervical cancer is not often given" (Mann 1984, 213). Furthermore, despite a change of policy in England and Scotland in the 1960s and 1970s that assumed an inherent mental instability and illness of women prisoners, treatment is difficult to obtain and when obtained is rarely helpful (Dobash et al. 1986).

Women defendants, as noted in Chapter 4, face a number of restrictions in the legal system en route to prison. One study found that 50 percent of incarcerated women saw their public defenders for fifteen minutes or less, most didn't even know the names of their public defenders, and those who saw public defenders for more than fifteen minutes were charged with a capital crime, and even then only met with their defenders for about an hour (Pendergrass 1975). Incarcerated women's legal battles begin well before incarceration and extend well into their incarceration. Legal cases in the 1980s challenged why women prisoners had to have their lights out earlier than male prisoners, and why they only received vocational training in sewing prison clothes while male prisoners in the same state received training in a variety of vocational skills (such as electronics or carpentry) (Leonard 1983). Limitations for current-day incarcerated women include disadvantages (relative to incarcerated men) in access to law libraries, jail house lawyers, and, consequently, the courts (Alpert 1982; Carlen 1983; Haft 1980; Wheeler et al. 1989). In fact, only about half of U.S. women's prisons have law libraries available for prisoner use (American Correctional Association 1990). One study found a lack of legitimate channels for incarcerated women to report abuses or seek effective help for their problems, reinforcing their belief that they are not taken seriously (Carlen and Tchaikovsky 1985).

One of the worst legal problems incarcerated women and girls have faced involves reproductive freedom. Not only have many imprisoned and institutionalized women and girls had abortions against their will (Holt 1982; Leonard 1983; McHugh 1980), but those who want abortions, particularly indigents, are not necessarily guaranteed access to them (Haft 1980; Holt 1982; Knight 1992; McHugh 1980; Resnick and Shaw 1980; Vitale 1980; Vukson

1988). Additionally, girls in juvenile institutions and women prisoners are encouraged and sometimes forced to give up their babies for adoption (Baunach 1992; Haft 1980; Haley 1980; Mann 1984; Ross and Fabiano 1986), even if they became pregnant while incarcerated (Mann 1984).

Incarcerated pregnant women and girls often face considerable hostility, resentment for their special medical and physical needs, and discrimination by the staff (Holt 1982; McHugh 1980). Although pregnancy tests do not appear to be routine in the intake of women prisoners, a recent study stated that 6 percent of U.S. women are pregnant at intake (American Correctional Association 1990). Other researchers estimate that one-quarter of women prisoners either were pregnant at intake or gave birth during the previous year (Church 1990). Given the large and growing number of incarcerated females, this is not an insignificant number.

Finally, current research on the incarceration of women and girls rarely mentions sexual abuse by the male staff. Although sexual abuse likely has decreased from earlier times, there has been no systematic research to determine the extent to which it still exists. Research published as recently as the 1970s, however, documented the high risk of women in southern U.S. jails being sexually assaulted by male sheriffs and jail trustees (Sims 1976). In addition to outright rape, it was not unusual for male staff to coerce or force women and girls into doing sexual "favors" in order to get their basic needs met (for example, food, and family contact). Sexual assault of jailed females in the South was overlooked until 1974, when Joan Little, an African American in jail appealing a larceny conviction, struggled with an Anglo male jailer who was trying to orally rape her. During the struggle, the jailer fell on the ice pick he was using to assault her, and died. Little's case received national recognition when she claimed she couldn't get a fair trial in Beaufort County, North Carolina, and she was acquitted after a change of venue (Feinman 1986).

There have been recent allegations of women prisoners being sexually assaulted and sexually harassed by male staff (Van Ochten 1993). Despite the fact that female prisoners are far more likely to be sexually abused by male guards than male prisoners are to be abused by female guards, there is more sex integration of workers in women's than men's prisons (Goetting 1987). This is due to the unfounded belief that women workers pose a security risk in men's prisons.

RATES OF IMPRISONMENT

The media, academics, and prison reformers have noted the surge in incarceration rates in recent years. Although women's recent incarceration rates are growing at a faster pace than men's, the discussions on the rates frequently fail to account for women, or simply lump them in with the men. Increases in women's incarceration rates have exceeded men's every year since 1981 (Kline 1993; Pollock-Byrne 1990). The number of women in U.S. prisons tripled during the 1980s (Church 1990; Fletcher and Moon 1993a; Immarigeon and

Chesney-Lind 1992; Kline 1993), while the number of incarcerated men about doubled (Kline 1993). Similar incarceration rate explosions for women have occurred in England (Morris 1987).

There are a number of interesting points regarding women's disproportionately high increases in incarceration rates. First, there does not appear to be a corresponding increase in women's criminality overall (Immarigeon 1987a; Morris 1987). Second, the proportion of women imprisoned for violent crimes has actually decreased (Immarigeon and Chesney-Lind 1992). In fact, most of the increase in women's imprisonment can be accounted for by minor property crimes (mostly larceny/theft), and drug and public order offenses (Chesney-Lind 1991; Immarigeon 1987a; Immarigeon and Chesney-Lind 1992; Kline 1993; Mann 1984; Sarri 1987). Two-thirds of women are in prison for such minor offenses as larceny, theft, prostitution, and disturbing the peace (Immarigeon 1987a). There is some indication in England, however, that younger women are committing more serious offenses today than three or four decades ago (Morris 1987).

A third important point is that the growth in the building of women's prisons and the addition of female units in existing prisons are unprecedented (Immarigeon 1987a; Immarigeon and Chesney-Lind 1992; Sarri 1987), although "nearly all imprisoned women are nondangerous, property offenders, drug abusers and/or victims of domestic violence" (Immarigeon 1987a, 4). Some reports say sentence lengths have not increased (Immarigeon 1987a), while others say that women's sentence lengths have increased along with their increased likelihood of incarceration (Sarri 1987). Overall, there appears to be an increasing willingness to incarcerate women (Immarigeon and Chesney-Lind 1992).

Fourth, women's increased incarceration rates can be traced to implicit policy changes. Chesney-Lind (1991) believes the "war on drugs" has been translated into a "war on women," given the extreme growth of women's incarcerations for drug crimes. She attributes the increase in women's imprisonment to this war on drugs/women and to changes in decision making in the crime-processing system (such as the implementation of new sentencing guidelines) .

Finally, despite the huge increase in women's incarceration, women constituted only about 6 percent of incarcerated persons in the United States in 1990 (U.S. Department of Justice 1992). Because this proportion is small, the special problems of women prisoners continue to be minimized, and their rising incarceration growth rate is overlooked.

WHO IS IN WOMEN'S PRISONS?

Until recently, little effort has been made to describe female prisoners. This section briefly summarizes research describing incarcerated females.

The most obvious characteristic distinguishing women and girls who have been incarcerated from those who have not is *race*. The women's prisons, like the men's, have a long history of racism. Even prior to 1865, African American women were disproportionately incarcerated, and after the Civil War the rate of imprisoned African American women swelled even more (Rafter 1985). It has been pointed out that the recent media and academic recognition of the highly disproportionate incarceration of African Americans has focused almost exclusively on males, although there have often been higher rates of blacks in women's prisons than in men's prisons (Binkley-Jackson et al. 1993; Goetting and Howsen 1983; Rafter 1985). Moreover, the rate of women of color in prison is increasing over time (Sarri 1987). Although collecting data on class is more difficult than gathering data on race, it is painfully apparent that poor women of all races are vastly overrepresented in women's prisons (Morris 1987).

In addition to race and class, a distinguishing characteristic of incarcerated females is their significantly increased likelihood of having survived sexual and/or physical violence, particularly by a male relative or intimate partner (American Correctional Association 1990; Arnold 1990; Carlen 1983; Chesney-Lind and Rodriguez 1983; Fletcher et al. 1993; Gilfus 1992; Immarigeon 1987a, 1987b; Sargent et al. 1993). Research also shows that women in prison have experienced unusually high rates of extremely abusive "discipline" from parents, involvement in drugs, and prostitution, whether they were imprisoned for these crimes or not (Chesney-Lind and Rodriguez 1983). Many of the incarcerated women and girls report that they believe their offending/incarceration, sexual victimization, drug abuse, and prostitution are all interrelated (Chesney-Lind and Rodriguez 1983; Gilfus 1992; Sargent et al. 1993).

GIRLS' "CORRECTIONAL" INSTITUTIONS

Although separate penal institutions were developed for adult women in the mid-1800s, separate facilities for girls date from the early 1900s (Sarri 1987). To date, women and girls in jails are usually placed in what are essentially male facilities. For the arrested girl, this usually amounts to solitary confinement in jail, which places youths at high risk for suicide, particularly given girls' high rates of prior sexual and physical victimizations (Chesney-Lind and Shelden 1992). Not only are girls more likely than boys to be placed in jail for trivial (status) offenses, but the conditions for girls in jail is worse than those for boys. In addition to experiencing high rates of solitary confinement, they appear to be at risk of being sexually assaulted by the male staff and other jail inmates (Chesney-Lind and Rodriguez 1983).

Like women's prisons, juvenile girls' institutions often reinforce gender stereotypes and roles (Gelsthorpe 1989; Kersten 1989; Smart 1976). The girls are subject to greater rule rigidity and control and offered fewer vocational and other programs than the boys (Kersten 1989; Mann 1984). A British study comparing incarcerated boys and girls found that despite no set gender differences in policies, the gender differences practiced in treatment and activities were quite severe (Gelsthorpe 1989). The girls were rewarded for feminine behavior such as acting maternal, being affectionate, showing sensitivity, and cry-ing. Moreover, even the activities were sex-prescribed: Boys swam, jogged, and played ping-pong, darts, soccer, and volleyball, while girls watched from the sidelines. If girls attempted to join in the "boys'" activities, they were negatively labeled "tomboys" or "unladylike." Conversely, the girls' activities included exercises to keep slim, sewing, and cooking, since the staff viewed the girls as "destined for marriage and family life" (Gelsthorpe 1989, 114).

Finally, like the jails, the "training schools" have proven to be dangerous for female juvenile offenders. "Studies of the conditions in the nation's detention centers and training schools indicate that rather than protecting girls, many neglect their needs and, in some instances, further victimize the girls" (Chesney-Lind and Shelden 1992, 164). This is particularly disturbing given that in 1989, 22 percent of girls and 3 percent of boys held in public juvenile facilities were there for nondelinquent reasons (for example, status offenses, abuse and neglect, and voluntary commitment) (U.S. Department of Justice 1991a). An important area of penal reform, then, is changing the institutionalization and treatment of female youth offenders. Given the vastly growing number of women prisoners, this could be an important preventive effort.

PSYCHOLOGICAL ASPECTS
OF WOMEN'S IMPRISONMENT

One of the most serious problems incarcerated females face is the institutional reinforcement of many of the early criminologists' (for example, Lombroso's) assumptions about their nature, "namely that women and girls who commit offenses are abnormal either biologically or psychologically" (Smart 1976, 144). Many of the treatment policies in women's prisons have been grounded in the assumption that convicted female offenders are "sick" individuals.

> Apparently policy-makers, like many criminologists, perceive female criminality as irrational, irresponsible and largely unintentional behavior, as an individual mal-adjustment to a well-ordered and consensual society.
> *(Smart 1976, 145)*

Such assumptions ignore the sexist implication that it is abnormal or "sick" for women—but not men—to commit crimes. The assumption of female offenders as "sick" also ignores the growing amount of research cited earlier of their high rates of violent victimization (usually by males), poverty, and other hardships (see also Carlen 1983).

A disturbing aspect of women's and girls' confinement is the relatively high rate of self-mutilation. Some speculate that incarcerated women's disproportionately high suicide attempts, cell destruction, and self-mutilation are a result of women's tendency to internalize anger, while incarcerated men are more likely to externalize anger by assaulting other prisoners or prison staff (see Dobash et al. 1986; Fox 1975). One reason offered for the self-mutilation is that it is a way for incarcerated females to feel *something* (Morris 1987).

There is also considerable evidence that psychotropic drug prescriptions are far more common in women's than men's prisons (Heidensohn 1985; Mann 1984; Morris 1987; Ross and Fabiano 1986). Incarcerated women's and girls' increased levels of psychotropic and tranquilizer drug prescriptions may be due to (1) females experiencing imprisonment more severely than males (Morris 1987); (2) women experiencing more pain due to separation from children (Morris 1987); and/or (3) an increased likelihood of prison staff to value or justify the social control of females relative to males (Fletcher and Moon 1993b; Sarri 1987). Unfortunately, there is some indication that the medical staff frequently prescribe these drugs without checking to see if the woman is pregnant, although these drugs can be quite harmful to fetuses (McHugh 1980).

Women's rate of incarceration for drug offenses has grown (Immarigeon and Chesney-Lind 1992; Moon et al. 1993; Morris 1987). Additionally, many women incarcerated for nondrug offenses report drug and alcohol addiction problems (Chesney-Lind and Rodriguez 1983). In fact, in a 1989 survey of jail inmates, women were significantly more likely than men to report drug use in general, as well as more frequent use and use of more serious drugs, such as LSD, heroine, crack cocaine, and methadone (U.S. Department of Justice 1991b). It has been noted, however, that little research has been conducted to examine the effectiveness of various chemical dependency programs for incarcerated females (Ross and Fabiano 1986).

Incarcerated women commonly worry about how they will stay off drugs after completing their prison sentences. Unfortunately, the programs to aid in confronting alcohol and drug addiction (including the twelve-step programs) have been sorely lacking in women's prisons and jail sections, relative to males' institutions. This is particularly disturbing for two reasons: (1) The extensive physical and sexual abuse women prisoners have survived may require special consideration in chemical dependency treatment, and (2) drug-abusing convicts have a high rate of reoffending and returning to prison (Moon et al. 1993).

Another source of psychological stress that will be dealt with in more detail in the next section is guilt and worry about separation from their families, especially their children. Women prisoners are more likely than men to feel guilty about their incarceration because of the lack of contact with their children. Women prisoners are more likely to worry that grandparents, foster parents, and others given temporary custody of their children may not adequately supervise the children (see Baunach 1992). Women who believe that their convictions were unjust are likely to feel doubly traumatized by the separation from their children.

Finally, the geographic isolation of women's prisons is not the only reason women prisoners get so few visits. The different values families place on the male members (husbands, fathers, sons, and brothers) as opposed to the female members (wives, mothers, daughters, and sisters) is evident in that incarcerated females receive fewer visits from family members than men receive. "Even while women are still at the county jail level (before being sent off to the remote prisons), they are not visited and stuck by with the same loyalty as men are by families, partners, and friends" (Swain 1994).

PARENTHOOD: A GENDER
DIFFERENCE AMONG PRISONERS

Incarcerated women are far more likely than incarcerated men to be the emotional and financial providers of children. Although four out of five women and three out of five men entering prison are parents, almost all incarcerated women have custody of their children prior to imprisonment, while fewer than half of the men do (Church 1990; Koban 1983). Thus, one of the greatest differences in stresses for women and men serving time is that the separation from children is generally a much greater hardship for women than for men. "Unlike men sentenced to prison, women seldom have been able to rely on a spouse to care for their children; therefore they have suffered more anxiety about the welfare of their families" (Rafter 1985, 179). One study found that only 10 percent of incarcerated women's children are taken care of by the children's fathers (Glick and Neto 1982).

Not only do women prisoners exhibit more concern than men about their children, but children are far more likely to be affected by an incarcerated mother than an incarcerated father. The general acceptance that children whose parents go to prison are likely to be far more affected by their mothers' than their fathers' incarceration is apparent from the titles of the books on this topic: *Unfit Mothers* (Mahan 1982), *When Mothers Go to Jail* (Stanton 1980), and *Why Punish the Children? A Study of Children of Women Prisoners* (McGowan and Blumenthal 1978). In fact, it is difficult to find studies on parenting issues with regard to incarcerated fathers.

Most women prisoners want to take an active role in determining where their children will stay while they are incarcerated, and when given a choice, they most frequently request their own mothers. This is largely because the maternal grandmothers often play a large role in the children's lives, and the incarcerated mothers will have fewer difficulties regaining custody after release (Baunach 1992). The children of incarcerated women run a high risk of having to change schools (as well as caretakers) and are less well off financially after their mothers' incarceration (Stanton 1980). There is also no guarantee that the initial placement of a child, say with a family member, will last the duration of the mother's incarceration (McCarthy 1980). Some incarcerated women report fearing to apply for financial help for the relatives caring for their children while they are imprisoned, because it may lead to institutionalizing the children rather than letting them live with their relatives (Carlen 1983).

The average number of dependent children per incarcerated woman is between two and three (American Correctional Association 1990; Baunach 1985; Fletcher et al. 1993; McGowan and Blumenthal 1976, 1978), and the percent of incarcerated women with children is growing (Sarri 1987). One of the most controversial debates surrounding the imprisonment of women is whether they should be allowed to keep infants and small children with them in prison. On the one hand, some argue that innocent children shouldn't be raised in prisons. On the other hand, others claim that it is unfair for innocent children to be separated from their mothers. A comprehensive book on children of prisoners states: "Often they are removed abruptly from their homes, schools, and communities, shuttled from one caretaker to another, deprived of seeing their parents or siblings, teased and avoided by their peers, and left to comprehend on their own what is happening" (McGowan and Blumenthal 1978). It is not surprising that these children's school performance and behavioral problems begin or get worse after their mothers' incarceration (Stanton 1980). Although a small number of women are imprisoned specifically for neglecting, abusing, or killing their children, a far greater number are in prison for stealing or prostituting in order to provide for themselves and their children. Notably, those few women in prison for harming or killing their children face more ostracism from the other prisoners than anyone else (Kaplan 1988; Mahan 1984).

Prisons and jails have varying policies regarding visitation with children and placement of babies born to incarcerated women. Many of the early women's reformatories allowed babies and young children to stay in the prisons with their mothers until they were two years old (Lekkerkerker 1931). A reformatory in Massachusetts built a nursery in 1880 and encouraged *all* of the women to visit and care for the babies. "This 'communal' maternal care proved to be, in many ways, the most effective therapy" (Janusz 1991, 11). More recently, social workers have decided whether babies born to pregnant prisoners would be cared for by relatives or put up for adoption (Baunach and Murton 1973). Overall, flexibility to allow contact and maintain the mother–child relationship appears to be limited in the United States. Only two out of five prisons allow extended visits between mothers and children (American Correctional Association 1990). A few U.S. women's prisons still allow infants to live in the prisons, sometimes up to the age of two (Baunach 1982, 1992; Haft 1980; Haley 1980; Heidensohn 1985; Holt 1982; McCarthy 1980; Schupak 1986).

The preceding policies also hold true for Denmark, England, Russia, Taiwan, and Jamaica. Peru, India, and Canada allow women to keep children up to five or six years old (Henriques 1994; Vachon 1994; Weintraub 1987). A comparative study of women's prisons reported that children forbidden from living with their incarcerated mothers frequently ended up on the streets (Weintraub 1987).

Most U.S. women's prisons with nurseries only house the babies temporarily, until placement with foster parents or other caregivers is determined (Boudouris 1985). Fewer than half of the jails allow women contact visitation (where they can touch, hold, and move freely) with children, but all U.S. women's prisons allow mothers contact visitation with their children (American Correctional Association 1990). Over half of incarcerated women in a recent study reported that their children had *never* visited them in prison, with the most cited reason being the great distance between the children's home and the prison (Bloom 1993). It can be disconcerting to children, especially young children, to have limited communications with their mothers, especially if they are feeling abandoned. Moreover, it is not uncommon for U.S. prisoners to be allowed only one fifteen-minute (collect) phone call per month.

Most incarcerated women's children are cared for by relatives, state foster homes, or other institutions. "One of the most painful problems confronting mothers in prison is the possibility of gradual loss of their children.... There is also the feeling of helplessness arising from concern for the welfare of children" (Fox 1975, 192). Many women justifiably worry that it will be difficult or impossible to retain custody from a foster parent or relative when they are released from prison. There are also cases of fathers who "disappear" with the children during the mothers' incarceration. Child welfare laws allow "termination of parental rights if the parent has failed to maintain an adequate relationship with a child who is in foster care. Imprisonment, by its very nature, poses serious obstacles to the maintenance of the mother–child relationships" (Bloom 1993, 66). Prison sentences alone have been used as reasons to negate parental rights for women (Haley 1980; Knight 1992; Pollock-Byrne 1990). Incarcerated women are more likely than incarcerated men to have their parental rights revoked (Fletcher and Moon 1993b). Furthermore, it is usually difficult for incarcerated women to respond to legal custody hearings:

> Obviously, if the mother is in prison she will not be able to appear at a hearing concerning the child's welfare and defend herself. Legal help is often nonexistent and consequently no one is there to represent the woman's interests. It is possible in some states for the woman to lose all rights and to lose the child completely to adoption proceedings, despite her objections.
>
> *(Pollock-Byrne 1990, 67)*

Consequently, one of the first goals of many women released from prison is to reestablish custody of their children. They may first be required to prove that they have stable housing and employment, which is difficult for anyone leaving prison. Even getting back on welfare can be time consuming because of the enormous amounts of "red tape." Often the woman is placed in a position of having to borrow from loan sharks or friends and family (Stanton 1980). Moreover, a number of jailed mothers report desertion or divorce by their male partners or husbands while they were incarcerated (Stanton 1980).

In conclusion, it is ironic that prisons have unabashedly programmed female offenders into their "proper" gender roles as wives and mothers, but simultaneously make few or no provisions for them to maintain contact with even their youngest children (Haft 1980; Knight 1992; Sarri 1987).

EDUCATIONAL, VOCATIONAL, AND RECREATIONAL PROGRAMS

Women prisoners have typically been viewed as unworthy or incapable of training or education, thus confirming their dependent status in and out of prison. "In general, treatment and training programs for female offenders are distinctively poorer in quantity, quality, and variety, and considerably different in nature from those for male offenders" (Ross and Fabiano 1986). Moreover, "women are frequently excluded from work release programs, halfway houses, and furloughs in many of the state correctional systems" in the United States (Janusz 1991). (This is not to imply that education and training programs in men's prisons are adequate or should be the model.)

The justifications offered for discrimination against women prisoners include that they are not major "breadwinners" or in need of remunerative employment (Smart 1976). The prisons still tend to reflect society's bias that the most acceptable role for women is as mother and wife (Carlen 1983; Feinman 1983; Natalizia 1991). The focus on women as domestic servants or wives and mothers clearly belies the vast and growing number of single women who are heads of households. Furthermore, assumptions about who "deserves" jobs and programs are often sexist. Other excuses offered for the lack of women's prison programs are that women make up a small portion of prisoners and that they are in prison for relatively short time periods, compared to men. Few work assignments are available to women incarcerated in the United States; those that exist "are not considered prison industries with marketable job skills" (American Correctional Association 1990, 38). It should be noted that programs in jails are even more limited for incarcerated women than in the prisons (Glick and Neto 1982), and that work release programs are far more available to incarcerated men than to incarcerated women (Ross and Fabiano 1986).

Few changes have been made in the programs and opportunities offered to women prisoners since the beginning of this century (Sarri 1987).

> Far less than half of women inmates are enrolled in educational programs, although most are educationally disadvantaged; there are few non-traditional jobs in the limited prison industries which exist. Most spend their days in idleness subjected to monotonous control and discipline
>
> *(Sarri 1987, 416)*

Most women's prisons have programs in cosmetology, office skills, typing, sewing, hairdressing, and homemaking, but few train women in skills to help them become legitimately independent on their release. This is particularly troubling when examining the gender differences in educational and vocational programs in prisons:

> [T]he vocational and educational programs available to males far exceed those available to females. Typically, women's programs are small in number and usually sex stereotyped. Thus, whereas men may have access to programs in welding, electronics, construction, tailoring, computers, and plumbing, and to college programs, women may have cosmetology, and child-care, keypunch, and nurse's aide programs, and often high school is the only education available to women.
>
> *(Pollock-Byrne 1990, 168–169)*

Furthermore, women prisoners who have questioned policies and attempted to change their restricted educational and vocational opportunities are often punished—sometimes with long periods in solitary confinement

(Sarri 1987). While some legal cases have successfully challenged the sex discrimination in prison vocational programs and educational opportunities, the decisions of the federal courts "have had little impact because of prison overcrowding, the dominance and resistance of male administrators, the punitive attitudes of legislators and court officials, and the fact that many social action organizations have ignored the plight of these offenders" (Sarri 1987, 417).

Both the prisoners and the staff rank education as the most valuable resource for women during incarceration (Glick and Neto 1982; Mawby 1982). This is not surprising given that less than one-third of all incarcerated females hold a high school degree at intake (American Correctional Association 1990). A study on coed prisons found that the women were more likely than the men to request academic programs, while women and men were equally likely to request vocational programs (Wilson 1980). One study found, however, that the women with more education prior to incarceration were the most likely to participate in prison educational programs (Mawby 1982).

Research has also found sex discrimination in the availability of *activities* for incarcerated men and women. A study in Scotland found that male prisoners were allowed to play darts, cards, ping-pong, dominoes, and so on, whereas these activities were unavailable to imprisoned women (Carlen 1983). Another study reported, as if this were perfectly normal and acceptable, that an activity called the "Hen House" provided an opportunity for the women in a coed prison to get together with the staff wives, to make Christmas cookies and spend the evening sewing, knitting, and talking (Campbell 1980). Men's prisons have vastly better recreational facilities and programs, based on the myth that men need more physical exertion than women (Goetting 1987). Apparently there is a related assumption that men are more in need of heterosexual contact than women, given that some states allow male prisoners conjugal visits, while providing no such opportunity for female prisoners (Boudouris 1985).

HEALTH CARE SERVICES

Incarcerated women may have more serious health problems than women outside of prison because of their increased likelihood of living in poverty, limited access to preventive medical care, poor nutrition, chemical dependency, and limited education on health matters (see Ross and Fabiano 1986). One of the major problems in women's prisons is the lack of skilled and available medical care (Fletcher and Moon 1993a; Pollock-Byrne 1990; Resnick and Shaw 1980). In fact, most lawsuits filed by or on behalf of incarcerated women are for problems in receiving medical services (American Correctional Association 1990; Aylward and Thomas 1984). Access to medical care is difficult for women prisoners, and the staff often patronizes and minimizes their requests for medical care (Dobash et al. 1986). One study found that women prisoners claimed it was easy to get illegal drugs while in prison, but very difficult to get needed prescribed medications. Furthermore, transportation and scheduling limit the women's access to physicians (Mahan 1984). For emergency situations, women frequently must be transported from rural prisons to city hospitals (Pollock-Byrne 1990). Again, the small number of women prisoners relative to men prisoners is the justification used for not having extensive medical services on prison grounds.

A study comparing incarcerated women's and men's medical care at Riker's Island Correctional Complex in New York City found that while men and women had similar reasons for requesting medical care (with the exception of obstetrics and gynecological problems for women), incarcerated males were four times as likely as female prisoners to see a physician (instead of a nurse), more likely to receive treatment, and half as likely to be given psychotropic drugs (Shaw et al. 1982). Moreover, the medical staff held the general perceptions that female prisoners were "mostly healthy complainers," while male prisoners were viewed as "stoic sufferers more in need of services" (Shaw et al. 1982, 6).

The shortage of medical care for women is further exacerbated when one acknowledges women's greater medical needs. Given that most of women's increased needs for medical attention are related to gynecological issues, it is problematic that one in five U.S. women's prisons do not have gynecological/obstetrical services available at least once a week (American Correctional Association 1990). In addition to standard medical treatment, some of the concerns include, "the detection and treatment of sexually transmitted infections; cancer examinations (breast and pelvic); general gynecological care; prenatal, childbirth and postpartum care; abortion; menstrual problems; and problems associated with poor nutrition and the abuse of drugs" (Ross and Fabiano 1986, 52). The epidemic of women with AIDS is apparent in women's prisons, particularly given the prostitution and drug abuse backgrounds of many of these women. In fact, female prisoners are more likely than male prisoners to test HIV positive (Lawson and Fawkes 1993). This is yet another area where the medical facilities are sorely lacking in responding to incarcerated women (see Clark and Boudin 1990; Lawson and Fawkes 1993).

Especially poignant are the medical needs of incarcerated pregnant women who often receive little or no prenatal care, or even appropriate nutrition, such as milk (Barry 1991; Mann 1984; McHugh 1980; Resnick and Shaw 1980). There is also some indication that women with gynecological complaints are too frequently given unnecessary hysterectomies (McHugh 1980). Ironically, while the prison system seems to be intolerant of offending women procreating, and has a history of forced abortions and adoptions, there appears to be little effort to educate incarcerated women and girls on birth control and their gynecological health. Additionally, there is little evidence that health care is provided for pregnant incarcerated women addicted to drugs, nor for their infants (McHugh 1980).

A recent survey of U.S. women's prisons found that (1) less than half provided prenatal care; (2) only 15 percent provided special diets and nutritional programs for pregnant women; (3) only 15 percent provided counseling to help mothers find suitable placement for the infant after birth; and (4) only 11 percent provided postnatal counseling (Wooldredge and Masters 1993). Additionally, the wardens listed the following as problems not addressed in the survey: (1) inadequate resources for false labors, premature births, and miscarriages; (2) a lack of maternity clothes; (3) a requirement for prisoners in labor to wear belly chains on the way to the hospital; and (4) the housing of minimum security pregnant women in maximum security prisons (Wooldredge and Masters 1993). Research has established that the conditions for pregnant women housed in jails are equally deplorable (Barry 1991).

One study found that social workers were more accessible than the medical personnel. Unfortunately, the social workers' time was consumed with responding to the women's practical concerns (such as contact with children, legal and court problems, and securing employment and housing on release), limiting their abilities to provide counseling (Dobash et al. 1986). The psychiatrists available to the prisoners were more concerned with the women's criminal and mental health histories than with the stresses of incarceration, and the women requesting psychiatric help were often labeled mentally unstable. Therapy, consistent with other programs in women's reformatories, was considered "successful" when gender stereotypes, such as dependence and compliance, were reestablished (Dobash et al. 1986).

THE PRISONER SUBCULTURE

There is speculation that males adapt to incarceration by isolating themselves, while females, conversely, adjust to imprisonment by forming close relationships with other prisoners (Fox 1975). Some rather dated research suggests that females' socialization to be caring and value family relationships has resulted in the structuring of "pseudofamilies" in women's prisons and girls' juvenile institutions (see Carter 1981; Ford 1929; Giallombardo 1966, 1974). "Having been socialized to concentrate their energies on family relationships, women presumably miss these relationships more than men do and therefore create pseudo families to replace lost familial relationships" (Bowker 1981, 415). Both heterosexual and lesbian girls and women are in these "family" systems (Mann 1984), although not all incarcerated females are in a "family."

> Kinship relationships vary in size dependent upon the family network and the number of "relatives" in the family. The basic dyad, of course, consists of the parents. Then there are children, aunts, uncles, grandparents, cousins, in-laws, and the like. The second major variable requisite in the understanding of this social system is the male role played by the female inmate—for example, husband, brother, uncle, or grandfather.
> *(Mann 1984, 188)*

More recent research suggests that the pseudofamilies were either exaggerated in earlier studies or are less common in women's prisons today (Bowker 1981; Mahan 1984; Mawby 1982).

The partnerships in these families are not necessarily sexual. Furthermore, while some women and girls arrive at prison or juvenile institutions already identifying themselves as lesbians, others assume a lesbian status only while incarcerated, and others "come out" as lesbians while institutionalized and maintain this status after their release. As in the world outside of prison, this confirms a high degree of both lesbianism and bisexuality. Research indicates that approximately one in four incarcerated women report involvement in a lesbian relationship (Mawby 1982; Moyer 1978). These relationships typically end when one of the partners is released from prison or the staff separate the women (Moyer 1978). Notably, one study found that a strict policy against homosexuality in women's prisons is more likely to foster than discourage homosexuality (Mahan 1984). Moreover, the staff's obsession with deterring homosexuality often results in women being penalized simply for forming friendship bonds with other prisoners. Subsequently, many women report a fear of developing emotional ties with other prisoners, which exacerbates their feelings of isolation and loneliness and their inability to cope with imprisonment (Moyer 1980).

Prison experts and laypeople alike often mistakenly lump homosexuality and rape together. This is most prevalent when discussing prisons. It is important, however, to distinguish consensual homosexual sex from homosexual rape. Given the gender roles and misogyny in the outside world, it is hardly surprising that the subculture in men's prisons views homosexual rape as acceptable, while consensual gay relationships are considered taboo (see Bowker 1980; Wooden and Parker 1982). The opposite is true in women's prisons; consensual lesbian relationships are more common and less taboo. The rape of women in prison is almost unheard of, and when it does occur it is almost always by a male guard. In fact, many of the lesbian relationships reported in prison are based more on affection with a sexual connotation than actual sexual activity (Pollock-Byrne 1990).

Finally, future research needs to compare and contrast the supportive bonds that both women and men prisoners form that help them survive prison. It is possible that male prisoners' bonds have been overlooked by researchers with stereotypical views of gender, emotions, and friendship. One woman who was incarcerated in a federal prison and now works with female and male prisoners states:

> I think there are some differences between the way women bond with each other in prison and the way men bond to each other in prison, but I know that it happens in both populations. And I believe it is what allows both men and women to survive prison with at least a little bit of our emotional beings intact.
>
> *(Swain 1994)*

COCORRECTIONS

While the original and primary goal of women's prison reformers was sex-segregated prisons, in the early 1970s this was offered as the major reason for gender inequality in prisons. The first attempt in almost a hundred years to reestablish coed prisons occurred in 1971 in Fort Worth, Texas. Although men and women are still housed in separate buildings or cottages, they share some or all prison programs and services in *cocorrections* (Schweber 1985). Five federal co-correctional institutions opened in the 1970s, and fifteen state cocorrectional facilities operated in 1977. By 1984, however, only six states had cocorrectional facilities (Ryan 1984). Long-term policies toward cocorrections in both state and federal prisons appear to have fizzled out by 1989 (Mahan 1989).

A recent survey by the American Correctional Association (1990), however, found that 45 percent of "correctional" facilities currently house both males and females. The availability of programs for women in cocorrections and the degree of interaction allowed between the male and female prisoners vary among institutions (Schweber 1985). Only about one-third of these facilities allow interactions between females and males during such activities as recreation/leisure, prison programs, dining, and work crews, and 13 percent allow men and women to work together in prison industry (American Correctional Association 1990, 95). These percentages suggest that the programs and opportunities probably remain separate and unequal.

An examination of the early literature on cocorrections suggests that prison administrators and feminists perceived very different potential advantages of cocorrections. Prison administrators who implemented cocorrections in the 1970s hoped that sex integration would normalize the prison experience, making reintegration of ex-prisoners into society easier. To these administrators, an added benefit of cocorrections would be a supposed decrease in homosexual activity. To feminists, the two potential advantages of cocorrections were (1) reducing sex discrimination in prison experiences and increasing women's access to educational, vocational, work, social, and medical programs and activities; and (2) decreasing the chances that women will be detained at a great geographic distance from their children, other family, and friends.

While there is little information to support or refute that cocorrections has increased incarcerated women's likelihood of being near friends and family members, the remaining perceived potential advantages of cocorrections have not been realized. It is difficult, however, to assess most of the research on cocorrections, because the research itself is often based on sexist and homophobic assumptions. It is apparent, however, that cocorrections has done little to make things better for imprisoned women (and they may in fact be worse).

The traditional gender roles continue to be encouraged in cocorrections (see Campbell 1980; Heffernan and Krippel 1980). For example, women are likely to be given positions subservient to men, who dominate the high-status positions in the prison community (Schweber 1985); cocorrections men are more likely than cocorrections women to rank the furlough and work/education programs as positive and fairly distributed (Almy et al. 1980); cocorrections men have more freedom to move around the facility than cocorrections women (Chesney-Lind and Rodriguez 1983); cocorrections women are more likely than cocorrections men to be disciplined (Chesney-Lind and Rodriguez 1983; Wilson 1980); cocorrections rarely decreases the traditional women's programs; and when men prisoners are "added" to women's prisons to make them cocorrectional, the men get many of the best prisoner jobs (Ross and Heffernan 1980). One study in a cocorrectional facility found that women were routinely denied access "to virtually all programs at the facility" (Chesney-Lind and Rodriguez 1983).

> Critics have noted that co-corrections "normalizes" in another way—it places women in a minority situation in which their needs are subordinated in a male-dominated environment. There is nothing about a co-correctional institution which prohibits management from deciding in allotting programs and services to focus on the needs of the majority—the men.
>
> *(Ross and Fabiano 1986, 66–67)*

Nowhere in cocorrections is sex discrimination more obvious than in sexual control. Both homosexual and heterosexual activity are against institutional regulations; however, both homosexual and heterosexual activity still occur. In fact, there is evidence not only of pregnancies occurring during incarceration in cocorrectional facilities, but also of prostitution, where women are coerced or agree to do sexual favors in return for cigarettes or contraband (Chesney-Lind and Rodriguez 1983; Heffernan and Krippel 1980; Ruback 1980). There has been some variation in what heterosexual romantic activity is allowed, although no homosexual romantic behaviors are allowed. For example, for heterosexuals some institutions don't allow any physical contact, others allow hand holding, and still others allow hand holding and putting arms around each other as long as the couple isn't lying down (Anderson 1978). Notably, cocorrections does not appear to have decreased the rate of homosexuality in the prisons for either women or men (Campbell 1980; Ross and Fabiano 1986).

Women in the cocorrectional facilities who are "caught" having heterosexual sex are more likely than men to receive punishment. The burden of upholding the "no sexual contact" policy in cocorrectional facilities falls more heavily on the women, which has resulted in closer observation of the women than the men in these facilities (and closer observation of the women in cocorrections than in women-only prisons) (Schweber 1985). One study reported that while twenty-nine men and twenty-nine women were written up for being in a "compromising sexual situation," twenty-nine women and only seven men were written up for having sexual intercourse. This discrepancy was attributed to the fact that women who get pregnant are automatically "caught," and that even when caught "in the act," men are somehow better able to avoid identification (Anderson 1978). In a similar study, a staff member reported: "When a female gets pregnant by another inmate in here, it's all hers. There are no attempts to make the father take responsibility for the child after the initial disciplinary hearings are over" (Mahan 1984, 235).

Finally, the obsession with keeping the women and men prisoners separated in the cocorrectional facilities does not prevent the male *staff* from sexually harassing and exerting pressure for sexual favors on the women prisoners (Chesney-Lind and Rodriguez 1983). One study confirmed reports of staff–prisoner sexual relations in cocorrections, but did not discuss its exploitative nature (Mahan 1989).

SUMMARY

This chapter traced the beginnings of the punishment of women and the treatment of incarcerated women historically, to current responses to convicted females. The development of women's reformatories during the nineteenth and early twentieth centuries has had long-term effects on the institutionalization of female offenders. While the reformatories were important in providing safety from sexual abuse, they were built on a foundation that stereotyped women and girls into roles of homemakers and maids. To this day, women's prisons are fraught with programs and activities that reaffirm women's "appropriate" role as in the home. Gender differences in women's and men's prison experiences and access to services and activities generally show discrimination against incarcerated females. Although the implementation of cocorrections was perceived as a means to decrease gender discrimination in prison opportunities, this does not appear to have happened. Finally, the issues of pregnancy and parenting for incarcerated women are some of the most difficult and heartrending in the prison system today.

REFERENCES

Almy, Linda, Vikki Bravo, Leslie Burd, Patricia Chin, Linda Cohan, Frank Gallo, Anthony Giorgianni, Jeffrey Gold, Mark Jose, and John Noyes. 1980. "A Study of a Co-Educational Correctional Facility." Pp. 120–149 in *Co-Ed Prison,* edited by J. O. Smykla. New York: Human Services Press.

Alpert, Geoffrey P. 1982. "Women Prisoners and the Law: Which Way Will the Pendulum Swing?" Pp. 171–182 in *The Criminal Justice System and Women,* edited by B. R. Price and N. J. Sokoloff. New York: Clark and Boardman.

American Correctional Association. 1990. *The Female Offender: What Does the Future Hold?* Arlington, VA: Kirby Lithographic Company.

Anderson, David C. 1978. "Co-corrections." *Corrections Magazine* Sep. 4: 33–41.

Arnold, Regina. 1990. "Processes of Victimization and Criminalization of Black Women." *Social Justice* 17:153–166.

Aylward, Anna, and Jim Thomas. 1984. "Quiescence in Women's Prison Litigation." *Justice Quarterly* 1:253–276.

Barry, Ellen M. 1991. "Jail Litigation Concerning Women Prisoners." *The Prison Journal* 71:44–50.

Baunach, Phyllis Jo. 1982. "You Can't Be a Mother and Be in Prison... Can You? Impacts of the Mother–Child Separation." Pp. 155–170 in *The Criminal Justice System and Women,* edited by B. R. Price and N. J. Sokoloff. New York: Clark and Boardman.

—————. 1985. *Mothers in Prison.* New Brunswick, NJ: Transaction Books.

—————. 1992. "Critical Problems of Women in Prison." Pp. 99–112 in *The Changing Roles of Women in the Criminal Justice System,* edited by I. L. Moyer. Prospect Heights, IL: Waveland Press.

Baunach, Phyllis Jo, and Thomas O. Murton. 1973. "Women in Prison: An Awakening Minority." *Crime and Corrections* 1:4–12.

Binkley-Jackson, Deborah, Vivian L. Carter, and Garry L. Rolison. 1993. "African-American Women in Prison." Pp. 65–74 in *Women Prisoners: A Forgotten Population,* edited by Beverly R. Fletcher, Lynda D. Shaver, and Dreama G. Moon. Westport, CT: Praeger.

Bloom, Barbara. 1993. "Incarcerated Mothers and Their Children: Maintaining Family Ties." Pp. 60–68 in *Female Offenders: Meeting the Needs of a Neglected Population.* Laurel, MD: American Correctional Association.

Boudouris, James. 1985. *Prisons and Kids.* College Park, MD: American Correctional Association.

Bowker, Lee. 1980. *Victimization in Prisons.* New York: Elsevier.

_____. 1981. "Gender Differences in Prisoner Subcultures." Pp. 409–419 in *Women and Crime in America,* edited by L. H. Bowker. New York: Macmillan.

Campbell, Charles F. 1980. "Co-Corrections—FCI Fort Worth After Three Years." Pp. 83–109 in *Co-Ed Prison,* edited by J. O. Smykla. New York: Human Services Press.

Carlen, Pat. 1983. *Women's Imprisonment: A Study in Social Control.* London: Routledge & Kegan Paul.

Carlen, Pat, and Chris Tchaikovsky. 1985. "Women in Prison." Pp. 182–186 in *Criminal Women,* edited by P. Carlen, J. Hicks, J. O'Dwyer, and D. Christina. Cambridge: Polity Press.

Carter, Barbara. 1981. "Reform School Families." Pp. 419–431 in *Women and Crime in America,* edited by L. H. Bowker. New York: Macmillan.

Chesney-Lind, Meda. 1991. "Patriarchy, Prisons, and Jails: A Critical Look at Trends in Women's Incarceration." *The Prison Journal* 71:51–67.

Chesney-Lind, Meda, and Noelie Rodriguez. 1983. "Women Under Lock and Key." *Prison Journal* 63:47–65.

Chesney-Lind, Meda, and Randall G. Shelden. 1992. *Girls, Delinquency, and Juvenile Justice.* Pacific Grove, CA: Brooks/Cole.

Church, George. 1990. "The View from Behind Bars." *Time Magazine* (Fall) 135:20–22.

Clark, Judy, and Kathy Boudin. 1990. "Community of Women Organize Themselves to Cope with the AIDS Crisis: A Case Study from Bedford Hills Correctional Facility." *Social Justice* 17:90–109.

Dobash, Russell P., R. Emerson Dobash, and Sue Gutteridge. 1986. *The Imprisonment of Women.* Oxford: Basil Blackwell.

Feinman, Clarice. 1981. "Sex-Role Stereotypes and Justice for Women." Pp. 383–391 in *Women and Crime in America,* edited by L. H. Bowker. New York: Macmillan.

_____. 1983. "An Historical Overview of the Treatment of Incarcerated Women: Myths and Realities of Rehabilitation." *Prison Journal* 63:12–26.

_____. 1986. *Women in the Criminal Justice System,* 2nd ed. New York: Praeger.

Fletcher, Beverly R., and Dreama G. Moon. 1993a. "Introduction." Pp. 5–14 in *Women Prisoners: A Forgotten Population,* edited by Beverly R. Fletcher, Lynda D. Shaver, and Dreama G. Moon. Westport, CT: Praeger.

_____. 1993b. "Conclusions." Pp. 5–14 in *Women Prisoners: A Forgotten Population,* edited by Beverly R. Fletcher, Lynda D. Shaver, and Dreama G. Moon. Westport, CT: Praeger.

Fletcher, Beverly R., Garry L. Rolison, and Dreama G. Moon. 1993. "The Woman Prisoner." Pp. 15–26 in *Women Prisoners: A Forgotten Population,* edited by Beverly R. Fletcher, Lynda D. Shaver, and Dreama G. Moon. Westport, CT: Praeger.

Ford, C. 1929. "Homosexual Practices of Institutionalized Females." *Journal of Abnormal and Social Psychology* 23:442–448.

Fox, James G. 1975. "Women in Crisis." Pp. 181–205 in *Man in Crisis,* edited by H. Toch. Chicago: Aldine-Atherton.

Freedman, Estelle. 1974. "Their Sisters' Keepers: An Historical Perspective on Female Correctional Institutions in the United States, 1870–1900." *Feminist Studies* 2:77–95.

——————. 1982. "Nineteenth-Century Women's Prison Reform and Its Legacy." Pp. 141–157 in *Women and the Law: A Social Historical Perspective,* Vol. I, edited by D. Kelly Weisberg. Cambridge, MA: Schenkman Publishing.

Gelsthorpe, Loraine. 1989. *Sexism and the Female Offender.* Aldershot, England: Gower.

Giallombardo, Rose. 1966. *Society of Women: A Study of a Women's Prison.* New York: John Wiley .

——————. 1974. *The Social World of Imprisoned Girls.* New York: Wiley.

Gilfus, Mary E. 1992. "From Victims to Survivors to Offenders: Women's Routes of Entry and Immersion into Street Crime." *Women and Criminal Justice* 4:63–90.

Glick, Ruth M., and Virginia V. Neto. 1982. "National Study of Women's Correctional Programs." Pp. 141–154 in *The Criminal Justice System and Women,* edited by B. R. Price and N. J. Sokoloff. New York: Clark and Boardman.

Goetting, Ann. 1987. "Racism, Sexism, and Ageism in the Prison Community." *Federal Probation* 49:10–22.

Goetting, Ann, and Roy M. Howsen. 1983. "Women in Prison: A Profile." *The Prison Journal* 63:27–46.

Haft, Marilyn G. 1980. "Women in Prison: Discriminatory Practices and Some Legal Solutions." Pp. 320–338 in *Women, Crime, and Justice,* edited by S. K. Datesman and F. R. Scarpitti. New York: Oxford Press.

Haley, Kathleen. 1980. "Mothers Behind Bars." Pp. 339–354 in *Women, Crime, and Justice,* edited by S. K. Datesman and F. R. Scarpitti. New York: Oxford Press.

Hancock, Linda. 1986. "Economic Pragmatism and the Ideology of Sexism: Prison Policy and Women."

Women's Studies International Forum 9:101–107.

Hannah-Moffat, Kelly. 1994. "Unintended Consequences of Feminism and Prison Reform." *Forum on Corrections Research* 6:7–10.

Heffernan, Esther, and Elizabeth Krippel. 1980. "A Co-Ed Prison." Pp. 110–119 in *Co-Ed Prison,* edited by J. O. Smykla. New York: Human Services Press.

Heidensohn, Frances M. 1985. *Women and Crime: The Life of the Female Offender.* New York: New York University Press.

Henriques, Zelma W. 1994. "Imprisoned Mothers and Their Children: A Cross-Cultural Perspective." Paper presented at "Prisons 2000," an International Conference on the Present and Future State of Prisons. Leicester, England, April.

Holt, Karen E. 1982. "Nine Months to Life: The Law and the Pregnant Inmate." *Journal of Family Law* 20:523–543.

Immarigeon, Russ. 1987a. "Women in Prison." *Journal of the National Prison Project* 11:1–5.

——————. 1987b. "Few Diversion Programs Are Offered Female Offenders." *Journal of the National Prison Project* 12:9–11.

Immarigeon, Russ, and Meda Chesney-Lind. 1992. *Women's Prisons: Overcrowded and Overused.* San Francisco: National Council on Crime and Delinquency.

Janusz, Luke. 1991. "Separate but Unequal: Women Behind Bars in Massachusetts." *Odyssey* (Fall):6–17.

Kaplan, Mildred F. 1988. "A Peer Support Group for Women in Prison for the Death of a Child." *Journal of Offender Counseling, Services, and Rehabilitation* 13:5–13.

Kersten, Joachim. 1989. "The Institutional Control of Girls and Boys." Pp. 129–144 in *Growing Up Good: Policing the Behavior of Girls in Europe,* edited by M. Cain. London: Sage.

Kline, Sue. 1993. "A Profile of Female Offenders in State and Federal Prisons." Pp. 1–6 in *Female Offenders: Meeting the Needs of a Neglected Population*. Laurel, MD: American Correctional Association.

Knight, Barbara. 1992. "Women in Prison as Litigants: Prospects for Post Prison Futures." *Women and Criminal Justice* 4:91–116.

Koban, Linda A. 1983. "Parent in Prison: A Comparative Analysis of the Effects of Incarceration on the Families of Men and Women." *Research in Law, Deviance and Social Control* 5:171–183.

Lawson, W. Travis, and Lena Sue Fawkes. 1993. "HIV, AIDS, and the Female Offender." Pp. 43–48 in *Female Offenders: Meeting the Needs of a Neglected Population*. Laurel, MD: American Correctional Association.

Lekkerkerker, Eugenia C. 1931. *Reformatories for Women in the United States*. J. B. Wolters' Groningen–The Hague: Batavia.

Leonard, Eileen B. 1983. "Judicial Decisions and Prison Reform: The Impact of Litigation on Women Prisoners." *Social Problems* 31:45–58.

Mahan, Sue. 1982. *Unfit Mothers*. Palo Alto, CA: R and E Associates.

_____. 1984. "Imposition of Despair: An Ethnography of Women in Prison." *Justice Quarterly* 1:357–384.

_____. 1989. "The Needs and Experiences of Women in Sexually Integrated Prisons." *American Journal of Criminal Justice* 13:228–239.

Mann, Coramae Richey. 1984. *Female Crime and Delinquency*. University of Alabama Press.

Mawby, R. I. 1982. "Women in Prison: A British Study." *Crime and Delinquency* 28:24–39.

McCarthy, Belinda R. 1980. "Inmate Mothers: The Problems of Separation and Reintegration." *Journal of Offender Counseling, Services and Rehabilitation* 4:199–212.

McClellan, Dorothy S. 1994. "Disparity in the Discipline of Male and Female Inmates in Texas Prisons." *Women and Criminal Justice* 5:71–97.

McGowan, Brenda, and Karen L. Blumenthal. 1976. "Children of Women Prisoners: A Forgotten Minority." Pp. 121–136 in *The Female Offender*, edited by L. Crites. Lexington, MA: D. C. Heath.

_____. 1978. *Why Punish the Children? A Study of Children of Women Prisoners*. Hackensack, NJ: National Council on Crime and Delinquency.

McHugh, Gerald A. 1980. "Protection of the Rights of Pregnant Women in Prisons and Detention Facilities." *New England Journal on Prison Law* 6:231–263.

Moon, Dreama G., Ruby J. Thompson, and Regina Bennett. 1993. "Patterns of Substance Use Among Women in Prison." Pp. 45–54 in *Women Prisoners: A Forgotten Population*, edited by Beverly R. Fletcher, Lynda D. Shaver, and Dreama G. Moon. Westport, CT: Praeger.

Morris, Allison. 1987. *Women, Crime and Criminal Justice*. Oxford: Basil Blackwell.

Moyer, Imogene L. 1978. "Differential Social Structures and Homosexuality Among Women in Prison." *Virginia Social Science Journal* 13:13–19.

_____. 1980. "Leadership in a Women's Prison." *Journal of Criminal Justice* 8:233–241.

_____. 1984. "Deceptions and Realities of Life in Women's Prisons." *Prison Journal* 64:45–56.

Natalizia, Elana. 1991. "Feminism and Criminal Justice Reform." *Odyssey* (Fall):19–20.

Pendergrass, Virginia E. 1975. "Innovative Programs for Women in Jail and Prisons." Pp. 67–81 in *The Female Offender*, edited by A. M. Brodsky. Beverly Hills, CA: Sage.

Pollock-Byrne, Joycelyn M. 1990. *Women, Prison, and Crime*. Pacific Grove, CA: Brooks/Cole.

Rafter, Nicole Hahn. 1985. *Partial Justice: Women in State Prisons, 1800–1935*. Boston: Northeastern University Press.

Resnick, Judith, and Nancy Shaw. 1980. "Prisoners of Their Sex: Health Problems of Incarcerated Women." Pp. 319–413 in *Prisoners' Rights Sourcebook,* Vol. 2, edited by Ira P. Robbins. New York: Clark Boardman.

Ross, James, and Esther Heffernan. 1980. "Women in a Co-Ed Joint." Pp. 248–261 in *Co-Ed Prison,* edited by J. O. Smykla. New York: Human Services Press.

Ross, Robert R., and Elizabeth A. Fabiano. 1986. *Female Offenders: Correctional Afterthoughts.* Jefferson, NC: McFarland.

Ruback, Barry. 1980. "The Sexuality Integrated Prison." Pp. 33–60 in *Co-Ed Prison,* edited by J. O. Smykla. New York: Human Services Press.

Ryan, T. A. 1984. *Adult Female Offenders and Institutional Programs: A State of the Art Analysis.* Washington, D.C.: U.S. Department of Justice.

Sargent, Elizabeth, Susan Marcus-Mendoza, and Chong Ho Yu. 1993. "Abuse and the Woman Prisoner." Pp. 55–64 in *Women Prisoners: A Forgotten Population,* edited by Beverly R. Fletcher, Lynda D. Shaver, and Dreama G. Moon. Westport, CT: Praeger.

Sarri, Rosemary. 1987. "Unequal Protection Under the Law: Women and the Criminal Justice System." Pp. 394–426 in *The Trapped Woman: Catch-22 in Deviance and Control,* edited by J. Figueira-McDonough and R. Sarri. Newbury Park, CA: Sage.

Schupak, Terri L. 1986. "Comments: Women and Children First: An Examination of the Unique Needs of Women in Prison." *Golden Gate University Law Review* 16:455–474.

Schweber, Claudine. 1985. "Beauty Marks and Blemishes: The Co-Ed Prison." *Prison Journal* 64:3–15.

Shaw, Nancy S., Irene Browne, and Peter Meyer. 1982. "Sexism and Medical Care in a Jail Setting." *Women and Health* 6:5–24.

Sims, Patsy. 1976. "Women in Southern Jails." Pp. 137–148 in *The Female Offender,* edited by L. Crites. Lexington, MA: D. C. Heath.

Smart, Carol. 1976. *Women, Crime and Criminology: A Feminist Critique.* London: Routledge & Kegan Paul.

Stanton, Ann M. 1980. *When Mothers Go to Jail.* Lexington, MA: Lexington Books.

Swain, Lorry. Personal correspondence, May 19, 1994.

U.S. Department of Justice. 1991a. *Children in Custody, 1989.* Office of Juvenile Justice and Delinquency Prevention. NCJ-127189. Washington, D.C., January.

—————. 1991b. *Drugs and Jail Inmates, 1989.* Special Report NCJ-130836. Bureau of Justice Statistics. Washington, D.C., August.

—————. 1992. *Census of State and Federal Correctional Facilities, 1990.* NCJ-137003. Bureau of Justice Statistics. Washington, D.C.: Government Printing Office.

Vachon, Marla M. 1994. "It's About Time: The Legal Context of Policy Changes for Female Offenders." *Forum on Corrections Research* 6:3–6.

Van Ochten, Marjorie. 1993. "Legal Issues and the Female Offender." Pp. 31–36 in *Female Offenders: Meeting the Needs of a Neglected Population.* Laurel, MD: American Correctional Association.

Vitale, Anne T. 1980. "Inmate Abortions: The Right to Government Funding Behind the Prison Gates." *Fordham Law Review* 48:550–567.

Vukson, Todd M. 1988. "Inmate Abortion Funding in California." *California Western Law Review* 24:107–126.

Ward, David A., and Gene G. Kassebaum. 1965. *Women's Prison: Sex and Social Structure.* Chicago: Aldine.

Weintraub, Judith F. 1987. "Mothers and Children in Prison." *Corrections Compendium* 11:1, 5.

Weisheit, Ralph A. 1985. "Trends in Programs for Female Offenders: The Use of Private Agencies as Service Providers." *International Journal of Offender Therapy and Comparative Criminology* 29:35–42.

Wheeler, Patricia A., Rebecca Trammell, Jim Thomas, and Jennifer Findlay. 1989. "Persephone Chained: Parity of Equality in Women's Prisons." *The Prison Journal* 69:88–102.

Wilson, Nancy K. 1980. "Styles of Doing Time in a *Co-Ed Prison*: Masculine and Feminine Alternatives." Pp. 150–171 in *Co-Ed Prison*, edited by J. O. Smykla. New York: Human Services Press.

Windschuttle, Elizabeth. 1981. "Women, Crime, and Punishment." Pp. 31–50 in *Women and Crime,* edited by S. K.

Mukherjee and J. A. Scutt. North Sydney, Australia: Allen & Unwin.

Wooden, Wayne S., and Jay Parker. 1982. *Men Behind Bars: Sexual Exploitation in Prison.* New York: Plenum.

Wooldredge, John D., and Kimberly Masters. 1993. "Confronting Problems Faced by Pregnant Inmates in State Prisons." *Crime and Delinquency* 39:195–203.

PART III

Female Victims
of Male Violence

6

✳

The Image of the Female Victim

The image of the female victim has changed considerably in recent years. Until the 1970s, female victims were relatively invisible. Although roughly 2 million women are battered annually in the United States, the term *battered woman* did not exist until 1974 (Schechter 1982, 16). Similarly, *sexual harassment* was not a labeled behavior until 1975 (Evans 1978), and *date rape* was first identified as a problem in the early 1980s. Although many people still believe the stereotypes surrounding female victimization, the frequency and facts about the sexual and physical victimization of women and girls have been increasingly documented. This chapter is an overview of how women victims of male violence have been viewed historically and how awareness of their victimization has changed over time.

The focus of the next few chapters is on the victimizations most frequently associated with women and girls: sexual victimization and battering. Rape and battering are the "most underreported crimes against persons in the criminal justice system" (Gelles 1979, 121). Unfortunately, it is beyond the scope of this book to address some of the other victimizations associated with women, particularly those involving reproductive freedom. There is substantial evidence not only of "botched" legal and illegal abortions, but also of coerced and forced sterilization of women, especially poor women and women of color (see Davis 1981; Gordon 1977).

Both the physical and sexual victimization of women and girls have been shrouded in beliefs that these occurrences are *rare*, the *victim's fault*, and *shameful* for the victim. The understanding of sexual victimization has been muddled because of puritanical views of rape as an "unmentionable" crime (Sanders 1980). Historically, battered women have been thought of as deserving victims, "nags," and inadequate wives. Although the stereotype of the "real" rape victim usually assumed the victim to be Anglo and middle class or upper class, the stereotype of a battered woman was of a woman involved in a "family disturbance" in a working-class or poor neighborhood. Research has shown that these stereotypes are myths: All women and girls are at risk of male violence, regardless of race, age, or ethnicity.

Although male violence against women and girls has been a historical constant, recognition of the epidemic proportions of these crimes has been relatively recent. Russell (1984) has traced the recognition of various phenomena as identified *social problems*. Social problems are phenomena that have often occurred for centuries, but were not labeled as problematic or common until data were collected and a critical mass of society accepted them as problematic. Russell (1984, 20) identifies, in order of their appearance from the 1960s to the early 1980s, the following social problems that came to the public's attention: (1) nonsexual child abuse, (2) the rape of women by strangers and other nonintimates, (3) nonsexual wife abuse, and (4) the sexual abuse of children (particularly incest). The identification of each of these social problems helped set the stage for the others to follow. Since the publication of Russell's (1984) book, the threats and reality of physical and sexual dating violence, marital rape, sexual harassment, and satanic cult victimization of women and girls have been increasingly documented.

Sexual abuse and battering are not always distinct victimizations. Homes where woman battering occurs may also be homes where children are physically and sexually abused. Additionally, physical and sexual violence in dating or courtship relationships often go hand in hand. Many men who batter their wives or girlfriends also sexually victimize these women (Finkelhor and Yllo 1985; Russell 1982, 1984; Schechter 1982).

DETERMINING THE FREQUENCY AND NATURE OF FEMALE VICTIMIZATION

A number of (male) researchers have claimed that males are much more likely to be victims of crime in general than are females (for example, Cohen and Felson 1979; Gottfredson 1986; Miethe et al. 1987). Other research has consistently shown that females have higher *fear of crime* than males (Braungart et al. 1980; Clemente and Kleiman 1976; LaGrange and Ferraro 1989; Ortego and Myles 1987). Recent research stated that "women *think* they are more likely [than men] to be the victim of a personal crime" (LaGrange and Ferraro 1989). Given the low rates of female victimization reported in most statistics, some criminologists have suggested that women's higher fear of crime is irrational.

The major problems with this rationale are that (1) awareness of the *extent* and *frequency* with which females are victimized is relatively recent and often ignored, and (2) the *nature* of the victimization is different for crimes associated with female victims (rape and battering). Regarding the first point, the extent and frequency of females' victimizations are not clearly known because sexual victimization and battering are the least likely offenses to be reported to the police (Young 1992). The most comprehensive, valid study of rape victimization found that 44 percent of women reported being the victims of rape or attempted rape at least once, and only 8 percent of those victimized reported it to the police (Russell 1984). Other researchers estimate that 40 to 50 percent of women in the United States experience battering at the hands of intimate male partners (Smith 1994; Walker 1979).

If crimes such as rape and battering were reported to the police (or even the National Crime Survey) as consistently as the types of crimes males tend to experience, statistics would likely begin to define females as significantly *more* at risk of violence than males. Females' high levels of fear and low *reported* victimizations are likely due to researchers' unwillingness to accept fear levels as realistic assessments of risk (Young 1992). Other research found that most women rarely tell anyone about physical and sexual intrusions because of fear, humiliation, and self-blame. Moreover, when they do tell someone, a decision is usually made to keep the incident "private" (Stanko 1992). A number of reasons have been offered as to why women don't report physical and sexual abuse to researchers or to the police: too personal to discuss, embarrassment or shame, fear of reprisal by the abuser, or repression due to the trauma (Smith 1994).

Although improved statistics would likely show the high risk of female victimization compared to male victimization, quantity alone is not sufficient to address gender differences in these crimes. It is vital to address the *nature* of crimes regularly perpetrated against females (Riger 1981). With the exception of murder, rape is the most fear-inducing crime (Brodyaga et al. 1975). The severity and threat of rape cannot be overemphasized. Similarly, not only is battering violent, but it is additionally disturbing for the victim to receive abuse from a person who is supposed to love and care for her, and on whom she and her children may be economically dependent.

Stanko (1990) views fear of danger as so commonplace in women's lives that they simply learn to manage it. In fact, fear is so routine that it is almost unrecognizable. A 63-year-old widow whom Stanko (1990, 11) interviewed about safety was sure that she would have nothing to contribute:

> When the interview was complete, she recalled being fondled by a shop owner when she was 8, feeling physically threatened by her brother as an adult, being attacked as a nurse while working at night in a hospital and being hassled by men for sexual favors after the death of her husband.

Thus, the threat of potential victimization restricts and controls the freedom of women and girls. But before addressing the restrictions that the threat of male violence poses on women and girls, the effect of culture on gender roles and gender power differences will be discussed.

EFFECT OF CULTURE ON GENDER ROLES

Sex-role stereotyping begins even before birth. Not only do the names parents choose for their children often differ depending on the child's sex, but frequently parents' expectations of that child depend on the child's sex. The societal image of women as weaker, less intelligent, and less valued influences the likelihood of victimization. Women and girls have frequently been objectified and perceived "to be almost wholly passive, devoid of both judgment and decision" (Sanders 1980, 22). Historically, men have been viewed as *people,* whereas women have been viewed as *property* (Sanders 1980). Laws historically defined rape as theft, and rape laws were designed to protect upper- and middle-class Anglo men in the case of their "property" (daughters and wives) being devalued by rape.

In a sense, then, many women and girls have been socialized to be victims of male violence. Girls are rewarded for passivity and "feminine" behavior, whereas boys are rewarded for aggressiveness and "masculine" behavior. These stereotypes are often reaffirmed in the media, where strong, independent female characters are rare, while violent, controlling male characters are abundant. Moreover, these images affect both males' and females' perceptions of males' dominance and females' (in)ability to resist male dominance. A woman or girl resisting an attacker is in need of resistance techniques that she has often been conditioned or instructed not to use (Estrich 1987).

Our culture often suggests that women need men for protection and financial security. For example, a social expectation is that women on dates usually assume their dates will take care of them. This expectation leaves women vulnerable to date rapists who often plan situations where the woman has little control (Medea and Thompson 1974). To compound this, men who perpetrate physical and sexual violence against women they know, or are even intimately involved with, often receive peer support from male friends who may encourage the abuse (DeKeseredy 1988; Gwartney-Gibbs and Stockard 1989; Martin and Hummer 1989).

There is a tendency to view instances of male aggressiveness (violence) against women and girls as somehow "natural," just as females are supposedly inherently passive. Explanations of women experiencing male violence often center around whether male aggression was "natural" in relation to the *woman's* behavior (Stanko 1985, 10). This implies that there are particular behavioral patterns and roles inherent biologically in both males and females that encourage and justify the victimization of females by males. Furthermore, it implies that women are the precipitators of men's violence, and that in some cases men are justified in their violent behavior. In 1993, a judge in Ohio released a man with a criminal record to shock probation who had severely beaten his estranged wife and her daughter (from another relationship) with a crow bar. He blamed the woman because she'd allegedly been in bed with another man when her estranged husband barged into her home. Such an image of male and female roles and behavior clearly deters the correct assignment of blame and the inhibition of male violence. A recent study of college students found that women were less likely than men to hold false beliefs inherent in rape myths. Those who believed rape myths (mostly males) were also more likely to blame the victims and support conservative gender roles (Fonow et al. 1992).

Gender stereotyping perpetuates mythical perceptions of both sexual assault *offenders* and *victims*. There is a tendency to think that only certain types of women and girls are sexually victimized and battered, and certain types of men are batterers and rapists. Raped women are often stigmatized for being "provocative" and sexually uncontrolled, and for not knowing where to draw the line (Stanko 1985). These stereotypes are frequently associated with racist and classist assumptions, such as that poor, African American women are more likely to be battered women, and young, Anglo, middle-class women are more likely to be sexual assault victims. Similarly, rapists and batterers are frequently assumed to be poor, black men, often mentally ill or drug-addicted. Such perceptions are not based on reality and inhibit our ability to understand and protect ourselves from sexual victimizations. In the United States, most rapists are Anglo, and 90 percent of rapes are *intra*racial (within race); yet African American men are disproportionately convicted of rape (Fonow et al. 1992).

GENDER DISPARITIES IN POWER

Susan Brownmiller's book *Against Our Will: Men, Women and Rape* (1975) received a great deal of attention. As well as enlightening its many readers on the history and terror of rape, *Against Our Will* exposed the anger many women feel about living in a culture where rape is minimized, ignored, or joked about. *Against Our Will* was a path-breaking book and the first widely read feminist analysis of rape. Unfortunately, despite the power of this book in raising awareness about rape, it has also been criticized for sometimes reinforcing myths about black rapists (Davis 1981; Tong 1984; Williams 1981). However, Brownmiller addresses how lynchings of blacks in the United States were racially motivated, targeting black men for fabricated rapes of Anglo women. Overall, *Against Our Will* has had a significant impact on the discourse of rape.

A controversial contention in *Against Our Will* is the statement that rape "is nothing more or less than a conscious process of intimidation by which *all men* keep *all women* in a state of fear" (Brownmiller 1975, 5). Brownmiller, then, views rape as a conscious means by which men control women. Russell (1984, 153), on the other hand, views rape and other male violence against women, as "a *consequence* of the power disparity between the sexes that has existed as long as recorded history." Brownmiller sees rape as causing the disparity between women and men, whereas Russell views the power disparity between the sexes as causing rape. Consistent with Russell's (1984) belief, a cross-cultural study found that rape levels were related to the levels of society's adherence to patriarchal roles. Rape-prone societies were associated with lower levels of female power and authority, including women's lack of participation in public decision making (Sanday 1981).

A more accurate depiction of the preceding debate is that female victimization and gender-power disparity reinforce each other (see the figure below on this page). More specifically, victimization and the threat of victimization of females decrease the power of women and girls. Simultaneously, inequalities in power between males and females make females more likely to be victims, and males more likely to be aggressors/offenders. There are many ways in which society, culture, and the crime-processing system contribute to this cycle of female victimization and gender-power disparity, such as advertisements linking sex and violence, images of women as passive, and police and court officials who blame victims. Thus we need to simultaneously construct the empowerment of women and girls as equal to that of men and boys, in the minds of both females and males.

This power disparity is not limited to physical power, but pervades most facets of our lives—men also tend to have higher economic, political, and social status than women. A study of fifty U.S. cities found that as the economic, political, and legal status of women decreased, the rape rate increased (Baron and Straus 1987). These more obvious power differences result in less obvious social and psychological power disparities between men and women. The aggregated gender status differences are equally obvious at the individual level. The verbal and psychological abuses of battered women exemplify this:

> Battered women consistently complain of degrading verbal abuse: "You can't do anything right"; "How could I have ever married a pig like you!" Verbal assaults, like physical ones, may go on for hours in a relentless attack on a woman's sense of dignity and self worth and almost always include threats: "I'll cut your throat from one end to another"; "If you try to leave me, you're dead."
>
> *(Schechter 1982, 17)*

Thus, power may be asserted in many forms: physically (battering), sexually, economically, and verbally. Male power, perceived and real, limits the freedom and rights of women and girls.

Sexual victimization, like woman battering, is an act of power. Sexual offenders are motivated by a desire to dominate, not simply to achieve sexual gratification. The forced sexual submission is clearly a manner of controlling and humiliating a victim; it is a way for a victim to experience that she does not have control over her own body, while the rapist does.

Cycle of Female Victimization and Gender Disparity

female victimization   gender-power disparity

THREAT OF VIOLENCE

Although both male and female children lead lives that are restricted because they are vulnerable and need protection, such limitations often follow females for the rest of their lives. Women are constantly reminded of their vulnerability by messages from friends, family, and the media. "Such fear can induce a continuing state of stress in women and can lead to the adoption of safety precautions that severely restrict women's freedom, such as not going out alone at night or staying out of certain parts of town" (Riger and Gordon 1981, 73). Similarly, the threat of rape may deny women employment, keep them off the streets at night, and influence them to be "passive and modest for fear that they will be thought provocative" (Griffen 1971, 35). The message of the vulnerability of women and girls is deeply and culturally embedded: Females should restrict their behavior, actions, and clothing, or something dreadful will happen. Women are reminded of their vulnerability and male violence every time they read or hear of another woman being raped. Moreover, women are rarely able to predict when a threatening or intimidating form of male behavior will escalate to violence. As a result, many women are frequently on guard to the possibility of men's violence, particularly if they have already been victimized (Stanko 1985, 1990).

The battering of women by their husbands or boyfriends, similar to their sexual victimization, keeps women under the control of men. The belief that a man is the "king of his castle" is still accepted by many people in society. Battering, both actual and threatened, reduces the control the battered woman has over her life, while increasing the batterer's control. Just as sexual assault is more likely in a culture with large power disparities between the sexes, the same can be expected of the battering of women. The more authority men are perceived to hold over women, the more likely that battering will occur. The implications of woman battering are significant:

> Violence signifies crossing a boundary in which violation and degradation, previously unacceptable in a loving relationship, are now used as tools of power and coercion. Battering is far more than a single event, even for the woman who is hit once, because it teaches a profound lesson about who controls a relationship and how that control will be exercised.…
> Self-consciously exercised, violence temporarily brings a man what he wants—his wife acquiesces, placates him, or stops her demands. As a form of terrifying intimidation, violence signifies that the man's way will prevail even when the woman struggles against this imposition. Leaving her in a constantly vigilant state, violence forces a woman to worry about the time, place, or reason for the next attack.
>
> *(Schechter 1982, 17)*

The threatened and actual victimization of women and girls (whether it is sexual, physical, or verbal) serves to define the "place" of females in the culture. It restricts the freedom and quality of life of women and girls. Brownmiller's (1975) assertion that all men benefit from rape is more understandable when one recognizes that *it is not necessary for all men to victimize all women in order for all women to be afraid of male violence.* The fact that *some* men victimize *some* women serves to control most females' lives through at least some degree of fear.

This fear affects many aspects of women's lives, such as enrolling in day classes, deciding to walk on the opposite side of the street when they see an unknown male walking toward them, or deciding not to wear certain clothes for fear of being perceived as "fair game" to all men. "Women worry more than men do in the same situations: going to laundromats, using public transportation, or being downtown alone after dark" (Gordon and Riger 1989, 14). Many women report that the fear of rape crosses their minds regularly (Gordon and Riger 1989). Compounding the fear of victimization by strangers is the growing awareness that women and girls are more likely to be victimized by males they know.

VICTIM BLAMING

Women and girls who don't follow society's unwritten rules are often blamed if they are raped. Persons who believe that women and girls *should* lead restrictive lives also tend to believe that a woman or girl who "violates" these "rules" is at least partially responsible if she is victimized. "The effect of women's greater fear of crime is to produce social constraints upon them; women not heeding those constraints may be punished not only by direct victimization, but also by being blamed for their own victimization" (Riger et al. 1978, 282). Notably, a recent national survey found that rape victims are concerned about having their families and other people find out they were raped, having people think they were at fault, and having the media release their names (National Victim Center 1992, 4).

Victims of rape and battering are more likely to be blamed than victims of any other crimes. Both battered women and sexual assault victims are frequently accused of having provoked the abusive behavior. In fact, "battered wives and rape victims are often accused of 'asking for,' 'deserving,' or 'enjoying' their victimization" (Gelles 1979, 121). If a batterer tells the police he hit his wife because she wasn't home when he got home from work, the police officer may ask the battered woman, "Why weren't you home when your husband got home from work?" Similarly, the police officer investigating a sexual assault may ask the victim why she left her door unlocked.

Rape victims are blamed for wearing certain clothing, failing to lock doors or windows, drinking alcohol, waiting for buses late at night, or hitchhiking. It is important for potential victims to know what situations increase their risk of victimization, but it is also important to remember that women don't always have access to their own transportation, and that *offenders,* not victims, are responsible for violence. Furthermore, although reliable statistics inform us that women are most at risk of being raped by husbands and boyfriends (see Russell 1984), few people are prepared to tell women and girls not to date and marry.

It is not only the "person on the street" who often has preconceived ideas of what "kinds of" people get victimized. Persons responsible for the treatment of victims and punishment of offenders also are frequently misinformed. One study on the perception of sexual assault victims' reputations in court found that divorced women, women of color, and women out alone at night are stereotyped as more readily consenting, to more men, in more situations (Burt and Albin 1981). "Having assumed a generalized propensity to consent and attached it to whole classes of women, this line of reasoning then particularizes the argument to *this* woman (victim) in *this* situation (alleged rape) and infers consent to *this* man (alleged assailant). Therefore, following this reasoning, this situation is not a rape" (Burt and Albin 1981, 214). The implication is that certain women are "fair game" to be sexually victimized, and therefore they cannot be assessed as legitimate rape victims. Such women have supposedly lost their rights to determine with whom they are sexual. Obviously, this is an absurd notion. Moreover, women and girls are expected to be "sexy, but modest; attractive, but not provocative" (Gordon and Riger 1989, 53).

Similar to females who are sexually victimized, battered women are frequently blamed for the abuse they receive. "When activists speak about battered women, even sympathetic audiences continually scrutinize the victim's behavior, moral 'failings,' or 'stupid' reactions, returning repeatedly to the question, 'Why do these women stay?' " (Schechter 1982, 16). One myth is that violence is a "way of life" for some people; therefore, women who are members of these "violence-prone" groups will not be as traumatized by rape or battering as other women. There are inherently classist and racist overtones in this assertion. Victimization hurts regardless of who it happens to, and violence is appropriate only when used in self-defense. The following is an excerpt from a 1984 journal article in *Victimology* depicting the abused wife's "responsibility" in her own victimization:

> The husband, perhaps burdened with a childhood in which violence was a fact of life, strikes the wife; she insults him, perhaps assaulting his masculinity or dredging up an incident from the past, or cringes, begging him to please stop, or runs away with him in hot pursuit, or laughs, or returns the blow. Any of these responses—it's a no-win game—leads to further blows, followed by further counters, etc. In a few weeks or months, the couple is locked into the twisted sequence of regenerative feedback, with no easy way out, rather like two super-powers maniacally escalating an arms race.
>
> *(Erchak 1984, 251)*

This is not only an example of relieving the offender of responsibility (he was abused as a child) and blaming the victim (she insults him, insults his masculinity, and laughs at him), but is a clear example of ignoring gender-power disparity. It is unrealistic to refer to the husband and wife as "two super-powers." This is not a situation of two equals "battling it out." In analyses of why some men are violent, a common problem is claiming they are violent because of the violence that has occurred to them. Why then aren't most females violent, since they have experienced so much more victimization?

Why are some victims blamed for their victimization? One explanation is Lerner's (1965) "just world" hypothesis, which states that most people want to believe that we get what we deserve (Karmen 1984). Therefore, when we hear of bad things happening to people, we often question behaviors that put them more at risk. In this way, we comfort ourselves by thinking "This won't happen to me because I didn't do ..." For instance, often when we hear that someone has cancer, one of our first thoughts is "Did she (or he) smoke?" This makes some sense, since we know smoking may lead to cancer (but it is certainly not a very sensitive question!). In cases of rape, people often ask "What was she wearing?" This denies that violence is random and rarely predictable. "Assuming that women can predict their rapists' behavior sets up a situation where sexually assaulted women are blamed for not avoiding what these advisors suggest could have been avoided" (Stanko 1985, 39).

The "just world" approach not only results in the assumption that only certain types of people can be victimized, but also serves as a way for people to deceive themselves that they are free from victimization because of who they are and how they behave. Unfortunately, this is not the case—*anyone* can be a victim. Studies of rape victims and battered women have a difficult time determining who is most at risk because the focus of research has often been on what is unusual about the victims rather than what is it about offenders that makes them likely to rape or batter. Much of the research on woman battering has been sexist, where "aberrant behavior" is more likely to be attributed to the victim than to the offender (Wardell et al. 1983).

In line with having to accept that violence is random, it is also necessary to acknowledge that the battering and sexual victimizations of most women and girls are committed by persons known to them. Research suggests that about four in five rape victims know their assailants (National Victim Center 1992; Russell 1984). Estrich (1987, 10) explains how the "simple" rape cases, "the cases where a woman is forced to have sex without consent by only one man, whom she knows, who does not beat her or attack her with a gun" are far more common than the "aggravated" rape cases, in which there is extrinsic violence, multiple assailants, or no prior relationship between the victim and the offender. The issue of victim blaming is exemplified through Wolfgang's (1958) coining of the term *victim precipitation,* which focuses on the "role" victims play in their own victimization. This approach implies that victims are at least partially responsible. In 1975, a psychiatrist published the following statement in the respected *British Journal of Criminology*: "Apparently, some pedophilia offenses never lead to prosecution and consequently are not recorded by courts. Obviously, this is the case in particular when the offense is a minor one and the *victim's precipitation very strong*" (Virkkunen 1975, 178).

Victim blaming for the battered woman usually comes in the form of the question "Why does she stay with him?" The implication is that if she doesn't want to be battered, she should leave her partner. This view ignores the economic and, more important, the psychological dependence and fear many battered women have developed. There is also the issue of family, friends, and the crime-processing system workers who often ignore the offense or encourage the *victim* to try to work things out. Again, victim blaming often includes asking the *woman* what she did to precipitate the violence. She is often blamed for starting the violence and for staying in the battering relationship. This keeps the focus from the real problem: the offender.

VICTIMIZATION OF WOMEN OF COLOR

The diversity of the U.S. population is such that cultural differences and the effects of racism and classism often provide vastly different life experiences. Lynora Williams (1981, 18–19) claims that Third World women in the United States (in which she includes African Americans) are disproportionately victims of rape, battering, and sterilization abuse. A recent study of homeless women found that women of color were more victimized overall—and raped in particular—than Anglo women (Costin 1992). Black women have been particularly vulnerable to sexual assault historically, in slavery, and because of the negative images associated with them, such as being "hot-natured" and morally "loose" (Giddings 1984, 31). Compounding this is the fact that it is not unusual for society or for crime-processing workers to treat women of color as if they aren't really victims. Thus, women of color appear to have disproportionately high victimization rates, yet they are much less likely to have their victimizations acknowledged.

"Racism and the rape laws are unquestionably inseparable" (Schwendinger and Schwendinger 1983, 110). Even the laws well into the twentieth century "stated that women who worked outside the home, or whose race had a history of sexual exploitation, were outside the realm of 'womanhood' and its perogative" (Giddings 1984, 49). Thus, the law implied that women of color weren't legally capable of being raped. In fact, rape laws were originally mandated to protect upper-class Anglo men whose wives and daughters could be assaulted (Davis 1981). Thus, in addition to the rape laws emerging because of a view of women as men's property, there were significant racist and classist components in the development of these laws.

The crime-processing system and society as a whole, then, tend to minimize female victims of male violence, and this is particularly true if the victims are of color and/or poor. The incongruity between high victimization rates and low validation rates for persons of color in this society serves to further victimize and oppress this group. The lack of response by the crime-processing system may lead victims to take matters into their own hands to protect themselves. However, *any* female victim of sexual assault or battering who uses self-defense runs the risk of being charged with a crime herself. This is most evident for women of color, as Williams (1981) exemplifies through a large number of cases of women of color who were incarcerated for protecting themselves against violent men. These women failed to be taken seriously as victims, but were taken extremely seriously as so-called offenders in their efforts to protect themselves and their children.

Chapter 1 discusses the dichotomy of women into madonnas or whores (Feinman 1986). Women more consistent with the madonna image (for example, virgins and Anglo women) are more likely to be viewed as legitimate victims than women in the "whore" category. None of Young's (1986) categories of black women portrays a woman who could be perceived as a legitimate victim: *Amazons* are viewed as capable of protecting themselves; *sinister sapphires* are viewed as vindictive or as precipitating the violence against them; and *seductresses* receive no validation as credible victims. Similarly, Tong (1984 155) discusses how the view of black women as "less sexually puritanical than white women" is objectionable and racist, and it furthermore implies that black women do not want or need protection against male violence. Clearly, these mythical views of African American women victims affect how they are treated (or not treated) by the crime-processing system.

The black community and feminists need to join forces in fighting both racism and violence against women (Matthews 1993; Tong 1984; Williams 1981). Historically, there has been a cleavage between Anglo and African American women fighting male violence, since the black women have also had to fight the stereotype of black male offenders. In the late 1800s, black activist Ida B. Wells publicly stated that there was a focus on accusing black males of raping white females, whereas the rape of black girls and women by Anglo males was overlooked (Giddings 1984). "While slave masters and other white men raped black women freely, death was the punishment for a black man convicted of raping a white woman" (Schwendinger and Schwendinger 1983, 108). The abolishment of slavery did not abolish capital punishment for black men who raped white women. Black males, "the guilty and innocent alike," are still indiscriminately brought to "justice" for rape (Davis 1981). More recent research confirms the disproportionately harsh treatment of African American males charged with rape compared to the treatment of Anglo males (Walsh 1987). Davis (1981) discusses how it has been difficult for African American women to be active in the antirape movement, given the treatment of black men (particularly innocent black men) charged with rape. The antirape movement in the United States began at the same time as black feminism, and as African American women began feeling distrustful of Anglo feminists (Matthews 1993). In more recent years, however, rape crisis centers and battered women's shelters have become more integrated and more dedicated to combating racism as well as sexism and male violence.

SUMMARY

The foremost image of the female victim has been invisibility. Battering and sexual victimization are the most underreported crimes against persons in the crime-processing system. Information on the victimization of females is becoming more widespread, including knowledge that it happens more frequently than once thought, and the *nature* of these victimizations are more threatening and violent than once acknowledged. Moreover, culture and society tend to support gender roles that encourage the likelihood of male violence against females. Women and girls are encouraged to be passive and "ladylike," while men and boys are encouraged to be aggressive.

Determination of the causes of the victimization of females is grounded in the acceptance of gender disparities in power. This chapter discussed how the *victimization of females is both a result and a reinforcement of gender-power disparity.* That is, the threat and existence of the victimization of females decreases the power of women and girls; simultaneously, this power disparity encourages victimization. Furthermore, the threat of violence against females restricts the freedom of women and girls. Fear of sexual victimization influences where, when, and how women will work, take classes, socialize, and live. Women learn they are not safe alone, at night, in certain areas of town, and with certain types of people. Compounding these restrictions is the more recent acknowledgment of the high degree of sexual victimization perpetrated by persons known, often well known, to the victim. Awareness of the prevalence and controlling nature of woman battering has also grown.

Stereotypical images in society imply that some women "ask for" rape through their clothing, behavior, and even race or class. Therefore, this view perpetuates the myth that the "real" rape victims are Anglo, wealthy, virgins who resisted the attack. Similarly, stereotypical images imply that women who "nag," who commit adultery, or who engage in other "demasculizing" or "obnoxious" behavior precipitate their battering victimizations. Victim blaming not only holds victims responsible for the violence and exploitation against them, but mistakenly assures persons that violence is not random.

Finally, the chapter concluded with an analysis of women of color. Black women, in particular, suffer extreme repercussions from the stereotypes associated with them. All of the stereotypes are negative, and once victimized, black women often face even greater problems of being taken seriously by the crime-processing system. Additionally, they are discouraged by some feminists who fail to make a connection between the exploitation of women and the exploitation of people of color.

This chapter described societal images of women and girls and how these images affect the victimization of females. Also discussed was how these victims are perceived by society and the crime-processing system. The exposure of female victimization has fostered an understanding of the extent and nature of the victimization women and girls face. These negative images and responses are particularly strong concerning women of color. To fight the victimization of women and girls, it is necessary to battle gender disparity, to make changes in responses by the crime-processing system, and to fight racism, classism, and sexism.

REFERENCES

Baron, Larry, and Murray A. Straus. 1987. "Four Theories of Rape: A Macrosociological Analysis." *Social Problems* 34: 467–489

Bowker, Lee. 1981. *Women and Crime in America.* New York: Macmillan.

Braungart, Margaret M., Richard G. Braungart, and William J. Hoyer. 1980. "Age, Sex, and Social Factors in Fear of Crime." *Sociological Forces* 13:55–66.

Brodyaga, A. L., M. Gates, S. Singer, M. Tucker, and R. White. 1975. *Rape and Its Victims: A Report for Citizens, Health Facilities and Criminal Justice Agencies.* Washington, D.C.: Government Printing Office.

Brownmiller, Susan. 1975. *Against Our Will: Men, Women and Rape.* New York: Simon & Schuster.

Burt, Martha R., and Rochelle S. Albin. 1981. "Rape Myths, Rape Definitions, and Probability of Conviction." *Journal of Applied Social Psychology* 11:212–230.

Clark, Anne. 1987. *Women's Silence, Men's Violence.* London: Pandora Press.

Clemente, Frank, and Michael B. Kleiman. 1976. "Fear of Crime Among the Aged." *Gerontologist* 16:211–219.

Cohen, L. E., and M. Felson. 1979. "Social Change and Crime Rate Trends: A Routine Activity Approach." *American Sociological Review* 44:588–608.

Costin, Charisse T. M. 1992. "The Influence of Race in Urban Homeless Females' Fear of Crime." *Justice Quarterly* 9:721–730.

Davis, Angela Y. 1981. *Women, Race, and Class.* New York: Vintage Press.

DeKeseredy, Walter S. 1988. *Woman Abuse in Dating Relationships: The Role of Male Peer Support.* Toronto: Canadian Scholars Press.

Erchak, G. M. 1984. "The Escalation and Maintenance of Spouse Abuse: A Cybernetic Model." *Victimology* 9:247–253.

Estrich, Susan. 1987. *Real Rape.* Cambridge, MA: Harvard University Press.

Evans, Laura J. 1978. "Sexual Harassment: Women's Hidden Occupational Hazard." Pp. 202–223 in *The Victimization of Women,* edited by J. Roberts-Chapman and M. Gates. Beverly Hills, CA: Sage.

Feinman, Clarice. 1986. *Women in the Criminal Justice System.* New York: Praeger.

Finkelhor, David, and Kersti Yllo. 1985. *License to Rape: Sexual Abuse of Wives.* New York: Free Press.

Fonow, Mary Margaret, Laurel Richardson, and Virginia Wemmerus. 1992. "Feminist Rape Education: Does It Work?" *Gender and Society* 6:108–121.

Frohmann, Lisa. 1991. "Discrediting Victims' Allegations of Sexual Assault: Prosecutorial Accounts of Case Rejection." *Social Problems* 38:213–226.

Gelles, Richard J. 1979. *Family Violence.* Beverly Hills, CA: Sage.

_____. 1983. "An Exchange/Social Control Theory." Pp. 151–165 in *The Dark Side of Families,* edited by D. Finkelhor, R. J. Gelles, G. T. Hotaling, and M. A. Straus. Beverly Hills, CA: Sage.

Giddings, Paula S. 1984. *When and Where I Enter: The Impact of Black Women on Race and Sex in America.* Toronto: Bantam Books.

Gordon, Linda. 1977. *Women's Body, Women's Right: A Social History of Birth Control in America.* New York: Penguin Books.

Gordon, Margaret, and Stephanie Riger. 1989. *The Female Fear.* New York: Free Press.

Gottfredson, Michael R. 1986. "Substantive Contributions of Victimization Surveys." In *Crime and Justice: An Annual Review of Research.* Chicago: University of Chicago.

Griffen, Susan. 1971. "Rape: The All-American Crime." *Ramparts* (September): 26–35.

_____. 1981. *Pornography and Silence.* New York: Harper Colophon Books.

Gwartney-Gibbs, Patricia, and Jean Stockard. 1989. "Courtship Aggression and Mixed-Sex Peer Groups." Pp. 185–204 in *Violence in Dating Relationships,* edited by M. Pirog-Good and J. E. Stets. New York: Praeger.

Karmen, A. 1984. *Crime Victims: An Introduction to Victimology.* Monterey, CA: Brooks/Cole.

Krulewitz, J. E., and J. E. Nash. 1979. "Effects of Rape Victim Resistance, Assault Outcome, and Sex of Observer on Attributions About Rape." *Journal of Personality* 47:557–574.

LaGrange, Randy L., and Kenneth F. Ferraro. 1989. "Assessing Age and Gender Differences in Perceived Risk and Fear of Crime." *Criminology* 27:697–718.

Lerner, M. 1965. "Evaluation of Performance as a Function of Performer's Reward and Attractiveness." *Journal of Personality and Social Psychology* 1:355–360.

Martin, Patricia Y., and Robert A. Hummer. 1989. "Fraternities and Rape on Campus." *Gender and Society* 3:457–473.

Matthews, Nancy A. 1993. "Surmounting a Legacy: The Expansion of Racial Diversity in a Local Anti-Rape Movement." Pp. 177–192 in *Violence Against Women: The Bloody Footprints,* edited by P. B. Bart and E. G. Moran. Newbury Park, CA: Sage.

Medea, Andra, and Kathleen Thompson. 1974. *Against Rape.* New York: Farrar, Straus and Giroux.

Miethe, T. D., M. C. Stafford, and J. S. Long. 1987. "Social Differentiation in Criminal Victimization: A Test of Routine Activities/Lifestyle Theories." *American Sociological Review* 52:184–194.

National Victim Center. 1992. *Rape in America.* Arlington, VA, 18 pp.

Ortega, Suzanne T., and Jessie L. Myles. 1987. "Race and Gender Effects on Fear of Crime: An Interactive Model with Age." *Criminology* 25:133–152.

Riger, Stephanie. 1981. "On Women." Pp. 47–66 in *Reactions to Crime,* edited by D. A. Lewis. Beverly Hills, CA: Sage.

Riger, Stephanie, and Margaret T. Gordon. 1981. "The Fear of Rape: A Study in Social Control." *Journal of Social Issues* 37:71–92.

Riger, Stephanie, Margaret T. Gordon, and R. K. LeBailly. 1978. "Women's Fear of Crime: From Blaming to Restricting the Victim." *Victimology* 3:274–284.

Rush, Florence. 1980. *The Best Kept Secret: Sexual Abuse of Children.* New York: McGraw-Hill.

_____. 1983. "Foreword." In *I Never Told Anyone,* edited by E. Bass and F. Rush. New York: Harper & Row.

Russell, Diana E. H. 1982. *Rape in Marriage.* New York: Collier Books.

_____. 1984. *Sexual Exploitation: Rape, Child Sexual Abuse, and Workplace Harassment.* Beverly Hills, CA: Sage.

Sanday, Peggy R. 1981. "The Socio-Cultural Context of Rape: A Cross-Cultural Study." *Journal of Social Issues* 37:5–27.

Sanders, William B. 1980. *Rape and Woman's Identity.* Beverly Hills, CA: Sage.

Schechter, Susan. 1982. *Women and Male Violence.* Boston: South End Press.

Schwendinger, Julia R., and Herman Schwendinger. 1983. *Rape and Inequality.* Beverly Hills, CA: Sage.

Smith, Michael D. 1994. "Enhancing the Quality of Survey Data on Violence Against Women: A Feminist Approach." *Gender and Society* 8:109–127.

Spencer, Cassie C. 1987. "Sexual Assault: The Second Victimization." Pp. 54–73 in *Women, Courts, and Equality,* edited by L. L. Crites and W. L. Hepperle. Newbury Park, CA: Sage.

Stanko, Elizabeth A. 1985. *Intimate Intrusions: Women's Experience of Male Violence.* London: Routledge & Kegan Paul.

_____. 1990. *Everyday Violence: How Women and Men Experience Sexual and Physical Danger.* London: Pandora.

_____. 1992. "The Case of Fearful Women: Gender, Personal Safety and Fear." *Women and Criminal Justice* 4:117–135.

Tong, Rosemarie. 1984. *Women, Sex, and the Law.* Totawa, NJ: Rowman & Allanheld.

Virkkunen, M. 1975. "Victim-Precipitated Pedophilia Offenses." *British Journal of Criminology* 15:175–180.

Walker, Lenore E. 1979. *The Battered Woman.* New York: Harper & Row.

Walsh, Anthony. 1987. "The Sexual Stratification Hypothesis and Sexual Assault in Light of the Changing Conceptions of Race." *Criminology* 25:153–174.

Wardell, Laurie, Dair L. Gillespie, and Ann Leffler. 1983. "Science and Violence Against Wives." Pp. 69–84 in *The Dark Side of Families,* edited by D. Finkelhor, R. J. Gelles, G. T. Hotaling, and M. A. Straus. Beverly Hills, CA: Sage.

Williams, Lynora. 1981. "Violence Against Women." *The Black Scholar* (January/February):18–24.

Wolfgang, Marvin. 1958. *Patterns in Criminal Homicide*. Philadelphia, PA: University of Pennsylvania Press.

Young, Vernetta D. 1986. "Gender Expectations and Their Impact on Black Female Offenders and Victims." *Justice Quarterly* 3:305–328.

——————. 1992. "Fear of Victimization and Victimization Rates Among Women: A Paradox?" *Justice Quarterly* 9:419–442.

7

❊

Sexual Victimization

DEFINING SEXUAL VICTIMIZATION

Problems arise from the limitations implied when defining the word *rape*. From 1770 to 1845 in England, rape was defined as penetration of the vagina by the penis, where ejaculation had taken place (Clark 1987, 8–9). This was extremely difficult to prove in court. The traditional, common-law definition of rape states: "A man commits rape when he engages in intercourse … with a woman *not his wife*; by force or threat of force; against her will and without her consent" (Estrich 1987, 8). Rape, then, has most commonly been defined as forced penile–vaginal intercourse, committed by an adult male stranger against an adult female.

There is growing awareness, however, that the majority of sexual victimizations do not fit this definition. Nevertheless, there is a tendency to minimize or redefine situations that do not meet the criteria of the traditional definition of rape. In fact, "many rape situations might be misconstrued as traditional heterosexual behavior rather than as rape. This would be especially likely when the victim offers less than extraordinary resistance" (Krulewitz and Nash 1979, 558).

It is necessary to broaden the definition of rape. In reality, rape can occur between a variety of persons (female and male, young or old) and in many forms. Although most states have worked to expand the legal definition of rape or "sexual conduct," there still tends to be a focus on penile–vaginal penetration, as well as on violence and brutality as "proof." This definition excludes all sexual victimization of males as well as molestation, attempted rape, oral and anal rape, and sexual assaults using foreign objects. In fact, in a study of 100 women who reported rape to University Hospital in Cincinnati, Ohio, in 1985, there were 87 penile–vaginal rapes, 24 oral rapes, and 9 anal rapes.[1] Clearly, it is vital to recognize the existence and devastating effects of oral, anal, and other forms of sexual victimization. For instance, attempted rapes are often minimized as "near misses" by society, by the crime-processing system, and by the victims themselves. However, victims of attempted rapes frequently experience the psychological trauma associated with "completed" rapes.

For these reasons, it is necessary to redefine rape. Russell (1984, 21) believes that the term *sexual assault* is too restrictive, because some forms of sexual conduct (in particular some instances of child sexual abuse and of sexual harassment) are *violating* rather than *violent*. Russell (1984) prefers the term *sexual exploitation* over *sexual assault* because rape, child sexual assault, and sexual harassment all include abuse of *power* by the offender over the victim, whether that power is economic, physical, and/or status in nature. Similarly, Medea and Thompson (1974, 12) define rape as "any sexual intimacy forced on one person by another."

Restricting the definition of sexual victimization (or rape) decreases understanding of the problem and overlooks many cases of sexual victimization. It is important to recognize that sexual victimization consists of a variety of forms, and occurs between a wide variety of persons. Because the term *rape* is associated with such a restrictive definition, the term *sexual victimization* will be used in this book in order to include the various forms of sexual violations discussed. Thus, sexual victimization will include penile–vaginal rape, anal and oral rape, molestation, sexual harassment, attempted rape, and sexual assault with foreign objects. For the purposes of this book, *sexual victimization* is any forced or coerced sexual intimacy.

HISTORICAL ISSUES
IN DEFINING SEXUAL VICTIMIZATION

Few words in the English language have as powerful an impact as the word *rape*. Historically, children have not been educated about the meaning of rape. In spite of ignorance of its meaning, girls are raised to know that rape restricts them and is something to fear. Stanko (1985, 2) claims that "female children are even taught to be on guard for male strangers who wish to offer them candy or money to do something unspeakable (unspeakable, because, of course, few of us were ever told why male strangers might wish to offer us goodies)." The lifestyles of girls and women are affected by the specter of potential rape. They learn that their vulnerability restricts their options: where and how they live, and where and when they work and go out. They learn the conflicting messages that men are to be both feared *and* depended on for protection. The fine line between victimization and protection regarding women, men, and rape has been compared to the victimization and "protection" in the Mafia; the Mafia is often feared by the very people who depend on it for protection (Griffen 1971). Similarly, women are frequently victimized by men, and yet are socialized to view men as their protectors. It is assumed that "known men will protect women from aberrant strange men's violence" (Stanko 1992), *yet women are more likely to be victimized by known men.*

The ancient *lex talionis,* better known as "an eye for an eye" system of crime processing, viewed women and girls as men's (fathers' and husbands') property. A "rape for a rape" meant that the father of a raped daughter was permitted to rape the rapist's wife (Brownmiller 1975). "Bride capture," where a male staked a claim to a woman by raping her, was the earliest form of permanent mating relationships (Brownmiller 1975). Brownmiller (1975) points out that rape has been so ingrained and accepted as part of society that Hebrew law did not include "Thou shalt not rape" in the Ten Commandments (although, significantly, the Ten Commandments warn against committing adultery).

Throughout history, rape laws were aimed mostly at protecting virginal daughters in wealthy families (Brownmiller 1975). In the late eighteenth century, rape was used to "justify" women's "place" in the home (Clark 1987). The system went from trivializing rape to using it as an excuse to restrict women from working or traveling outside of the home.

In eighteenth-century England, sexually victimized women were in a double-bind if they wished to involve the court system to receive justice (Clark 1987). Being raped itself caused a woman to lose her credibility. Any woman charging rape had by admittance had sex (although forced) with a man not her husband. By raping a woman, a man not only victimized her, but also stripped her of her credibility as a victim. Subsequently, conviction was extremely rare unless (1) the woman proved her chastity was preserved by being "only" the victim of an attempted rape (it was much more difficult to obtain convictions for completed rapes because they implied the victim's culpability), or (2) a husband or father of a raped woman went to court to challenge *his* loss of property value (Clark 1987, 47). Unfortunately, some men still view women as their property. This will be addressed more thoroughly in the next chapter.

In the 1970s, when sexual victimization was first becoming defined as a social problem, the focus was on adult stranger rapes. The effort to acknowledge two broad categories of sexual victimizations based on the victim–offender relationship has been more recent. *Stranger rapes* are those sexual victimizations where the victim and offender had no prior relationship. *Acquaintance rapes* are forced or coerced sexual intimacy by someone the victim knows. Their prior relationship could be as distant as "a friend of a friend," a neighbor, or a fellow student, or as intimate as a boyfriend, husband, or father.

Sexual victimization runs on a continuum from coercion to force. *Force* is a physical method to obtain power, such as hitting or stabbing. *Coercion* is a psychological method to obtain power. Using coercion, a rapist may achieve sexual intimacy through varoius threats. For instance, a man may threaten a girl with telling her mother that she was smoking if she doesn't comply sexually. A boyfriend may tell his girlfriend he will break up with her if she won't have sex with him. A foster father may threaten a girl with removal of support if she does not submit to his sexual demands. These examples of coercion show how physical force is not always necessary in order to sexually victimize.

STATISTICS ON SEXUAL VICTIMIZATION

Determining the rates of sexual victimization has been problematic for a number of reasons. First, it has been difficult to gather sexual victimization statistics. Until the National Crime Survey (NCS) was implemented in 1973, the Uniform Crime Reports (UCR) provided most of the victimization data in the United States. The UCR data are limited for any crime because they only include crimes reported to the police. This is particularly problematic for sexual victimizations, since these are the most underreported of the index crimes. The humiliation and intimate violation involved in sexual victimizations make them difficult to report to strangers, even research interviewers. Because many victims do not report rapes to the police or even to interviewers, the statistics on sexual victimization are often invalid.

A second limitation of sexual victimization statistics is that some victimization cases are disproportionately reported to the police depending on *characteristics of the victim and the assailant*. Sexual victimizations that the culture and the crime-processing system view as "real" rapes—those occurring between strangers, those where the victim is white, those where the offender is black, those where the victim has a "good reputation," and so on—are disproportionately reported to the police. Acquaintance rapes are underreported to the police because they are often more difficult to prove and the victim is more likely to feel some responsibility. "Pressure not to involve the police, fear of causing an embarrassing situation for themselves in a relatively closed community, and fear that their names will not be kept confidential often prevents victims from reporting" acquaintance rape (Parrot 1986, 2). Similarly, although many prostitutes experience sexual victimization, these assaults are rarely reported to the police because they usually are not taken seriously.

Sexual victimization is particularly troublesome when the victims are children. Children and youth typically are less informed of their rights, and access to crime-processing authorities is more limited. Furthermore, they are usually in less powerful positions than adults to report, particularly if the rapist is related to them.

Another significant problem concerns acquaintance rapes in which the victim and the offender had a consensual sexual relationship prior to the rape. Victims of date and marital rape sometimes fail to define their experiences as rapes or sexual victimizations. Even if they do, they believe (often correctly) that the police and the courts will not define them as rapes, so they do not report them.

Just as characteristics of the victim and the offender influence reporting to the police, *characteristics of the sexual victimization itself* also influence the validity of rape statistics. For instance, anal and oral sexual assaults, as well as sexual victimizations with a foreign object, are less likely to be reported to the police because of the additional humiliation sometimes associated with these experiences. Also, many rape statistics don't "count" these as "real" rapes. Another reason that sexual victimization statistics are difficult to collect accurately is that there is a tendency among some victims (especially victims of attempted rape) to believe that their victimizations are not "important enough" to report to the police. Finally, many times rape victims fail to label their own victimizations as rapes. They don't consider it rape because they don't want to admit that a man they would go out with is a rapist.

As mentioned in Chapter 6, Russell's (1984) San Francisco study found that 44 percent of the 930 randomly sampled women age 18 and older had been victims of completed or attempted rape (defined as completed or attempted forced penile–vaginal penetration) at some point in their lives. (24 percent had experienced completed rapes.) We refer to these rates over a person's lifetime as *prevalence rates.* Similarly, 53 percent of women in a study in Charleston County, South Carolina, reported experiencing sexual assault at least once in their lives (Murphy et al. 1988). A recent study, termed *The National Women's Study,* conducted a national probability sample of over 4,000 women in the United States (National Victim Center 1992). Rape was defined as force or threat of force to penetrate the victim's vagina, mouth, or rectum. The researchers projected that over 12 million U.S. women (or 1 in 8) have been the victims of rape at some point in their lives.

Incidence rates, on the other hand, are measured as rates within some period, usually a year, prior to the interview or survey. The NCS and UCR statistics are incidence rates. Russell (1984) compared her 1974 incidence rates with the 1974 UCR and NCS incidence rates, since all of these methods measured rape and attempted rape in the traditional method (penile–vaginal). Russell (1984) found that the incidence rate in her study (3 percent in the prior year) was thirteen times greater than the UCR incidence rate, and over seven times greater than the NCS incidence rate.[2] Although NCS techniques, unlike those of the UCR, capture some rapes not reported to the police, even the NCS questionnaire design is fraught with problems, bringing into question the validity of this rape measure (see Eigenberg 1990). The NCS interviewers never directly ask respondents whether they have been raped or sexually victimized. This information is assumed to be volunteered when the respondents are asked if they have been assaulted. Nonetheless, it was recently suggested that NCS data are a likely approximation of trends in rape frequencies, while the UCR statistics better reflect police organizations' management of rape cases (Jensen and Karpos 1993). Even Russell's (1984) findings, however, are limited because of her restricted definition of rape as penile–vaginal, and because her sample excluded such high-risk women as those confined in prison and mental institutions.

WHO ARE THE VICTIMS?

Traditionally, "real" rape has tended to be viewed as something that happens in alleys to young, Anglo women who are alone late at night. The offenders are often viewed as insane perverts, usually black. Chapter 6 dealt with many of these stereotypes. These misleading portrayals have been largely perpetuated by the media. Research, on the other hand, portrays all women at risk, regardless of age, race, or class. *Anyone can be a victim.*

Females are much more likely to be victims of sexual assault than males. Statistics from the NCS covering a ten-year period between 1973 and 1982 reported that 762 females were victims of rape or attempted rape. (Information on other sexual victimizations was not collected.) For this same time period, only thirty-six males reported rape or attempted rape.[3] Because of gender-power inequalities (see Chapter 6) and the societal view of women and girls, it is not surprising that females are more likely to be sexually victimized than males.

Research has also pointed out some commonalities regarding who is most at risk of rape. It is important to remember, however, that official statistics on sexual victimization overrepresent stranger assaults (since they are disproportionately reported); most sexual victimizations occur between nonstrangers. The statistics imply that rape tends to occur to women between the ages of 16 and 24 (Amir 1971; Belknap 1987; Russell 1984; Skogan 1976). Black females appear to be more at risk of rape than Anglo females (Amir 1971; Costin 1992; Schram 1978; Skogan 1976). Russell (1984) found that black females were more at risk of stranger rapes, while Anglo females were more at risk of acquaintance rapes. Women and girls have a high risk of being raped in their own homes—even by strangers (Belknap 1987; Sanders 1980; Schram, 1978). Research focusing on stranger rapes also finds that rapes are more likely to occur at night and in the summer months (Amir 1971; Belknap 1987; Sanders 1980).

WHO ARE THE OFFENDERS?

Groth's (1979) research on convicted sex offenders warns against describing rapists as simply "oversexed." In fact, one-third of the rapists in his study were sexually active with their wives at the time of the rapes. Similarly, many mothers of incest victims are shocked on discovering that their husbands sexually abused their daughter(s), given that their own sex lives with the perpetrator were very active (Russell 1986). Sexual victimization is fundamentally a *power* issue—a need to dominate. Groth (1979, 13) describes rape as "sexual behavior in the primary service of non-sexual needs." Thus, domination is the goal, and sex is the means through which domination is achieved.

Groth's (1979) attempts to categorize types of rapists have been somewhat limited because of his focus on convicted rapists. Since only a small percentage of rapists are convicted, it is highly unlikely that convicted rapists are representative of rapists at large. Nonetheless, his three categories are useful to examine. *Anger rapes* are characterized by physical brutality, where sex is used to express rage and anger. Excessive force is used to dominate the victim. The second pattern, *power rapes,* are characterized not by the rapist wishing to harm his victim, but rather by the rapist wanting to "possess her sexually" (Groth 1979, 25). The goal is sexual conquest, and only the amount of force necessary to achieve this is used. The final pattern, the *sadistic rape,* fuses sexuality and aggression such that aggression itself becomes eroticized (Groth 1979, 44). This type of rapist finds the victim's suffering sexually gratifying. Groth's (1979, 58) study found that 55 percent of the cases were power rapes, 40 percent were anger rapes, and about 5 percent were sadistic rapes. He contends that if his sample weren't restricted to *convicted* rapists, he would have seen more power rapists and fewer anger and sadistic rapists, given that anger rapes are more likely than power rapes to include corroborating evidence, and sadistic rapes are more likely to provide evidence of force—both of which increase conviction rates.

Another study of convicted rapists' perceptions of themselves and their victims found that most of the men experienced no guilt or shame regarding their behavior (Scully 1988). Furthermore, their inability to empathize influenced their self-control, or lack thereof. Scully (1988, 211) identified two groups of rapists: "Some of the men viewed women as opponents to be reduced to abject powerlessness. Others, adopting the cultural view of women as sexual commodities, reduced their victims to meaningless objects."

Although the crime statistics tend to show black males overrepresented as sexual offenders, Tong (1984, 166) suggests that this is because black offenders are more likely to be reported to and taken seriously by the crime-processing system. Despite the fact that the vast majority of rapes are *intra*racial (white on white, black on black, and so on), the U.S. legal system has followed a legacy from slavery to the present day that treats the rape of white women by black men "with more harshness than any other kind of rape" (Wriggins 1983, 116). Wriggins (1983) argues that this is a result of patriarchal values (controlling both Anglo women and African American men). Moreover, she points out the numerous consequences of focusing on black on white rapes: (1) It denies all sexual victimizations of African American women; (2) it denies the majority of sexual victimizations of Anglo women (those perpetrated by Anglo men); and (3) it falsely depicts rape as largely black on white and stranger oriented (given the highly segregated U.S. society). This focus on black on white rapes discriminates against black men and leaves out victims who are other women of color in addition to African American. As Wriggins (1983, 117) states, "[R]ape is painful and degrading . . . regardless of the attacker's race."

The "typical rapist" frequently has been portrayed as "crazy," "sexually starved," or "psychotic." However, empirical research is unable to confirm these beliefs, and rapists are no more likely to be mentally ill than nonrapists (see Bart and O'Brien 1985; Russell 1984). Interviews with men who confessed to raping, as well as with men who hadn't raped, represented how many men who aren't rapists often (1) blame women for "turning them on," (2) link sex and violence, and (3) report wanting to be violent toward women they perceive as trying to "tease" them (Beneke 1982). Just as with sexual assault victims, rapists come from every racial, ethnic, and economic group. They include doctors, lawyers, ministers, priests, professors, politicians, and many others. Thus, just as anyone can be a rape victim, so too, anyone can be a rapist.

Why, then, do we have the common image of rapists as abnormal, African American, and oversexed? First, the media often portrays them as such. Second, women are socialized to be wary of strangers, especially strange men. And third, akin to the previously discussed "just world" hypothesis, it is probably another attempt to feel control over one's environment. We feel safer if we think we can determine whether someone is a rapist by his appearance. Unfortunately, this is not the case.

THE VICTIM–OFFENDER RELATIONSHIP

Research reports vary in the stranger versus acquaintance rates of sexual victimizations. This is largely a result of how the studies were conducted. For example, 42 percent of the rapes in a study of police reports were committed by strangers (Amir 1971), whereas 50 percent of the single-offender and 58 percent of the multiple-offender ("gang") attempted and completed rapes were committed by strangers in a NCS study (Belknap 1987). Russell's (1984, 59) random study of women found that only 16 percent of completed and attempted rapes were committed by strangers.

Russell's (1984) study no doubt has the highest rates of nonstranger rapes because of her data collection method (a process that did not rely on cases reported to the police, as did UCR statistics), and because she used a random sample where the respondents were directly asked whether they were raped (unlike NCS statistics). In any sexual victimization situation, it is difficult for the victim to report it to the police, or even to an interviewer. This is particularly the case if the offender is known to the victim. First, the victim is likely to feel ashamed to admit that a friend or loved one sexually victimized her. Second, she may fear retaliation if the offender finds out that she reported him (particularly to the police, but also to an interviewer or a friend). Finally, the victim of acquaintance rape may not define the situation as rape or sexual victimization.

> Many acquaintance rape victims feel that they were forced to have intercourse, but deny that they were raped. This discrepancy in terms stems from our socialization and cultural standards, which leads to the common notion that rape only happens when a stranger jumps out of the bushes.
> *(Parrot 1986, 4)*

CHILD SEXUAL VICTIMIZATION

One of the most disturbing aspects of sexual victimization is the high degree to which children are victims. This was once thought to be a rare occurrence, particularly cases of incest. Child sexual abuse was reported to social service agencies during the 1800s, but it was not labeled as a "social problem" until the early 1980s (Gordon and O'Keefe 1984). The National Women's Study found "the majority of rape cases occurring during childhood and adolescence. Twenty-nine percent of all forcible rapes occurred when the victim was less than 11 years old, while another 32 percent occurred between the ages of 11 and 17" (National Victim Center 1992, 3). Regarding incest, Russell (1984) found that 12 percent of the women reported familial child sexual abuse occurring when they were under 14, and 16 percent reported it occurred when they were under 18. The offenders were most likely to be fathers or uncles. An article in *Psychology Today* claimed that 40 million Americans (about 1 in 6) may have been sexually victimized as children (Kohn 1987, 54). "There is scarcely a study, report or investigation into aspects of human sexuality which does not indicate that child–adult sex is an active, prevalent pastime" (Rush 1980, 5). These are extremely high rates for a crime that we know has such devastating psychological, and often physical, effects. A review of empirical research on the prevalence of child sexual abuse states:

> [T]here is considerable variation in the prevalence rates for child sexual abuse derived from the various North American studies. Reported rates range from 6% to 62% for females and from 3% to 31% for males. Although even the lowest rates indicate that child sexual abuse is far from an uncommon experience, the higher reported rates would point to a problem of epidemic proportions.
>
> *(Peters et al. 1986, 19)*

Probably no other area of crime processing has remained so hidden and protected from the public eye as child sexual abuse, particularly incest. While statistics suggest that female children are more at risk of child sexual victimization (70 percent of cases), than boys (30 percent of cases), boys—unlike men—are under substantial risk (Finkelhor and Baron 1986, 60–64). Ninety-five percent of the perpetrators of sexual abuse against girls and approximately 80 percent of the perpetrators of sexual abuse against boys are male (Finkelhor and Baron 1986; Russell 1984). Thus, the victims of child sexual abuse tend to be girls, and the abusers tend to be men.

As mentioned previously, child sexual victimization was not acknowledged as a social problem until the 1980s. Prior to this, it was viewed as a taboo that rarely occurred. Just as it has been extremely difficult for adult women to "speak out" about sexual victimization, this has also been the case for children. The power of children is even further minimized by their increased psychological, emotional, and financial dependencies, in addition to their small physical statures. Given these conditions, it is not surprising that the crime of child sexual victimization has remained so invisible, despite its wide occurrence. Most child sexual abuse victims do not report their victimizations until they are adult survivors. Even then, many choose to keep it a secret or even repress the memory.

> Why is it that children who have been molested, sexually abused, or even raped rarely or never tell? They never tell for the same reason that anyone who has been helplessly shamed and humiliated, and who is without protection or validation of personal integrity, prefers silence. Like the woman who has been raped, the violated child may not be believed (she fantasized or made up the story), her injury may be minimized (there's no harm done, so let's forget the whole thing), and she may even be held accountable for the crime (the kid really asked for it).
>
> *(Rush 1983, 13)*

Psychiatrist and pioneer of psychoanalysis Sigmund Freud is partly to blame for the coverup of child sexual abuse. He was amazed at the large numbers of women who reported having experienced sexual victimization as children, most often naming their fathers as the offenders. Although he initially believed his clients, other psychologists doubted him. He then restructured his theories and proposed the *Oedipus complex,* which is "the theory of innate erotic attraction of children to parents" (Rush 1980, 84).

Although it is unusual for a child to wish to be "seduced," as children do not understand sexuality and sexual feelings, it is apparent that sometimes children's behavior is sexual. Often this is a "natural" curiosity, customarily "acted out" by exploring their own and often their peers' bodies (for example, playing "doctor"). People who work with children who have been sexually abused note that these children have heightened and often troubling sexual behavior. This is hardly surprising given that they have learned that this is "appropriate." This sexual behavior might also make these children more at risk for revictimization. It is the adult's responsibility to make sure that he or she does not cross sexual boundaries with the child. Unfortunately, the child victim often feels guilty about the crime that was committed against her or him. One adult survivor claims the following about her victimization:

> I felt enormously guilty about my participation in the incest, as if I had been responsible. I know now I was not. It was my father's responsibility as an adult and as a parent to prevent sexual contact between us, but I didn't understand that at the time.
>
> *(Forward and Buck 1978, 1)*

Similar to the other victimizations discussed previously, the sexual abuse of children occurs in all races, neighborhoods, and income levels, and it happens with alarming frequency. It is difficult to determine patterns and realistic statistics because child sexual abuse is a covered-up crime. However, researchers have uncovered some tendencies: Abusers are usually male and usually well known to the child, the abuse is often not limited to a single episode, and the abuser rarely uses force (Gomes-Schwartz et al. 1990; Kohn 1987).

Why do some people sexually abuse children? Just like motivations for battering and the sexual victimization of adult women, the sexual victimization of children is strongly related to power and inequality. Children are particularly at risk: "With their naivete and their natural capacity for affection, children are far more capable of idolatry than any of the adults the abuser knows" (Crewdson 1988, 63). Groth (1979, 154) discusses how perpetrators of child sexual abuse use sex as a weapon to discharge power and/or anger in order to control their victims. "Such offenders capitalize on the relative helplessness of a child to coerce her or him into the sexual activity" (Groth 1979, 154). Children abused by parents, on whom they are economically and emotionally dependent, are in extremely powerless and vulnerable positions.

> Father–daughter incest is not only the type of incest most frequently reported but also represents a paradigm of female sexual victimization. The relationship between father and daughter, adult male and female child, is one of the most unequal relationships imaginable. It is no accident that

incest occurs most often precisely in the relationship where the female is most powerless. The actual sexual encounter may be brutal or tender, painful or pleasurable; but it is always, inevitably, destructive to the child. The father, in effect, forces the daughter to pay with her body for affection and care which should be freely given.

(Herman 1981, 4)

Society has been blamed for encouraging child sexual abuse through advertisements, media, and pornography, which frequently blur distinctions between adult women and girl children—women are photographed to look childish, and girls are photographed to look sensuous (Bass 1983). It is not unusual for pedophiles to photograph their victims and exchange the photographs with other pedophiles. *Playboy* published a cartoon of a lecherous worker in a doll factory assembly line who changed one doll's voice from "Momma" to "Wanna have a party, big boy?" (Crewdson 1988, 249). Such forms of "entertainment" perpetuate the *myth* that children are willing participants and are not being assaulted, abused, exploited, and raped when they have sex with adults. In reality, children are not in a position to make decisions about sex with adults.

Similar to men who rape adult women, the child sexual abuser is indistinguishable in the population (Crewdson 1988, 55). In fact, as evidence to contradict the myth that child sexual abusers are "dirty old men," one study found that 71 percent of child sexual abusers were under the age of 35 (Groth 1979). One trait that seems to be prevalent among (although not exclusive to) child sexual abusers is a high propensity toward *narcissism* (Crewdson 1988). The abusers may feel unworthy and powerless, but they attempt to portray an image of importance and superiority. They often have inflated views of their appearance, abilities, and intelligence (Crewdson 1988, 61). Additionally, the narcissist is better able to overcome the taboos associated with child sexual abuse because "he secretly believes that rules and laws are meant for others," and thus is less concerned with the consequences of being apprehended (Crewdson 1988, 64). In this view, the child sexual abuser is primarily focused on his own well-being and gratification, and sees himself as above the law.

A further disturbing aspect of child sexual abusers is the movement among some to publicly encourage adult–child sex as "healthy" and "natural." There are a number of groups such as the Rene Guyon society, which was founded in 1962 and boasts thousands of members, who advocate legalizing sex with children (Crewdson 1988, 97). Their slogan is "sex by year 8, or else it's too late." Child sexual abuse quadrupled between the early 1900s and the early 1970s (Russell 1986, 82). Five explanations for this epidemic increase include (1) an increase in *child pornography and the sexualization of children*; (2) the *sexual revolution* with its "all-sex-is-okay" philosophy; (3) the *backlash against sexual equality* (men who can't cope with women as equals turn to girls); (4) the recycling of *untreated child sexual abuse,* in which victims grow up to become victimizers; and (5) the increase in *stepfamilies,* where girls are especially at risk of incest (Russell 1986).

Research has shown that initial reactions to child sexual abuse include anxiety, depression, fear, anger and hostility, and inappropriate sexual behavior

(Browne and Finkelhor 1986). While some victims of child sexual abuse become quite withdrawn, many victims react by becoming very sexual; they have "learned" that their most important asset is to service others sexually. Other research on the immediate impact of child sexual abuse found differing ranges of the effects, ranging from very serious damage to apparently unaffected children (Conte and Schuerman 1987). In the long term, most adults and children psychologically survive child sexual abuse, but its effects can be extremely painful.

In addition to the trauma and danger that victims of child sexual abuse experience during and immediately after abuse, they frequently also experience long-term effects. Adult survivors of child sexual abuse report depression, self-destruction, anxiety, isolation, stigma, negative feelings about men, fear, and mistrust (Browne and Finkelhor 1986; Murphy et al. 1988; Russell 1984). Long-term behaviors that are associated with adult survivors of child sexual abuse include drug and alcohol abuse and sexual dysfunction (Browne and Finkelhor 1986). Research also shows that sexually abused children have an extremely high rate of rape revictimization (Browne and Finkelhor 1986; Murphy 1991; Murphy et al. 1988; Russell 1986, 158). Revictimization may be associated with low rates of self-esteem and high rates of chemical dependency. Low self-esteem and chemical dependency are associated with *surviving sexual victimization* as well as *being sexually victimized*. That is, rapists often "pick" victims who look vulnerable, and vulnerability is often an effect of sexual victimization.

In summary, child sexual abuse can occur to anyone, and its effects are often devastating.

> The sexual abuse of children spans all races, economic classes, and ethnic groups. Even babies are its victims—hospitals treat three-month old infants for venereal disease of the throat. Sexually abused children are not more precocious, pretty, or sexually curious than other children. They do not ask for it. They do not want it. Like rape of women, the rape and molestation of children are most basically acts of violation, power, and domination.
> *(Bass 1983, 24)*

The frequency and prevalence with which child sexual abuse occurs is outrageous. Again, power plays a tremendous role, as it does in other forms of sexual assault and sexual harassment.

DATE RAPE

Date rape is forced or coerced sexual intimacy by someone with whom one has had a romantic or dating relationship, but does not include someone with whom one has been living as a spouse. Thus, date rape is one type of acquaintance rape; the victim and the assailant have experienced a relationship including some kind of romantic involvement, however briefly. Sexual victimization may occur on the first date or years into a dating relationship. It is distinct from *marital rape* in that the victim and the offender are not married nor living as spouses. Date rape is not a recent phenomenon, although it has only re-

cently been made public. Clark (1987) traces sexual assault in England between 1770 and 1845 and found that rape in courtship was not particularly
unusual. She examined why some men raped the women they dated and found
it was *not* because the women had refused them sexually, but rather the men
"refused to acknowledge women's right to desire or refuse themselves, and believed they had a right to women's bodies" (Clark 1987, 85). Some of the
women raped during courtship felt pressured into marrying the rapist, since
views were such that a woman should be sexual only with her husband. Unfortunately, more recent research has also found that some women who are
raped by their boyfriends or fiancés feel an obligation to marry them, since
they have already been sexual with them, however forced (Russell 1982, 1984).

In 1957, Kanin published an article in a well-known sociology journal
claiming that 62 percent of first-year college women reported experiencing
some level of "offensive erotic intimacy" in the twelve months prior to starting college. Nonetheless, date rape remained unrecognized publicly until Mary
P. Koss's study in conjunction with *MS.* magazine, published early in the 1980s
(Barrett 1982). In studies of college women, 70 to 80 percent reported having
a man misinterpret the degree of sexual intimacy they desired or having a man
use sexual aggression (Koss and Oros 1982; Muehlenhard and Linton 1987).
Furthermore, 15 percent of the women and 7 percent of the men reported
being involved in sexual intercourse against the woman's will, or rape, as it is
commonly defined. In a more recent and larger scale study of over 6,000 students at thirty-two U.S. colleges and universities, 12 percent of the women
had experienced attempted rape, and another 15 percent had experienced
completed rape. Six and one-half percent of the women reported experiencing completed rape in the twelve months prior to the study. Approximately 3
percent of men reported committing attempted rapes, and 4 percent admitted
committing completed rapes (Koss et al. 1987).

It is apparent that roughly three-fourths of college women have experienced sexual victimization (excluding sexual harassment). Approximately one
in four has experienced completed or attempted rape since the age of 14.
Eighty-four percent of these rapes were acquaintance rapes, and "[f]ifty-seven
percent of the rapes happened on dates" (see Warshaw 1988, 11).

College students may be particularly vulnerable, "[s]ince the majority of
acquaintance rape victims are between the ages of 15 and 24," with the average age of 18 (Glavin 1986). In fact, college women are less likely to be victims of acquaintance rape the longer they are in college: Freshmen women are
most at risk, and senior women are least at risk (Parrot 1986). Culture and society have been blamed for the high rates of date and acquaintance rapes. Our
dating scheme often sets up conditions where the woman is at risk. For instance, if she is expected to have her date pick her up and bring her home, she
is somewhat dependent on him. There are additional unwritten assumptions
adopted by some men (and women) that if he pays for dinner, movies, and so
on, then she "owes" him sex.

In addition to dating practices negatively affecting gender differences in
power, there are also the more fundamental beliefs regarding "masculinity" and
"femininity." Women are "supposed" to be passive, weak, dependent, and yet in

control of sexual encounters with men. They are in the double-bind of having to appear attractive to men, but to not be sexual. Men, on the other hand, are expected to be aggressive, strong, and independent, and to take control with women (and other men). Despite recent awareness surrounding date rape, there are still many people who believe women don't "mean it" when they say "no" to sex with men.

Women who have been using drugs or alcohol, who wear "revealing" clothing, who have a reputation for being sexually "free," or who have been intimate with the rapist prior to the rape are even less likely to be viewed as "legitimate" rape victims—that is, as women who had a legitimate right to say "no." Men's and women's different socialization may result in different interpretations of the same behaviors. Some behaviors that women interpret as friendly or showing some interest in a man, men interpret as an invitation to sex; such behaviors include a woman visiting a man's apartment or accepting a ride home from a party (Spencer 1987).

Date rapes on college and university campuses may be related to the environment of fraternities and other campus parties (Ehrhart and Sandler 1985; Sanday 1990). Although most male students do not gang rape, it is important to respond to those who do. The campus gang rape can take many forms; however, there is usually a pattern. They tend to take place during parties where there is a free flow of alcohol (and often drugs), the music is loud, and women can be easily controlled and isolated. Gang rapes are particularly humiliating in that these rapes are often watched by others, are photographed, and otherwise occur with a multitude of witnesses who either decide to participate or refuse to take action (Warshaw 1988, 102). Most victims of such gang rapes transfer to another college or drop out.

> At one Maine school, fraternity members participated in *ledging:* That's where, in the words of one woman graduate, "a fraternity member invites all his brothers to watch his conquest of a naive freshman woman, and then she hears about it for months afterward." The name "ledging" for this practice refers to the woman's being driven to the point of suicide by the harassment.
>
> *(Warshaw 1988, 109)*

Gang rapes exhibit a bonding between the rapists, where the participants feel a need to "perform" in front of their peers. Instigators of gang rape place pressure on onlookers to participate (Groth 1979). This pressure is probably particularly apparent between fraternity brothers. Also, male athletes' disproportionately high rates of sexual assaults have been attributed to the intense bonding of living and playing with other male athletes (Eskenazi 1990). A combination of high-status privilege (often attributed to male athletes) and a "pack mentality" likely influences male athletes' rape-prone behavior. It is also disturbing that these onlookers (whether they are fraternity brothers, friends, and so on) usually choose to join in or at least watch, but rarely feel an obligation to stop the victimization.

[I]n some gang rapes each offender in turn becomes more aggressive than his predecessor and forces more degrading acts onto his victim, in part to prove his toughness to his cohorts, but also because it seems that, in his eyes, the victim is a whore because she is having sex with all the men in the gang. The fact that she is submitting under duress seems irrelevant. *(Groth 1979, 114)*

Frequently, the assailant will purposely work to create an environment that minimizes the victim's control. Two factors often associated with acquaintance rapes are (1) the consumption of alcohol/drugs prior to the victimization, and (2) the playing of loud music (Parrot 1986, 10). One study on campus rape found that almost all campus gang rapes involved alcohol or drugs, and *every one* of the fraternity gang rapes they identified involved drugs or alcohol, which helped decrease men's inhibitions and weakened women's ability to determine threatening situations and resist sexual victimizations (Ehrhart and Sandler 1985).

The playing of loud music is probably used in acquaintance rapes to "cover the victim's non-compliant sounds and increase the victim's feeling of helplessness" (Parrot 1986, 10). Alcohol and drug use and the playing of loud music serve to further debilitate the woman's ability to resist sexual victimization. Many date rapists actually plan the situation in advance, in order to maximize their advantages and limit their victims' resistance (Warshaw 1988, 87). It is not unusual for these men to invite their dates to their own or a friend's apartment on the pretext of seeing the friend or picking something up. The victim later realizes her victimization was planned, often in collusion with the "friend" who vacated the apartment. Even more disturbing, 84 percent of the men in one study "who committed rape said that what they did was *definitely not rape*" (Warshaw 1988, 90).

Miscommunication is often blamed for the occurrence of date rapes. While the woman may perceive her own flirtatious behavior as simply meaning "I may be interested in you," or even "I am interested in you," she likely does not mean it to be interpreted as "I will have sex with you under any conditions." He may believe (for reasons stated above) that he has the "license" to force sex with her. After a date rape, even though she knows she said "no" and didn't want sex with him, and he physically forced her, she may still not define the behavior as rape. Fear, shock, confusion, guilt, disbelief, degradation, and loss of control are some of the common reactions of acquaintance rape victims. Many women, so overcome with guilt, often don't realize that they have been raped. Some victims are so preoccupied with blaming themselves for wanting to be with their date that they view the entire episode as their fault. If there were any romantic exchanges prior to the attack, such as innocent hugging or kissing, the victim often feels that she went "too far" before she said "no" and therefore caused the rape to occur by pushing the man to the edge of sexual frustration (Glavin 1986, 3).

Although it is important to address the role of miscommunication in the occurrence of date rapes, as well as the accompanying gender differences associated with this miscommunication, it is also important not to use miscommunication as *the* explanation of date rapes. Clearly, many date rapists proceed to rape despite significant communication from victims that they are not consenting, or when the victims are asleep or passed out and unable to consent.

Nonetheless, perceptions about *consent* are at the crux of almost every rape trial, and nowhere is this more complex than date rapes—she invited him out, she let him pay for dinner, she invited him to her apartment, she let him kiss her, and so on. But, "a gender gap in sexual communication exists" (Weiner 1983, 147), and considerable research documents that males are more likely than females to interpret various behaviors and verbal communications as sexual (Abbey 1987; Miller and Marshall 1987; Muehlenhard 1989).

Some studies show that women tend to be more at risk of date rape the longer they have been dating someone (Henton et al. 1983; Muehlenhard and Linton 1987). However, date rape can also occur early on in the dating relationship, even on the first date. The reason for many date rapes occurring later in the dating relationship may be that men feel more entitled to sex in a long-term relationship (Weis and Borges 1973).

To better understand date rape, it is important to study men, as well as women. One study of college men found that over half thought it was somewhat justifiable to force kissing with tongue contact, and over one-fifth thought it was somewhat justifiable to touch the woman's genitals against her wishes (Muehlenhard et al. 1985). Thirty-five percent of college males in a study in the United States and Canada reported that they would commit rape if they knew they could get away with it (Malamuth 1981). Still another study of male college students found that 15 percent reported forcing intercourse at least once, 28 percent reported using directly coercive methods at least once, and only 39 percent denied coercive sexual involvement. Consistent with the above contention that some men do not listen when a woman says "no" or "stop," over one-third of college men reported *ignoring a woman's protests* (Rapaport and Burkhart 1984).

Data in recent years have shown the extent to which date rape affects young women's lives. To date, most of this research has been carried out on college campuses. While a few date rape studies have been conducted in high schools, none have been conducted on older women or younger women not in college. Future research needs to address this class and institutionalized bias. Additionally, research on fraternity rapes and rapes committed by male athletic "stars" suggests that *some* fraternity members and sports stars perceive that their fraternity or "star" association allows them to have sex with whomever they desire, whether it is voluntarily, coercively, or forcefully. Future research must address these perceived "privileges" and how they are fostered.

MARITAL RAPE

Many people still view "marital rape" as a "contradiction in terms," believing that husbands should have complete say on when, how, and how often they have sex with their wives. Persons who adhere to these beliefs, however, are often unaware of the extreme brutality in many marital rapes, as well as the effects of routinely having sex against one's will with someone who is supposed to be loving. Unfortunately, media images of marital rape as simply a "conflict over sex" or an "unpleasant, but not particularly serious, marital squabble" have resulted in a *sanitary stereotype* of marital rape (Finkelhor and Yllo 1985, 13). Marital rape is either minimized as a petty conflict (Finkelhor and Yllo 1985) or romanticized as highly erotic for the husband and the wife (for example, in movies such as *Gone with the Wind* and *The Thorn Birds*).

Most research conducted on marital rape defines it as rape in a marital relationship, including common-law marriages and sometimes persons living together as spouses although not legally married. Rape occurs in marriage with alarming frequency (Finkelhor and Yllo 1983, 1985; Russell 1982, 1984; Shields and Hanneke 1983). In fact, Russell's (1984, 62) random sample found that *12 percent* of the married women had experienced sexual assault by a husband. While there is still a lot to learn, research starting in the 1980s has begun to address the issues surrounding marital rape.

Researchers have identified two typologies of marital rape. The first, by Finkelhor and Yllo (1985), categorizes marital rapes as *battering rapes, nonbattering rapes,* and *obsessive rapes.* In *battering rapes,* sexual violence occurs in addition to verbal and physical violence, or rather, as part of the battering. *Nonbattering rapes* are marital rapes in relationships where there is little nonsexual physical violence, but rape occurs (usually as a result of sexual conflicts). *Obsessive rapes* are marital rapes that involve "bizarre sexual obsessions," largely perpetrated by men who consume considerable amounts of pornography (Finkelhor and Yllo 1983, 123–125).

The second typology of marital rapes, by Russell (1982), is a result of her belief that Finkelhor and Yllo's typology is too limiting and not exhaustive. Russell is concerned that the Finkelhor and Yllo typology neglects the less extreme forms of wife rape. In fact, Russell (1982, 145) believes that although many men who physically abuse their wives also sexually abuse them, "there are probably many more wives who are raped by their husbands but not [physically] battered" in extreme and repeated forms. Therefore, Russell (1982, 133–143) proposes the following typology of husbands in relation to wife rape:

1. Husbands who prefer raping their wives to having consensual sex with them

2. Husbands who are able to enjoy both rape and consensual sex with their wives or who are indifferent to which it is

3. Husbands who prefer consensual sex with their wives, but are willing to rape when their sexual advances are refused

4. Husbands who would like to rape their wives, but don't act on these desires

5. Husbands who have no desire to rape their wives

Rape by intimates is difficult to uncover. The victims themselves often redefine what they experience, believing it cannot be *rape* if the offender is a husband, a boyfriend, or a relative. Marital rape victims often attempt to minimize or forget that they were sexually abused by their husbands (Kelly 1988).

In fact, many times it is not until years later, looking back at a situation, that a woman recognizes that the forced sex she experienced with her husband was indeed rape (Kelly 1988; Sheiner 1987).

SEXUAL HARASSMENT

- A woman is walking by a construction site, and one of the workers whistles at her.
- A student goes to her professor to discuss a paper she is writing for his class, and he asks her on a date.
- A woman's supervisor tells her she has "nice legs."

These are all examples of sexual harassment. Sexual harassment is typically viewed as something that happens only in the workplace or on the street. However, sexual harassment can occur anywhere, including in a college classroom, in a doctor's office, and at social gatherings. Sexual harassment can gradually erode the victim's sense of self-respect and privacy, whether it's a junior executive looking down one's blouse, an obnoxious drunk at the next table making lewd comments, or a construction worker whistling and cat-calling (Medea and Thompson 1974, 50). Similar to discussions on other victimizations of women and girls, power plays a huge role in sexual harassment. The unwanted, intrusive, and insulting behaviors included in sexual harassment have the effect of controlling, angering, and humiliating women and girls.

Most research on sexual harassment has focused on sexual harassment in the workplace. In fact, Stanko (1985, 60) defines sexual harassment as "many forms of unwanted sexual attention that occur in working situations: visual (leering) or verbal (sexual teasing, jokes, comments or questions) behavior; unwanted pressure for sexual favors or dates; unwanted touching or pinching; unwanted pressure for sexual favors with implied threats of retaliation for non-cooperation." The most comprehensive study on sexual harassment in the workplace was conducted by the Merit Systems Protection Board and initiated by the Subcommittee on Investigations of the House Committee on Post Office and Civil Service. This 1981 report involved questionnaires completed by 20,000 randomly selected federal employees. They found that 15 percent of all male employees and 42 percent of all female employees reported sexual harassment on the job.

The coercion involved in sexual harassment cannot be overstated. Just as a woman may decide to take a less convenient route to her destination to avoid sexual harassment on the street, women students or women workers may reasonably fear they will do poorly in a class, or be fired or denied promotions at work, if they refuse to put up with the sexual harassment. It has been suggested that such women keep their jobs at the expense of their self-respect (Farley 1978). Women are increasingly deciding to confront their harassers, either informally or through university or job policies, or laws. The 1991 U.S. Senate confirmation hearings regarding the appointment of Clarence Thomas helped advance awareness on sexual harassment more than anything to date. Thomas was confronted with accusations of sexually harassing Anita Hill, a former employee, at the Equal Employment Opportunity Center office. Although Thomas was confirmed, much of the country was moved by Hill's integrity, and many victims and survivors of sexual harassment came forward to tell their stories as well.

Many people view sexual harassment as harmless, or even worse, flattering. Besides having an effect that is often *demeaning* (making victims feel "cheap," or like a "piece of meat" or a "sexual object"), sexual harassment is yet one more manner in which women are *controlled*. The threat behind sexual harassment cannot be minimized. The victim is often unsure as to what degree the harasser will go to attempt to demean or control her. If she confronts the harasser for whistling, might she end up being physically sexually assaulted? The severity of sexual harassment is witnessed in a study where more than one in five women reported being sexually *assaulted* (that is, raped) by someone they knew from work (Schneider 1991). Fear of losing jobs or promotions, or failing courses, and so on, keeps women and girls from pursuing their goals and careers. The threat of sexual harassment also serves to keep women from pursuing or maintaining jobs traditionally held by males, which are also the jobs that pay the most. This is not to imply that jobs traditionally held by women are free from sexual harassment.

> In such [traditionally female] jobs a woman is employed as a woman. She is also, apparently, treated like a woman, with one aspect of this being the explicitly sexual. Specifically, if part of the reason the woman is hired is to be pleasing to a male boss, whose notion of a qualified worker merges with a sexist notion of the proper role of women, it is hardly surprising that sexual intimacy, forced when necessary, would be considered part of her duties and his privileges.
>
> *(MacKinnon 1979, 18)*

Clearly, *sexual harassment is not harmless* when it has such devastating effects. Some research has been conducted at universities in order to determine levels of sexual harassment. One such study at the University of Rhode Island randomly surveyed the entire university community: faculty, undergraduate and graduate students, administrators, and staff (Lott et al. 1982). Their random sample of students found that 30 percent of the women and 82 percent of the men reported that they had never been sexually insulted on campus; 56 percent of the women and 17 percent of the men reported rare or occasional insults; 13 percent of the women and *none* of the men reported being insulted often or very often. Similarly, the men considered sexually related behavior on the job and at school to be more natural, more to be expected, and less problematic and serious than the women did.

Sexual harassment is a problem that occurs on the job, on the street, in the classroom, in the library, and many other places. Sexual harassment demeans women; it poses a threat, thus serving as a control over women; and it limits women economically from pursuing certain careers, or causes them to lose jobs, wages, or promotions. Sexual harassment can be as "mild" as leering and as extreme as a physical sexual assault. It occurs in many environments to many women.

SEXUAL VICTIMIZATION AND THE CRIME-PROCESSING SYSTEM

The sexual assault victim has frequently been referred to as being twice victimized: once by her assailant and once by the crime-processing system. But not just police, judges, and juries have been reported to be ignorant about sexual victimization and hostile to the victims. There are also accounts of doctors, nurses, therapists, and administrators who behave insensitively to victims, often failing to take victimizations seriously. An analysis of 100 years (from 1880 to 1980) of medical indexes found a recurring theme, particularly in indexes prior to 1960, of advice to view rape victims as *liars*, and to "be extremely meticulous in your examination and history, as many women and girls falsely accuse men of sexual assault; if you make erroneous hasty conclusions, you may be responsible for sending an innocent man to his death" (Mills 1982, 53). Fortunately, Mills (1982) reports improvements by physicians and hospitals since then.

The sexual assault victim is likely not to have any witnesses to her assault. If she decides not to inform anyone of her victimization, it is usually "easy" for her to keep her victimization a secret. Unfortunately, this lack of witnesses has served to further hurt her chances of being viewed as a victim if she decides to report the incident. The victim may decide not to tell anyone, to tell only a close friend or relative, to tell the police, and/or to tell a rape crisis center. Rape crisis centers have proven helpful in providing the victim with a variety of services. In addition to emotional support, they usually provide volunteers to accompany the victim to the hospital, to the police department, and to court if she opts to use any of these services.

Victims who formally report the assault will likely have to deal with responses from a variety of persons, including physicians, counselors, family, and friends, as well as the various actors of the crime-processing system. Making their victimizations public, then, often requires survivors to deal with various persons' views and beliefs, as well as myths associated with rape. Regardless of responses by the police and courts, the *community* response is important. If there are no community services for rape victims, or if the community values sexist and rape-supportive myths, "then the victims' needs will undoubtedly go unaddressed" (Koss and Harvey 1991, 95). However, a study of fraternity gang rapes found that people who publicly condemned "the brothers" received obscene calls and death threats over the phone (Sanday 1990).

The Police

Sexual victimization is particularly difficult for the victims to make public because of the shame involved, the fear of retaliation by the assailant, and the need to convince others (sometimes even themselves) that they did not "ask for" or deserve the assault. The first contact most victims have with the criminal justice system is the police. The police serve an important function, not only in that they are the first contact, but that victims are dependent on the police to "make" the case for them. Victims' fears of the way police view rape, rapists, and the rape victims themselves often inhibit them from formally reporting the crime (LeDoux and Hazelwood 1985, 211). Rape victims, unlike other victims, must often prove nonconsent, with the assumption that most women lie when charging rape (Spencer 1987, 56).

Consistent with this, researchers argue that rape is far more susceptible to unfounding than other crimes (Brownmiller 1975; Russell 1984). *Unfounding* refers to the practice by which police determine that a "victim" is making false charges. As a result, the case is dropped. Rape is more susceptible to unfounding because of the mistaken belief that women "cry" rape after consensual sex in order to protect their reputations. More recently, some departments have forbidden the unfounding of rape cases.

One study in Indianapolis found that the reasons police unfounded rape cases were due to complaints about the victim's moral character or conduct (71%), lack of victim cooperation (20%), and technical reasons (such as the rape occurring outside of the departmental jurisdiction) (9%) (LaFree et al. 1985). Notably, "nonconforming" victims—women who hitchhiked, had sex outside of marriage, went to bars without male escorts, and willingly went to the defendant's apartment—were less likely to have their cases result in arrests (LaFree et al. 1985).

One study of over 2,000 police officers found that although police officers are not insensitive to rape victims overall, they "are suspicious of victims who meet certain criteria, such as previous and willing sex with the assailant, or who 'provoke' rape through their appearance or behavior" (LeDoux and Hazelwood 1985, 219). Furthermore, some of these officers strongly agreed with statements such as "Nice women do not get raped," and "Most charges of rape are unfounded." Rapes that police determine to be unfounded never appear in official statistics of victimization (such as the UCR), thus increasing the invisibility of sexual victimization. Significantly, a study of police officers, counselors, rapists, and citizens found that both citizens and the police were more closely aligned with *rapists'* attitudes toward rape than they were to *counselors'* views of rape (Feild 1978).

Russell (1984) found that only 8 percent of attempted or completed rapes were reported to the police, and the National Victim Center (1992) found that 16 percent of forcible rapes were reported to the police. As expected, stranger rapes are far more likely than acquaintance rapes to be reported (Russell 1984). Furthermore, 86 percent of U.S. women reported they would be less likely to report a rape to the police if the media disclosed victims' names (National Victim Center 1992). Other studies found that on the average, only 5 percent of the child sexual assault cases and 5 percent of date rape cases were reported to the police (Russell 1984; Warshaw 1988). Problems of credibility, insensitivity, and invisibility are not restricted to the adult sexual assault victim. The crime-processing system has been criticized for its inadequate treatment of and response to the victims of child sexual abuse, particularly incest victims. A 1979 journal published the following:

> Most police officers, however, use an adversary approach when conducting an interview with a child-victim because it is an approach with which they are familiar. The police officer also employs this approach because the child victim must convince the officer that an offense has been committed. Furthermore, the officer must determine the victim's potential effectiveness as a courtroom witness.
>
> *(Kirkwood and Mihaila 1979, 681)*

The Court Process, or "Whose Trial Is It, Anyway?"

Assuming that her sexual assault case is not unfounded by the police and a suspect has been identified, the victim may choose to prosecute if there is an identifiable offender. However, the unfounding pattern may not have ended with the police. Now it is the prosecutor's turn to determine whether the accuser is "really a victim" and whether the case is worth the *prosecutor's* time (not taking the victim's wants or needs into account). Like police, prosecutors rely on gender stereotypes in their efforts to assess "credible" female victims (Stanko 1982). Thus, the prosecutor's reliance on irrelevant characteristics about the victim, and the prosecutor's acceptance of rape myths, may result in the victim not being able to prosecute. In short, prosecutors and judges have been accused of having the same limited attitudes about rape that many police hold (LaFree 1989).

Less than 35 percent of arrests for rapes end up in convictions (Estrich 1987, 17); the rest are dismissed or acquitted. Of the 670 attempted and completed rapes reported in Russell's (1984) study, only 2 percent resulted in arrests, and 1 percent resulted in convictions. LaFree (1989) found that 37 percent of rape cases reported to the police ended in arrests, 12 percent resulted in guilty pleas or verdicts, 6 percent went to trial, and less than 5 percent resulted in a prison sentence. Another study analyzed prosecutors' unfounding of rape cases, and found that of victims who report to the police, rape victims are just as likely to want to take their cases to court as aggravated assault, robbery, and burglary victims. However, rape victims are more likely to be perceived as lying by prosecutors than are aggravated assault, robbery, and burglary victims. "[R]ape victims are as willing to undergo the ordeal of the court process as are other victims, despite the fact that it may be more grueling for them. However, they are less frequently believed than other victims" (Williams 1981, 32).

Prosecutors' ignorance of the dynamics surrounding sexual victimization negatively affects victims who attempt to secure prosecution of their rapists. A study of prosecutors' screening of sexual assault cases found a centrality of *victim discredibility* in the prosecutors' decisions to reject many rape cases (Frohmann 1991). This was done through looking for discrepancies in the victim's account or between the victim's account and the police report, and trying to determine if the victim had ulterior motives for filing a false report (for example, not wanting to tell her boyfriend she got a venereal disease from consensual sex with another man). These decisions were heavily based on the often incomplete and mistaken police reports, and on the victim's criminal connections. Rap sheets chronicling a person's arrests and convictions were routinely run on victims who were homeless, who were involved in illegal activities, or who simply lived in African American and Latina neighborhoods, but they were not run on women from the wealthier, Anglo part of the city (Frohmann 1991). Typifications of the victim's behavior and knowledge of the victim's personal life also influenced prosecutors' decisions to reject rape cases. What prosecutors may think is "typical" rape behavior is likely inaccurate, yet it often affects their perceptions of victims' credibility. "Unless we are able to challenge the assumptions on which these typifications are based, many rape cases will never get beyond the filing process because of unconvictability" (Frohmann 1991, 224).

A number of factors influence whether a rape charge results in a conviction. Estrich (1987; 18–19) identifies three such factors: (1) the victim–offender relationship, (2) the amount of force used by the defendant and the level of resistance offered by the victim, and (3) the quality of the evidence (that is, the perceived plausibility of the victim's testimony and whether her account can be corroborated).

Studies on the relationship between the victim and the offender in sexual assault cases consistently find that convictions are less likely in cases where the victim knows the offender than in "stranger rapes" (Estrich 1987; Russell 1984; Williams 1981). Although victims are much more likely to be able to identify the assailant in acquaintance rapes, stranger rapes are much more likely to be taken seriously by the crime-processing system (and most of the public) and to result in convictions. This is particularly troubling given that most sexual assaults are perpetrated by men known to the victim. Similarly, evidence about the victim's lifestyle, such as drinking, drug use, or extramarital sexual activity, also affects the verdict (LaFree et al. 1985). In fact, rape trials often seem more concerned with the victims' than the offenders' accountability, responsibility, and personal characteristics. Ironically, one study found that while the *defendant's* criminal history did not affect the likelihood of his conviction, the *victim's* criminal history significantly affected whether the offender was convicted (Williams 1981).

Research has also addressed how levels of both offender aggression and victim resistance influence perceptions that a rape actually occurred. Predictably, both influence impressions of rape culpability. The greater the level of force used by the offender, the more likely the behavior will be labeled rape (Burt and Albin 1981; Goodchilds and Zellman 1984). Similarly, the more actively a woman resists, the better chance she has of being viewed as a legitimate victim (Deitz et al. 1984; Gilmartin-Zena 1988).

Regarding the quality of the evidence in rape cases, Williams (1981) found that witnesses and traces of physical evidence (such as torn clothing and the presence of sperm) positively affected the likelihood of conviction. Similarly, a review of empirical research found that medical corroboration and corroboration by a witness significantly improved the chances of conviction in sexual victimization cases (Estrich 1987, 17). Conditions for child sexual abuse victims also tend to lack adequate crime-processing system responses. One problem is that even when conclusive medical evidence exists, the child is frequently too young to testify. If the child does testify, she or he is not exempt from the typical abrasiveness and victim blaming of defense lawyers. Finally, given the alarming number of child sexual abusers, it is not unlikely that at least one will end up on a jury (Crewdson 1988).

The process of making her victimization public is likely to be a painful process for the sexually assaulted victim. In addition to shame and depression, she is likely to experience frustration and anger toward persons who are supposed to be helping her bring the offender to justice. However, there are costs to not prosecuting. A victim may experience a sense of denial of her victimization if she doesn't prosecute, as well as inhibiting the possibility of punishing the rapist. The victim who does not report may also feel a sense of responsibility that the rapist is free to continue assaulting other victims. On the other hand, deciding to take the case through the crime-processing system may not necessarily result in a sense of vindication. As stated previously, many women who have experienced sexual victimization fear how the police, lawyers, judges, and juries will respond to them.

The sexual assault victim, then, may suffer not only at the hands of the rapist, but also through her experiences with the police department and the court system. Both the movie *The Accused,* starring Jodie Foster, and the real-life rape trial of William Kennedy Smith portrayed how women who charge rape are often treated in court. It is evident that we need to educate these actors of the crime-processing system so that they may understand sexual victimization and help the victim rather than further victimize her.

SUMMARY

This chapter started by explaining the limitations inherent in how the term *rape* has traditionally been defined. To fully understand and measure sexual victimization, it is necessary to acknowledge that people are sexually victimized in many ways in addition to forced penile–vaginal penetration between adult strangers. The rate of sexual victimization in this country is much higher than once thought, particularly between acquaintances. Increased awareness of the probability of stranger rapes of adult women occurred in the 1970s. Next, the uncovering of acquaintance rapes of adult women occurred. Finally, in the early 1980s, the sexual abuse of children, particularly incest, became defined as a social problem, if not a national epidemic. Awareness of date and marital rape followed shortly after the identification of child sexual abuse as a social problem.

Of the eight index crimes, rape is the least likely to be reported. In addition to the humiliation associated with sexual victimization, victims may fear the offenders' retaliation or lack of support by the crime-processing system, and/or they may blame themselves for the assault. In the case of child sexual abuse, the victim may not be in a situation to report the behavior or even to understand that she or he has been victimized. Thus, in spite of increased attention by the media and researchers, for many reasons sexual victimization remains a highly invisible crime.

Determination of rates of sexual victimization has been hampered by some of the following factors: (1) Rape is one of the crimes that victims are least likely to report to the police; (2) stereotypical characteristics of the victim and the offender (such as whether they are strangers, whether she has a "bad reputation") often are mistakenly used to determine whether the rape was "real"; (3) the nature of the sexual victimization (that is, the increased humiliation of having been anally or orally raped, or raped by a husband) may deter the victim from reporting; and (4) the victims of attempted rapes may perceive their victimizations as "not important enough to report," since they weren't "really" raped.

While the NCS data collection method provides a more accurate assessment than the UCR of the degree to which rapes occur in the United States, neither the NCS nor the UCR adequately assesses the frequency of sexual victimization because of their methods of questioning, and in the case of the UCR, data collection. (Specifically, the UCR relies on rapes reported to the police, which presents a skewed picture of the overall distribution of rapes.) Improved data collection methods have uncovered the high likelihood of U.S. females being sexually victimized, particularly by their families, close friends, and dates.

It was not until the 1980s that child sexual abuse was labeled a social problem. In a relatively short period of time we have become aware that it may occur to as many as 62 percent of female children and 31 percent of male children (Peters et al. 1986). Child sexual victimization has remained invisible for the same reasons that the sexual victimization of adult women has remained invisible. However, in most cases, children are even less empowered than adult women to physically resist sexual victimization and to be able to report their victimizations.

Young women who have recently left home (for college or work) are also a high-risk group for sexual victimization. Date rape has recently been identified as a sexual problem. Research has also highlighted gang rapes on college campuses, where the victim and rapists knew each other prior to the assault. This appears to be particularly prevalent during fraternity and dormitory parties, and by male athletes. These rapes are frequently planned, using alcohol, drugs, and loud music to debilitate the victim (Parrot 1986).

Sexual harassment is a form of sexual victimization. It is behavior that is sexual in nature and empowers the harasser by demeaning the victim. Occurrence of this behavior is most frequently associated with the workplace, but more recently, it is recognized as occurring anywhere: in educational settings, at work, in social settings, and on the streets. Sexual harassment is one more method by which women are threatened and their lives are shaped.

Unfortunately, many persons experiencing sexual victimization are further victimized through their encounters with the crime-processing system. Police and courts have frequently been found to be suspicious of any women, and often children, who claim to have been sexually victimized. Disbelief and cynicism on the part of the crime-processing authorities is most prevalent in the cases that occur most frequently and in which the victim is most likely to be able to identify the offender: acquaintance rapes. It is necessary for police officers, judges, and lawyers to be educated about the realities of sexual victimization. This education is also necessary for the public, not only because they serve on juries, but in order that they may stop their own rape-prone behaviors and/or be supportive when someone they know experiences sexual victimization. Rape awareness education may reduce women's and girls' sexual victimization by making them aware of what makes them most at risk, as well as educating males about what constitutes rape and why it is illegal and immoral.

NOTES

1. *Cincinnati Magazine,* December, 1986. These do not add up to 100, because some women were victims of more than one category of sexual victimization.

2. Russell (1984) had to extrapolate her data to make the necessary comparisons with the UCR and NCS findings, based on differences in sampling and reporting techniques. For instance, Russell's (1984) data are for persons 18 years old and older, the NCS is for persons 12 and older, and the UCR includes persons of all ages.

3. This is from analysis by the author on ten years of NCS data (1973–1982).

REFERENCES

Abbey, Antonia. 1987. "Misperceptions of Friendly Behavior as Sexual Interest." *Psychology of Women Quarterly* 11:173–194.

Amir, Manachem. 1971. *Patterns in Forcible Rape.* Chicago: University of Chicago Press.

Barrett, Karen. 1982. "Date Rape: A Campus Epidemic?" *Ms. Magazine* (September): 49–51, 130.

Bart, Pauline B., and Patricia H. O'Brien. 1985. *Stopping Rape: Successful Survival Strategies.* New York: Pergamon Press.

Bass, Ellen. 1983. "Introduction: In the Truth Itself, There Is Healing." Pp. 23–61 in *I Never Told Anyone,* edited by E. Bass and L. Thornton. New York: Harper & Row.

Belknap, Joanne. 1987. "Routine Activity Theory and the Risk of Rape: Ana-lyzing Ten Years of National Crime Survey Data." *Criminal Justice Policy Review* 2:337–356.

Beneke, Timothy. 1982. *Men on Rape: What They Have to Say About Sexual Violence.* New York: St. Martin's Press.

Browne, Angela, and David Finkelhor. 1986. "Impact of Child Sexual Abuse: A Review of the Research." *Psychological Bulletin,* 99:66–77.

Brownmiller, Susan. 1975. *Against Our Will: Men, Women and Rape.* New York: Simon & Schuster.

Burt, Martha R., and R. S. Albin. 1981. "Rape Myths, Rape Definitions, and Probability of Conviction." *Journal of Applied Social Psychology* 11: 212–230.

Clark, Anne. 1987. *Women's Silence, Men's Violence: Sexual Assault in England, 1770–1845.* London: Pandora Press.

Cluss, Patricia A., Janice Broughton, Ellen Frank, Barbara Duffy Stewart, and Deborah West. 1983. "The Rape Victim: Psychological Correlates of Participation in the Legal Process." *Criminal Justice and Behavior* 10:342–357.

Conte, John R., and John R. Schuerman. 1987. "The Effects of Sexual Abuse of Children." *Journal of Interpersonal Violence* 2:380–390.

Costin, Charisse T. M. 1992. "The Influence of Race in Urban Homeless Females' Fear of Crime." *Justice Quarterly* 9:721-730.

Crewdson, John. 1988. *By Silence Betrayed: Sexual Abuse of Children in America.* Boston: Little, Brown.

Deitz, Sheila R., Madeleine Littman, and Brenda J. Bentley. 1984. "Attribution of Responsibility for Rape: The Influence of Observer Empathy, Victim Resistance, and Victim Attractiveness." *Sex Roles* 10:261–280.

Ehrhart, Julie K., and Bernice R. Sandler. 1985. *Campus Gang Rape: Party Games?* Washington, D.C.: Association of American Colleges.

Eigenberg, Helen M. 1990. "The National Crime Survey and Rape: The Case of the Missing Question." *Justice Quarterly* 7:655–672.

Eskenazi, Gerald. 1990. "The Male Athlete and Sexual Assault." *New York Times,* June 30, p. 27.

Estrich, Susan. 1987. *Real Rape.* Cambridge, MA: Harvard University Press.

Farley, L. 1978. *Sexual Shakedown: The Sexual Harassment of Women on the Job.* New York: Warner.

Feild, H. S. 1978. "Attitudes Toward Rape: A Comparative Analysis of Police, Rapists, Crisis Counselors, and Citizens." *Journal of Personality* 36:156–179.

Finkelhor, David, and Larry Baron. 1986. "High Risk Children." Pp. 60–88 in *A Sourcebook on Child Sexual Abuse,* edited by D. Finkelhor. Beverly Hills, CA: Sage.

Finkelhor, David, and Kersti Yllo. 1983. "Rape in Marriage: A Sociological View." Pp. 119–131 in *The Dark Side of Families: Current Family Violence Research,* edited by D. Finkelhor, R. J. Gelles, G. T. Hotaling, and M. A. Straus. Beverly Hills, CA: Sage.

——————. 1985. *License to Rape: Sexual Abuse of Wives.* New York: Free Press.

Forward, Susan, and Craig Buck. 1978. *Betrayal of Innocence: Incest and Its Devastation.* Middlesex, England: Penguin Books.

Frohmann, Lisa. 1991. "Discrediting Victims' Allegations of Sexual Assault: Prosecutorial Accounts of Case Rejection." *Social Problems* 38:213–226.

Gilmartin-Zena, Pat. 1988. "Gender Differences in Students' Attitudes Toward Rape." *Sociological Focus* 21:279–292.

Glavin, A. P. 1986. *Acquaintance Rape: The Silent Epidemic.* Massachusetts Institute of Technology, Campus Police Department, March.

Gomes-Schwartz, Beverly, Jonathan M. Horowitz, and Albert P. Cardearelli. 1990. *Child Sexual Abuse: The Initial Effects.* Newbury Park, CA: Sage.

Goodchilds, Jacqueline D., and Gail L. Zellman. 1984. "Sexual Signaling and Sexual Aggression in Adolescent Relationships." Pp. 233–243 in *Pornography and Sexual Aggression,* edited by N. M. Malamuth and E. Donnerstein. Orlando, FL:Academic Press.

Gordon, Linda, and Paul O'Keefe. 1984. "Incest as a Form of Family Violence: Evidence from Historical Case Records." *Journal of Marriage and Family* 46:27–34.

Griffen, Susan. 1971. "Rape: The All-American Crime." *Ramparts* (September): 26–35.

Groth, A. Nicholas. 1979. *Men Who Rape: The Psychology of the Offender.* New York: Plenum Press.

Henton, J., R. Cate, J. Koval, S. Lloyd, and S. Christopher. 1983. "Romance and Violence in Dating Relationships." *Journal of Family Issues* 4:467–482.

Herman, Judith L. 1981. *Father–Daughter Incest.* Cambridge, MA: Harvard University Press.

Jensen, Gary F., and MaryAltani Karpos. 1993. "Managing Rape: Exploratory Research on the Behavior of Rape Statistics." *Criminology* 31:363–386.

Kanin, Eugene J. 1957. "Male Aggression in Dating–Courtship Relations." *American Journal of Sociology* 63:197–204.

Kelly, Liz. 1988. "How Women Define Their Experiences of Violence." Pp. 114–132 in *Feminist Perspectives on Wife Abuse,* edited by K. Yllo and M. Bograd. Newbury Park, CA: Sage.

Kirkwood, L. J., and M. E. Mihaila. 1979. "Incest and the Legal System: Inadequacies and Alternatives." *University of California–Davis Law Review* 12:673–699.

Kohn, Alfie. 1987. "Shattered Innocence." *Psychology Today* (February): 54–58.

Koss, Mary P., C. A. Gidycz, and N. Wisniewski. 1987. "The Scope of Rape: Incidence and Prevalence of Sexual Aggression and Victimization in a National Sample of Higher Education Students." *Journal of Consulting and Clinical Psychology* 55:162–170.

Koss, Mary P., and Mary R. Harvey. 1991. *The Rape Victim: Clinical and Community Interventions,* 2nd ed. Newbury Park, CA: Sage.

Koss, Mary P., and C. J. Oros 1982. "Sexual Experiences Survey: A Research Instrument Investigating Sexual Aggression and Victimization." *Journal of Consulting and Clinical Psychology* 50:455–457.

Krulewitz, J. E., and J. E. Nash. 1979. "Effects of Rape Victim Resistance, Assault Outcome, and Sex of Observer on Attributions About Rape." *Journal of Personality* 47:557–574.

LaFree, Gary D. 1989. *Rape and Criminal Justice: The Social Construction of Sexual Assault.* Belmont, CA: Wadsworth.

LaFree, Gary D., Barbara F. Reskin, and Christy A. Visher. 1985. "Jurors' Responses to Victims' Behavior and Legal Issues in Sexual Assault Trials." *Social Problems* 32:389–407.

LeDoux, J. C., and R. R. Hazelwood. 1985. "Police Attitudes and Beliefs Toward Rape." *Journal of Police Science and Administration* 13:211–220.

Lott, B., M. E. Reilly, and D. R. Howard. 1982. "Sexual Assault and Harassment: A Campus Community Case Study." *Signs* 8:296–319.

MacKinnon, Catherine A. 1979. *Sexual Harassment of Working Women.* New Haven, CT: Yale University Press.

Malamuth, Neil M. 1981. "Rape Proclivity Among Males." *Journal of Social Issues* 37:138–157.

McCarty, M. 1986. "Rape." *Cincinnati Magazine,* December, pp. 58–64.

Medea, Andra, and Kathleen Thompson. 1974. *Against Rape.* New York: Farrar, Straus and Giroux.

Merit Systems Protection Board. 1981. *Sexual Harassment in the Federal Workplace: Is It a Problem?* Office of Merit Systems Review and Studies. Washington D.C.: Government Printing Offices.

Miller, Beverly, and Jon C. Marshall. 1987. "Coercive Sex on the University Campus." *Journal of College Student Personnel* 28:38–47.

Mills, Elizabeth A. 1982. "One Hundred Years of Fear: Rape and the Medical Profession." Pp. 29–62 in *Judge, Lawyer, Victim, Thief,* edited by N. H. Rafter and E. A. Stanko. Stoughton, MA: Northeastern University Press.

Muehlenhard, Charlene L. 1989. "Misinterpreted Dating Behaviors and Risk of Rape." Pp. 241–256 in *Violence and Dating Relationships,* edited by M. A. Pirog-Good and J. E. Stets. New York: Praeger.

Muehlenhard, Charlene L., D. E. Friedman, and C. M. Thomas. 1985. "Is Date Rape Justifiable? The Effects of Dating Activity, Who Initiated, Who Paid, and Men's Attitudes Toward Women." *Psychology of Women Quarterly* 9: 297–310.

Muehlenhard, Charlene L., and M. A. Linton. 1987. "Date Rape and Sexual Aggression in Dating Situations: Incidence and Risk Factors." *Journal of Counseling Psychology* 34:186–196.

Murphy, John E. 1991. "An Investigation of Child Sexual Abuse and Consequent Victimization: Some Implications of Telephone Surveys." Pp. 79–88 in *Abused and Battered: Social and Legal Responses to Family Violence,* edited by D. D. Knudsen and J. L. Miller. New York: Aldine De Gruyter.

Murphy, Shane M., Dean G. Kilpatrick, Angelynne Amick-McMullan, Lois J. Veronen, Janet Paduhovich, Connie L. Best, Lorenz A. Veilleponteaux, and Benjamin E. Saunders. 1988. "Current Psychological Functioning of Child Sexual Assault Survivors." *Journal of Interpersonal Violence* 3:55–79.

National Victim Center. 1992. *Rape in America.* Arlington, VA, 18 pp.

Parrot, Andrea. 1986. *Acquaintance Rape and Sexual Assault Prevention Training Manual.* Department of Human Services Studies. Ithaca, NY: Cornell University.

Peters, Stefanie D., Gail E. Wyatt, and David Finkelhor. 1986. "Prevalence." Pp. 15–59 in *Sourcebook on Child Sexual Abuse,* edited by D. Finkelhor. Beverly Hills, CA: Sage.

Rapaport, K., and B. R. Burkhart. 1984. "Personality and Attitudinal Characteristics of Sexually Coercive Males." *Journal of Abnormal Psychology* 93:216–221.

Rush, Florence. 1980. *The Best Kept Secret: Sexual Child Abuse of Children.* New York: McGraw-Hill.

_____. 1983. "Foreword." Pp. 13–14 in *I Never Told Anyone,* edited by E. Bass and L. Thornton. New York: Harper & Row.

Russell, Diana E. H. 1982. *Rape in Marriage.* New York: Collier Books.

_____. 1984. *Sexual Exploitation: Rape, Child Sexual Abuse, and Workplace Harassment.* Beverly Hills, CA: Sage.

_____. 1986. *The Secret Trauma: Incest in the Lives of Girls and Women.* New York: Basic Books.

Sanday, Peggy Reeves. 1990. *Fraternity Gang Rape: Sex, Brotherhood, and Privilege on Campus.* New York: New York University Press.

Sanders, William B. 1980. *Rape and Woman's Identity.* Beverly Hills, CA: Sage.

Schneider, Beth E. 1991. "Put Up and Shut Up: Workplace Sexual Assault." *Gender and Society* 5:533–548.

Schram, Donna D. 1978. "Rape." Pp. 53–80 in *The Victimization of Women,* edited by J. R. Chapman and M. Gates. Beverly Hills, CA: Sage.

Scully, Diana. 1988. "Convicted Rapists' Perceptions of Self and Victim: Role Taking and Emotions." *Gender and Society* 2:200–213.

Shields, Nancy M., and Christine R. Hanneke. 1983. "Battered Wives' Reactions to Marital Rape." Pp. 132–148 in *The Dark Side of Families: Current Family Violence Research,* edited by D. Finkelhor, R. J. Gelles, G. T. Hotaling, and M. A. Straus. Beverly Hills, CA: Sage.

Sheiner, Marcy. 1987. "Battered Women: Scenes from a Shelter." *Mother Jones* (November): Pp. 15–19, 43–44.

Skogan, Wesley G. 1976. "The Victims of Crime: Some National Survey Findings." In *Criminal Behavior in Social Systems,* edited by A. L. Guenther. Chicago: Rand-McNally.

Spencer, Cassie C. 1987. "Sexual Assault: The Second Victimization." Pp. 54–73 in *Women, Courts, and Equality,* edited by L. L. Crites and W. L. Hepperle. Newbury Park, CA: Sage.

Stanko, Elizabeth A. 1982. "Would You Believe This Woman? Prosecutorial Screening for 'Credible' Witnesses and a Problem of Justice." Pp. 63–82 in *Judge, Lawyer, Victim, Thief,* edited by N. H. Rafter and E. A. Stanko. Stoughton, MA: Northeastern University Press.

_____. 1985. *Intimate Intrusions: Women's Experience of Male Violence.* London: Routledge & Kegan Paul.

_____. 1992. "The Case of Fearful Women: Gender, Personal Safety and Fear of Crime." *Women and Criminal Justice* 4:117–135.

Tong, Rosemarie. 1984. *Women, Sex, and the Law.* Totowa, NJ: Rowman & Allanheld.

Warshaw, Robin. 1988. *I Never Called It Rape*. New York: Harper & Row.

Weiner, Robin D. 1983. "Shifting the Communication Burden: A Meaningful Consent Standard in Rape." *Harvard Women's Law Journal* 6:145–161.

Weis, K., and S. S. Borges. 1973. "Victimology and Rape: The Case of the Legitimate Victim." *Issues in Criminology* 8:71–115.

Williams, Kirk M. 1981. "Few Convictions in Rape Cases." *Journal of Criminal Justice* 9:29–40.

Wise, Sue, and Liz Stanley. 1987. *Georgie Porgie: Sexual Harassment in Everyday Life*. London: Pandora Press.

Wriggins, Jennifer. 1983. "Rape, Racism, and the Law." *Harvard Women's Law Journal* 6:103–141.

8

Battered Women

DEFINING BATTERING

Naming the phenomenon of males who assault their intimate female partners has been problematic. Defining it as *domestic violence* confuses the issue of separating child abuse, "elder" abuse,[1] and sibling abuse, from woman battering. Defining the phenomenon as *spouse abuse* hides the fact that women are the victims and men are the perpetrators approximately 95 percent of the time (Berk et al. 1983; see Browne 1987; Dobash et al. 1992). Defining this phenomenon as *wife abuse* or *wife battering* ignores the fact that many of the couples are dating or cohabiting, and are not married (even if we include common law marriages). Thus, the label *woman battering* is most appropriate to refer to the violence between heterosexual intimates.[2]

One force that keeps woman battering invisible is that the victims themselves are often reluctant to define themselves as victims or battered (Walker 1979). They may believe that since it happens "only" once or twice a year, they aren't really victims. As was stated in Chapter 6, once the woman has been abused, she knows that potential is always there, and the threat of violence frequently serves to guide her relationship from then on. Furthermore, research has found that battered women usually understate the degree of violence or injury they incur (Browne 1987, 15).

The tendency of battered women to minimize their victimization is further exacerbated by batterers' tendencies to minimize the frequency and seriousness of their violence. Studies of batterers found that batterers use *excuses* and *justifications* when confronted with their culpability (Dutton 1988; Ptacek 1988). Batterers use excuses in order to deny responsibility (Ptacek 1988). Excuses are related to situational characteristics of the assault (Dutton 1988). Batterers' excuses may include being drunk, being frustrated, or losing control. Justifications, on the other hand, are used to deny wrongness (Ptacek 1988) and tend to include characteristics about the victim (Dutton 1988). Justifications for battering include blaming the victim for "causing" the battering because she is a bad cook, is not sufficiently sexually responsive, is not deferential to the batterer, is not "faithful," and does not know when to "shut up" (Ptacek 1988). Clearly, none of these excuses and justifications legitimizes abuse. Notably, batterers are more likely to use justifications than excuses. That is, batterers are more likely to blame their victims for "making" them violent than they are to offer situations to explain their violence (Dutton 1988).

Four categories of battering have been developed (see Tong 1984, 125–126). It is not uncommon for more than one of these to occur within the same battering relationship. The first category is *physical battering,* which consists of slapping, hitting, burning, kicking, shooting, stabbing, or any other form of nonsexual physical violence. This is battering as it has been traditionally viewed. The second category, *sexual battering,* occurs when there is a sexual nature to the violence, such as beatings on the breasts or genitals, and oral, anal, or vaginal rape. Marital rape is discussed in more detail in Chapter 7.

The third category of battering, *psychological battering,* is often minimized but is potentially extremely harmful. Many battered women report psychological battering as the most damaging type of abuse. This exists where the offender threatens, demeans, and otherwise discredits the victim. The final category is *the destruction of pets and property.* It is not unusual for batterers to destroy the woman's property (anything from minor clothing to automobiles or even their houses) and abuse or kill animals belonging to the woman. Underlying the clear loss of a beloved animal or cherished property is the message that the victim and her/their children are also capable of being cruelly destroyed. One of the most disturbing aspects for the jury in listening to Francine Hughes's defense for killing her abusive husband (the famous "Burning Bed" case) was when her husband would not allow the pregnant family dog into the house during a cold snap in Michigan, and the dog and her puppies died (McNulty 1980).

There are three commonalities among the four categories of battering: They all result in harm to the victim, all are manifestations of domination and control, and all occur in an intimate relationship (Tong 1984, 126). Nonetheless, there is not complete agreement on what qualifies as battering. Researchers have suggested disagreement over such issues as to whether "only" psychological battering makes a woman battered. There is also disagreement as to whether a woman who is hit "only" once is battered. Some researchers' definitions of battering require a systematic occurrence where battering is an ongoing aspect of the relationship. In most cases, it appears that the violence and threat of violence *are* ongoing, and that the different categories of violence operate simultaneously within battering relationships. That is, it is not uncommon for a battered woman to be physically, sexually, and psychologically abused, as well as to experience destruction of property or pets.

HISTORY OF IDENTIFYING
BATTERING AS A SOCIAL PROBLEM

Chapter 6 stated that the nonsexual physical abuse of women was not identified as a social problem until the 1970s. However, attempts had been made prior to the 1970s to bring attention to the problem of battering. Physical abuse by men toward their wives not only has been recorded for hundreds of years, but often has been portrayed as acceptable, even expected, behavior (Martin 1976). Although there were a few laws criminalizing wife beating in the United States in the 1600s and 1700s, formal complaints numbered only one or two *per decade* (Pleck 1989). In 1776, Abigail Smith Adams wrote a letter to her husband, John Adams, requesting the freedom of women by restricting the power men held in marriages (Dobash and Dobash 1979, 4). This plea apparently was ignored.

During the struggle for women's suffrage during the latter part of the nineteenth century, liberal feminists Elizabeth Cady Stanton and Susan B. Anthony spent considerable time attempting to bring the plight of battered women into the public eye (Pleck 1983). However, their efforts were less effective than those of conservative feminists Lucy Stone and her husband, Henry Blackwell. Unlike Stanton and Anthony, Stone and Blackwell did not advocate divorce as a necessary solution; rather, they simply advocated suffrage and protective legislation. The second time that wife beating was addressed was as a part of the platform by British and U.S. suffragists during the beginning of this century (Dobash and Dobash 1979).

The most recent and successful movement questioning the violence against wives began in 1971 in a small English town (Dobash and Dobash 1979). A group of over 500 women and children and one cow marched to protest rising food costs and the reduction of free milk for children. Although the march was not deemed a success regarding the problems it set out to address, it was a success and a historical event in that it led to solidarity among the women marching. This solidarity resulted in a community gathering place for local women, the Chiswick's Women's Aid. During discussions at Chiswick's Women's Aid, women began revealing and discussing the systematic violence they had experienced from their husbands. Woman battering and its frequency, then, were accidentally discovered, changing the focus of Chiswick's Women's Aid to woman battering (Dobash and Dobash 1979).

Feminists in the United States followed the lead set out by British feminists. Public information on battering increased with Chiswick's Women's Aid founder, Erin Pizzey's, 1974 publication in England of *Scream Quietly or the Neighbors Will Hear,* and Del Martin's 1976 publication in the United States of *Battered Wives.* Since the mid-1970s, shelters for battered women have been established all over the United States, England, Canada, and many European and other countries. These early shelters were very basic, starting as grass-roots, community-based efforts by feminists. Often the shelters were individual women's homes, which they volunteered as sanctuaries for battered women. Such make-do shelters still operate in some rural communities. Thus, the first step in the current battered women's movement was the setting up of emergency shelters by women within each community. "Since 1975, the movement has made substantial headway in three areas, besides emergency shelter: legislation, government policy and programs, and research and public information" (Tierney 1983, 208). However, even today woman battering remains invisible to a large degree, and shelters are regularly underfunded and overpopulated, turning women and children away in large numbers.

Since the 1980s, literature has emerged portraying the widespread existence of what is labeled courtship violence. *Courtship violence* is sexual or other physical violence or threats of violence (emotional violence) that occur in dating relationships. A study that compared battering in premarital, marital, and ex-spousal relationships reported to the police found that unmarried couples resort to physical violence and use weapons somewhat more frequently than the other types of couples (Erez 1986). While the premarital relationships have a higher percentage of assaults than the other two categories, the marital, and particularly postmarital (ex-spousal), relationships have the most serious assaults and injuries (Erez 1986; Mahoney 1991). Studies on the rates of courtship violence suggest that between one-fifth and one-third of college students report experiencing nonsexual, physical courtship violence (Bogal-Allbritten and Allbritten 1985; Cate et al. 1982; Knutson and Mehm 1986; Lane and Gwartney-Gibbs 1985; Makepeace 1981, 1986; Matthews 1984; Stets and Pirog-Good 1987).

FREQUENCY OF BATTERING

Dobash and Dobash (1988, 69) claim that "25 percent of all violent crimes are wife assaults." Other researchers believe that as many as half of all women will be victims of battering by a husband or boyfriend (Mills and McNamar 1981; Walker 1979). Determining the prevalence of battering is difficult, as is evident from the range these statistics present. Problems inherent in determining the prevalence of battering are exemplified by researchers' frustrations in trying to find a control group of nonbattered women to compare with a group of battered women; they often find battered women in their "control group" (Browne 1987, 5). The degree and frequency of violence differ among relationships where battering occurs, but it usually begins early on in marriages (Dobash and Dobash 1979, 124), or even during the courtship stage (Dobash and Dobash 1979, 84; Erez 1986; Makepeace 1981).

One of the most often asked questions regarding battering is "What about men who are battered by women?" Some research views men and women as "mutually combative," or inflicting fairly equal amounts of violence on each other in intimate relationships (Steinmetz 1977/1978; Straus and Gelles 1986; Straus et al. 1980). The police receive calls where women have abused men, or where the battering occurs in lesbian or gay couples. However, regardless of whether data are collected via police reports or self-reported victim surveys, research has consistently shown that men tend to batter women in approximately 95 percent of the battering situations (Berk et al. 1983; see Browne 1987, 8; Dobash et al. 1992). Furthermore, women usually resort to violence out of self-defense, where the violence was initiated and escalated by the man (Saunders 1988; Schwartz 1987), and women are more likely to incur serious injury than men in battering incidents (Berk et al. 1983; Loving 1980; Oppenlander 1982; Stets and Straus 1990). Furthermore, the violence husbands direct at wives is not comparable to the violence wives direct at husbands: Battering damages women's self-esteem, whereas men's self-esteem often appears unaffected by violence from their wives (Mills 1984). Finally, men's greater economic resources decrease their need for shelters (Straus 1991).

Research stating that men and women are "mutually combative" (Steinmetz 1977/1978; Straus and Gelles 1986; Straus et al. 1980) has been disputed. Much of the criticism of these findings has centered around the *Conflict Tactic Scale* (CTS), which has been criticized by many as incomplete and inadequate to measure battering (Berk et al. 1983; Dobash and Dobash 1988; Kurz 1993; Schwartz 1987; Stark and Flitcraft 1983; Yllo 1988). Specifically, the CTS oversimplifies the complexities of battering, focusing solely on behaviors and ignoring consequences of the social contexts in which the behaviors occur and their meanings to the victim and the offender (Ferraro and Johnson 1983; Smith 1994). For example, the CTS fails to take into account the difference between a 250-pound man slamming a 100-pound woman into a wall and her shoving him back forcefully. Moreover, in a public opinion poll, respondents tended to blame women for battering whether they were the ones who hit or the ones who got hit (Greenblat 1983). Thus, researchers and nonresearchers alike have had a tendency to blame women as equally responsible, if not more so, for battering.

WALKER'S CYCLE THEORY OF VIOLENCE

Psychologist Lenore E. Walker (1979) is credited with developing the "cycle theory of violence," which describes the pattern of battering over time. She identified three phases in the continuous cycle of battering. Phase one is the *tension-building stage*. This is a sort of "calm before the storm." The victim feels that the pressure is mounting and that a violent explosion is inevitable. While "minor" battering incidents may occur during this time (for example, shaking or slapping), a major abusive assault is what she most fears. She may try to calm him down with something that worked in the past, such as cooking his favorite meal or keeping the children quiet.

Phase two of Walker's (1979) battering cycle is the *acute battering incident*. Phase two is when the major battering actually occurs, and is usually the briefest of the three phases in the cycle. If the police are notified at all (only 10 percent of Walker's sample had done so), it is usually during this phase. However, by the time the police arrive, the cycle has usually moved on to phase three.

Phase three is characterized by *kindness and contrite loving behavior* from the batterer. "He begs her forgiveness and promises her that he will never do it again" (Walker 1979, 65). Usually, both the man and the woman want to believe that this violence was some fluke, and that it will not occur again. It is easier for them to believe this when the battering first starts, as opposed to after years of battering. The batterer often appears very sincere in his apology and in his commitment to change. He may lavish the woman with gifts, quit drinking, or do other things to convince her that he really loves her and that the battering will never happen again. "It is during this phase that the woman gets a glimpse of her original dream of how wonderful love is.... The traditional notion that two people who love each other surmount overwhelming odds against them prevails" (Walker, 1979, 67–68). This phase is usually longer than phase two, but shorter than phase one. At the beginning of a battering relationship women are often confused, shocked, depressed, and in need of reassurance, making them vulnerable to the batterers' promises to stop the abuse (Browne 1987, 62–63).

As phase three ends, phase one begins again, and the cycle continues. Other researchers have noted that over time the violence tends to increase in frequency, severity, and injuries, and thus more formal social agency assistance becomes necessary (Dobash and Dobash 1979, 179). "Each successive violent episode leaves the woman with less hope, less self-esteem, and more fear" (Dobash and Dobash 1979, 140). In more recent research, Walker (1983a, 44) has found that the length of the three phases in battering relationships changes over time. As the battering relationship progresses, tension building (phase one) is longer and more evident, and loving and contrition (phase three) decline. Batterers are less likely to apologize for their violence over time, and more likely to blame the victims for "making" them violent (Dobash and Dobash 1979, 117–123). This implies that once the batterer has established his power over the victim, he feels less of a need to apologize to keep her. Thus, *hopefulness* (the belief that he may change) may be replaced with fear (that he will kill or severely harm her and/or her/their children if she leaves) as the motivation for staying in the relationship.[3]

WHY DO (SOME) MEN BATTER?

Many men do not batter women, regardless of how angry they may feel toward them. So why do some men batter? Most researchers focus on the family structure in attempts to explain battering. For instance, Goode (1971) stresses the importance of viewing the *family as a power system,* where power is unequally distributed. He points out that such characteristics as being male, being older, and having control over property, money, and gifts serve to enhance the power of the father/husband in the family system. Additionally, there are fewer restraints against aggression in the family than exist in other social settings, because fights between family members are viewed as more socially acceptable (Sebastian 1983). Furthermore, the dependency of some family members on others requires that they tolerate the abuse. This is particularly apparent regarding child abuse.

It is necessary to assess the battering of women and the family structure within a sociohistorical context. Gender disparities in the culture, the economy, and politically have an inherent impact on the family (Bograd 1988; Breines and Gordon 1983, 508; Dobash and Dobash 1979; Stark and Flitcraft 1983; Yllo 1983, 1988). Focusing on family inequality independent from the political context leads to an image of battered women dominated by rotten husbands. This removes the focus from such issues as inadequate governmental policies (such as welfare and child care) that encourage female subordination and patriarchal dependency (Stark and Flitcraft 1983, 336). Similarly, Bograd (1988, 14) claims: "The reality of domination at the social level is the most crucial factor contributing to and maintaining wife abuse at the personal level." The family cannot be analyzed independently from the social, political, and economic structure of a society. These outside forces serve to reinforce the power disparity and dependency of women in marriage.

Stereotypical gender differences discussed earlier in this book are related to the expectations by some that men should be aggressive and women passive; these expectations have an impact on woman battering. While aggression may have many aims, "one of the aggressor's objectives is the injury of the target" (Berkowitz 1983, 179). Men's violent and aggressive behavior is often viewed as "typical" and therefore goes unquestioned (Stanko 1985). Similarly, there is a tendency to view both *sexism* and *violence* as an inevitable part of culture (Klein 1981). Male violence, then, is more conforming than aberrant behavior (Bograd 1988, 17). Men are socialized to dominate women, and male aggression is not only encouraged, but often glorified. This can be seen in male sports such as football, hockey, and boxing, as well as in the media, with movies such as *True Lies, Lethal Weapon, Rambo,* and *Robocop.* Woman battering, then, has not occurred as an isolated event from the community, or against the general principles of acceptable behavior; rather, it is an institution in its own right (Dobash and Dobash 1981, 565). Not only is male violence in general often tolerated by the media and culture, but male violence directed against females, specifically, is frequently tolerated, and even glorified.

What benefits do batterers obtain? It is clear that violence or the threat of violence result in a strong sense of power and dominance for the batterer. Batterers may not always be conscious of their need to control, but violence may be a result of their discomfort when they feel the lack of control they have been socialized to believe they deserve (Schechter 1982, 219). Batterers may have a sense that their behavior is justified—their victims "needed" to be punished or "taught a lesson." Batterers often view their victims as their property or as children who need discipline. These men usually feel threatened by any indication of their victims' autonomy—even time these women spend with their families or other women friends. It is not unusual for batterers to inflict violence when the victims are pregnant, or when they feel jealous of attention the victims have given to their children. There is some belief that batterers act out of their own insecurities and become abusive to counteract feelings of powerlessness (Finkelhor 1983).

Goolkasian (1986) claims that there are two reasons why woman battering continues to exist. First, "violence is a highly effective means of control" (Goolkasian 1986, 2). Thus, men batter in order to gain and maintain control over women. Second, "men batter because they can; that is because in most cases no one has told batterers that they must stop" (Goolkasian 1986, 2). Although the victim and her/their children may make attempts to communicate to the batterer that his behavior is unacceptable, the batterer often gets messages from many others that he is the "king of his castle" and can treat "his woman" in whatever manner he pleases. These messages often come from the media, friends, family, and even the crime-processing system.

WHO ARE THE BATTERERS?

Who are the batterers? The stereotype of the unemployed, alcoholic, lower class abuser is not necessarily accurate. Batterers as well as battering victims come from a range of backgrounds and experiences. Research in the 1970s attempted to refute the myth that batterers were all mentally ill or had a psychological disorder (Gelles 1980, 876). Numerous researchers have pointed out that battering occurs in all socioeconomic and educational levels (Brisson 1981; Flynn 1977; Goolkasian 1986).

While a batterer may come from any background, the description of batterers by battered women suggests that batterers "all went to the same training school" (Walker 1983a). Although this study found no "victim-prone women" (or types of women who were likely to become battering victims), "violence-prone" personalities for men were identified, including adherence to traditional views of women, possessiveness, and abuse of alcohol (Walker 1983a). As stressed in Chapter 6, no nonviolent behavior, perceived or real on the part of the victim, justifies violent behavior from the batterer. However, it is still useful to examine how batterers perceive their own behavior. Researchers have found batterers strongly motivated by *jealousy* (Brisson 1981; Browne 1987; Dobash and Dobash 1979; Straus et al. 1980; Walker 1979, 1983a). This relates to the batterers' belief that their wives or girlfriends "belong" to them, and this "justifies" their violent behavior. Regarding alcohol abuse, most researchers agree that violence is not *caused* by substance abuse, but that such use and abuse may disinhibit violence. Most men who beat their wives when they are drunk also beat them when they are sober. One study on battering found that "alcohol use at the time of violence is far from a necessary or sufficient cause for wife abuse despite the stereotype that all drunks hit their wives or all wife hitting involves drunks" (Kantor and Straus 1987, 224).

One attitude about battering that is increasingly being disputed is that it is a result of *loss of control* on the part of the batterer. In fact, groups who have organized to try to help batterers end their violent behavior concentrate on teaching batterers that battering is a *choice,* and they may choose *not* to batter. Others have pointed out that battering is indeed controllable if we assess battering via the "targets" of the battering (where the offenders place their blows) and the locations in which battering occurs (whether the assault takes place in public or at home). For instance, a batterer may attempt to excuse his violence because he was angry at something his boss did that day. It is important to note, however, that the target of his violence was not his boss, but rather his wife or girlfriend. Thus, if it is a matter of simply losing control, how is it that he is able to control himself from hitting his boss, who provoked his anger? Also, batterers are often controlled enough to restrict their blows to places on the body that are least likely to be visible to other people, such as the stomach, breasts, and thighs.

Marital rape is also viewed as an effective "tool of control" by the batterer, because the damage is not visible, and the victim is likely to be too ashamed to report it, even to friends or family, and particularly to law enforcement officials. The fact that most batterers refrain from abusive behavior in public places also indicates a degree of control on the batterer's part in determining his own violent behavior.

> It seems reasonable to conclude that the men know their behavior is inappropriate, because they keep battering such a private affair. According to reports from the battered women, only the batterers can end the second phase. The woman's only option is to find a safe place to hide. Why he stops is also unclear. He may simply have become exhausted and emotionally depleted. It is not uncommon for the batterer to wake the woman out of a deep sleep to begin his assault. If she answers his verbal harangue, he becomes angrier with what she says. If she remains quiet, her withdrawal enrages him. She gets the beating no matter what her response is.
>
> *(Walker, 1979:61-62)*

A number of researchers have focused on a hypothesized *intergenerational transmission of violence,* in an attempt to explain why men batter (Dutton and Painter 1981; Fagan et al. 1983). This theory contends that children who witness violence learn that violence is an acceptable way to resolve conflict (Dutton and Painter 1981, 142). The intergenerational transmission of violence theory, then, views battering as a learned behavior that is passed down from one generation to another within the family system. In applying this theory, it is important to acknowledge that the experiential learning is likely to be different for males and females. While both males and females may learn that physical conflict is a legitimate response to family or interpersonal conflict, males may learn to be the oppressors, whereas females learn to be the victims. One study found that adult male survivors of child abuse by their parents, or adult males who had watched their fathers abuse their mothers, were more likely than adult males from nonabusive homes to view violence as an adequate response to family conflict and to abuse their own wives or girlfriends later in life (Fagan et al. 1983).

However, the theory of intergenerational transmission of violence has received criticism, too. For instance, it is possible that living in a violent home may result in an adult survivors' strong commitment to disallow violence in her or his own home. Adult survivors of homes where woman battering occurred may not all behave uniformly. Although witnessing parental violence increases the likelihood of a boy growing up to be a batterer, "the majority of wife assaulters have never witnessed parental violence" (Dutton 1988, 47). The studies testing the intergenerational transmission of violence have been accused of committing "clinical fallacy," by only examining adult batterers and failing to include the effects of childhood violence on nonviolent adults (Breines and Gordon 1983). An exception to this is a study that found that persons (male and female) raised in homes with "spousal violence" were at risk of being *victims,* not offenders, of battering as adults; and "*vulnerability* to aggression was transmitted more than the learned role of perpetrator" (Cappell and Heiner 1990, 135). In conclusion, while there are likely some implications for condoning violence if one grows up with it, overall the impact on later violent behavior is unclear.

INHIBITORS TO LEAVING
A VIOLENT RELATIONSHIP

Much of the writing on battering, and even responses by the public as well as by the crime-processing system, have focused on asking why a woman stays in a battering relationship. This response tends to be *victim blaming* in that it implies she would leave if she really didn't like to be battered. Battering is a complex phenomenon, and it is important to understand why some women stay in or return to battering relationships.

First, we must ask why the focus is on "Why does she stay?" rather than on "Why does he batter?" Focusing on why battered women stay has resulted in the labeling of such women as "deviant" (Loseke and Cahill 1984). Perhaps it would be more fruitful to ask questions such as "Why are men violent?" "Why are women so easily victimized?" "Why are violent men allowed to stay?" and "Why should the victims rather than the assailants be expected to leave?" (Hoff 1990).

Second, it is rarely acknowledged that many women do leave battering relationships. There is a tendency to hear only about women who stay in battering relationships. Many women have left battering relationships, even after the first violent episode. However, shame and the tendency of others to discount their victimizations keep these survivors from identifying themselves as ex-battered women. In fact, 70 percent of 251 battered women who had contacted a counseling unit associated with the county attorney's office decided to leave their abusive partners (Strube and Barbour 1984). Nonetheless, many women do stay for a period of time or indefinitely. Thus, it is important to understand the numerous obstacles these women face.

Third, some women stay in battering relationships because they face overwhelming restrictions in their attempts to leave. The previous section discussed the importance of looking at aggregate political and social realities that maintain men's power over women, particularly within the institutions of marriage and the family. Economic and psychological factors also help to explain why women stay. Forces restricting women's autonomy, then, function at aggregate levels in the political and social structure, as well as at individual economic and psychological levels.

Economic Restrictions

Frequently, it is simply not economically feasible for a woman to leave the man who batters her. This is particularly problematic for women who have children. It is not uncommon for a battering man to control all of the money they both earn, and to place the woman on a miniscule allowance for which she must justify all spending. Furthermore, many women do not possess the skills or education necessary to support themselves and their children. Research has shown that unemployed women are less likely to leave the battering relationship than employed women (Gelles 1976; Strube and Barbour 1984). Some experts believe that battered women not only need access to shelters and adequate police and court protection, but also need to be able to obtain skills and financial resources in order to be free of the batterers (Tong 1984).

Many batterers are so jealous and possessive that they do not want their wives or girlfriends to work outside of the home, for fear that they will start having affairs. However, even batterers who confine their victims to the home frequently accuse the victims of having extramarital affairs.

Sociological Restrictions

Women are confined to battering relationships in a number of cultural ways. First, people seem to have a need to believe that battering isn't happening, or if it is happening, that the victims deserve it. (This parallels Lerner's "just world" hypothesis discussed in Chapter 6.) Second, attitudes about marriage negatively affect a woman's ability to leave a battering relationship. Battered women frequently claim that their relatives, neighbors, and friends deny the battering, and if confronted with it, imply to the victim that she is somehow responsible, and that she must work harder on her marriage. This is also true of many women who turn to religious guidance, such as priests, ministers, or rabbis. To some clergy, marriage is viewed as sacred, to be held together at all costs, however dangerous doing so may be to women and children. The children not only witness their mother's victimization (a form of emotional child abuse), but may be physically abused themselves (Bowker et al. 1988; Jaffe et al. 1986; Jaffe et al. 1990; Walker 1989).

Battered women frequently report a feeling of "no escape." They may have exhausted every resource in order to leave a battering relationship. Many battering survivors have discussed attempts to gain help from their own relatives, the batterer's relatives, the police, and the courts (such as through divorces or restraining orders). Batterers continue to threaten and violate many of these victims, and sometimes their children. One study of battered women reported:

> Almost all [of the battered women] have sought help from a variety of sources. Most have, at some time, called the police for physical protection. Over two-thirds had received counseling from marriage counselors or clergy at some point. Few women, however, reported that their husbands were willing to cooperate with counseling. Over one-half had consulted with attorneys and almost half turned to divorce for resolution of the problem. However, divorce was not always found to be the successful resolution, as occasionally the assaulter continued to seek out his former wife to assault her or assaults occurred at the time of visitation with the children.
>
> *(Flynn 1977, 18)*

In fact, some studies have shown that batterers' violence often escalates when the victims attempt to leave the abusive relationship (Mahoney 1991). Instead of asking "Why do (some) battered women stay?" perhaps we should be asking: "What happened to you when you left? What support did you get?" (Mahoney 1991).

Psychological Restrictions

Many psychologists have suggested various explanations for staying in a battering relationship. The victims themselves sometimes describe the psychological effects of abuse and exploitation as "brainwashing" (Finkelhor 1983, 20). Efforts to determine which women are "victim-prone"—or likely to become battered women—not only are victim blaming, but have proven to be fruitless. Researchers have been unable to establish what types of women are battered (Walker 1983a). This implies that *any* woman could become a battered woman—a frightening thought and counter to those who want to believe a "just world" exists.

Walker (1979) uses the social learning theory called *learned helplessness* to explain the battered woman's behavior. She bases this on (ethically questionable) studies of animals where all options of escape are closed off. The animals in these tests experience uncontrollable pain or harm on a random, unpredictable basis. Learned helplessness is characterized by persons (or animals) who have learned through repeated failure that they cannot control their destiny. Because they have no control over their environments, there is no point in trying. Therefore, even when faced with what outsiders may view as viable escapes, the person or animal with learned helplessness cannot identify these alternatives as escapes. In a later study, Walker (1983a) claimed that this learned helplessness may occur early or later in life. For instance, it may be a result of women growing up in a violent family and viewing battering as a coping strategy for family conflict. Or, learned helplessness may occur later in life within the confines of a battering relationship. "Thus, learned helplessness has equal potential to develop at either time in the battered woman's life" (Walker 1983a, 35).

Walker's (1979, 1983a) learned helplessness theory has been criticized by some feminists (Dobash and Dobash 1988; Gondolf and Fisher 1988; Wardell et al. 1983). These critics believe that the learned helplessness approach suggests too strongly that battered women have wrongly assumed they cannot leave a battering relationship. The battered woman's recognition of a lack of alternatives is often rational, not simply a poor self-image, after she has sought help repeatedly from friends, family, the police, and the courts and is still in a threatening position (Wardell et al. 1983). Social learning theory focuses on battered women overlooking some of the alternatives available to them. Even if such such alternatives exists (1) people under conditions of high anxiety or terror may not see them; and (2) people often make decisions that appear illogical to others, such as keeping their houses although their neighbors have been burglarized twice, or getting a Ph.D. when universities are not hiring (Wardell et al. 1983).

The theory of learned helplessness diverts attention from the abuse to the victim, by labeling her response as "unreasonable" (Wardell et al. 1983, 76). The focus is on what the *victim* is doing wrong, rather than on the batterer's behavior and the woman's lack of alternatives. For these reasons, it has been suggested (tongue-in-cheek) that the police and judges who do nothing to help battered women may be the ones with learned helplessness (Gondolf and Fisher 1988).

Another psychological theory used to explain deterrents to women leaving battering relationships is that of *traumatic bonding*. Dutton and Painter (1981, 146–147) define this as "the development and course of strong emotional ties between two persons where one person intermittently harasses, beats, threatens, abuses or intimidates the other." This approach has been used to explain why hostage victims, children abused by their parents, or members of malevolent cults frequently bond with their aggressors. If viewed within this context, the relationship between battered women and their abusers may not be an isolated phenomenon, but rather is an example of traumatic bonding (Dutton and Painter 1981, 146). The two common features of the various forms of traumatic bonding are (1) power imbalance and (2) intermittent abuse. It is not uncommon for the power imbalance to grow as a relationship becomes increasingly violent: The violent person feels more powerful and the victim less powerful as the violence progresses. The intermittent nature of the abuse may be exemplified in battering if we examine Walker's cycle, where violence is intermittently dispersed among expressions of sorrow, love, and affection (Dutton and Painter 1981, 150).

Closely related to the traumatic bonding approach, the *Stockholm syndrome* has been used as an explanation of battered women's reluctance to leave violent relationships: "In particular, when threatened with death by a captor who is also kind in some ways, hostages develop a fondness for the captor and an antipathy toward authorities working for their release. The captor may also develop a fondness for the hostages" (Graham et al. 1988, 218). The Stockholm syndrome was developed to describe the behavior of hostages, specifically bank robbery kidnap victims. This behavior includes bonding with one's captor (or abuser), often to the degree of wanting to protect the captor or abuser from punishment. The Stockholm syndrome is seen as a survival strategy. Indeed, hostages who develop it are more likely to survive captivity. It is hypothesized that four conditions allow the Stockholm syndrome to develop (Graham et al. 1988, 218–219):

1. A person threatens to kill another and is perceived as having the capability to do so.

2. The other cannot escape, so her or his life depends on the threatening person.

3. The threatened person is isolated from outsiders so that the only other perspective available to her or him is that of the threatening person.

4. The threatening person is perceived as showing some degree of kindness to the one being threatened.

Others claim that the experts on battered women have created a new problem in labeling battered women who stay as *deviant*: "It is typically marital stability, 'staying,' which is normatively expected and marital instability, 'leaving,' which requires an account. However, as far as the experts on battered women are concerned, once wife assault occurs, it is marital stability which requires explanation" (Loseke and Cahill 1984, 297). Battering relationships, then, are not unlike nonbattering relationships in that marital stability is often accorded higher priority than marital quality. Men and women in long-term but low-quality relationships (low quality in other ways than violence) often stay together because an attachment exists, and they believe their mate is truly the only one for them (Loseke and Cahill 1984). Given this attitude, battered women who stay are not so unusual; rather, they are typical.

Scholarly publications often focus on the battered woman as inadequate and somehow deserving of her abuse, because this "supports the conclusion that wife battering can be managed by offering social and psychological services to the victim, rather than through law enforcement efforts or socioeconomic changes in the status of women" (Morash 1986, 258). However, in tracing the various theoretical and historical perspectives on what causes battering, it is clear that confronting battering must occur in many contexts. These include adequate divorce laws, services available to battered women and their children to help them leave and start over again, adequate legislation, and appropriate responses by the crime-processing system. Additionally, similar to the contention in Chapter 7 that sexual victimization and gender inequality reinforce each other, battering and gender inequality do so as well. As men and women become more equal, we should expect women to have more economic, psychological, and societal resources to leave battering relationships.

The Process of Victimization

In an interesting study of over 100 battered women in a shelter, Ferraro and Johnson (1983) identified six *rationalizations* battered women use to explain to themselves why they stay in violent relationships:

1. *Appeal to the salvation of an ethic:* The woman overidentifies with a nurturing gender role and wants to "save" the batterer from some internal problem (for example, chemical dependency).

2. *Denial of the victimizer:* Battering is viewed as a result of some force external to the relationship (for example, his job stress).

3. *Denial of injury:* Battering pain is viewed as normal or tolerable, and the woman focuses on everyday rituals (such as work and child care) to ignore the memory of the abuse.

4. *Denial of victimization:* The woman doesn't believe the violence against her was justified, but she blames herself for not avoiding it by being more conciliatory or passive.

5. *Denial of options:* Practical options (such as alternative housing or economic independence) and emotional options (such as outside supportive relationships) exist, but the woman doesn't believe that she can make it on her own (the abuser often ingrains this in her).

6. *Appeal to higher loyalties:* The woman endures the violence because of a religious or traditional commitment (such as a belief that divorce is wrong or children should live with both their mothers *and* fathers).

These categories are not mutually exclusive; a battered woman could adhere to one or more of the rationalizations at the same time. To leave a battering relationship, the woman must reject these rationalizations and view herself as a victim of abuse.

Ferraro and Johnson (1983) further identified *six catalysts* that help battered women redefine their experiences and view themselves as victims:

1. *An increase in the level of violence:* They realize the abuse is serious and may be fatal.

2. *A change in resources:* They find employment, housing, or a shelter.

3. *A change in the relationship:* Walker's (1979) loving and remorseful phase no longer occurs, and they see no positive aspects of the relationship.

4. *Despair:* They lose hope that things could ever improve.

5. *A change in the visibility of the violence:* The violence is more apparent to family, friends, or even strangers.

6. *External definitions of the relationship:* Friends, relatives, police officers, or others condemn the violence and tell her she is a victim.

These six catalysts not only help battered women redefine their experiences and relationships with batterers, but also motivate women to leave the relationships. These catalysts—especially numbers 2 and 6—also emphasize the importance of shelters for battered women.

In summary, the dynamics behind why men batter and the limitations women face in attempting to escape violent relationships are complex. We cannot just use economic explanations, nor can we simply settle on sociological or psychological explanations; rather, a variety of factors must be considered.

THE CONSTANT THREAT OF DANGER

All of the inhibitors (economic, sociological, and psychological) addressed in the preceding section are influenced by a constant threat of danger once the violence has begun. If the batterer threatens to assault or actually does assault the victim, they both become aware of his potential to harm her. One study found that almost all battered women report a fear that their batterers may completely "lose control" and kill them during a beating (Star et al. 1979). Even if none of the other negative conditions, such as those suggested earlier (economic, sociological, and psychological), exists for the victim, *the danger is still present.* For instance, if a woman is beaten up by her husband and decides to leave him, she may feel assured in doing this on many levels—she may hold a good job, his family and her family and friends may support her leaving him, and she may not have fallen victim to some of the psychological syndromes previously addressed. Even if her parents and friends do not support her break-up with him, she may have access to a battered women's shelter. *However, he may still pose a powerful threat of danger.* He may tell her he will kill her, her/their children, and/or her parents if she does not return to him. She has learned he is capable of violence, and she likely has reason to believe he may follow through on his threats. Even if she is not completely convinced he will carry out his threats, the risk of destruction to loved ones is logically perceived as too great to gamble.

If she is staying in a shelter or hotel, or hiding out with friends or relatives, she may have to quit her job, since he could locate her at work. It is not unusual for women who have left batterers to have the batterers show up at their places of employment or trace their new residences through friends, family, coworkers, or private detectives. When the victim is staying with her family to escape from the batterer, he often will use sufficient threats and pressure that one or more members of her own family might begin to advise the victim to "work it out" with him. Although a victim may have received a restraining order from the court, not allowing the husband on her property, he may still have rights to child visitation, so avoiding him is almost impossible (McCann 1985; Walker 1989). Many battered women survivors have had to move to a new city or state and change their names in order to be free of the violence. Clearly, such women often lose their family and friends, in addition to their possessions, which is often some batterers' goal.

Evidence shows that batterers' promises to kill their victims are not merely idle threats—some batterers *do* eventually kill the women they have battered. In fact, much of the worst violence battered women experience occurs *after* they have separated from or divorced their husbands (Mahoney 1991). This may be most dangerous for unmarried battered women, whose rates of being murdered by their batterers increased from 1976 to 1987 (Browne and Williams 1993).

WOMAN BATTERING AND
THE CRIME-PROCESSING SYSTEM

A historical account of community-wide and crime-processing system responses to the battering of women leads one to believe that men were more likely to be punished for *not* dominating their wives than for beating them. A portrayal of community regulations of domestic authority since the fifteenth century states:

> Men could be subjected to ritualized rebukes if they were thought to be doing "women's work," were "henpecked," cuckolded, or believed to have been beaten by their wives—that is, when there was a perceived inversion of patriarchal authority and domination.... In addition to being ridiculed by the community for failing to maintain authority, men thought to have domineering or wayward wives were supported in their attempts to regain or retain dominance by ridiculing and shaming the woman publicly and/or by punishing her physically.
>
> (Dobash and Dobash 1981, 566)

Thus, it was not acceptable for men and women to have any semblance of an equal relationship, and certainly not one where women exhibited any sense of power. Woman battering was viewed as acceptable behavior, particularly in cases where women "needed" to be disciplined (by men) in order to understand their "rightful" place.

To challenge the accepted public beliefs and laws regarding battered women, we must challenge the contention that wives (women) belong to husbands (men). It was not until the latter half of the nineteenth century that such challenges began to appear in the legal code.

The Police

The police are usually the first, and often the only, contact battering victims and offenders face. Most research in the area of battering has criticized the police for their failure to respond adequately to battered women's calls for help. These calls are often viewed as frustrating and unimportant to police officers. Because most persons who aspire to become police officers do so with the idea that they are going to "fight crime," the aspects of their job that are viewed as more mundane, or "peace keeping," are often resented. Most assaults are viewed as a crime by the police; historically, however, woman battering has not been defined as *criminal* in the context of policing, but rather is viewed as a "mild disturbance." Ironically, the police simultaneously perceive these as the most dangerous calls for them.

A recent analysis of FBI statistics showed that estimates of police deaths during "domestic disturbances" were inflated by about 200 percent (Garner and Clemmer 1986). This study laid to rest the belief that domestic violence calls were the most dangerous calls to which police respond. The error in prior studies was the manner in which "domestic disturbances" were operationalized. In addition to "family violence," domestic disturbance calls also included "bar fights, gang calls, general disturbances…, and incidents where a citizen is brandishing a firearm" (Garner and Clemmer 1986, 2). In fact, if more accurate measures are used, analysis shows that between 1973 and 1984, more officers were killed accidentally as a result of their own or other police officers' actions (sixty-five officers) than were killed in "domestic disturbances" (fifty-six officers) (Garner and Clemmer 1986).

Before the 1960s, police training in domestic violence was rare, and few departments had policies on how the police should respond to these calls. In the 1960s, *mediation* training and policies were implemented in many departments. Mediation policies and training encouraged police officers to treat woman battering as merely a breech of the public peace and to calm the parties down. However, a mediation response communicates to everyone involved—the victim, the offender, the children, witnesses, and the police—that a serious crime has not occurred. The batterer's violence goes unpunished, and in some respects is actually sanctioned by the police department, since they know what has occurred and still fail to restrict or punish the offender.

The problem with law enforcement tends to start even prior to the police officers' arrival on the scene. Police dispatchers often downplay woman-battering calls, even when the assault is reported as "in progress" (Oppenlander 1982). When dispatchers describe the call as an "assault" rather than a "disturbance," officers' response is more immediate because the call is seen as a potential arrest (Stanko 1985, 108–109). Moreover, the implementation of the 911 number and computer-aided dispatching has increased the likelihood that calls are screened out and that the individual needs of victims are ignored (Manning 1992). Officers often justify slower response times to woman battering cases because of their own personal (not departmental) policies and hope that the offender will have left and/or the dispute will be resolved by the time they arrive (Oppenlander 1982).

The *potential* for danger in responding to battering is uncontested. First, the police are responding to a man who has already proven he is capable of violence. Second, the offender also probably believes that nobody, including the police, has any right to tell him how to treat his wife or girlfriend. Most batterers resent anyone telling them what do do or coming to their victims' aid. Clearly, these are potentially explosive situations. Given that responding to violent calls is part of the job, police training needs to address the importance of responding to *all* calls, including battering, in a professional and effective manner.

Evidence that mediation does not deter battering is apparent from the vast amount of calls police get to return to relationships where there is a history of battering. Furthermore, research suggests that mediation is not even a temporary solution. One study found that "[e]ven when the patrol officer leaves the scene of conflict, nearly a fourth of the domestic assault victims remain in a state of distress" (Oppenlander 1982, 455). At the same time, National Crime Survey data analysis reports that 37 percent of the battered women who call the police do so to prevent an incident from happening (Langan and Innes 1986). Also disturbing are research findings that the police tend to focus most concern on the offender, rather than to adapt to the needs of the victim (Oppenlander 1982). In short, police response to woman battering, unlike other assaults, has traditionally included a formal or informal policy of arrest avoidance (Dobash and Dobash 1979; Erez 1986; Finesmith 1983; Gondolf and Fisher 1988; Hanmer et al. 1989; Oppenlander 1982; Rowe 1985; Schechter 1982; Stanko 1985; Tong 1984; Zorza 1992).

In addition to police officers frequently failing to arrest batterers, other options they make available to battered women often have been frustrating and ineffective. For instance, police officers are known to encourage battered women to obtain a peace bond or restraining order, although these same police officers "rarely devote time or energy to enforcing them" (Tong 1984, 135). *Restraining orders* were developed in order to reduce battering and to provide a remedy in addition to prosecution (Grau et al. 1985, 15). However, there are numerous limitations with the current structure of most restraining orders. Acquiring restraining orders normally places the burden on the victim. This is unrealistic in many battering situations in which a batterer leaves his victim with no access to transportation, and the fear of getting "caught" trying to acquire the order overrides the desire to obtain it.

Temporary restraining orders (TROs) have been found to be more useful to fiscally independent women in less severe battering relationships, but have not proven useful in more violent relationships with long histories of abuse (Chaudhuri and Daly 1992; Grau et al. 1985). (TROs are court orders limiting a batterer's or stalker's access to any place that can be defined as the woman's "sphere of activity" [Ferraro 1993, 173].) Although battered women's acquisitions of TROs may increase police responsiveness and empower women with more emotional and financial independence to leave abusive relationships, some women are at increased risk of violence by the batterer for retaliation for acquiring the TRO (Chaudhuri and Daly 1992).

Four factors helped to change the traditional police response of nonintervention in woman-battering calls. First, it was clear that mediation was as ineffective as nonintervention (Finesmith 1983; Gee 1983; Rowe 1985; Stanko 1985; Tong 1984). Second, the feminist movement was gaining momentum and organizing around male violence against women, including the implementation of the first battered women's shelters and rape crisis centers. This was related to the third factor—court cases aimed at police departments.

Battered women, often in class action suits, began taking police departments to court for failing to arrest their batterers and leaving them in dangerous and life-threatening situations (see Eppler 1986). The battered women were successful in the court outcomes, using the Fourteenth Amendment to contend that they were not treated equally by the police as persons assaulted by strangers. Probably the most famous of these is the 1984 *Thurman* v. *City of Torrington* case, where Tracey Thurman's repeated calls to the police and the restraining order she obtained were ineffective in acquiring police protection. During Thurman's final battering, the police not only delayed in responding to the call, but watched for some time as her batterer severely assaulted her. Thurman suffered severe and permanent physical damage.

The fourth and final factor influencing police policy changes in response to woman battering was research finding that arresting batterers "works." Sherman and Berk (1984) conducted the first of these studies in Minneapolis, Minnesota, where offenders were randomly assigned to three options: (1) arrest, (2) mediation, or (3) an order that the offender leave the premises. This research found that arrested batterers were the least likely to recidivate, and stated that "an arrest should be made unless there are good, clear reasons why an arrest would be counterproductive" (Sherman and Berk 1984, 270).

Sherman and Berk's (1984) "Minneapolis experiment" was replicated, and their findings were confirmed throughout the 1980s (Berk and Newton 1985; Jaffe et al. 1986). These four factors (mediation's ineffectiveness, feminists organizing against male violence, battered women's successful lawsuits against police departments, and research findings that arrest deters batterers) resulted in the adoption of pro-arrest (presumptive or mandatory arrest) policies in most large U.S. cities.

However, since the 1990s, a number of replications of the "Minneapolis experiment" (including ones conducted by the original researchers, Sherman and Berk) have found no differences in repeat violence by batterers who were and were not arrested (see Dunford 1992; Dunford et al. 1990; Hirschel and Hutchison 1992; Hirschel et al. 1991; Sherman 1992). There is a current effort, seemingly led by Sherman, to withdraw the pro-arrest policies, given the more recent studies on their perceived ineffectiveness. This repeal effort is troubling to feminists for many reasons.

First, just because arresting batterers may not stop their battering does not in and of itself justify not arresting them. When many robbers keep robbing after being arrested, we don't throw our hands in the air and say, "Oh we might as well not bother arresting them!" (robbery analogy made by Zorza [1992]). Second, arresting batterers gives battered women and their children an opportunity to escape, if the batterers spend at least a few hours being processed and in jail. Given this assumption, it is not surprising that an Oregon study found that the implementation of a state pro-arrest policy resulted in a significant decrease in the number of domestic homicides, women or men killing their spouses (Jolin 1983). This study points out two important issues: (1) There is more than one way to measure the effectiveness of arrest, and (2) not only might pro-arrest policies save battered women's lives, but these policies are also likely to reduce the number of women forced into a situation where they kill their batterers in self-defense. (Interestingly, Jolin's research has received no attention by the same police scholars who are currently involved in evaluating pro-arrest policies.) A fourth area of concern is that research evaluating pro-arrest policies has found that police often fail to comply with the policy; officers still tend *not* to arrest batterers even in jurisdictions with pro-arrest policies (Balos and Trotzky 1988; Ferraro 1989; Lawrenz et al. 1988).

This does not mean that all feminists blindly support pro-arrest policies. There is concern that these policies are implemented discriminately—that batterers of color and from less wealthy neighborhoods are more likely to be arrested than their wealthier, Anglo counterparts (Edwards 1989; Hoff 1990; Miller 1989; Stanko 1989). A second feminist concern with the pro-arrest policies is that they take decision making completely away from the victim, who may already feel powerless (Hoff 1990; Rowe 1985; Stanko 1989). There is also evidence that the police arrest some *victims* who resist or fight back their batterers (Stanko 1989). While some feminists are also concerned that arresting batterers may increase violence toward the victim, there is too little research to verify this.

These feminist criticisms of pro-arrest policies do not necessarily mandate a withdrawal of the policies. Rather, they suggest that the policies need to be implemented fairly and that officers who fail to do so should be punished. Moreover, the crime-processing system should not avoid arresting batterers because of their potential to become more violent. Instead, police departments and the remainder of the crime-processing system must become more responsible for protecting battered women and their children. Unfortunately, the current efforts to repeal the pro-arrest policies have diverted attention from other important responses to woman battering, such as police use of referrals for victims, batterers, and their children; shelter funding and availability; and medical professionals' and court officials' responses to woman battering.

The Courts

The police are not the only actors in the crime-processing system who often fail to respond to the plight of battered women. A study in Minnesota and Illinois found that arrested batterers are convicted of felonies less than 10 percent of the time (Blodgett 1987, 68). Furthermore, Barbara Hart, founder of the National Coalition Against Domestic Violence, stated, "Judges don't usually do anything the first time a man violates an order of protection" (quoted in Blodgett 1987).

The courts' condoning of woman battering is not a recent phenomenon. In fact, court responses have improved, although a great deal of change is still necessary to protect battered women adequately. Early British Common Law established the "rule of thumb," a ruling that allowed husbands to beat their wives with rods no larger than the thickness of their thumbs. In 1824, the Mississippi Supreme Court upheld this ruling. "Progress" was made in 1864 with North Carolina's "curtain rule": The law could interfere with a husband's chastisement of his wife (go beyond the curtain of the home), but only where the husband's violence resulted in permanent injury to the wife (Tong 1984, 128). Thus, courts have historically defined some forms of wife abuse as legal.

With the implementation of pro-arrest policies, there has been a large increase in the number of battering cases that reach the court system (Goolkasian 1986, 3). While battered women vary in what they want from prosecution, they have in common the experience of facing "significant barriers to safe and effective participation as victim-witnesses in the criminal justice process" (Hart 1993, 625). Battered women frequently feel frustrated when they have made it to court, but the judge decides to take no action, to dismiss the case, or to acquit the batterer. This lets victims know that one more source of help has failed them. It is important to note that police officers also complain of the courts' failure to act. Understandably, police often wonder why they should bother trying to help the victim and make an arrest if the judge isn't going to sentence the batterer. Similarly, some battered women's shelter workers have ambivalent feelings about encouraging victims to take the batterers to court, knowing the likelihood that nothing will be accomplished. Unfortunately, the courts, as well as the police, have tended to favor mediation as an appropriate response to battering (see Goolkasian 1986).

A particularly vulnerable time for women who have decided to press charges and follow through is the pretrial period. During this time, it is not unusual for the batterer to attempt to "woo" his estranged victim back, by promising they can start over and that he won't be violent anymore. If this doesn't work, he is likely to try to intimidate her with threats of what he will do to her or to her loved ones if she goes to court. One study found that many women who went in to drop battering charges were escorted by their batterers, and *fear* was the major reason battered women gave for dropping charges against batterers (Quarm and Schwartz 1985).

To address the lack of response to woman battering, many scholars and activists have pushed for a more community-oriented and comprehensive approach to handling this violence. Currently, the police, courts, and corrections often have conflicting goals. The police are often frustrated by judges' dismissal of the often dangerous cases they diligently pursued. Judges sometimes fail to grant TROs in an effort to protect *batterers'* rights, and even when they are granted they're often not enforced (McCann 1985). Therefore, there is a need to coordinate the police, judiciary, and social services in order to respond effectively to woman battering (Gamache et al. 1988). Battered women who prosecute "frequently report that criminal justice system personnel appear to consider them 'unworthy victims' who are clogging up the courts with unimportant family matters" (Hart 1993, 626). There is evidence that battered women are more likely to testify when they have support from and access to community referrals and advocates assigned to their cases (Goolkasian 1986). In fact, social workers can serve as effective conduits of information between the police, the prosecutor, and the victim, as well as help establish trust between the victim and the crime-processing personnel (Martin 1988; Mullarkey 1988).

Just as police officers tend to focus on the offenders, judges also tend to "side" with batterers (Crites 1987). This is likely due to the judges' own sexist attitudes regarding a man's right to privacy, the desirability of keeping families intact, and even the husbands' justifications and excuses for abuse. Battered women and their advocates hold realistic concerns that pursuing charges against batterers may result in repeated and even escalated violence. Moreover, an acquittal by the court likely empowers batterers to continue the abuse (Crites 1987). In fact, battered women appear to be at an elevated risk for retaliatory violence compared to other victim-witnesses who prosecute (Hart 1993).

Evaluation of the *battered women's syndrome* (BWS) as a defense for women who kill their batterers is a current focus of the crime-processing system. Before defining BWS, it is important to address the dynamics behind women killing their batterers.

> In some cases, the batterer may eventually become a victim of his own violence, particularly if the woman uses force to defend herself or others from his attacks. There are homes where the violence reaches lethal levels and it is difficult to predict who might ultimately die, although statistics suggest the victim will most likely be the woman.
>
> *(Walker 1983b, 102)*

Men are more likely to kill battered women than women are to kill their batterers, even in self-defense (Browne and Williams 1993). Ironically, it has been noted that the same court system and judges who have refused to take the victims of battering seriously, "appear to exercise little leniency toward women who kill their husbands in self-defense or after years of abuse" (Crites 1987, 45). Women who are released from charges of killing their batterers have typically had to plead insanity or temporary insanity; however, the insanity plea is problematic. First, the insanity plea could result in a stigma almost as harsh as criminality (Marcus 1981, 1711). Second, the insanity plea is problematic in that most evidence shows these women were acting sanely, using the only means they had left to get themselves, and possibly their children, out of a lethal situation. Thus, the insanity plea negates the fact that women frequently have no other alternative but to kill their batterers.

> In other words, the battered woman is a victim of battering and of the criminal justice system's seeming lack of responsibility in responding to and prosecuting wife abusers. In case after case, documentation exists which consistently shows that police were called more than one time (generally an average of ten times) to intervene in a domestic violence dispute. Documentation exists which graphically depicts the woman who is battered over a period of years and when she reaches out for help from friends, family, social service agencies and the police, the stance taken by those outsiders is one of nonintervention.
>
> *(Kuhl 1985, 202)*

Frequently, women who have left (or divorced) their batterers experience even more severe battering after leaving (Mahoney 1991). It is not unusual for the batterer to threaten the victim's life after she has left him, or when he suspects or knows she is planning to leave (Browne 1987, 66). When no one helps the victims keep the batterers away, the women often logically conclude that their lives will be less violent if they return to the batterers. This is frequently the case of women who eventually kill their batterers. Even divorcing the batterer and moving to a different state does not always stop the violence.

What factors influence the likelihood of a woman killing her batterer? Research comparing women who killed and women who haven't (yet) killed their batterers shows some characteristic distinctions between the two. First, battered women who kill are more likely to be involved with a batterer who physically and, often, sexually abuses her/their children (Browne 1987; Ewing 1987; Walker 1989). Second, battered women who kill have perceived a more immediate sense of danger, usually involving violence that has increased in frequency, severity, and injury (Browne 1987; Ewing 1987; Walker 1989). Finally, battered women who kill are more likely to have received death threats and been terrorized with weapons (often firearms) (Browne 1987; Ewing 1987). It is useful to note that these findings suggest that the factors that "trigger" a battered woman to kill have more to do with actions of the batterer than actions of the victim.

While *self-defense* has been increasingly used as a defense in trials where women kill their batterers, it is also problematic with the courts. In three out of four cases where battered women kill, the homicide takes place during Walker's phase two, the battering incident, and often using the batterer's own weapons (Maguigan 1991). However, one in five cases do not occur during confrontations. What occurs in the remaining 5 percent of cases is unknown (Maguigan 1991). If one accepts Walker's cycle of violence theory, it should not be surprising to find that one-fifth of the killings of batterers by victims takes place during nonconfrontations, probably the tension-building phase, in which the batterer often makes threats to kill the woman and/or her/their children. One study of battered women who kill found that 83 percent of these women's batterers had threatened to kill somebody. "Given their experience with the men's capacity for violence, the women took what they said quite seriously" (Browne 1987, 65). Because she believes this threat, she may decide at the least to provide a defense and possibly to kill him. This is often after many requests to the police and others for help have not been granted. She realizes that for survival, she has to take matters into her own hands. Frequently, battered women who kill, use weapons because they lack the physical strength to overpower their batterers. They may in fact simply be trying to stop the batterer temporarily (not to kill him); however, the use of weapons may lead to the batterer's death (Flynn 1977, 17).

Although the victim realizes that a violent and possibly deadly interaction is probably inevitable in the near future, she does not know exactly when it will occur. She doesn't know if she'll come home from work, be wakened in the middle of the night, or be in the middle of a family reunion when he finally "blows." In some cases, a victim may take steps to defend herself prior to an attack, when she has more control over the situation. Pleading self-defense for a murder charge when the woman had clearly prepared for assault, and particularly where her violence did not occur during an incident where the batterer was actually hitting her, poses culpability problems to judges and jurors.

One battered woman in Browne's (1987) study was told by her husband that he was going to kill her if she did not find out what had happened to his current lover whom he'd also abused and who had left him. This woman had no idea where her husband's other victim had fled, but she believed his threat. In this instance, she had prepared to defend herself by locating one of his guns. She did not shoot him even when he was shooting at her (with another one of his guns). She did not shoot him until he attempted to kill their child.

It is difficult to question a woman's rationality in the vast majority of these situations. Women who kill their batterers usually do so only after having exhausted alternatives, including leaving him and contacting the crime-processing system. These women have usually come to the conclusion that the batterer will never leave her alone—she can't stop him and the crime-processing system can't—or won't stop him. Thus, the victim might decide it is safer and more rational to kill the batterer before the violence escalates to Walker's phase two, when her chances of having any control in the confrontation are significantly diminished. The following experience of one woman who killed her batterer exemplifies how battered women who kill have frequently exhausted all "legitimate" resources:

> She had been shot by her husband six times, four bullets aimed at her, the last two at her young son, whose body she shielded with her own. The man was given *six months* in jail. She divorced him, had a restraining order, and had moved to another county. A few weeks before our interview she had seen her ex-husband on her property and called the police, who replied, "We can't help you. He hasn't done anything yet." When I asked the woman what she was going to do, she replied bitterly, "I bought a gun. Nobody's going to take care of me. If he comes back, I'm going to use my gun."
>
> *(Rosewater 1988, 205)*

In some cases where women have killed their batterers, experts have been brought in to explain BWS. BWS has three components: Walker's cycle of violence, learned helplessness, and post-traumatic stress disorder (PTSD). The former two components were discussed earlier in this chapter. PTSD, developed to explain responses of U.S. Vietnam War veterans, claims that certain psychological symptoms result from experiencing severe and unexpected trauma or being unexpectedly and repeatedly exposed to abuse. These expert witnesses educate judges and juries about the dynamics behind battering (Attorney General's Task Force on Family Violence 1984, 41). Testimony regarding BWS is usually used to provide evidence that the woman was indeed battered, as suggested by psychological indicators. Although feminists in part have supported the use of expert witnesses in cases where women have killed their batterers, the result is that battered women often don't have the chance to tell their own stories. The case of *People* v. *Eleuterio* (1975) portrays this:

> At the time of this killing she was 25 years of age, had an above average I.Q. and had attended college. She had been married to the decedent for five years and had two infant daughters…. [T]he decedent worked only irregularly and the support of the family was left largely to appellant…. [Her husband] had physically assaulted her frequently. She tried on several occasions to leave him but he refused to permit it. Shortly before the killing she left decedent, moved to Watertown and instituted divorce

proceedings. Decedent followed her and insisted that she terminate the divorce action. Fearing injury to herself and her children she allowed him to move in with the family again…. On the night of the killing decedent and appellant argued again about separating. Decedent refused to do so, verbally abused her and struck her in the face. He then got his .22 caliber pistol, cleaned it and placed it on his pillow next to him before going to sleep. During the night appellant awoke and using her husband's gun fired two shots into his head. She then drove to the police station with the gun and turned herself in.

(*People* v. *Eleuterio*, 1975, as cited by Marcus 1981, 1728)

The defendant in this case received an "indeterminate sentence of up to twelve years, despite medical testimony that appellant needed psychiatric treatment on an outpatient basis rather than institutionalization" (Marcus 1981, 1728). In this case and many others where battered women have killed their abusers, they have little or no say in the trial. Their lawyers are often unlikely to let them take the stand to tell their own stories, in spite of the fact that they wish to do so. Thus, the judge or jury may base the facts only on events recorded in the police reports, which do not identify a pattern of victimization against the accused victim. This is an effective way of silencing victimized women, and appears to have resulted in extremely harsh sentences.

Many women survivors who have killed their batterers in self-defense have received life imprisonment, in spite of an otherwise clean record. In fact, it is common for battered women who kill not only to admit that they killed, but also to notify the police. Although usually in a state of shock, they often assume that it will be apparent to the police and courts that they acted in self-defense. This, unfortunately, is not often the case, as was discussed in Chapter 4. The heartbreak of these cases is further confounded by women who have killed in order to save their own and their children's lives, only to be in prison and have their children placed in foster homes, or possibly with relatives of the batterer.

Most court cases of battered women who kill have resulted in convictions with no appeals (Gillespie 1989). Some scholars believe that the BWS defense is necessary because the current interpretation of the self-defense law is largely patriarchal and fails to understand the threat of great bodily harm and death that victims experience (see Gillespie 1989). However, a number of costs are associated with using BWS as a defense. Although it goes beyond insanity and self-defense claims to help women who kill their batterers, it perpetuates stereotypical images of women.

The aspect of BWS that has been most severely criticized by feminists is *learned helplessness*, because it perpetuates images of women as passive and weak. An adoption of this view stereotypes women who kill their batterers as "abnormal," although their responses are quite normal compared to victims in similar situations (see Sheehy et al. 1991). Moreover, the guilt, low self-esteem, self-blame, and depression these women report might be a result of the failure of family, police, judges, and physicians to provide help (Gondolf and Fisher 1988). Some women's justifiable *anger* at being abused and not being protected by the crime-processing system at least partially explains why they kill their batterers. By definition, this anger fails to fit the "learned helplessness" model (see Allard 1991; Mahoney 1991). In fact, it has been noted that BWS is less likely to work for African American women, since they are more likely to be viewed as angry by judges and juries (Allard 1991). Another cost of the BWS defense is that when women are viewed as abnormal, irrational, weak, mentally ill, or angry, they are at increased risk of losing custody of their children (Stark 1992).

HEALTH PROFESSIONALS

Although health professionals are not direct operators in the crime-processing system, they have key interactions with victims. The training on battering that physicians, welfare and mental health professionals, and the clergy traditionally receive "reflects a bias toward keeping the family together at all costs" (Goolkasian 1986, 3). Because of the severe injuries battered women frequently receive, it is not unusual for them to require help from their private physicians or emergency medical personnel. Although the potential for the medical field to deter battering is great, the response has been "slow and sporadic" (Kurz and Stark 1988, 249). When workers in the health care professions—physicians, nurses, and social workers—fail to ask the cause of battered women's injuries, they perpetuate the invisibility of battering and contribute to the women's rationalization that they are not really victims (Campbell 1991; Dobash and Dobash 1979). Additionally, mental health clinicians and counselors frequently deal with battered women as their clients. It is important for all of these actors to label the act for what it is—*violence.*

Although physicians, particularly emergency room physicians, may be acutely aware that the woman they are treating is a battering victim, they are unlikely to address how the injury was caused (Star et al. 1979). Research in nursing journals claims a lack of sensitivity and appropriate action in treating battered women on the part of nurses as well as doctors (Drake 1982). One study of emergency department staff workers found three responses to battered women: 11 percent had *positive* reactions, where they showed concern for the battered woman's safety as well as providing medical care; 49 percent provided a *partial response* where medical provisions were "brief" and "routine" and had low priority; and 40 percent of the staff *did not respond* to the battering aspect of the case (Kurz 1987). This exemplifies how the invisibility of battered women is maintained among medical professionals. If one goal of medicine is prevention, then failure to address the cause is particularly problematic. Just as police officers should act professionally in response to battering calls, health care workers also have professional responsibilities to determine the cause of the injury and to plan for prevention of further injury. Responding similarly to many law enforcement officals, many health care workers lose their patience with victims who leave the hospitals with their batterers or have returned to the hospital with injuries, presumably from the same batterer. That health care professionals are "fed up" with battered women is not a legitimate excuse for ignoring their injuries.

Medicalization is a process by which medical professionals define an emerging social problem as belonging within their professional expertise (Kurz 1987). Medical professionals are reluctant to medicalize woman battering, and often view responding to battering as detracting from their proper role (Kurz 1987). (This is similar to police officers who view the appropriate response to woman battering as "peace keeping," and who resent peace keeping because it is not considered "real" police work.) It is unusual for emergency room physicians to take detailed histories of women who are obviously victims of battering, even when serious wounds or injuries are present. These physicians rarely open up a discussion for such crucial questions as how the abuse occurred and who did it, often reinforcing some battered women's efforts to minimize the reality and severity of their abuse (Warshaw 1993). One example of how negatively the emergency room professionals view battered women is that "battered women who attempted suicide were significantly more likely than non-battered women to be sent home and/or to receive no referral of any kind after a suicide attempt" (Kurz and Stark 1988, 253). Relative to the rest of the population, it is not uncommon for battered women or battering men to attempt suicide. Both the batterer and the victim in these cases believe (and it would seem logically so) that the violence is not going to stop until one of them dies.

In sum, both crime-processing and health professionals tend not only to keep woman battering hidden, but to condone it through their own failure to respond adequately. Any other phenomenon that occurred as frequently and caused the degree of injury as woman battering would likely result in a national outrage and an effort to treat the victim or control the cause (Star et al. 1979).

SUMMARY

Many of the myths and problems surrounding woman battering are discussed in this chapter. Battering may take place in many forms, but its results are always devastating. When exploring the causes of battering, it is not enough to simply examine batterers or the family system; rather, battering must be viewed in a sociohistorical context. Battering must be deterred not only by reacting to individuals, but by building a political, economic, and social system that is more equitable to women, and a crime-processing and health system that is more responsive to battering. The current situation leaves battered women with little recourse to escape abusive relationships safely. Additionally, the culture provides an environment that accepts male violence as "normal." Not until gender equality and male violence are confronted on a more global and pervasive level will battering be viewed as unacceptable and, indeed, criminal.

NOTES

1. I placed *elder* in quotation marks because many advocates for older people find the term *elder* offensive, particularly when referring to persons in their sixties.

2. Battering in lesbian and gay relationships has been documented, although insufficient research exists to compare this to the rate of battering in heterosexual relationships. For more information on lesbian battering see Lobel (1986) and Renzetti (1992).

3. Consistently throughout this chapter I refer to the children as "her/their" since the batterer is not always the father of all or any of the children the battered woman is raising.

REFERENCES

Allard, Sharon A. 1991. "Rethinking Battered Woman Syndrome: A Black Feminist Perspective." *UCLA Women's Law Journal* 1:191–207.

Attorney General's Task Force on Family Violence. 1984. *Final Report,* September, 157 pp.

Balos, Beverly, and Katie Trotzky. 1988. "Enforcement of the Domestic Abuse Act in Minnesota: A Preliminary Study." *Law and Inequality* 6:83–125.

Belknap, Joanne, and K. Douglas McCall. 1994. "Woman Battering and Police Referrals." *Journal of Criminal Justice* 22:195–208.

Berk, Sarah F., and Donileen R. Loseke. 1981. " 'Handling' Family Violence: Situational Determinants of Police Arrest in Domestic Disturbance." *Law and Society* 15:317–346.

Berk, Richard A., Sarah F. Berk, Donileen R. Loseke, and David Rauma. 1983. "Combat and Other Family Violence Myths." Pp. 197–212 in *The Dark Side of Families: Current Family Violence Research,* edited by D. Finkelhor, R. J. Gelles, G. T. Hotaling, and M. A. Straus. Beverly Hills, CA: Sage.

Berk, Richard A., Alec Campbell, Ruth Klap, and Bruce Western. 1992. "The Deterrent Effect of Arrest in Incidents of Domestic Violence: A Bayesian Analysis of the Colorado Springs Spouse Abuse Experiment." *Journal of Criminal Law and Criminology* 83:170–200.

Berk, Richard A., and Phyllis J. Newton. 1985. "Does Arrest Really Deter Wife Battery? An Effort to Replicate the Findings of the Minneapolis Spouse Abuse Experiment." *American Sociological Review* 50(2):253–262.

Berk, Richard A., David Rauma, and Donileen R. Loseke. 1982. "Throwing the Cops Back Out: The Decline of a Local Program to the Criminal Justice System More Responsive to Incidents of Domestic Violence." *Social Science Research* 11: 245–279.

Berkowitz, Leonard. 1983. "The Goals of Aggression." Pp. 166–181 in *The Dark Side of Families: Current Family Violence Research,* edited by D. Finkelhor, R. J. Gelles, G. T. Hotaling, and M. A. Straus. Beverly Hills, CA: Sage.

Blodgett, Nancy. 1987. "Violence in the Home." *ABA Journal* (May, 1):66–69.

Bogal-Allbritten, Rosemarie, and William L. Allbritten. 1985. "The Hidden Victims: Courtship Violence Among College Students." *Journal of College Student Personnel* 26:201–204.

Bograd, Michele. 1988. "Feminist Perspectives on Wife Abuse: An Introduction." Pp. 11–27 in *Feminist Perspectives on Wife Abuse,* edited by K. Yllo and M. Bograd. Newbury Park, CA: Sage.

Bowker, Lee H., Michelle Arbitell, and J. Richard McFerron. 1988. "On the Relationship Between Wife Beating and Child Abuse." Pp. 158–174 in *Feminist Perspectives on Wife Abuse,* edited by K. Yllo and M. Bograd. Newbury Park, CA: Sage

Breines, Wini, and Linda Gordon. 1983. "The New Scholarship on Family Violence." *Signs: Journal of Women in Culture and Society* 18:490–531.

Brisson, Norman J. 1981. "Battering Husbands: A Survey of Abusive Men." *Victimology* 6:338–344.

Browne, Angela. 1987. *When Battered Women Kill*. New York: Free Press.

Browne, Angela, and Kirk R. Williams. 1993. "Gender, Intimacy, and Lethal Violence: Trends from 1976 through 1987." *Gender and Society* 7:78–98.

Burris, Carole Anne, and Peter Jaffe. 1983. "Wife Abuse as a Crime: The Impact of Police Laying Charges." *Canadian Journal* 25:309–318.

Buzawa, Eve S., and Carl G. Buzawa. 1990. *Domestic Violence: The Criminal Justice Response*. Newbury Park, CA: Sage.

Campbell, Jacquelyn C. 1991. "Public-Health Conceptions of Family Abuse." Pp. 35–48 in *Abused and Battered*, edited by D. D. Knudsen and J. L. Miller. New York: Aldine De Gruyter.

Cappell, Charles, and R. Heiner. 1990. "The Intergenerational Transmission of Family Violence." *Journal of Family Violence* 5:135–152.

Cate, Rodney M., June M. Henton, James Koval, F. Scott Christopher, and Sally Lloyd. 1982. "Premarital Abuse: A Social Psychological Perspective." *Journal of Family Issues* 3:79–90.

Chaudhuri, Molly, and Kathleen Daly. 1992. "Do Restraining Orders Help? Battered Women's Experience with Male Violence and Legal Process." Pp. 227–252 in *Domestic Violence: The Changing Criminal Justice Response*, edited by Eve S. Buzawa and Carl G. Buzawa. Westport, CT: Auburn House.

Cohn, Ellen G., and Lawrence W. Sherman. 1987. "Police Policy on Domestic Violence, 1986: A National Survey." *Crime Control Institute, Crime Control Reports,* No. 5.

Crites, Laura L. 1987. "Wife Abuse: The Judicial Record." Pp. 38–53 in *Women, the Courts, and Equality,* edited by L. L. Crites and W. L. Hepperle. Newbury Park, CA: Sage.

Davidson, Terry. 1978. *Conjugal Crime: Understanding and Changing the Wife Beating Pattern*. New York: Hawthorne Books.

Davis, E. G. 1971. *The First Sex*. New York: Putnam.

Davis, P. W. 1981. "Structured Rationales for Non-Arrest: Police Stereotypes of the Domestic Disturbance." *Criminal Justice Review* 6(2):8–15.

Dobash, R. Emerson, and Russell Dobash. 1979. *Violence Against Wives*. New York: Free Press.

————. 1988. "Research as Social Action: The Struggle for Battered Women." Pp .51–74 in *Feminist Perspectives on Wife Abuse,* edited by K. Yllo and M. Bograd. Newbury Park, CA: Sage.

Dobash, Russell P., and Rebecca E. Dobash. 1981. "Community Response to Violence Against Wives." *Social Problems* 28:563–581.

————. 1983. "The Context-Specific Approach." Pp. 261–276 in *The Dark Side of Families: Current Family Violence Research,* edited by D. Finkelhor, R. J. Gelles, G. T. Hotaling, and M. A. Straus. Beverly Hills, CA: Sage.

Dobash, Russell P., R. Emerson Dobash, Margo Wilson, and Martin Daly. 1992. "The Myth of Sexual Symmetry in Marital Violence." *Social Problems* 39:71–91.

Dolon, Ronald, James Hendricks, and M. Steven Meagher. 1986. "Police Practices and Attitudes Toward Domestic Violence." *Journal of Police Science and Administration* 14:187–192.

Drake, Virginia K. 1982. "Battered Women: A Health Care Problem in Disguise." *Image* 24:40–47.

Dunford, Franklyn W. 1992. "The Measurement of Recidivism in Cases of Spouse Assault." *Journal of Criminal Law and Criminology* 83:120–136.

Dunford, Franklyn W., David Huizinga, and Delbert S. Elliott. 1990. "The Role of Arrest in Domestic Assault: The Omaha Police Experiment." *Criminology* 28:183–206.

Dutton, Donald G. 1988. *The Domestic Assault of Women.* Boston, MA: Allyn & Bacon.

Dutton, Donald G., and Susan L. Painter. 1981. "Traumatic Bonding: The Development of Emotional Attachments in Battered Women and Other Relationships of Intermittent Abuse." *Victimology* 6:139–155.

Edwards, Susan S. M. 1989. *Policing "Domestic" Violence: Women, the Law and the State.* London: Sage.

Eppler, Amy. 1986. "Battered Women and the Equal Protection Clause: Will the Constitution Help Them When the Police Won't?" *Yale Law Review* 95:788–809.

Erez, Edna. 1986. "Intimacy, Violence, and the Police." *Human Relations* 39(3):265–281.

Ewing, Charles P. 1987. *Battered Women Who Kill.* Lexington, MA: Lexington Books.

Fagan, Jeffrey A., Douglas K. Stewart, and Karen V. Hansen. 1983. "Violent Men or Violent Husbands? Background Factors and Situational Correlates." Pp. 49–68 in *The Dark Side of Families: Current Family Violence Research,* edited by D. Finkelhor, R. J. Gelles, G. T. Hotaling, and M. A. Straus. Beverly Hills, CA: Sage.

Ferraro, Kathleen J. 1989. "Policing Woman Battering." *Social Problems* 36(1):61–74.

Ferraro, Kathleen J. 1993. "Cops, Courts, and Woman Battering." Pp. 165–176 in *Violence Against Women: The Bloody Footprints,* edited by P. B. Bart and E. G. Moran. Newbury Park, CA: Sage.

Ferraro, Kathleen J., and John M. Johnson. 1983. "How Women Experience Battering." *Social Problems* 30:325–339.

Finesmith, Barbara K. 1983. "Police Responses to Battered Women: A Critique and Proposals for Reform." *Seton Hall Law Review* 14:74–109.

Finkelhor, David. 1983. "Common Features of Family Abuse." Pp. 17–28 in *The Dark Side of Families: Current Family Violence Research,* edited by D. Finkelhor, R. J. Gelles, G. T. Hotaling, and M. A. Straus. Beverly Hills, CA: Sage.

Flynn, J. P. 1977. "Recent Findings Related to Wife Abuse." *Social Casework* (January):13–20.

Gamache, D. J., Edleson, J. L., and Schock, M. D. 1988. "Coordinating Police, Judicial, and Social Service Response to Woman Battering." In *Coping with Family Violence,* edited by G. T. Hotaling, D. Finkelhor, J. T. Kirkpatrick, and M. A. Straus. Beverly Hills, CA: Sage.

Garner, Joel, and Elizabeth Clemmer. 1986. "Danger to Police in Domestic Disturbances—A New Look." *National Institute of Justice, Research in Brief Report* (November):1–8.

Gee, Pauline W. 1983. "Ensuring Police Protection for Battered Women: The Scott v. Hart Suit." *Signs: Journal of Women in Culture and Society* 8(3):554–567.

Gelles, Richard J. 1976. "Abused Wives: Why Do They Stay?" *Journal of Marriage and the Family* (November):659–668.

——————. 1980. "Violence in the Family: A Review of Research in the Seventies." *Journal of Marriage and the Family* (November):873–885.

Gillespie, Cynthia K. 1989. *Justifiable Homicide: Battered Women, Self-Defense, and the Law.* Columbus, OH: Ohio State University Press.

Gondolf, Edward W., with Ellen R. Fisher. 1988. *Battered Women as Survivors.* New York: Lexington Books.

Goode, W. J. 1971. "Force and Violence in the Family." *Journal of Marriage and the Family* (November):624–636.

Goolkasian, Gail A. 1986. "Confronting Domestic Violence: The Role of Criminal Court Judges." *National Institute in Justice/ Research in Brief* (November):1–8.

Graham, Dee L. R., Edna Rawlings, and Nelly Rimini. 1988. "Survivors of Terror: Battered Women, Hostages and the Stockholm Syndrome." Pp. 217–233 in *Feminist Perspectives on Wife Abuse,* edited by K. Yllo and M. Bograd. Newbury Park, CA: Sage.

Grau, Janice, Jeffrey Fagan, and Sandra Wexler. 1985. "Restraining Orders for Battered Women: Issues of Access and Efficacy." Pp. 13–20 in *Criminal Justice Politics and Women: The Aftermath of Legally Mandated Change,* edited by C. SchWeber and C. Feinman. New York: Haworth Press.

Greenblat, Cathy S. 1983. "A Hit Is a Hit Is a Hit … Or Is It?" Pp. 235–260 in *The Dark Side of Families: Current Family Violence Research,* edited by D. Finkelhor, R. J. Gelles, G. T. Hotaling, and M. A. Straus. Beverly Hills, CA: Sage

Hanmer, Jalna, Jill Radford, and Elizabeth A. Stanko. 1989. "Policing, Men's Violence: An Introduction." Pp. 1–12 in *Women, Policing, and Male Violence: International Perspectives,* edited by J. Hanmer, J. Radford, and E. A. Stanko. London: Routledge & Kegan Paul.

Hart, Barbara. 1993. "Battered Women and the Criminal Justice System." *American Behavioral Scientist* 36:624–638.

Hirschel, J. David, and Ira W. Hutchison, III. 1992. "Female Spouse Abuse and the Police Response: The Charlotte, North Carolina, Experiment." *Journal of Criminal Law and Criminology* 83:73–119.

Hirschel, J. David, Ira W. Hutchison, III, and Charles W. Dean. 1991. "The Charlotte Spouse Abuse Study." *Popular Government* (Summer): 11–16.

Hoff, Lee Ann. 1990. *Battered Women as Survivors.* London: Routledge & Kegan Paul.

Jaffe, Peter G., David A. Wolfe, Anne Telford, and Gary Austin. 1986. "The Impact of Police Charges in Incidents of Wife Abuse." *Journal of Family Violence* 1:37–49.

Jaffe, Peter G., David A. Wolfe, and Susan Kaye Wilson. 1990. *Children of Battered Women.* Newbury Park, CA: Sage.

Jolin, Annette. 1983. "Domestic Violence Legislation: An Impact Assessment." *Journal of Police Science and Administration.* 11:451–456.

Kantor, Glenda K., and Murray A. Straus. 1987. "The 'Drunken Bum' Theory of Wife Beating." *Social Problems* 3:213–230.

Klein, Dorie. 1981. "Violence Against Women: Some Considerations Regarding Its Causes and Its Elimination." *Crime and Delinquency* 27:64–80.

Knutson, J. F., and J. G. Mehm. 1986. "Transgenerational Patterns of Coercion in Families and Intimate Relationships." Pp. 67–90 in *Violence in Intimate Relationships,* edited by G. Russell. New York: PMA Publishing Corporation.

Kuhl, Anna F. 1985. "Battered Women Who Murder: Victims of Offenders." Pp. 197–216 in *The Changing Roles of Women in the Criminal Justice System,* edited by I. L. Moyer. Prospect Heights, IL: Waveland Press.

Kurz, Demie. 1987. "Emergency Department Responses to Battered Women: Resistance to Medicalization." *Social Problems* 34:69–81.

——————. 1993. "Social Science Perspectives on Wife Abuse: Current Debates and Future Directions." Pp. 252–269 in *Violence Against Women,* edited by P. B. Bart and E. G. Moran. Newbury Park, CA: Sage.

Kurz, Demie, and Evan Stark. 1988. "Not-So-Benign Neglect: The Medical Response to Battering." Pp. 249–268 in *Feminist Perspectives on Wife Abuse,* edited by K. Yllo and M. Bograd. Newbury Park, CA: Sage.

Lane, K. E., and P. A. Gwartney-Gibbs. 1985. "Violence in the Context of Dating and Sex." *Journal of Family Issues* 6:45–59.

Langan, Patrick A., and Christopher A. Innes. 1986. "Preventing Domestic

Violence Against Women." Bureau of Justice Statistics Special Report, August.

Lawrenz, Frances, James F. Lembo, and Thomas Schade. 1988. "Time Series Analysis of the Effect of a Domestic Violence Directive on the Number of Arrests Per Day." *Journal of Criminal Justice* 16:493–498.

Lobel, Kerry (Ed.). 1986. *Naming the Violence: Speaking Out About Lesbian Violence.* Seattle, WA: Seal Press.

Loseke, Donileen R., and Spencer E. Cahill. 1984. "The Social Construction of Deviance: Experts on Battered Women." *Social Problems* 31:296–309.

Loving, N. 1980. *Responding to Spouse Abuse and Wife Beating: A Guide for Police.* Washington, D.C.: Police Executive Research Forum.

Maguigan, Holly. 1991. "Battered Women and Self-Defense: Myths and Misconceptions in Current Reform Proposals." *University of Pennsylvania Law Review* 140:379–486.

Mahoney, Martha. 1991. "Legal Images of Battered Women: Redefining the Issue of Separation." *Michigan Law Review* 90:2–94.

Makepeace, J. M. 1981. "Courtship Violence Among College Students." *Family Relations* 30:97–102.

_____. 1986. "Gender Differences in Courtship Violence Victimization." *Family Relations* 35:383–388.

Manning, Peter K. 1992. "Screening Calls." Pp. 41–48 in *Domestic Violence: The Changing Criminal Justice Response,* edited by Eve S. Buzawa and Carl G. Buzawa. Westport, CT: Auburn House.

Marcus, M. L. 1981. "Conjugal Violence: The Law of Force and the Force of the Law." *California Law Review* 69:1657–1733.

Martin, Del. 1976. *Battered Wives.* San Francisco, CA: Glide.

Martin, Margaret. 1988. "A Social Worker's Response." Pp. 53–61 in *The Violent Family,* edited by N. Hutchings. New York: Human Sciences Press.

Matthews, William J. 1984. "Violence in College Couples." *College Student Journal* 18:150–158.

McCann, Kathryn. 1985. "Battered Women and the Law: The Limits of Legislation." Pp. 71–96 in *Women-in-Law: Exploration in Law, Family and Sexuality,* edited by J. Brophy and C. Smart. London: Routledge & Kegan Paul.

McNulty, Faith. 1980. *The Burning Bed.* New York: Harcourt Brace Jovanovich.

Miller, Susan L. 1989. "Unintended Side Effects of Pro-Arrest Policies and Their Race and Class Implications for Battered Women: A Cautionary Note." *Criminal Justice Policy Review* 3:299–317.

Mills, Billy G., and Mary L. McNamar. 1981. "California's Response to Domestic Violence." *Santa Clara Law Review* 21:1–19.

Mills, Trudy. 1984. "Victimization and Self-Esteem: On Equating Husband Abuse and Wife Abuse." *Victimology* 9:254–261.

Morash, Merry. 1986. "Wife Battering." *Criminal Justice Abstracts* (June): 252–271.

Mullarkey, Edward. 1988. "The Legal System for Victims of Family Violence." Pp. 43–52 in *The Violent Family,* edited by N. Hutchings. New York: Human Sciences Press.

Oppenlander, Nan. 1982. "Coping or Copping Out." *Criminology* 20:449–465.

Pizzey, Erin. 1974. *Scream Quietly or the Neighbors Will Hear.* Middlesex, England: Penguin.

Pleck, Elizabeth. 1983. "Feminist Responses to 'Crimes against Women,' 1868–1896." *Signs: Journal of Women Culture and Society* 8:451–470.

_____. 1989. "Criminal Approaches to Family Violence, 1640–1980." Pp. 19–58 in *Family Violence,* edited by L. Ohlin and M. Tonry. Chicago: University of Chicago Press.

Ptacek, James. 1988. "Why Do Men Batter Their Wives?" Pp. 133–75 in *Feminist Perspectives on Wife Abuse,* edited by K. Yllo and M. Bograd. Newbury Park, CA: Sage.

Quarm, Daisy, and Martin D. Schwartz. 1985. "Domestic Violence in Criminal Court: An Examination of New Legislation in Ohio." Pp. 29–46 in *Criminal Justice Politics and Women: The Aftermath of Legally Mandated Change,* edited by C. SchWeber and C. Feinman. New York: Haworth Press.

Renzetti, Claire M. 1992. *Violent Betrayal: Partner Abuse in Lesbian Relationships.* Newbury Park, CA: Sage.

Rosewater, Lynne B. 1988. "Battered or Schizophrenic? Psychological Tests Can't Tell." Pp. 200–216 in *Feminist Perspectives on Wife Abuse,* edited by K. Yllo and M. Bograd. Newbury Park, CA: Sage.

Rowe, Kelly. 1985. "The Limits of the Neighborhood Justice Center: Why Domestic Violence Cases Should Not Be Mediated." *Emory Law Journal* 34:855–910.

Saunders, Daniel B. 1988. "Wife Abuse, Husband Abuse, or Mutual Combat? A Feminist Perspective on the Empirical Findings." Pp. 90–113 in *Feminist Perspectives on Wife Abuse,* edited by K. Yllo and M. Bograd. Newbury Park, CA: Sage.

Schechter, Susan. 1982. *Women and Male Violence: The Visions and Struggles of the Battered Women's Movement.* Boston: South End Press.

Schwartz, Martin D. 1987. "Gender and Injury in Spousal Assault." *Sociological Focus* 20:61–75.

Sebastian, Richard J. 1983. "Social Psychological Determinants." Pp. 182–191 in *The Dark Side of Families: Current Family Violence Research,* edited by D. Finkelhor, R. J. Gelles, G. T. Hotaling, and M. A. Straus. Beverly Hills, CA: Sage.

Sheehy, Lisa, Melissa Reinberg, and Deborah Krichway. 1991. *Commutation for Women Who Defended Themselves Against Abusive Partners: An Advocacy Manual and Guide to Legal Issues.*Philidelphia, PA: National Clearinghouse for the Defense of Battered Women.

Sherman, Lawrence W. 1992. *Policing Domestic Violence: Experiments and Dilemmas.* New York: Free Press.

Sherman, Lawrence W., and Richard A. Berk. 1984. "The Specific Deterrent Effects of Arrest for Domestic Assault." *American Sociological Review* 49:261–272.

Sherman, Lawrence W., Janell D. Schmidt, Dennis P. Rogan, Douglas A. Smith, Patrick R. Gartin, Ellen G. Cohn, Dean J. Collins, and Anthony R. Bacich. 1992. "The Variable Effects of Arrest on Criminal Careers: The Milwaukee Domestic Violence Experiment." *Journal of Criminal Law and Criminology* 83:137–169.

Smith, Douglas A., and Jody R. Klein. 1984. "Police Control of Interpersonal Disputes." *Social Problems* 31:469–481.

Smith, Michael D. 1994. "Enhancing the Quality of Survey Data on Violence Against Women." *Gender and Society* 8:109–127.

Stanko, Elizabeth A. 1985. *Intimate Intrusions.* London: Routledge & Kegan Paul.

—————. 1989. "Missing the Mark? Policing Battering." Pp. 46–69 in *Women, Policing, and Male Violence: International Perspectives,* edited by J. Hanmer, J. Radford, and E. A. Stanko. London: Routledge & Kegan Paul.

Star, B., C. G. Clark, K. M. Goetz, and L. O'Malia. 1979. "Psychological Aspects of Wife Battering." *Social Casework: The Journal of Contemporary Social Work* (October):479–487.

Stark, Evan. 1992. "Framing and Reframing Battered Women." Pp. 271–292 in *Domestic Violence: The Changing Criminal Justice Response,* edited by Eve S. Buzawa and Carl G. Buzawa. Westport, CT: Auburn House.

Stark, Evan, and Anne Flitcraft. 1983. "Social Knowledge, Social Policy, and the Abuse of Women: The Case Against Patriarchal Benevolence."

Pp. 330–348 in *The Dark Side of Families: Current Family Violence Research,* edited by D. Finkelhor, R. J. Gelles, G. T. Hotaling, and M. A. Straus. Beverly Hills, CA: Sage.

Stark, Evan, Anne Flitcraft, and W. Frazier. 1979. "Medicine and Patriarchal Violence: The Social Construction of a 'Private' Event." *International Journal of Health Sciences* 9:461–493.

Steinmetz, Suzanne. 1977/1978. "The Battered Husband Syndrome." *Victimology* 2:499–509.

Stets, Jan E., and Maureen A. Pirog-Good. 1987. "Violence in Dating Relationships." *Social Psychology Quarterly* 50:237–246.

Stets, Jan E., and Murray A. Straus. 1990. "Gender Differences in Reporting Marital Violence and its Medical and Psychological Consequences." In *Physical Violence in American Families,* edited by M. A. Straus and R. J. Gelles. New Brunswick, NJ: Transaction Press.

Straus, Murray A. 1991. "Physical Violence in American Families." Pp. 17–34 in *Abused and Battered,* edited by D. D. Knudsen and J. L. Miller. New York: Aldine De Gruyter.

Straus, Murray A., and Richard J. Gelles. 1986. "Societal Change and Change in Family Violence from 1975 to 1985 as Revealed by Two Surveys." *Journal of Marriage and the Family* 48:465–479.

Straus, Murray A., Richard J. Gelles, and Suzanne Steinmetz. 1980. *Behind Closed Doors: Violence in the American Family.* New York: Anchor Books.

Strube, M. J., and L. S. Barbour. 1984. "Factors Relate to the Decision to Leave an Abusive Relationship." *Journal of Marriage and the Family* (November):837–844).

Tierney, K. J. 1983. "The Battered Women Movement and the Creation of the Wife Beating Problem." *Social Problems* 29:207–220.

Tong, Rosemarie. 1984. *Women, Sex, and the Law.* Totowa, NJ: Rowman & Allanheld.

Walker, Lenore E. 1979. *The Battered Woman.* New York: Harper & Row.

——————. 1983a. "The Battered Woman Syndrome Study." Pp. 31–49 in *The Dark Side of Families: Current Family Violence Research,* edited by D. Finkelhor, R. J. Gelles, G. T. Hotaling, and M. A. Straus. Beverly Hills, CA: Sage.

——————. 1983b. "Victimology and the Psychological Perspectives of Battered Women." *Victimology* 1–2:82–104.

——————. 1989. *Terrifying Love: Why Battered Women Kill and How Society Responds.* New York: HarperPerennial.

Wardell, Laurie, Dair L. Gillespie, and Ann Leffler. 1983. "Science and Violence Against Wives," Pp. 69–84 in *The Dark Side of Families: Current Family Violence Research,* edited by D. Finkelhor, R. J. Gelles, G. T. Hotaling, and M. A. Straus. Beverly Hills, CA: Sage.

Warshaw, Carole. 1993. "Limitations of the Medical Model in the Care of Battered Women." Pp. 134–146 in *Violence Against Women: The Bloody Footprints,* edited by P. B. Bart and E. G. Moran. Newbury Park, CA: Sage.

Worden, Robert E., and Alissa A. Pollitz. 1984. "Police Arrests in Domestic Disturbances: A Further Look." *Law and Society Review* 18(1):105–119.

Yllo, Kersti. 1983. "Using a Feminist Approach in Quantitative Research: A Case Study." Pp. 277–288 in *The Dark Side of Families: Current Family Violence Research,* edited by D. Finkelhor, R. J. Gelles, G. T. Hotaling, and M. A. Straus. Beverly Hills, CA: Sage.

——————. 1988. "Political and Methodological Debates in Wife Abuse Research." Pp. 28–50 in *Feminist Perspectives on Wife Abuse,* edited by K. Yllo and M. Bograd. Newbury Park, CA: Sage.

Zorza, Joan. 1992. "The Criminal Law of Misdemeanor Domestic Violence, 1970–1990." *Journal of Criminal Law and Criminology* 83:46–72.

PART IV

Women Workers

9

Resistance to Change

Part IV of this book examines the U.S. legal movement toward women's equality and women professionals in the crime-processing system. This chapter provides a historical account of how women have broken into the nondomestic labor force and of changes in the labor market that have occurred. It describes the movement of women from the private sphere (the home) to the public sphere (society and the paid labor force).

One of the most pronounced gender differences is that of sex segregation in the labor market; women and men still tend to be employed in different occupations. Although this is changing, we still see a tendency for men to be in higher paying jobs and also in jobs that require more physical labor. This gender occupational difference is especially evident in employment in the crime-processing system.

Before specifically addressing the topic of women working in the crime-processing system (Chapter 10), it is useful to examine how women's work outside the home has at times been criminalized or at least made "deviant" through legislation, policies, court decisions, and the culture. These forces have severely limited women's participation in the world outside of the home. Although there has been significant improvement, particularly through court cases since the 1970s, barriers still exist to women's equal employment opportunities.

This chapter introduces the issue of women workers in the crime-processing system within the larger context of the forces that have restricted and shaped female labor force participation. It will be shown that discrimination against women has been based on both sex *and* gender distinctions, as well as assumptions that all women marry (and stay married), have children, and are in traditional sex roles.

MOVEMENT FROM THE PRIVATE TO THE PUBLIC SPHERE

To understand social and legal resistance to women's employment outside the home, it is necessary to examine sex discrimination in the historical context of women's and men's lives and rights. It is also important to understand that sex discrimination does not occur in a vacuum; it often accompanies race, class, ethnicity, sexual preference, and other forms of discrimination. "Discrimination is the perpetration of unjustifiable inequality in consequence of bigotry" (Campbell 1988, 16). Behavior does not have to be purposeful, conscious, or direct to classify as discrimination. Sex discrimination is when sex or gender specification is used to the disadvantage of one sex (definition adapted from Campbell, 1988, 22). Sex discrimination is overwhelmingly against women and girls.

There are political, economic, and social aspects to women's (and men's) lives in both the public (outside the home) and private (within the home) spheres (Bradley and Khor 1993). This section of the chapter will explore the public and private spheres of women's lives; however, the focus will be on the *economic* aspects of the *public* domain, given that these make up most of the sex discrimination cases brought by both women and men regarding gender equality. Sex discrimination cases have also been brought regarding access to athletic training/programs and exclusively male clubs, and have questioned statutory rape laws and drinking-age laws that apply differently to the sexes.

History of Women's Movement into the Public Sphere

When the nation's founding fathers spoke of "We the People" they were not using the term generically. Although subject to the Constitution's mandates, women were unacknowledged in its text, uninvited in its formulation, unsolicited in its ratification, and, before the last quarter-century, largely uninvolved in its interpretation.

(Rhode 1990, 121)

Women have traditionally been limited to the private sphere, while men have generally enjoyed more freedom in the public sphere. The *private sphere* includes the home and care of the family, while the *public sphere* includes life outside the home, such as in the paid labor force, the voting booth, and bars. Religiosity and sexuality were also tied to the separate spheres, where predictably, women were expected to be more religious, pure, and sexually chaste than men (see Welter 1978). Separate spheres for women and men can be traced back to Aristotle, St. Paul, and Thomas Aquinas, who believed the only purpose for women was reproduction and marriage, while men were meant for loftier purposes (Harris 1978). The precedent for separate spheres was set and remained for centuries, with the assumptions that (1) men are (and should be) "breadwinners," and (2) women (should and do) care for the home and children—for free (Atkins and Hoggett 1984).

In addition to societal values, legal doctrine has "reflected and reinforced" men's dominance of the public sphere and women's confinement to the private sphere (Rhode 1987, 13). Even leading feminists of the nineteenth century had difficulty arguing that women should not have the primary responsibility of the home and family. This was apparent in the 1873 U.S. Supreme Court case *Bradwell* v. *Illinois*. Justice Bradley had the following opinion about Myra Bradwell's (unsuccessful) request to overturn the law forbidding married women in Illinois to practice law:

> It is true that many women are unmarried and not affected by any of the duties, complications, and incapacities arising out of the married state, but these are exceptions to the general rule. The paramount destiny and mission of woman are [sic] to fulfill the noble and benign offices of wife and mother. This is the law of the creator. And the rules of civil society must be adapted to the general constitution of things, and cannot be based upon exceptional cases.
>
> (*Bradwell* v. *Illinois*, 83 U.S. [16 Wall.] at 141–142 [1873]*)*

Smart (1989, 85, 88) states that law is "grounded in patriarchy" and "defines how we think about women." The importance of laws, legal precedence, and legislation cannot be overemphasized. "Women were—and are—kept in place by laws" (Epstein 1988, 121). While sex discrimination has been prevalent throughout history, sex discrimination as a legal concern is a recent phenomenon (Robinson 1988). An analysis of laws affecting women's rights found that even in the 1960s, the view of women's primary function as homemakers was used as a basis for treating men and women differently under the law. The effect was the relegation of women to a service class: to serve man and the state (Eastwood 1975, 327). Women and the laws affecting them have historically moved from the private sphere to the public sphere (Dahl 1987). However, it was not until the 1970s, as a result of the women's movement, that the Supreme Court agenda included sex discrimination cases. It has been stated that the legal status of U.S. women changed more in the past twenty-five years than in the prior two centuries (Hoff 1991, 229).

There are two important implications regarding women's work in the home: (1) the myth that all women have worked only in the home, and (2) the devaluation of women's work in the home. Although women have faced numerous restrictions to working outside of the home, many have done so; meanwhile their work inside the home often remains unrecognized and undervalued. Regarding the first point, women have worked outside of the home for many years, and many continue to do so, usually out of economic necessity. Frontier women, poor women, and slave women have always worked outside the home. "By 1930, one-quarter of all adult women and over half of all single women worked in the wage labor force" (Meyerowitz 1988, 5). Women who worked outside the home have tended to be single, black, and poor; but married, white, and middle-class women have increasingly been employed outside of the home since the 1940s. It has been argued that the public/private distinction is relevant only for upper- and middle-class Anglo women, given the government's historic interference in the public and private lives of the working class and the poor:

> Welfare programs and policies have discouraged family life, sterilization programs have restricted reproduction rights, government has drafted and armed disproportionate numbers of people of Color to fight its wars overseas, and locally, police forces and the criminal justice system arrest and incarcerate disproportionate numbers of people of Color. There is no such thing as a private sphere for people of Color except that which they manage to create and protect in an otherwise hostile environment.
> *(Hurtado 1989, 849)*

Now turning to the devaluation of women's work in the home, regardless of women's personal characteristics (marital status, race, and class), their work outside has rarely excused them from the onerous and devalued work inside the home. Domestic work in a woman's own home is unpaid, while domestic work in other people's homes is performed almost exclusively by women ("cleaning ladies") and poorly paid (Burrows 1988). There is no logical reason why women, and not men, perform these duties, and it is not a coincidence that they are severely underpaid. Moreover, the lack of acknowledgment of a person's or group's qualities and activities often results in a loss of dignity for the person or group (Dahl 1987, 367). Women's work in the home lacks recognition and support—it is work that others expect of them, and it is rarely appreciated. Housework is not covered by the Social Security Act, often leaving divorced and widowed full-time homemakers without security for their labors (Thomas 1991).

Meyerowitz (1988) accounts for "women adrift" between 1880 and 1930, when women's participation in the U.S. labor force increased from 2.6 million to 10.8 million. "Women adrift" were single, independent, wage-earning women who did not live with relatives or employers. "Women adrift" tended to be white, unmarried women from poor families who migrated to the cities, largely out of economic necessity, but also to escape abuse or stigma, or to find adventure. However, "women adrift" were a heterogeneous group that also included black women; separated, divorced, or widowed women; and women who deserted or had been deserted by their husbands. The wages of "women adrift" were extremely low—frequently below the poverty level—because women's wages were set for dependent wives and daughters who had access to additional (male) resources and income. These women challenged traditional views of women. "When they mingled freely with men in rooming houses, at work, and at places of recreation, they undermined the 'separation of spheres' that had segregated women from men by relegating them to the domestic world of the home" (Meyerowitz 1988, xix). "Women adrift" represent a significant pattern of the movement of women from the private to the public sphere:

> The "women adrift," then, stand at a juncture in U.S. women's history. They moved from a female domestic world in predominantly rural societies to a sexually integrated, urban environment. Bereft of family support and confronted with poverty, they created new subcultures, challenged

Victorian prescriptions, set patterns for contemporary sex roles, inspired social reformers, and influenced popular culture. Their history links together the history of women, work, sexuality, social reform, and popular culture in the late-nineteenth and early-twentieth century city.

(Meyerowitz 1988, xxiii)

Motivations for Restricting
Women to the Private Sphere

Various excuses have been given to restrict women from job opportunities and equality in general. These excuses often fall under the rubric of *protection*—protecting women "for their own good." Such a paternalistic attitude may "protect" women from certain physically grueling and dangerous jobs, but it often excludes women from many occupations and limits their ability to earn high wages. For instance, in 1948 the Supreme Court upheld a 1945 Michigan statute (*Goesaert* v. *Cleary*) that prohibited women from tending bars unless they were the daughters or wives of male bar owners. This was affirmed under the guise of protecting these women from unsafe patrons, despite evidence that showed that women had a civilizing influence on the patrons (Rhode 1989).

Thus, the "protection" of women often results in excluding women from employment opportunities and basic rights. Almost every government report on women workers between 1918 and 1944 mentioned the concern that women workers might resist and undercut men's opportunities (Atkins and Hoggett 1984, 20). Additionally, the policies and laws supposedly designed to protect women have not addressed health hazards in occupations traditionally occupied by women, such as brown lung disease in cotton mills (Epstein 1988, 129). Even a recent study of policies and court decisions attempting to exclude women of "fertile ages" (which includes most working women) from employment found that employers are concerned only about potential harm to fetuses for women working in traditionally male occupations. Notably, excluding women of childbearing ages from traditionally female jobs where harmful chemicals are abundant (such as beauty shops, nursing, cleaning, and garment industries) is unheard of (Draper 1993).

Atkins and Hoggett (1984) discuss three ways the legal system has attempted to justify limiting women's job opportunities. First is a belief in *women's "natural" inferiority*. This view suggests that women are too emotionally, intellectually, and physically weak to endure certain jobs, most of which are outside the home and often relatively lucrative. Seen as the "weaker sex," women have been excluded, for example, from high-paying positions involving the use of machines and a full work week, and have been relegated instead to low-paying and part-time employment. Particularly in the nineteenth century, but well into this century, judges upheld this "natural" inferiority to limit women's access to wages and job opportunities, including medicine (supposedly, women are too intellectually weak to be physicians). Women were traditionally barred from entering law schools and practicing law based on the assumption that females were inherently unable to perform the job and were best suited to their natural environment: the home.

Maternity is Atkins and Hoggett's (1984) second justification used to restrict women's work. This excuse was first posed in the 1847 House of Commons Factory Bill in England. The bill claimed that there was a danger to young infants whose mothers were working outside the home. If we combine the supposed inherent "weakness" of women with the idea that women are destined to stay home (since infants' well-being is supposedly dependent on their mothers not leaving the house), a bleak picture for women confronts us—women are trapped into staying home because society depends on them to do so. Until the mid-1970s, pregnant women workers were routinely "dismissed" (fired) and frequently were denied requests for reinstatement after giving birth. Additionally, most state unemployment and insurance programs excluded pregnant women (Rhode 1989). Notably, despite the weakness assumed to be inherent in women, they are seen as potentially powerful enough to dismantle a seemingly healthy society by "shirking" their "womanly duties" and not staying home. Unfortunately, such a commitment to women's "rightful" place in the home is not simply a belief of the past. Criminologists published the following statement implying women's responsibility in the rising crime rate:

> [T]he changing economic status of women [through their increased participation in the job market] could contribute to higher crime rates in four distinct ways: each family's control over its own children is reduced; control over neighborhood children is reduced when women are not at home during the day; empty homes are targets for crime; and the women themselves are exposed to new opportunities to commit crimes in the workplace.
>
> *(Chaiken and Chaiken 1983, 21)*

This statement suggests that a movement toward women's equality in the labor force will have a negative impact on society as a whole. "Women who seize their right to work outside the home, for instance, are being blamed for the break-down of the American family, when economic pressures are the true source of the problem" (Williams 1981, 19). Even if a woman's family could survive on income from her spouse, it is unfair to suggest that women carry the burden of society falling apart simply because they pursue a career outside of the home. This implies that careers are only, or more important, for men. Given the high rates of female, single-head-of-household families, this argument is outdated as well as unfair. Furthermore, more recent research points out that family income and the supports available to working women mediate any spurious relationship between women's work and delinquency, and women with full-time employment may be *less* likely to have delinquent children (see Currie 1985).

Marriage is Atkins and Hoggett's (1984, 18) third and final justification used to limit women's employment opportunities. This justification assumes that all women (should) marry, and that the man's job should be in the public sphere and the woman should remain in the private sphere. William Blackstone's eighteenth-century legal treatise on wives was based on the Bible, where husband

and wife were regarded as "one person in the law," where "the 'one' was the husband" (Rhode 1989, 10). At the beginning of the nineteenth century in England, single women had more legal abilities than married women, especially regarding property ownership (Fergus 1988). Similarly, in the United States, regardless of marital status, all women were barred from many professions and trades. However, married women fared much worse than unmarried women, because they were viewed as their husbands' property (Kirp et al. 1986, 31). In fact, most nineteenth- and early twentieth-century women had to choose between marriage and employment in the paid labor force, which is probably why as late as 1920, four in five women in the paid work force were unmarried (Rhode 1989, 13).

Even today, although most women and men marry, marriage generally influences women's lives and life choices much more than men's (Okin 1989). Some parties still propose that marriage is a justification for discriminating against women working outside of the home; they maintain that certain jobs should be left for men who have families to support. Not only does this discriminate against women seeking employment, but it ignores that access to paid labor enables women to avoid being economically "forced" into marriage, and gives them the means to leave bad marriages (Burrows 1988).

The belief that women should marry and raise children and let men have careers results in obvious discrimination against women. If men can be married (and have children) *and* have careers, why can't women? Furthermore, the number of dependents should not be a criterion in assigning jobs. Even if the number of dependents were a legitimate criterion, there is a need to acknowledge the vast and growing number of single-parent mothers. Also, male workers vary by need and number of dependents. It is highly doubtful that males would want jobs assigned on the basis of the number of dependents.

These assumptions and explanations lead one to believe that separate spheres for women and men still exist. One study of professionals in an industrial corporation found that marriage and motherhood were used as excuses for not promoting women. Employers assumed that women would not want to go on business trips, which were a requirement for promotion (Kanter 1977a). Even in the 1980s, the courts successfully used explanations of women's domestic roles to allow sex discrimination in terms of promoting only male teachers into administrative positions (*Gillespie* v. *Board of Education of North Little Rock* [1982]) and keeping women in lower paying, noncommissioned, dead-end sales jobs (*Equal Employment Opportunity Commission* v. *Sears, Roebuck, and Company* [1986]) (Eisenstein 1988; Schultz 1991).

MOVEMENT TOWARD GENDER EQUALITY

Women are discriminated against in a number of ways that perpetuate their lack of power in society. For women as a class to obtain political power, they must first obtain (1) equal treatment under the law, (2) protection from sex discrimination, and (3) physical self-determination (largely through reproductive freedom, such as access to birth control and abortion) (Eastwood 1975). The history of women's equality encompasses a wide variety of issues. Central to these is the equal access to employment opportunities and the autonomy that such employment provides through financial independence. Regardless of whether women are married, they usually work because they need to support themselves and their families. However, a woman's average pay is two-thirds of a man's for comparable work, and the more an occupation is populated by women, the lower the pay (Thomas 1991, 193).

Access Versus Influence and the Necessity of Both

Women's right to vote (suffrage) and the movement for women's equality were in many ways two separate battles. Although earlier efforts toward feminist activist outcomes existed before the 1920s, it was a long struggle for women to receive the right to vote in 1920 (Berger 1980). (However, in some individual states, women had the legal right to vote before 1920, just as some states had legal abortion statutes before *Roe* v. *Wade* [1973].) Why were they unsuccessful until 1920? One suggestion is that *group consciousness,* a necessary prerequisite to effecting change for an oppressed group, was lacking until 1920. "Women first needed to recognize that they faced certain problems precisely because they were women in order for the feminist movement to emerge" (Klein 1984, 3). Similarly, the wave of feminism in the 1960s has been attributed to "not only the increasing number of women in the work force who might experience discrimination, but also the increasing number of women who perceived it as such" (Rhode 1989, 55).

Legislative and Supreme Court rulings have been important avenues for effecting social change. Virtually all of the movement of women into the areas of law enforcement, the courts, and prison and jail work has been because of lawsuits (initiated by women). The initial opportunities, as well as some current ones, were the result of court decisions, not genuine opportunity or good-will on the part of the dominant group (wealthy, white males). *Reed* v. *Reed* (1971) was the first successful major sex discrimination case (O'Connor 1980). Sally Reed challenged an Idaho statute that favored males as estate administrators of the deceased. This case marked the first time that the equal protection clause of the Fourteenth Amendment was extended to women. Although this decision didn't directly tackle the separate spheres ideology, *Reed* v. *Reed* laid the groundwork for many other successful sex discrimination cases brought by women that explicitly condemned separate spheres. Nonetheless, the courts have been less understanding of "more subtle sex-based classifications that affect opportunities for and social views about women" (Bartlett 1991, 372).

Unfortunately, although legal changes are usually *necessary,* they are not always *sufficient* to actually bring about change. Many citizens are unaware of their own legal rights, and some institutions who discriminate may be unaware that they are breaking the law (or even discriminating). However, even when some employers are aware of the laws they are breaking, they use various forms of direct or indirect coercion to override the law. For instance, even though a police department may have a policy against sexual harassment, a policewoman may decide it is less costly emotionally and financially to "put up" with it than to take on the male-dominated police and court system. In the same vein, workers who know that they are being discriminated against may justifiably decide that to keep the job they have, or even to maintain a good record for a future job, it is important not to "rock the boat." This is particularly crucial when the victims of discrimination or harassment have no other means of supporting themselves (and perhaps their dependents) during the time-consuming and costly experience of a trial. These are examples of how laws may be necessary but not sufficient in order to effect change.

Similarly, it is important to have both *access* and *influence* in order to achieve equality (Klein 1984). Briefly, access involves acquiring recognition and rights, while influence is being in a position to use the rights and attain new advantages and power. For example, Title VII (a 1972 amendment to the 1964 Civil Rights Act) resulted in the hirings of many policewomen on patrol duties for the first time in U.S. history. However, because these women have, overall, remained in such small numbers (token status) and been in the lower strata of police departments (officers), it has been difficult for them to shape policing in a nonmale manner. Additionally, using the established law to fight discrimination can be "hazardous"; a backlash of countersuits and hostility—sometimes even violence—is often unleashed against oppressed groups and individuals who sue for basic rights (Smart 1989, 138).

With regard to the access issue during the early part of this century, suffragists expected overnight political results once women achieved the right to vote. They believed women's votes would have a powerful influence on elections. Unfortunately, most women did not vote after initially acquiring the right, and of those women who did vote, there was no identifiable "gender gap" (differential candidate support between men and women) until the 1980 presidential election between Ronald Reagan and Jimmy Carter. (Women were more supportive of Carter, and men of Reagan.) This achievement of women's right to vote (*access*), with no apparent resulting effect (*influence*), is an example of achieving access without influence. The limited influence of suffrage, then, may have been due to suffragists strictly limiting their goals in an effort to gain broad-based support.

> By struggling so single-mindedly for one formal guarantee, suffrage advocates failed to confront the other social and economic forces that constrained women's independence. In avoiding issues such as divorce, birth control, poverty, employment discrimination, working conditions, racism, and domestic violence, the major women's rights organizations remained one step removed from the problems and priorities of most women.
> *(Rhode 1989, 18)*

Overall, between 1920 and 1960, there appeared to be a lull in the fight for women's rights (Berger 1980; Klein 1984; Rhode 1989). This is not to say that there was no feminist political activity between 1920 and 1960. The Equal Rights Amendment was first submitted to Congress in 1923 and every year after that until it was passed by the House and the Senate in 1972. (It was assumed that acquiring ratification by three-fourths of the states would be perfunctory, but a backlash against its ratification headed by antifeminist Phyllis Schlafly was extremely successful.) Thus, although there was some political activity to improve the equality of women, it lacked the widespread momentum and support the suffrage battle had acquired. In the 1960s, renewed political advocacy for women's rights was stimulated by the 1964 Civil Rights Act and the progress made by the black movement.

Comparison of Racial and Gender Equality Activism

Comparisons and analogies are frequently made between political activism to promote racial equality and political activism to promote gender equality. Some people resist comparing gender to racial oppression, believing that since women do not make up a minority in the population, they should not require special legislative appeals used by African Americans and other people of color. Nonetheless, women are a disadvantaged group despite their numerical dominance; they have limited access to rewards and opportunities in a system where the male is viewed as "normal" and the female is often viewed as deviant (Laws 1975).

Comparing gender and racial oppression is complex. We need to keep in mind that the lynching of African Americans, the genocide of Native Americans, and the military conquest of Latinos are not identical to the physical abuse, discrimination, and cultural denigration experienced by women (King 1988, 15). However, both racial minority members and women experience "shared subordinate treatment on the basis of ascribed attributes and have internalized the social values that perpetuate such subordination" (Rhode 1987, 20–21). While members of an oppressed group usually understand and are frustrated by this oppression, it is also evident that oppression can effect members' self-esteem, self-confidence, and sense of self-worth.

A major distinction between racism and sexism is that people of color do not tend to share the private sphere as intimately with the empowered (that is, Anglo men), whereas Anglo women often benefit, particularly financially, from the advantages accrued to their Anglo fathers and Anglo husbands. Furthermore, racial and sex discrimination have been distinguished by motivation: Racial discrimination is more often motivated by the intent to degrade and disempower, while discrimination against women is more often motivated by paternalism (Rhode 1987, 21). Similarly, although the law has traditionally treated blacks with "unremitting antagonism," and women as "frail" and "nobler" than men and thus in need of men's protection, the impact on women and blacks has been the same: "a constraint on the choices open to individual blacks or individual women" (Kirp et al. 1986). Although the paternalism and protectionism supposedly guiding laws that restrict women are viewed more positively than the degrading laws restricting blacks, both paternalistic and degrading laws have extremely negative consequences. In some ways, the paternalistically motivated laws may be more difficult to fight, since there is some element that is claiming to be helpful. Unfortunately, they usually serve to restrict women's rights (to employment, jury duty, and so on) and help to perpetuate stereotypes of women as weaker than or less than men.

In short, despite their proportion in the population, women have been considered "minorities" in some legislation and policies. This is a recognition of women's "deviant" status when they try to obtain rights ranging from educational and job opportunities to opportunities to play on athletic teams. Legislation and court decisions overturning sex discrimination acknowledge that society is not gender-neutral, that boys and girls are raised with different attitudes about and access to rights and opportunities, and that males and females have different experiences. It is not surprising that one of the first successful sex discrimination cases in the United States, *Frontiero* v. *Richardson* (1973), compared the classification of sex to that of race. This case established sex as a "suspect class," similar to race, in that excuses unrelated to a group's abilities had been used historically to discriminate against members of the group (Hoff 1991; Lucie 1988). The Frontiero decision overturned regulations that denied female armed service workers the same dependents' rights as the male workers.

The impact of holding more than one stigmatized status at once can be more than cumulative. Occupying a subordinate status in both sex and race has been referred to as "double marginality," "double jeopardy," and "intersectionality." Similarly, poor women of color experience "triple jeopardy," based on sex, race, and class (King 1988). Examining the effects of racism *or* sexism fails to acknowledge that some individuals in society experience race discrimination and sex discrimination. For instance, the abysmally low wages earned by Anglo "women adrift" in the early decades of this century were lower still for African American "women adrift" (Meyerowitz 1988). Black women who were leaders and key organizers in the civil rights movement remain, for the most part, unrecognized and invisible (Barnett 1993). Even in the late 1980s, data from full-time workers indicate that the average Anglo woman college graduate earned significantly less than the average man with a high school degree, and the average college-educated African American woman earned about 90 percent of the average Anglo woman, "a figure roughly equivalent to a white male high school dropout" (Rhode 1989, 163).

The "intersectional experience" of being both black and female "is greater than the sum of racism and sexism" (Crenshaw 1989, 140). The history of tension between the African American and Anglo feminist movements was discussed earlier. More recently, most Anglo feminists have increased their attempts to acknowledge and fight racism as well as sexism. Although many African American women have traditionally viewed racism as a more powerful cause of their subordination than sexism, both black and white women are becoming more integrated in unified feminist and antiracist activities and goals (Lewis 1977).

Impact of Movement to the
Public Sphere on Women's Equality

Surprisingly, many persons (including some women) who believed women had a right to vote did not believe men and women were equal. (This may not be too different from today. It is likely that the majority of people opposed to the Equal Rights Amendment *do* believe women have a right to vote.) Thus, women's suffrage did not result in a movement for equality between the sexes. The catalysts for effecting a change in women's equality were the 1940s movement of women out of the home and the 1960s civil rights movement. The movement of women from the private sphere (the home) to the public sphere (society) has not simply been a result of feminist political activism. In fact, women's most successful movement to the public sphere was due more to economic conditions and technology than to feminist activism.

During World War II, when the labor supply was affected by "prime age" male workers who were fighting or being trained to fight, the U.S. government pursued a highly successful advertising campaign to attract women to "men's" jobs in factories, construction, and aviation. The government recruited women out of necessity, since there were too few men left to perform the jobs. Thus, the women were recruited through the lure of helping their country. These women temporarily enjoyed improved wages and government-sponsored day care for their children while they worked and helped their country. (It is not clear why they weren't perceived as helping their country with their work inside the home, too.) Most of these privileges were reneged, however, when the war ended and the men returned. Nonetheless, once many of the women experienced working in the public sphere, they were no longer satisfied to return to the lack of wages and the isolation of life at home. This belief in their right to work outside the home helped bring about group consciousness of the oppression of women's rights (as previously discussed by Klein [1984]).

The 1960s were significant in the struggle for women's equality. Data from this era indicate that many U.S. women were dissatisfied with full-time domestic work. At the same time, "marriage and motherhood were becoming less stable foundations for an entire lifetime" as the divorce rate increased from one in six marriages in 1940 to one in two marriages in the 1980s (Rhode 1989, 53). The number of women estimated never to marry increased to 10 percent in the late 1980s, while the percentage of single-parent families headed by a woman grew to almost twice that (Rhode 1989, 54). Rhode (1989, 54) identifies *status deprivation* as another motivating force for a new wave of feminism in the 1960s: "a perception that women had less opportunity for social recognition than men with comparable talents and training." During the mid-1960s, many women were displeased with their treatment in the civil rights, antiwar, and other leftist organizations. Consciousness-raising (CR) groups became popular, where small groups of women met to discuss, among other issues, "the personal as political." This slogan represented a belief that patriarchy dominates all aspects of women's lives, their personal lives (for example, sexual activity and housework) as well as their public participation (for example, employment outside the home) (Hurtado 1989; Jaggar 1983).

Consciousness-raising and similar groups helped organize the women's movement and push for women's equality.

Labor market conditions for women have changed very slowly. For example, women were relegated to the lowest paying jobs in the sex-segregated
labor market during industrialization and development of the service economy in the late nineteenth and early twentieth centuries in the United States
(Meyerowitz 1988). By the 1970s, half of all female employees were concen-
trated in seventeen occupations, while half of male employees were located in
sixty-three occupations (Kanter, 1977a). Moreover, current working conditions for women in England may also be applied to the United States:

> As far as women's employment is concerned, the majority of women
> workers are to be found in a small number of occupations. They tend to
> be employed in the catering or service industries; they work as cleaners,
> hairdressers, shop assistants or clerical workers, or they are involved in
> repetitive assembly or packaging work. They are also over-represented
> within the education, welfare and health occupations. Within each occu-
> pation, they are heavily concentrated in the lower grades [with far lower
> wages].
>
> *(Gregory 1987, 3)*

A recent analysis of African Americans' progress toward economic equality
notes that not only is employment outside the home necessary for single-
women head of households (who are predominantly black), but such employment is also often necessary for women (and their families) who are married to
black men (Geschwender and Carroll-Seguin 1990). African American women's
economic contributions to their families are relatively much greater than those
of Anglo women. The pressure of paid employment for married black women,
then, is usually greater than for married white women, given the reduced earn-
ing capacity of black men. The decline in real income in recent years, com-
bined with the lack of available educational and economic opportunities for
African Americans, not only has loosened their precarious hold on the middle
class acquired during the 1960s and 1970s, but has increased the proportion of
blacks living in poverty (Geschwender and Carroll-Seguin 1990).

In conclusion, despite feminist attempts to widen women's working opportunities, there remains a stubborn adherence to sex-segregated jobs, with
women's jobs being the lowest paid. This has the most severe impact on women
of color and their families.

LEGAL IMPLICATIONS

Sex-Neutral Legislation

Although men and women hold different positions in society, the laws tend to
be "unisex" in nature (Dahl 1987, 361). In contrast with the sex-specific legislation discussed below, most laws are sex neutral ("unisex"), even those created
with hopes of rectifying gender equality. That is, sex-neutral laws simply state
that a person should not be discriminated against based on her or his sex.

However, when the differing living conditions, needs, and potentials for men and women meet the unisex laws, the "legal rules will necessarily affect men and women differently" (Dahl 1987, 361). More simply, because men and women hold such different positions in society, unisex laws will have different results for women than for men. "Clearly the gender neutral terms of the federal constitution do not protect the rights of women to the same extent as they protect the rights of men" (Thomas 1991, 116).

Title VII, a 1972 amendment of the 1964 Civil Rights Act, is an example of such sex-neutral legislation. It is illegal to base any terms of employment (conditions, compensation, firing, hiring, and so on) on a person's sex, race, religion, or national origin. Ironically, although most employment sex discrimination suits have been brought via Title VII, "sex" was added to the list of nondiscriminatory characteristics listed in the amendment (after race, religion, and natural origin) at the last minute before its passage, as an attempt to derail the entire Civil Rights Act; that is, antiwoman sentiment was used to try to deny racial equality (Deitch 1993). In fact, when the inclusion of sex was read to Congress, it was met with laughter, and all but one of the men who had voted for including "sex" in the amendment voted against the whole bill (Deitch 1993). This is another example of racism and sexism operating simultaneously.

Title VII allowed the Equal Employment Opportunity Commission (the EEOC), a federal agency established in 1964, "the power to prosecute Title VII violators in the federal courts, a power it quickly utilized" (Zimmer 1986, 4). In fact, most employment discrimination suits have been brought pursuant to this amendment (Berger 1980). However, it has also been stated that it took ten years for Title VII to get some "teeth" and be effective (Hoff 1991, 234).

Despite its positive influence, Title VII has important limitations. First, the *bona fide occupational qualification* (or BFOQ) defense was designed for exceptions where it would be considered rational to prefer the employment of one sex over the other. (Notably, race never qualifies as a BFOQ [Blankenship 1993].) Some claim that the only rational BFOQs regarding sex are sperm donors and wet nurses. BFOQs, however, have been legally used to exclude women's employment from a variety of occupations, including prison chaplain, prison guard, and international oil executive (Epstein 1988). Second, Title VII is problematic in that it is costly to litigate; the cost of discovery (proof of differential employee treatment) and the need for expensive experts prohibit most workers from charging these suits on their own (Berger 1980, 39).

Third, even when female employees have had the resources to go to court, many of these decisions have been disappointing. In *Geduldig* v. *Aiello* (1974) and *General Electric Co.* v. *Gilbert* (1976), for example, the Supreme Court decided that a company's exclusion of pregnancy and pregnancy-related disorders from their disability plan "does not constitute a denial of equal protection... because *no pregnant man is treated differently from any pregnant woman*" (Berger 1980, 22). Although the disability plan covered sports injuries, elective cosmetic surgery, vasectomies, and disabilities incurred while committing a crime, absences associated with pregnancy and childbirth were excluded. Justice Rehnquist, in fact, viewed the decision as *promoting* gender equality, since women wouldn't be covered for anything men couldn't be covered for (Williams 1991). This ruling not only helps keep women in the private sphere, but has obvious class bias, given the additional burden for women (and their families) who are economically dependent on the job—they simply can't afford to have children.

Despite its unsuccessful outcome for the complainant, *General Electric Co.* v. *Gilbert,* was not a complete loss. The high visibility of the case prompted the American Civil Liberties Union (ACLU) to convince Congress to amend Title VII to include discrimination against pregnant women as a type of sex discrimination (Berger 1980; Eisenstein 1988; Minow 1993; Williams 1991). The 1978 Pregnancy Discrimination Act (PDA) required employers to treat pregnancy like any other temporary disability. Nonetheless, even ten years after the inception of the PDA, one-third of working women did not have access to protected leaves during pregnancy, "and even those with such protection could not count on returning to their same position at the time they wished" (Rhode 1989, 119).

The PDA also fails to protect women from pregnancy discrimination in situations other than employment. A 1990 ruling in *Pfeiffer* v. *Marion Center Area School District* found that it was acceptable for the high school's National Honor Society (NHS) to dismiss a pregnant student. It was decided that this was not sex discrimination because the basis for expulsion was premarital sex (obvious from her pregnant state), not the pregnancy itself. The testimony of a male NHS member who admitted to engaging in premarital sex and was not expelled was excluded. "Pregnant or not, it is unclear how premarital sex destroys one's academic achievement that warrants membership in the National Honor Society" (Thomas 1991, 137).

Another problem with Title VII is that its bifurcation of race and sex has served to *decrease* the employment protection for women of color. The wording of Title VII separates race and sex, giving people of color, as a group, different access to challenging employment discrimination than it provides for women as a group. In essence, the legislative history of Title VII suggests that women of color are not to be its beneficiaries (Blankenship 1993). For example, *DeFraffenreid* v. *General Motors* (1976) was brought by five black women employees because of the hiring and laying-off practices of General Motors. The court sided with GM because they showed that Anglo women and black men had not been discriminated against in hiring and laying off. Thus, black women may be protected only insofar as their discrimination experiences coincide with black men or white women (Crenshaw 1989).

Perhaps the greatest irony of the first fifteen years of sex discrimination Supreme Court rulings is that males have been more successful than females both in their access to the courts and in obtaining favorable decisions (Rhode 1987). The majority of cases recognizing sex discrimination overturned the few instances where the legal or social system was advantageous toward women (the men in these cases claimed to have been the victim of "reverse discrimination"). "When one looks at the actual holdings [of Supreme Court triumphs on sex discrimination], the constant thread that runs through these 'women's rights' cases is that most of the winners have been men, and that women have won only when it was not at the expense of a man" (Berger 1980, 19). Such legal cases granting men alimony eligibility (*Orr* v. *Orr,* 1979), social security benefits (*Califano* v. *Goldfarb,* 1977; *Weinberger* v. *Weisenfeld,* 1975), and access to all-female nursing schools (*Mississippi University for Women* v. *Hogan,* 1982) acknowledge what feminists have been arguing all along in their attempts to promote *women's* access: that persons should not be discriminated against because of their sex. Another example of "reverse discrimination" being overturned in court concerns airlines' policies against hiring male flight attendants in the 1970s and 1980s. While Pan American Airlines attempted to justify restricting flight attendant jobs to women because of their "maternal" role, Southwest Airlines built their case on the "sexy image" of female flight attendants in "hot pants" and high boots as a legitimate reason to exclude male workers. "In both cases, the courts reasoned that the 'essence' of the airline's business was safe transportation, and that other employment attributes were 'merely tangential' to that 'primary' function" (Rhode 1989, 94). The subsequent switch in title from the gendered "stewardess" to nongendered "flight attendant," along with the substantial hirings of male flight attendants are likely results of the courts' rulings.

The 1963 Equal Pay Act has also been fraught with problems. Reportedly designed to rectify gender wage discrimination by prohibiting pay discrimination for women and men performing the same job, it applies only where the jobs performed are substantiated as equal. Thus the Equal Pay Act can't be used to raise the abysmally low wages for traditional women's work, and thus is not applicable to nearly half of all employed women and over two-thirds of employed women of color (Berger 1980; Blankenship 1993).

In summary, although the courts are acknowledging discrimination based on sex, the most successful cases in court are those that *further advance males.* Or, put more simply, sex discrimination is more likely to be considered unconstitutional in instances where males are discriminated against than in situations where females are discriminated against. Unfortunately, of course, the vast amount of sex discrimination is against females, and apparently that is the least likely to be rectified. Additionally, two important legislative changes proposing to help discrimination against working women, Title VII and the Equal Pay Act, are written and applied in a manner that provides significantly less coverage for women of color.

Sex-Specific Legislation

As stated earlier, most laws are "unisex" (or sex-neutral). However, some laws are sex-specific, meaning that they identify the sex to which the laws apply, and restrict or give an advantage to one sex over the other. Historically, male judges' and male legislators' sex-specific rulings were almost completely to the disadvantage of women. A historical account of women's rights and the Supreme Court states: "What is perhaps most striking is the utter unselfconsciousness with which an exclusively male judiciary interpreted statutes adopted by exclusively male legislators to determine issues of male exclusivity" (Rhode 1987, 14). The year 1992 was called "the year of the woman" because of record high numbers of women, especially African American women, running for elected office, and yet resulted in only six women in the U.S. Senate and 47 in the U.S. House of Representatives. Furthermore, President Clinton's efforts to appoint more women to high offices resulted in the intense scrutiny of female nominees' child-care providers, an issue that had never been raised for elected or appointed men. This so-called "Nannygate" excluded many qualified women from offices if there was any hint that illegal aliens had been used as child-care workers, or if social security payments for the workers weren't appropriate. No one had ever examined this for male nominees.

In 1908, the U.S. Supreme Court reinforced women's place as in the home in *Muller* v. *Oregon* (cited in Rhode 1987), which made maximum-hour work weeks for women (but not men) constitutional. The motivation for this ruling was paternalistic: to protect women from being overworked. The ruling, however, resulted in limitation on women's hours at work outside of the home, income, and jobs at which they could be employed. This decision made women more expensive and less available for overtime and night shifts, limited their occupational choices and bargaining power, and increased their unemployment rates (Rhode 1987, 17).

Historically, organized labor supported sex-specific laws denying or restricting women's employment opportunities, supposedly in attempts to secure better labor standards for all workers (Eastwood 1975). Similarly, some current sex-specific legislation is labeled *benign discrimination* because the laws are supposedly designed to protect women. Predictably, this "protective" legislation has served to reinforce the separate spheres and stereotypical gender roles (Rhode 1989). Thus, there may be a cost to sex-specific legislation where the goal is to compensate for women's lack of equality.

Formal Versus Compensating Equality Laws

Two distinct strategies exist for achieving equality through laws: (1) formal equality and (2) compensating equality (Gregory 1987). *Formal equality* laws require that everyone is treated identically, regardless of sex or race. Thus, formal equality includes the sex-neutral legislation discussed above, but is designed to enhance equality. An example of a formal equality law is the Equal Rights Amendment, which states, "Equality of rights under the law shall not be denied or abridged by the United States or by any state on account of sex." Title VII is another example of a formal equality law.

Compensating equality laws, on the other hand, are an attempt to overcome the limitations of formal equality laws "by compensating for the social equalities suffered by certain groups" (Gregory 1987, 5). Thus, compensating equality laws may be sex-specific in giving women an advantage over men in an attempt to address historical exclusion. An example of a compensating equality law would be affirmative action laws. While the Equal Rights Amendment simply requires that everyone be treated the same regardless of their sex, affirmative action legislation is more pro-active and acknowledges that inequalities exist that need to be addressed and that require compensation. The formal equality laws request no differential treatment (that is, men and women should be treated identically), whereas the compensating equality laws request preferential treatment in order to acknowledge that women and people of color are at a disadvantage. Notably, compensating equality laws also exist for groups that have not faced oppression, such as veterans (Glasser 1988; Thomas 1991). Programs for veterans have existed for over 100 years and provide a lifetime preference for civil service jobs (Thomas 1991). Interestingly, these laws have rarely been questioned or judged, while affirmative action laws continue to be rigorously questioned and eroded.

Feminist scholars are not in agreement as to whether formal or compensating equality laws should be the preferred method to achieve women's equality. Some feminist scholars support compensating equality laws, believing that formal equality laws ignore the current gender differences in access and opportunity, and thus serve to perpetuate gender inequality (Dahl 1987; Finley 1993; Gregory 1987; Krieger and Cooney 1993). Others support compensating equality laws because the progress on equality in women's employment has been slow due to court decisions being based on precedent that has a history of supporting sex discrimination (McLean 1988; Mullen 1988). Still others believe that formal equality can effect only limited change and, for example, can't ensure that job structures allow both females and males to work outside the home *and* parent (Becker 1993).

Nonetheless, other feminist scholars have concerns about compensating equality laws. For example, although the formal and compensating equality laws were constructed as mutually exclusive, it is difficult to justify using formal equality laws for some circumstances and compensating equality laws for others. By promoting one it is impossible not to undermine the other (Smart 1989). Sex-specific compensating equality laws, then, often serve to affirm sex-based stereotypes, which in turn perpetuate sex-based inequality (Littleton 1991; Lucie 1988; Mezey 1990; Rhode 1989; Smart 1989; Williams 1991, 1993).

Feminist support for compensating versus formal equality laws has been dubbed the "equal treatment/special treatment debate," and this issue is especially apparent with regard to the rights of pregnant women (Williams 1993). Women are distinguished from men by their ability to become pregnant, lactate, and give birth, but not all women can or choose to do so. Although some women never become pregnant, no men ever become pregnant. There is a fine line between beneficiary and victim when it comes to legal classifications surrounding pregnancy, such that women must not be "trapped by the argument that pregnancy is unique" (Lucie 1988, 237). The federal PDA defines pregnancy as a "disability." Furthermore, the PDA can't stop states from *mandating* special maternity leaves, whether the woman wants one or not (Rhode 1990).

The equal treatment/special treatment debate focuses on the following concern: Can we assert that men and women are equal and need to be treated equally, and at the same time request special laws for women implying that women are different/special (not the same/equal)? This is particularly troubling when these "special" compensating equality laws reinforce gender stereotypes. Eisenstein (1988, 204) concurs with the ACLU's fear that protective pregnancy legislation reinforces the myth that women belong in the private sphere:

In the eyes of an employer, a woman is a potential mother whether or not she is pregnant. Pregnancy affects a woman's options in the labor force either by its absence (she is not pregnant now but she may become pregnant) or by its presence. Recognition of pregnancy through sex-specific legislation undermines discrimination at least as much as, if not more than, it enforced it.

Recent research has documented how women's *potential* to bear children has negatively affected their employment opportunities, and coerced some women to be sterilized in order to keep their traditionally male jobs (Draper 1993). One solution offered to the equal treatment/special treatment debate is to implement formal equality laws overall, and take account of biological differences (such as pregnancy) only when the differences are significant to the issue at hand. This approach views biological reproductive differences as "episodic and temporary" and thus should be relevant in legal cases only when they are relevant to the question at hand (Kay 1993). *Who* will determine relevancy and *how* it will be decided are problematic issues.

WOMEN JURORS

Serving on juries is an area in which women have been short-changed historically, and they continue to experience discrimination. Although many people view jury duty as annoying or inconvenient, it is a fundamental form of citizenship. It has been argued that excluding women from jury duty and the military draft in fact excludes women from full citizenship and feeds stereotypes about women's weakness and dependency on men (Eastwood 1975; Lucie 1988). We are thus forced to ask, "When is an advantage discrimination?" (Lucie 1988). For example, courts' restrictions of women from military service and some other occupations has "transformed biological distinctions into cultural imperatives" where biology becomes destiny (Rhode 1990, 121). Jury duty is an important service, and jury selection should not systematically disallow members of the population. When laws or *voir dire* policies exclude women from jury duty, "they limit both the woman's right to participate in the judicial process and the plaintiff's and defendant's right to a representative jury" (Mahoney 1987, 209).

An earlier portion of this chapter discussed the importance of achieving both *access* and *influence* in terms of power, in order to create social, political, and economic change. Jury duty is an excellent example of how access was a hard-fought battle for women, and a success that has not always included significant influence. The 1957 Civil Rights Act permitted women to serve on federal court juries, but had nothing to say about state courts (Mahoney 1987, 210). It was fairly common during this time period for states to have automatic exemptions for women. This meant that women could avoid jury duty simply because they were women (an example of sex-specific legislation). This automatic exemption may strike some people as an advantage for women, but it had two unfortunate results: (1) Juries were not representative (which may be unfair to complainants and defendants), and (2) in states where women had automatic exemption, clerks routinely and deliberately did not call women for jury duty because they assumed the women would want their exemption (Mahoney 1987).

An all-male jury convicted Gwendolyn Hoyt of the second-degree murder of her husband. Her counsel appealed this decision to the U.S. Supreme Court, charging that requiring women to register for jury duty at the courthouse had denied Hoyt equal protection and a jury of her peers in *Hoyt* v. *Florida* (1961) (Thomas 1991). The U.S. Supreme Court decided that despite the "advent of 'T.V.' dinners," women's domestic burdens were more important than their civil obligations; that is, women's "rightful" place in the home justified deterring them from jury duty. "The court found no suspicion of denial of equal protection when only 10 out of 10,000 jurors were women" (Mahoney 1987, 211). It was not until *Taylor* v. *Louisiana* (1975) that women could no longer be exempt from jury service based simply on their sex. Interestingly, in this case with a male defendant accused of aggravated kidnaping and rape, the Supreme Court decided an all-male jury was not equal protection. Thus, sexism in jury selection was not considered problematic for a woman defendant (Hoyt), but it was viewed as unacceptable for a male defendant (Taylor).

Even since women have legally achieved the right to serve equally on juries, the process of *voir dire*—the questioning of the various possible jury members by lawyers prior to the trial—has resulted in discrimination. Lawyers often base their questions and attitudes on stereotypical views of women. This process was challenged in *Bobb* v. *Municipal Court* (1983), when attorney Carolyn Bobb was notified for jury duty and refused to answer questions regarding her marital status and spouse's occupation during the *voir dire* process. Bobb was annoyed because the lawyer was asking these questions only of the females in the jury pool. She was "held in contempt of court and taken into custody… sentenced to one day in jail with credit for time served" (Mahoney 1987, 212).

A final example of access not being sufficient in jury duty to achieve women's equality is exemplified by the research finding that women serving on juries tend to be deferential to male jurists and more easily persuaded by other jury members' opinions (Constantini et al. 1983). Contrary to popular opinion, however, women jury members are not inherent enemies of or overly harsh to the women they are judging (Mahoney 1987).

SUMMARY

This chapter addresses the successes and failures of attempts to achieve gender equality, particularly in the public sphere of employment. Women's movement from the private to the public sphere has occurred in fits and starts. First, women's suffrage in 1920 did not automatically enhance women's place in the public sphere, and the Equal Rights Amendment still remains unratified. During World War II, women's aspirations to equality were encouraged when they were "allowed" to participate in the labor market in wider numbers and in a greater variety of jobs—at increased pay. The 1960s spurred a third revival of attempts to bring women into the workplace, this time as equals. Women's movement into the paid labor force has been the focus of discrimination; recognizing financial independence is necessary to free women's dependence on men (Burrows 1988).

Women have struggled with various legislations and court rulings in attempts to be active in the public sphere. This ranges from serving on juries to working in the same fields, and on equal footing, with men. Indeed, it has been noted that the concept "citizenship" is so fraught with male privilege and access that women are routinely excluded, and when included, they stand out as "gendered beings" (Jones 1990). This has been especially problematic in employment in the crime-processing system. Women's battle to overcome the barriers to work with male prisoners and serve as patrol officers in police departments has been grueling and continues to progress slowly. The resistance to change was not ended simply by "allowing" women to practice as lawyers, police officers, and correctional officers. It is a mistake to assume that legislation and communities committed to equality will in and of themselves remove all discrimination (McLean 1988, 3). The next chapter examines women's employment in law enforcement, in prisons and jails, and in courts as attorneys and judges.

REFERENCES

Atkins, Susan, and Brenda Hoggett. 1984. *Women and the Law*. New York: Basil Blackwell.

Barnett, Bernice M. 1993. "Invisible Southern Black Women Leaders in the Civil Rights Movement." *Gender and Society* 7:16–82.

Bartlett, Katherine T. 1991. "Feminist Legal Methods." Pp. 370–403 in *Feminist Legal Theory: Readings in Law and Gender,* edited by K. T. Bartlett and R. Kennedy. Boulder, CO: Westview Press.

Becker, Mary E. 1993. "Prince Charming: Abstract Equality." Pp. 221–236 in *Feminist Legal Theory,* edited by D. K. Weisberg. Philadelphia, PA: Temple University Press.

Berger, Margaret A. 1980. *Litigation on Behalf of Women: A Review for the Ford Foundation.* New York: Ford Foundation Publication.

Blankenship, Kim M. 1993. "Bringing Gender and Race In: U.S. Employ- ment Discrimination Policy." *Gender and Society* 7:204–226.

Bobb v. *Municipal Court,* 143 Cal. App. 3d 849, 192 Cal. Rptr. 260 (1983).

Bradley, Karen, and Diana Khor. 1993. "Toward an Integration of Theory and Research on the Status of Women." *Gender and Society* 7:347–378.

Bradwell v. *Illinois,* 83. U.S. (16 Wall.) 130 (1873).

Burrows, Noreen. 1988. "Employment and Gender." Pp. 102–118 in *The Legal Relevance of Gender,* edited by S. McLean and N. Burrows. Atlantic Highlands, NJ: Humanities International.

Califano v. *Goldfarb,* 430 U.S. 199 (1977).

Campbell, Tom. 1988. "Sex Discrimination: Mistaking the Relevance of Gender." Pp. 16–39 in *The Legal Relevance of Gender,* edited by S. McLean and N. Burrows. Atlantic Highlands, NJ: Humanities International.

Chaiken, Jan M., and Marcia R. Chaiken. 1983. "Crime Rates and the Active Criminal." Pp. 11–30 in *Crime and Public Policy,* edited by J. Q. Wilson. San Francisco, CA: ICS Press.

Constantini, E. M., M. Mallery, and D. M. Yapundich. 1983. "Gender and Jury Partiality: Are Women More Likely to Prejudge Guilt?" *Judicature* 67:124.

Crenshaw, Kimberle. 1989. "Demarginal- izing the Intersection of Race and Sex: A Black Feminist Critique of Anti-Discrimination Doctrine, Femi- nist Theory and Anti-Racist Politics." *University of Chicago Legal Forum* 14:139–167.

Currie, Elliott. 1985. *Confronting Crime: An American Challenge.* New York: Pantheon Books.

Dahl, T. Stang. 1987. "Women's Law: Methods, Problems, and Values." *Contemporary Crises* 10:361–372.

DeFraffenreid v. *General Motors,* 413 F. Supp. (E. D. M. 1976).

Deitch, Cynthia. 1993. "Gender, Race, and Class Politics and the Inclusion of Women in Title VII of the 1964 Civil Rights Act." *Gender and Society* 7:183–203.

Draper, Elaine. 1993. "Fetal Exclusion Policies and Gendered Constructions of Suitable Work." *Social Problems* 40:90–107.

Eastwood, M. 1975. "Feminism and the Law." Pp. 325–334 in *Women: A Feminist Perspective,* edited by J. Free- man. Palo Alto, CA: Mayfield.

Eisenstein, Zillah R. 1988. *The Female Body and the Law.* Berkeley, CA: University of California Press.

Epstein, Cynthia F. 1988. *Deceptive Dis- tinctions: Sex, Gender, and Social Order.* New Haven, CT: Yale University Press.

Equal Employment Opportunity Commission v. *Sears, Roebuck, and Company,* 628 F. Supp. 1264 (N. D. Ill. 1986).

Fergus, T. D. 1988. "Women and the Parliamentary Franchise in Great Britain." Pp. 80–101 in *The Legal Relevance of Gender,* edited by S.

McLean and N. Burrows. Atlantic Highlands, NJ: Humanities Interna- tional.

Finley, Lucinda M. 1993. "Transcending Equality Theory: A Way Out of the Maternity and the Workplace De- bate." Pp. 190–210 in *Feminist Legal Theory,* edited by D. K. Weisberg. Philadelphia, PA: Temple University Press.

Frontiero v. *Richardson,* 411 U.S. 677 (1973).

Gates, Margaret J. 1976. "Occupational Segregation and the Law." Pp. 61–74 in *Women and the Workplace: The Implications of Occupational Segregation,* edited by M. Blaxall and B. Reagan. Chicago: University of Chicago Press.

Geduldig v. *Aiello,* 417 U.S. 484 (1974).

General Electric Co. v. *Gilbert,* 429 U.S. 125 (1976).

Geschwender, James A., and Rita Carroll- Seguin. 1990. "Exploding the Myth of African-American Progress." *Signs: Journal of Women in Culture and Society* 15:285–299.

Gillespie v. *Board of Education of North Little Rock,* 692 F. 2d 529 (8th Circ. 1982).

Glasser, Ira. 1988. "Affirmative Action and the Legacy of Racial Injustice." Pp. 341–358 in *Eliminating Racism: Profiles in Controversy,* edited by P. A. Katz and D. A. Taylor. New York: Plenum.

Goesaert v. *Cleary,* 335 U.S. 464 (1948).

Gregory, Jeanne. 1987. *Sex, Race and the Law: Legislating for Equality.* London: Sage.

Harris, Barbara. 1978. *Beyond Her Sphere.* Westport, CT: Greenwood.

Hoff, Joan. 1991. *Law, Gender, and Injus- tice: A Legal History of U.S. Women.* New York: New York University Press.

Hoyt v. *Florida,* 368 U.S. 57 (1961).

Hurtado, Aida. 1989. "Relating to Privi- lege: Seduction and Rejection in the Subordination of White Women and Women of Color." *Signs: Journal of Women in Culture and Society* 14:833–855.

Jaggar, Alison M. 1983. *Feminist Politics and Human Nature.* Sussex, England: Rowman & Allanheld.

Jones, Kathleen B. 1990. "Citizenship in a Woman-Friendly Polity." *Signs: Journal of Women in Culture and Society* 15:781–812.

Kanter, Rosabeth M. 1977a. *Men and Women of the Corporation.* New York: Basic Books.

_____. 1977b. "Some Effects of Proportions on Group Life: Skewed Sex Ratios and Responses to Token Women." *American Journal of Sociology* 82:965–990.

Kay, Herma H. 1993. "Equality and Difference: The Case of Pregnancy." Pp. 180–189 in *Feminist Legal Theory,* edited by D. K. Weisberg. Philadelphia, PA: Temple University Press.

King, Deborah K. 1988. "Multiple Jeopardy, Multiple Consciousness: The Context of a Black Feminist Ideology." *Signs: Journal of Women in Culture and Society* 14:12–72.

Kirp, David L., Mark G. Yudof, and Marlene S. Franks. 1986. *Gender Justice.* Chicago: University of Chicago Press.

Klein, Ethel. 1984. *Gender Politics.* Cambridge, MA: Harvard University Press.

Krieger, Linda J., and Patricia N. Cooney. 1993. "The Miller-Wohl Controversy: Equal Treatment, Positive Action and the Meaning of Women's Equality." Pp. 156–179 in *Feminist Legal Theory,* edited by D. K. Weisberg. Philadelphia, PA: Temple University Press.

Laws, Judith L. 1975. "The Psychology of Tokenism: An Analysis." *Sex Roles* 1:51–67.

Lewis, Diane. 1977. "A Response to Inequality: Black Women, Racism, and Sexism." *Signs: Journal of Women in Culture and Society* 3:339–361.

Littleton, Christine A. 1991. "Reconstructing Sexual Equality." Pp. 35–56 in *Feminist Legal Theory: Readings in Law and Gender,* edited by K. T. Bartlett and R. Kennedy. Boulder, CO: Westview Press.

Lucie, Patricia. 1988. "Discrimination Against Males in the USA." Pp. 216–243 in *The Legal Relevance of Gender,* edited by S. McLean and N. Burrows. Atlantic Highlands, NJ: Humanities International.

Mahoney, Anne R. 1987. "Women Jurors: Sexism in Jury Selection." Pp. 208–224 in *Women, the Courts, and Equality,* edited by L. L. Crites and W. L. Hepperle. Newbury Park, CA: Sage.

McLean, Sheila A. M. 1988. "The Legal Relevance of Gender: Some Aspects of Sex-Based Discrimination." Pp. 1–15 in *The Legal Relevance of Gender,* edited by S. McLean and N. Burrows. Atlantic Highlands, NJ: Humanities International.

Meyerowitz, Joanne J. 1988. *Women Adrift: Independent Wage Earners in Chicago, 1880–1930.* Chicago: University of Chicago Press.

Mezey, Susan B. 1990. "When Should Difference Make a Difference: A New Approach to the Constitutionality of Gender-Based Laws." Pp. 105–120 in *Women, Politics and the Constitution,* edited by N. B. Lynn. New York: Harrington Park Press.

Minow, Martha. 1993. "The Supreme Court 1986 Term, Foreword." Pp. 301–319 in *Feminist Legal Theory,* edited by D. K. Weisberg. Philadelphia, PA: Temple University Press.

Mississippi University for Women v. *Hogan,* 458 U.S. 718 (1982).

Mullen, Tom. 1988. "Affirmative Action." Pp. 244–266 in *The Legal Relevance of Gender,* edited by S. McLean and N. Burrows. Atlantic Highlands, NJ: Humanities International.

O'Connor, Karen. 1980. *Women's Organizations' Use of the Courts.* Lexington, MA: Lexington Books.

Okin, Susan M. 1989. *Justice, Gender, and the Family.* Basic Books.

Orr v. *Orr,* 440 U.S. 268 (1979).

Pfeiffer v. *Marion Center Area School District,* 917 F. 2d 779 (1990).

Reed v. *Reed,* 404 U.S. 71 (1971).

Rhode, Deborah L. 1987. "Justice, Gender, and the Justices." Pp. 13–34 in *Women, the Courts, and Equality,* edited by L. L. Crites and W. L. Hepperle. Newbury Park, CA: Sage.

_____. 1989. *Justice and Gender: Sex Discrimination and the Law.* Cambridge, MA: Harvard University Press.

_____. 1990. "Gender Difference and Gender Disadvantage." Pp. 121–136 in *Women, Politics and the Constitution,* edited by N. B. Lynn. New York: Harrington Park Press.

Robinson, O. F. 1988. "The Historical Background." Pp. 16–39 in *The Legal Relevance of Gender,* edited by S. McLean and N. Burrows. Atlantic Highlands, NJ: Humanities International.

Roe v. *Wade,* 410 U.S. 179 (1973).

Schultz, Vicki. 1991. "Telling Stories About Women and Work: Judicial Interpretations of Sex Segregation in the Workplace in Title VII Cases Raising the Lack of Interest Argument." Pp. 124–155 in *Feminist Legal Theory: Readings in Law and Gender,* edited by K. T. Bartlett and R. Kennedy. Boulder, CO: Westview Press.

Smart, Carol. 1989. *Feminism and the Power of Law.* London: Routledge & Kegan Paul.

Taylor v. *Louisiana,* 419 U.S. 522 (1975).

Thomas, Claire S. 1991. *Sex Discrimination in a Nutshell.* St. Paul, MN: West.

Weinberger v. *Weisenfeld,* 420 U.S. 636 (1975).

Welter, Barbara. 1978. "The Cult of True Womanhood: 1820–1860." Pp. 224–250 in *The American Family in Social–Historical Perspective,* edited by M. Gordon. New York: St. Martin's Press.

Williams, Lynora. 1981. "Violence Against Women." *The Black Scholar* 12:18–24.

Williams, Wendy W. 1991. "The Equality Crisis: Some Reflections on Culture, Courts, and Feminism." Pp. 15–34 in *Feminist Legal Theory: Readings in Law and Gender,* edited by K. T. Bartlett and R. Kennedy. Boulder, CO: Westview Press.

_____. 1993. "Equality's Riddle: Pregnancy and the Equal Treatment/Special Treatment Debate." Pp. 128–155 in *Feminist Legal Theory,* edited by D. K. Weisberg. Philadelphia, PA: Temple University Press.

Zimmer, Lynn. 1986. *Women Guarding Men.* Chicago: University of Chicago Press.

10

※

On the Job

The preceding chapter examined women's struggle for equality, particularly with respect to the workplace. This chapter addresses how women's entrance as professionals into three areas within the crime-processing system has taken hold. In particular, women's occupations in prisons and jails, the courts, and policing are discussed. This chapter explores the advances these "pioneer" women workers made in the crime-processing system. It analyzes the breakthroughs, as well as the disappointing inhibitors for women workers' recognition and equality. Although laws discussed in Chapter 9 played a critical role in challenging policies that keep women from traditionally male jobs, "most occupations have remained highly gender-segregated or gender stratified" (Rhode 1989, 161). This includes jobs in the crime-processing system.

The term *correctional officer* will not be used in this chapter to describe persons working in prisons and jails (consistent with Zimmer [1986]). Given that U.S. prisons and jails do not train their employees in rehabilitation, nor hire significant numbers of employees with rehabilitative expertise, it seems inappropriate to call such workers "correctional officers." Similarly, the word *corrections* to discuss the jail and prison system was avoided in Chapter 5 given that there is little evidence that the system emphasizes treatment to correct behavior and rehabilitate prisoners. Therefore, the terms *prison and jail workers, prison officers,* and *guards* are used in place of *correctional officers.*

WOMEN AS TOKENS
IN THE WORKPLACE

Before an in-depth analysis of women in crime-processing professions begins, it is useful to examine the position of women as *outsiders* to the paid work force. Although legal breakthroughs resulted in women's increased participation in typically male jobs in the crime-processing system, women's participation is still relatively rare compared to men, particularly for women working in prisons and jails and policing. Women constitute 11.5 percent of prison guards, 9 percent of sworn law enforcement officers, and about 20 percent of practicing lawyers (Hagan et al. 1991; U.S. Federal Bureau of Investigation 1993; U.S. Federal Bureau of Prisons 1993). This discussion goes hand in hand with the last chapter's description of movement from the private sphere (the home) to the public sphere (the paid labor force).

Sociologist Robert K. Merton (1972) introduced the idea of viewing human behavior and organization through an *insider* versus *outsider* perspective. This perspective recognizes that some groups of people (insiders) have greater access to power and privilege than others (outsiders), and the distinctions between these groups is more likely based on *ascribed* rather than *acquired* characteristics. For example, a person may be more likely to receive a promotion because of race (an ascribed characteristic) than because of merit (an acquired characteristic). Being an insider (Anglo, in this case) allows one more access to privilege (promotion in this case) than one's work record. The insider/outsider doctrine recognizes that powerful network memberships and decision making are often more heavily influenced by who you know and your ascribed characteristics than by who you are and what you have accomplished.

Although programs such as affirmative action were developed to compensate for inequities, ascribed characteristics are still frequently the basis for hiring and promotional decisions. Additionally, outsiders hired into what have typically been insiders' jobs, whether or not their hirings were due to affirmative action policies, have often faced resistance. Women who break into male-dominated jobs are often viewed as "double deviants," first for being female and second for "aspiring to the attributes and privileges of the dominant class...[and] refusing the constraints of the ascribed status" (Laws 1975, 53).

In 1944, Everett C. Hughes published an interesting analysis of a somewhat mobile society and its affects on *status*. He claimed that new groups acquiring employment status in professions from which they had previously been excluded could only hope to *modify* stereotypes; their hirings alone could not *stop* stereotypes. *Tokens* in the workplace may be compared to Merton's (1972) outsiders. Kanter (1977a) examines women in male-dominated jobs through a token/dominant perspective, where tokens are analogous to Merton's outsiders, and dominants are analogous to Merton's insiders.

> Tokens are not merely deviants or people who differ from other group members along any one dimension. They are people identified by ascribed characteristics (master statuses such as sex, race, religion, ethnic group, age, etc.) or other characteristics that carry with them a set of assumptions

about culture, status, and behavior highly salient for majority category members.

(Kanter, 1977a, 968)

Furthermore, Laws (1975, 51) states:

Tokenism is likely to be found wherever a dominant group is under pressure to share privilege, power, or other desirable commodities with a group which is excluded. Tokenism is the means by which the dominant group advertises a promise of mobility between the dominant and excluded classes. By definition, however, tokenism involves mobility which is severely restricted in quantity, and the quality of mobility is severely restricted as well.... The Token is a member of an underrepresented group, who is operating on the turf of the dominant group, under license from it.

The pressure of being a token within one's profession is heightened by the responsibility borne of representing every other person of one's token group. For instance, a police department or law firm hiring its first woman may consciously or unconsciously base further hiring of women on this token's performance. In addition to standing out and being watched, this is a huge responsibility for a new token employee. The lack of logic should also be evident. Just as some Anglo males are incompetent workers, so will some women and people of color be incompetent workers. However, most people do not use incompetent Anglo male workers as a basis to form opinions on whether to hire other Anglo males. It is recognized that even with affirmative action, some incompetent workers have been hired, but it is also necessary to recognize that many incompetent Anglo males have been hired before and since affirmative action policies. Regardless of which hiring measures are used, some incompetent people of every racial, ethnic, sex, and class category will be hired. Unfortunately, there is a tendency to focus on the less competent employees of the outsider groups to "justify" discrimination in hiring.

Recent research evaluating gains and losses by African American and Anglo women and men from 1960 to 1980 found that while there were gains for African American and Anglo women and African American men, these gains were "highly questionable" in the male-dominated (best paying) professions (Sokoloff 1988). Regarding crime-processing system employment, all "positions should be fully available to *qualified* women, just as they should be *restricted* to qualified men" (Morris 1987, 159).

A person's token status is heightened when (1) her or his social category is obvious (that is, sex), and (2) her or his social category is new to the setting (Kanter 1977a, 969). Both of these "heightening" characteristics exist for women breaking into the crime-processing system work force. These "pioneer" women did so mostly by maintaining a gender-specific role within these male-dominated jobs. For instance, the first policewomen worked with juveniles and "wayward women," the first female prison and jail workers were "matrons" for female offenders, and the first women lawyers and judges tended to work in juvenile courts and were often married to male lawyers.

Hughes (1944, 358) claims that exceptions to jobs previously employing only Anglo males (or only males, or only Anglos) do so through "some elaboration of social segregation. The woman lawyer may become a lawyer to women clients, or she may specialize in some kind of legal service in keeping with women's role as guardian of the home and morals." Another example is hiring policewomen to work solely with juveniles and sexual assault victims. Thus, sex segregation is maintained to some degree, which additionally provides excuses for gender pay discrimination and limited promotions. For example, in policing, promotions and advancement are directly tied to patrol, detective, and investigative work, yet women were historically barred from these jobs. One study on policewomen found that their token status affected their experiences on the job (Belknap and Shelley 1993). For example, women from departments with 10 percent or fewer policewomen were more likely to report being seen as women first and police officers second.

Zimmer (1988) criticizes Kanter's (1977b) tokenism approach as overly simplified. She warns against perceiving male entrance into female-dominated jobs as identical to female entrance into male-dominated jobs. Tokenism alone will not account for problems women "pioneers" face as they advance into male jobs. For instance, Zimmer (1988) found that women integrated as guards in men's prisons faced substantial opposition from male coworkers. On the other hand, men recently hired in women's prisons reported no opposition from female staff or supervisors. In fact, the women's prison staff displayed appreciation for their addition. This may be because traditionally male jobs could be perceived as *losing* status by hiring more women, while traditionally female jobs may *gain* status by hiring more men (Yoder 1991). Further evidence suggests that men more rigorously exclude token women from "their domain" in traditionally male jobs, than women exclude token men in traditionally female jobs (Epstein 1988). Given these hypotheses, it is not surprising that a study comparing male nurses and policewomen found that policewomen faced more sex stereotyping, were less accepted, experienced more sexual harassment, and felt more visible than the male nurses (Ott 1989).

A related phenomenon is the "glass ceiling effect," which symbolizes a promotion block experienced by many women and people of color in jobs traditionally unavailable to them. Put another way, women and people of color may have gotten a foot in the door, but they are still unlikely to be police captains or prison wardens (especially in men's prisons), and even less likely to become judges and partners in law firms. On the other hand, a study of men in the predominately female professions of nursing, elementary education teaching, librarianship, and social work found that unlike token women, most of the prejudice the token men faced was from people *outside* of their professions. Furthermore, instead of the "glass ceiling" that women tokens usually experience, this study found that token men in female-dominated jobs experienced a "glass escalator": Token men were given fair and often preferential treatment that enhanced their positions relative to their female coworkers (Williams 1992).

Tokenism, then, must be examined in conjunction with sexism in order to understand women's experiences of entering male-dominated jobs. It is evident that it is not enough simply to increase women's proportions in male-dominated jobs—more important, gender-based attitudes on women's abilities and appropriateness in male-dominated jobs need to be changed. Clearly, this is not an easy feat. While increasing the number of women may help men to view women as competent, Zimmer (1988) fears a backlash with increased opposition to women, and cites evidence where women are more intimidated and discriminated against when they enter in larger numbers. For whatever reasons, some males feel threatened to realize women can adequately perform jobs previously available to males only.

HISTORY OF WOMEN PROFESSIONALS
IN CRIME PROCESSING

Women Lawyers

Although the status of attorney is much greater than that of police officer or jail or prison guard, women have been and continue to be more successful at breaking into the occupation of law than policing or "corrections." Perhaps this is because in law there is less actual physical contact with male offenders than is likely with policing and prison jobs. Arresting, deterring, and guarding male offenders is perhaps the ultimate in machismo, while lawyers have more physical distance from offenders. At any rate, women have practiced law in the United States since colonial times, despite active efforts to keep women out of the law field. In fact, in efforts to keep women out of law, "bar associations claimed women lacked the physical strength to handle heavy case loads, and newspapers charged that attractive women would unfairly sway juries" (Morello 1986, xi). Historical objections offered to restrict women from practicing law included accusations that women had inferior minds and bodies, an inability to be discreet, and a role conflict between career and wife and motherhood (Weisberg 1982). (These are consistent with the images of women discussed in Chapter 1.)

The first woman to practice law in the United States arrived in the "New World" in 1638 and acquired considerable real estate holdings. She was addressed as "Gentleman Margaret Brent" in person and in court records (Morello 1986). Brent was a highly successful attorney, particularly regarding land deals, and was consistently employed by the governor. Little is known about women practicing law from colonial times until the mid-1800s, except that they were denied acceptance to law schools and admission to the state bar. In the rare cases where women conducted litigation in court, they were usually there on their own behalf (Bernat 1992). Although men could receive legal training either through clerkship with an attorney or by attending law school, both of these avenues were routinely closed to women, unless a brother or husband "allowed" his sister or wife to clerk with him. "Males who oversaw the entrance of persons into law (judges, lawyers, law school professors and bar admission boards) argued that law was a hard-nosed, 'male' profession which could impugn the 'delicacy' of a female's biological character" (Bernat 1992, 310–311). Also, the case of *Bradwell* v. *Illinois* (1873), which is discussed in Chapter 9, barred married women from practicing the law.

Women lawyers were needed for the fight to acquire women's equality, and particularly to combat the discrimination that was inherent for married women, as discussed in the last chapter. In the 1800s, married women were unable to receive professional educations, hold elective offices, enter into contracts, obtain custody of their children, and control their own money—even when they had earned it (Morello 1986, 9). Ironically, women members of the legal profession "have used their expertise in courts and legislatures to gain the right to be admitted to law schools and state and federal bars, and to be permitted to plead cases before state and federal courts" (Feinman 1986, 104).

Two historical events are related to legal training becoming accessible to women and the less wealthy in the 1830s and 1840s (Morello 1986). First, as Anglos increasingly populated the western part of the United States, more women became lawyers. In fact, the first law schools open to women were in the West (Feinman 1986). The westward movement of Anglos gave European American women increasing amounts of freedom: The farther away women were from the staid northeastern society, the greater their independence (Morello 1986). The corresponding decrease in the prestige of legal practice, predictably, opened the door to women. The second historical event that increased women's access to legal training was the Civil War. With men off fighting in the war, women had the opportunity to fill the vacant clerkship and law school positions.

The first woman formally admitted to the bar in the United States, Arabella Mansfield, passed the Iowa bar in 1869 (Feinman 1986). Again, it was particularly difficult for married women to become lawyers, unless they happened to be married to a lawyer who was willing to train them. In fact, more than one in six women lawyers in 1890 were married to lawyers (Weisberg 1982). Still, even many married women who were legally permitted to practice law were often restricted by society and their own husbands and families who didn't believe women could have marriages and careers (Drachman 1989). In addition to the strong likelihood of having husbands and family members who were lawyers, another characteristic that the first women lawyers had in common was their tendency to come from wealthy families (Weisberg 1982).

Laws forbidding women to enter into contracts also stymied their ability to practice law. As might be expected, many of the first women practicing law in the United States were dedicated to fighting different aspects of discrimination, including women's issues (such as suffrage, birth control, and equal rights), and advocating for the poor, Native Americans, African Americans, and immigrants (Morello 1986). In the late 1800s, the first woman lawyer to argue a case before the U.S. Supreme Court, Belva Lockwood, obtained a $5 million settlement for the Cherokee nation from the U.S. government (Morello 1986).

The Ivy League law schools were the last to accept women students. One letter directed to Yale Law School in 1872 suggested that perhaps "ugly women" should be allowed to enroll, since they would not distract the male students (Morello 1986). Harvard Law School was one of the last law schools to accept women when it did so in 1950. Moreover, women lawyers weren't eligible for elective judgeships in most states until the Nineteenth Amendment (women's suffrage) was passed in 1920 (Cook 1978).

The first African American women lawyers were caught in the double-marginalization discussed in Chapter 9. Feminist activists had focused on Anglo women's rights, and African American activists focused on African American men's rights, a problem that still exists to some extent. Thus, African American women activists often felt ignored and forced to divide their loyalties (Morello 1986). Even traditionally black Howard University resisted admitting women to the law school. In the 1880s, Charlotte E. Ray, the first African American woman lawyer in the United States, gained entry to Howard Law School by using only her initials for her first and second names in her application. Nonetheless, being black and a woman, Ray was never permitted to join the ranks of practicing lawyers. She eventually resumed teaching in Brooklyn public schools and died in obscurity in 1911 (Morello 1986). In the 1940s, Constance Baker Motely, the second African American woman to attend Columbia, was active in many important civil rights cases, working with Thurgood Marshall and serving as counsel to the Reverend Martin Luther King, Jr.

Women Prison and Jail Guards

The first women working in the crime-processing system were predominantly from wealthier homes, and their work in the system tended to be volunteer (Morris 1987). There is a strong link between women's advancement into policing jobs and their advancement into prison and jail employment. Women prison reformers, however, "paved the way" for women to work in policing, as well as advancing women's roles from volunteer to paid/professional services (Schulz 1989).

Historically, male and female prisoners shared the same institutions and were guarded by men (as discussed in Chapter 5). Chapter 5 includes a description of the history of female prisoners being raped, beaten, and prostituted by male wardens (Freedman 1981). Although female prisoners were moved to separate prison wings in the late eighteenth century, they were still guarded by men (Zupan 1992). The first women entered prison and jail employment in the 1800s and were mostly middle- and upper-class Anglo citizens who wanted to reform society (Feinman 1986). The first women working in crime-processing professions "were admitted as women and not as professionals" (Morris 1987, 139).

Unlike the focus on women prisoners in Chapter 5, this section is concerned with the conditions of women who worked in prisons. However, changes in women's imprisonment affected both women as prisoners and women employed to work with women prisoners. The separate institutions designed for women prisoners in the late nineteenth and early twentieth centuries not only provided women prisoners with more attention, but also provided women with more opportunities to work with offenders (Zupan 1992). Significantly, the wardens of women's institutions have typically been men. Similar to policewomen on patrol, women were not hired to work as officers with *male* prisoners until the 1970s. Working in male prisons provides important opportunities for women aspiring to a career in "corrections" for four reasons: There are better posts and shifts, there are more promotional opportunities, there are more locations to work in prisons, and working in a men's prison appears to be necessary for advancement into administration (Zimmer 1986). The first three reasons are largely due to the fact that there are many more men's prisons than women's prisons (usually there is only one woman's prison per state), and the men's prisons are more highly populated, allowing for more positions in each rank, shift, and post.

Black women's experiences working in prisons have mirrored the racism and sexism outside the prisons. Before the Supreme Court decision in *Brown v. the Board of Education* (1954), "racial segregation existed as institutional policy and practice, de jure in the South and de facto in the North" (Feinman 1986, 141). Most superintendents and officers in the prisons were white, and when blacks were hired, it was usually to guard black prisoners, who were typically segregated and housed in the worst parts of prisons. Since the 1950s, African American women's (and men's) employment in penal institutions has significantly increased. It has also been noted that as more *nonprison* jobs opened for Anglo women, more African American women moved into the vacuum created by their absence in prison employment (Feinman 1986).

Women in Policing

The entrance of women into U.S. police work began in the late 1800s, spurred by increased problems with women and girls that policemen seemed uninterested in or unable to confront (for example, prostitution, disorderly conduct, and vagrancy) (Feinman 1986). During World War I in England, women conducted voluntary police patrol work to control other women such as prostitutes (Morris 1987). In 1905, Lola Baldwin was hired as a "safety worker" in Portland, Oregon, to "protect" women and girls from "approaching" male miners, lumberjacks, and laborers (Feinman 1986). Women prison reformers gained legitimacy for women professionals in public agencies caring for women, which "paved the way for the first police matrons and then policewomen to follow in establishing their own legitimacy in the criminal justice field" (Schulz 1989, 117).

The first woman to hold the title "policewoman" was Alice Stebbins Wells, in Los Angeles, California, in 1910 (Feinman 1986). Wells was a social worker and theologian who believed that she could accomplish more to help women and girls through police work than through volunteer work (Feinman 1986). Although the press negatively characterized Wells as "unfeminine" and "muscular," she also received some support (Feinman 1986). (This is an example of Rafter and Stanko's [1982] image of "the active woman as masculine," discussed in Chapter 1.)

Many of the first policewomen identified more as social workers than as "cops" and saw their role as helping women and children. The first two decades of this century were important in advancing women into police departments, albeit in stereotypical roles. Between 1910 and 1930, policewomen largely worked in specialist roles within the police departments, usually confined to traditionally female skills (Martin 1980). Overall, policing itself didn't change much between 1920 and the 1940s, including the hiring and roles of police-women. During the postwar period of the 1950s and 1960s, the number of policewomen increased, but increased variation in roles was not commensurate (Schulz 1993). Policewomen during this time, however, were actively attempting to broaden their roles. Title VII, therefore, did not create police-women's desire for equality, but rather provided legal support for changes that began in the 1950s (Schulz 1993). Nonetheless, prior to 1968, "no women were assigned to the backbone of policing, patrol duty" (Martin 1980, 48), and until 1972, policewomen's roles typically evolved around assisting policemen (Hale 1992).

WOMEN AS TOKENS IN CRIME-PROCESSING JOBS SINCE THE 1970s

Four Problem Areas for Women Professionals

Women have faced considerable opposition to working in the crime-processing system, largely from male professionals, and to a lesser degree from their clients. Baunach and Rafter (1982) identified four problem areas for women professionals in male-dominated crime-processing jobs. The first problem is the so-called *"preferential" treatment* women get when male coworkers and supervisors shield them from "real" work, such as female police officers and guards handling violent men (or even violent women), or women lawyers handling high-stress cases (including cases with violent men). A second problem area is that women tokens often face *higher expectations* than their male colleagues encounter, including the pressure of representing *all* women by any of their actions. For example, women lawyers and judges "have had to be smarter, work harder, and be better at what they do than their male colleagues" in order to succeed (Feinman 1986, 126).

Lack of access to the "old boy" network, Baunach and Rafter's third problem area, presents the damned-if-you-do, damned-if-you-don't dilemma of "fraternizing" with male colleagues. If women socialize with male coworkers, they are often assumed to be having sex with them, which results in negative assessments about the woman's, but not the man's, professionalism. Women who don't socialize with their male colleagues risk not receiving important information about the job or promotions, as well as being labeled "cold" or "lesbians." Some male supervisors report consciously spending less time with female supervisees so that people won't think they are sexually involved. This is an obvious cost to women employees.

The final problem area identified by Baunach and Rafter (1982) is *sex stereotyping* in the job assignment. Women lawyers often report being assigned cases with women and children; women prison and jail workers are often restricted to working with juveniles and incarcerated women; and policewomen have historically been given "lighter" duties more commensurate with "feminine" ideals. For example, long before becoming a U.S. Supreme Court judge, Sandra

Day O'Connor was unable to find a job other than working as a law clerk or secretary, after graduating at the top of her class at Stanford Law School.

Legal Pressure for Women's Employment in Crime Processing

The histories of women working in corrections and policing parallel each other almost identically. Pollock (1986, 5) compares the numerous similarities between the experiences of policewomen and women guards. Both have long histories of playing stereotypical roles (such as working in clerical roles or with juveniles or women offenders); both still represent small percentages of overall employees in their departments (particularly in administration), both attained their current status through court challenges and despite "strong male resistance"; and there is substantial evidence that both are as successful as their male counterparts. Similar resistance to women tokens in law school is exemplified by the fact that women and men taking the bar exam in New York had to sit separately until 1971 because women would "excite the men" and distract them from taking their exams (DeCrow 1974).

Legal pressure has been identified as the major impetus allowing equal entry of women into prison and jail employment (Jurik 1985). Specifically, Title VII, the 1972 legislation discussed in Chapter 9, is viewed as the greatest motivation for hiring women into nongendered jobs in policing and prisons (see Morton 1981). In 1971, there were only seven policewomen on patrol in the United States (Gates 1976), and the refusal to hire women to work in men's prisons was "unquestioned and unchallenged" until 1972 (Zimmer 1986, 1). Although Title VII's positive influence cannot be underestimated, there is concern that Justice Department and Supreme Court reinterpretations of Title VII in the 1980s will have a "chilling effect on potential plaintiffs, making it more costly and difficult to win subsequent employment discrimination cases in the 1990s" (Martin 1992, 285).

Unfortunately, while legislation has helped in many ways to improve women's opportunities, it has not provided clear guidelines allowing women equal opportunities. That is, while supporters of women working with male offenders have been somewhat successful in overturning height and weight requirements used to systematically deny women policing and prison employment, other blocks to women's equality in working with male offenders exist. For example, although Equal Employment Opportunity Commission and affirmative action programs resulted in women being hired as police officers on patrol and to work with male prisoners, these programs don't guarantee women's employment in large numbers in these fields (Morton 1981). Hiring women for police and prison work is still not the norm. Additionally, women police and prison workers have fallen victim to the last-hired, first-fired (or laid-off) practices. Presumably, the longevity of male workers' employment overrode the commitment to having female officers.

A study evaluating political factors related to hiring women police officers in urban departments found that departments experiencing budget reductions hired significantly fewer policewomen (Warner et al. 1989). Nonetheless, a growth in the number of available policing positions didn't result in a corresponding increase in the hiring of women. Notably, the more women on city council, the more women hired onto the police department. Furthermore, although *verbal* affirmative action commitments were unrelated to the rate of policewomen hired, *court-imposed* and *formal voluntary programs* were effective in increasing the number of policewomen (Warner et al. 1989). These findings suggest the importance of having women in political leadership roles and for formal policies to increase the rate of women in policing.

In 1973, policewoman Fanchon Blake, a twenty-five-year police force veteran, and some of her female coworkers brought a sex discrimination law, suit against the city, chief, and police department in Los Angeles two years after the police chief, Ed Davis, announced that "women were no longer wanted or needed by the L.A.P.D." (*Blake* v. *City of Los Angeles* as cited in Felkenes et al. 1993). Davis reorganized the department not only to stop the hiring of policewomen, but to relegate the existing female officers into receptionist and secretarial roles. The plaintiffs won the suit in an appeals court in 1979, and in 1981 "a mutually agreed-upon 'Consent Decree' was signed" requiring better representation of women of all races as well as African American and Hispanic men (Felkenes et al. 1993, 34). Although the decision resulted in an increase in the hiring of women, it was not within the required amount, and little was done to alleviate the daily hostility the policewomen experienced afterward.

Turning to the legal profession, the percent of women law students increased from 8.5 percent to 33.5 percent between 1970 and 1980, yet the percent of women lawyers increased only from 4.7 percent to 12.0 percent for the same time period (Epstein 1983). Moreover, in the 1970s, women went from "virtual invisibility" in Wall Street corporate firms to "significant numbers" (Epstein 1982). This is at least in part due to corporate firm members' fears of and experiences with sex discrimination lawsuits. In many ways, it seems that women lawyers have been accepted more easily than women working in policing and prisons.

Prisoner Privacy and Prison Safety

Although some legislation has proven to be powerful in dismantling restrictions on women workers in men's prisons, other legislation has been instrumental in emphasizing why differential assignments of female and male officers should be considered *bona fide occupational qualifications* (BFOQs). (BFOQs are the "acceptable" sex discrimination employment practices provided for in Title VII, as discussed in Chapter 9.)

There appear to be two major issues used in legislation defending women's restrictions in working with male prisoners: (1) male prisoners' rights to privacy, and (2) the impact of women officers on the security of the prison. This section first addresses the issue of prisoners' rights to privacy, and then briefly discusses the impact of women on prison security.

Over time, male prisoners' rights have been increasingly prioritized (over prison security) as a reason (or BFOQ) to exclude women from working in men's prisons (Morton 1981). In fact, questions about whether guards of the opposite sex are invading a prisoner's right to privacy in showers and bathrooms never occurred until women were employed in men's prisons—when women moved into the dominant sphere. Subsequently, the concern for prisoner privacy in legislation appears to be far more prevalent regarding male prisoners with female guards than for female prisoners with male guards (Morton 1981). Moreover, state guidelines developed to protect prisoner privacy have resulted in women officers being excluded from posts that have high contact with male prisoners (Zimmer 1986, 9).

However, two points are worth making here. First, a review of 1970s and 1980s court cases on prisoners' rights to privacy from guards of the opposite sex shows that the courts have tended to favor the officers' right to employment over the prisoners' right to privacy, regardless of the sex of the prisoner or the officer (see Bernat and Zupan 1989). Second, a 1993 court case found that while the use of male guards to perform body searches of female prisoners does not violate their right to privacy (the Fourth Amendment), such actions do violate women prisoners' rights to freedom from cruel and unusual punishment (the Eighth Amendment), given the high rate of women prisoners who have survived physical and sexual violence at the hands of men. It was found that such searches could exacerbate preexisting mental conditions resulting from prior victimizations (*Jordan* v. *Gardner* 986 F. 2d. 1521 U.S. App. 1993).

No set guidelines have been established to confront the problem of balancing prisoners' privacy with the employment of officers of either sex (Zimmer 1986). It is significant that most of the focus on this problem has centered around women working in men's prisons, despite the history (including recent documentations) of the stronger likelihood for male officers to violate women prisoners' privacy than for women officers to violate men prisoners' privacy. Finally, research on women working in male penal facilities has found that the job is often structured to deny women and men equal assignments, to the disadvantage of women workers (Belknap 1991; Zimmer 1986).

In addressing prisoners' rights to privacy and balancing this with women's rights to work in men's prisons (where there are the most job, shift, and promotional opportunities), we must ask a few questions. First, how is this different from having a doctor or nurse of the opposite sex? The appropriateness and right to privacy of this "intimate" professional interaction is rarely questioned. Second, is it really different or more degrading for men to have women, rather than other men, see them shower, undress, and so on? Presumably, if a doctor, nurse, or prison guard acts professionally and discreetly, the sex combination of the prisoner/patient and the professional should be irrelevant. Third, it might be argued that when one is imprisoned, certain rights and privileges are lost, including the privilege to choose the sex of the prison staff. (Obviously, it is important that prisoners have access to grievance procedures that are seriously looked into and enforced when a staff person of either sex behaves inappropriately.) Despite all of the fuss made over male prisoners' rights to privacy, research reports that the majority of male prisoners do *not* report that women officers violate their privacy (Kissel and Katsampes 1980; Zimmer 1986).

Denying women equal access to a career in "corrections" does not seem to be the answer to the prisoner privacy issue, especially given some of the advantages women officers might bring to these institutions (which is discussed later in this chapter). It has also been pointed out that opaque shower doors or partial barriers (where the prisoner's feet and head can be seen) could help balance prisoners' privacy with the employment of officers of either sex (Zimmer 1986).

Regarding the security aspect of women working in men's prisons, although *Dothard* v. *Rawlinson* (1977) eliminated minimum height and weight requirements for officers in men's prisons, it upheld that under at least some circumstances, men's prisons qualified for a BFOQ exception. This exemption was given because of the belief that even one woman officer present might threaten the security of the prison, although there was no evidence to support this (Zimmer 1986). In fact, recent research on men and women working in a male prison found that women perceive the prisons to be less dangerous than men do (Wright and Saylor 1991). Ironically, *Dothard* v. *Rawlinson* has not been successfully used in subsequent cases to deny women "guard" jobs (Bernat and Zupan 1989; Zimmer 1986).

Lawsuits about prison workers and sex discrimination in areas other than prisoners' rights to privacy and prison security have focused on discrimination in individual hiring, firing, and promotional decisions. These have routinely been decided in favor of men or against women (see Bernat and Zupan 1989). It is hoped that in the future, prison security and prisoners' rights to privacy will not be misused to keep women from exploring careers working with offenders. Flynn (1982, 331) stresses that "[n]ot only should qualified women be given the opportunity to work in any potentially dangerous situation if they want to, but their work assignments should not differ, to any degree, from the assignments of their male counterparts."

Institutionalized Sexism

Institutionalized sexism has also been instrumental in restricting women from crime-processing jobs. When a discriminatory behavior, policy, or law is institutionalized, it may not directly prohibit one group's rights, but rather does so indirectly. Title VII itself may not protect women applicants or employees from institutionalized sexism. A number of examples of institutionalized sexism affecting women's employment in crime processing follow.

The first example of institutionalized sexism is *height and weight requirements.* Height and weight requirements not only effectively exclude the vast majority of women, but also serve as institutionalized racism against Asian American and Hispanic men who are generally proportionately smaller than their Anglo counterparts. In 1975, in *The Officers for Justice et al.* v. *The Civil Service Commission of the City and County of San Francisco,* "a district court judge said that studies made by the police department failed to show any correlation between the height requirement and an officer's ability to perform police duties" (Gates 1976, 71). Similarly, in 1977, the U.S. Supreme Court upheld in *Dothard* v. *Rawlinson* that the minimum height and weight requirement in a penal facility was not job related, and thus could not be a condition for hiring.

The second example of institutionalized sexism in hiring women police and prison officers is the *physical agility test*. Any criteria used to screen out potential employees should be relevant to performing the job in question. However, the Work Sample Test developed for the Houston Police Department in 1977 included a physical agility test where a 7'6" wall had to be scaled—although there were no 7-foot walls within the city limits (Townsey 1982a). The focus on physical prowess in police and prison/jail recruiting tests ignores the importance of intelligence and communication skills, which are routinely necessary and probably more useful in policing and prison employment. Since the 1980s, more police departments have recognized this and developed physical agility tests that are less likely to discriminate against women.

The third example of institutionalized sexism is the *veterans preference system*—the "extra credit" for military service when making hiring and promotion decisions. Such a practice is far more likely to benefit males, given that women are neither expected nor encouraged to join the military, and should they enter the military, their jobs are more restricted than men's (Becraft 1993a, 1993b; Berger 1980).

The problem with establishing preferential treatment regarding military or some other status is deciding what factors should make one a preferential employee. For instance, a study of women working in a jail found that many women mentioned that one of the greatest assets women bring to the job is their experience raising children (Belknap 1991). Child-rearing experience teaches patience, responsibility, and how to deal with crises. Unfortunately, this prior experience probably serves as more of a disadvantage than an advantage in hiring women in the crime-processing system. Indeed, many people are *reluctant* to hire women, but not men, with young children.

Other Restrictions on Women in Crime-Processing Jobs

Even legislation supporting women police and prison officers' rights to equal employment cannot guarantee male prisoners', offenders', fellow officers', supervisors', administrators', and citizens' acceptance of women as police officers and prison guards. Flynn (1982, 307) states that "legislative and judicial decree is neither the most expeditious nor the most efficient means for bringing about change. This is because most social change comes about incrementally, at a snail's pace, and largely as a result of multi-institutional and societal forces."

The organizational structures of prisons and jails have also managed to restrict women's roles in numerous ways. Organizational barriers include gender differences (discrimination) in training, work assignments, and performance evaluations (Jurik 1985). Women guards continue to face barriers of gender stereotyping in treatment and job assignments, in addition to bias from the veterans' preference system, physical requirements, safety considerations, and prisoners' privacy rights (Flynn 1982).

In the same vein, a study of federal prison officers found that the security level of the prison predicts the acceptance of female officers more than any other variable—"as the level of security increases, personnel are less supportive of female officers. Moreover, the longer one has been employed in corrections, the less liberal his/her attitude toward women guards" (Simpson and White 1985, 291). Similarly, in policing, male officers' understanding of police work is often culturally centered around the importance of physical strength and aggressiveness. Thus, formal policies admitting women into policing do not guarantee that they will be culturally or professionally integrated into policing if their male coworkers automatically view them as incapable of performing the job (Morris 1987, 145). For women to work as true equals, then, legislation must be far reaching, and even then it cannot guarantee that everyone's behavior will be open and nonsexist. On the other hand, an African American woman describes the shock of acquiring an "honorary white pass" immediately after she began her job as a law professor:

> White students of the type who had been repulsed by me in law school (their own status threatened by the presence of blacks in their classes) now curried my favor. Secretaries who had once made me wait at the photocopying machine for hours now let me know I was too important to make a single copy myself. Restaurateurs wanted my business so badly that they shouted "Professor" as I came through the door (the better for the patrons to hear). Partners in law firms who made more in a year than my parents had made in their entire lifetimes sought me out at cocktail parties.
> *(Moran 1990–1991, 119)*

GENDER SIMILARITIES AND DIFFERENCES IN JOB PERFORMANCES

The vast majority of studies examining gender differences in crime-processing job performances have centered on policing. While a few exist concerning males and females working in prisons and jails, gender comparisons of job performances for attorneys are rare (perhaps because their actions are more difficult to follow and assess).

There have been a number of studies evaluating policewomen on patrol since 1972, and most report that women are as capable as men (Bartlett and Rosenblum 1977; Bloch and Anderson 1974; Grennan 1987; Sherman 1975; Sichel et al. 1978). This is particularly impressive given a study on the evaluations of women on patrol, which found that the studies themselves were sexist, valuing typically male traits and devaluing typically female traits—most of which were not shown to be meaningfully related to policing (Morash and Greene 1986). In sum, then, most of the evaluations of women on patrol in some manner assumed that policemen do the job right to see how well policewomen measure up. In fact, they "measured up" quite well.

Researchers evaluating policewomen often report that policewomen in general may bring positive aspects to the policing role. For example, some research found that policewomen tend to have more support from and improved relations with citizens than policemen (Bloch and Anderson 1974; Felkenes and Trostle 1990; Marshall 1973; Sichel et al. 1978). Other researchers suggest that policewomen and women prison and jail workers have a less aggressive style than policemen and male penal workers, and the women are better at deescalating potentially violent situations (Belknap 1991; Belknap and Shelley 1993; Bell 1982; Gates 1976; Grennan 1987; Kissel and Katsampes 1980). Research has also indicated that policewomen may be more likely to have traits that should be associated with "good policing," such as having empathy for rape victims and battered women, and possessing a broader and more creative outlook on policing (Feinman 1986; Homant and Kennedy 1985; Kennedy and Homant 1983; Price 1974).

While there have been far fewer attempts to evaluate women prison officers and to compare them to male officers (as in policing), most of these evaluations portray these women favorably. Further, despite women officers facing strong resistance from fellow officers, most male prisoners support women officers (Zimmer 1986). "Overall, the presence of female officers in men's institutions seems to have normalized the environment, relaxed tension, and led to improvements in the inmates' behavior, dress and language" (Morris 1987, 157). Perhaps instead of assessing how well women workers "measure up" to male workers, we should be asking how well male workers measure up to women workers.

Finally, one study comparing male and female trial judges in over 30,000 felony cases found that overall the only gender differences in judges' convicting and sentencing of male and female defendants were that women judges are less likely to find defendants guilty and more likely than male judges to send women defendants to prison (Gruhl et al. 1981). Perhaps women judges feel more pressure than male judges to appear to be not "siding" with defendants of their own sex.

MALE RESISTANCE TO WOMEN
WORKING IN CRIME-PROCESSING JOBS

Women Working in Prisons and Jails

The positive evaluations of policewomen on patrol have not sheltered them from considerable hostility from their fellow officers, and sometimes from administration (Balkin 1988; Belknap and Shelley 1993; Bloch and Anderson 1974; Christopher et al. 1991; Jacobs 1987; Marshall 1973; C. A. Martin 1983; S. E. Martin 1980; Remmington 1983; Rivlin 1981; Sherman 1973; Timmins and Hainsworth 1989; Wexler and Logan 1983). Some policemen believe many stereotypes about women in general and policewomen in particular. For example, research shows that some policemen believe that policewomen are emotionally and physically weak, that they are more likely to use deadly force, and that they get sick every month when they menstruate (Balkin 1988; Koenig 1978). Clearly these stereotypes are damaging for women who want to be taken seriously as police officers. Given these reported attitudes, it is hardly surprising that some policemen report that women as a group are unsuitable for employment in policing (Pope and Pope 1986; Remmington 1983).

Research on both female prison officers and policewomen has found that their male coworkers often perceive the job as "macho" and are thus confused and threatened when they see women capably performing the job (Balkin 1988; Martin 1980; Sherman 1973; Wexler and Logan 1983; Zimmer 1986). The result of this "macho" confusion is a no-win situation for the female officer: Male officers may reject competent female officers because they are threatened that a woman can do "their" job; at the same time, they believe that incompetent women officers are "better women"—but unacceptable officers (Gross 1984; Zimmer 1986).

There are other forms of sex discrimination and gender stereotyping of women working in prisons and policing. For instance, one study found that competent policewomen were rated more negatively than competent policemen (Deaux and Taynor 1973). A study of women prison officers found that their male coworkers frequently ignored them (acting as if they weren't present), assigned them the worst posts, and wrote them up for actions against prison policies that the male officers regularly violated and weren't sanctioned for (Zimmer 1986). Considering their reported experiences of dealing with male coworkers' hostility, it is not surprising that policewomen and women prison workers report higher stress levels than men in these professions (Martin 1983; Rivlin 1981; Van Voorhis et al. 1991; Wexler and Logan 1983; Wright and Saylor 1991). This stress may be largely due to dealing with male coworkers' hostility, but it may also be attributed to the constant pressure to prove competency (Martin 1983; Rivlin 1981; Timmins and Hainsworth 1989; Wexler and Logan 1983). Moreover, women in these jobs are pessimistic about the likelihood of their own and other women's advancements and promotions (Belknap 1991; Chapman et al. 1980; Nallin 1981; Poole and Pogrebin 1988). This is particularly acute for African American women (Townsey 1982b). Ironically, policemen view policewomen as receiving unfair advantages in their promotional climbs and assignments; this view is at least partly due to the policemen's negative attitudes about affirmative action (Weisheit 1987).

As expected, the limited accounts of women of color's employment experiences in policing, prison work, and legal careers suggest that the effects of racism *and* sexism are more than cumulative (Felkenes and Schroedel 1993; Christopher et al. 1991; Dreifus 1982; Moran 1990–1991; Townsey 1982b). That is, combining racism with sexism seems to result in more than twice the oppression.

A study of the first policewomen on patrol found that men's views of policewomen fell into three categories: traditionals, moderns, and moderates (Martin 1980). *Traditionals* believe that policewomen don't belong on patrol and if present should be protected and treated as junior partners. *Moderns* are willing to work with policewomen as equals. Finally, *moderates* are neither supportive nor negative toward policewomen; they tend to be ambivalent. Consistent with other research on token women, African American male coworkers were more supportive than Anglo male coworkers of policewomen as equals (Martin 1980).

A study of some of the first women working in a men's prison found that male officers believed that (1) women workers impair prison security because they are both physically and emotionally weaker; (2) women officers need male officers' protection; (3) women officers can only do some of the job; and (4) it is unfair for women officers to be placed only in those parts of the jobs that they are "suited" for (Zimmer 1986). Given this agenda, the only logical solution was to have no women working in the prison, according to many of the men (Zimmer 1986). Further, "rather than questioning the necessity of masculinity, most male guards question the ability of women to perform the job without it" (Zimmer 1986, 57). If a woman can do the job, her "feminine" identity is questioned, and she is seen as abnormal or lesbian.

Women Attorneys and Judges

The limited research conducted on the experiences of women attorneys suggests that they also face a considerable amount of male hostility. This is most likely to be perpetrated by male lawyers, followed by clients, judges, and other legal staff, respectively (Rosenberg et al. 1993). In one study women attorneys believed that if they were treated differently than men during the hiring process, it was to their own advantage. "In contrast, once the women lawyers were on the job, in salary, promotion, or task allocation, very few (from 1.5% to 10.2%) said they benefited from different treatment based on gender" (Rosenberg et al. 1993, 422). One in four of the attorneys in this study reported being sexually harassed in a professional situation, and this rate was significantly higher for women in private firms and in token positions in their practice (Rosenberg et al. 1993).

Women have fared much better as far as representation in law as compared to policing and corrections. A study of women and men in law firms in Canada, however, found that women continue to be overrepresented in family law, and underrepresented in corporate, commercial, and civil litigation. On the other hand, women are making some advances in large firms in corporate settings (Hagan 1990). Furthermore, while experience increased the earnings for both women and men, women gained "an annual average of about $3,000, compared to nearly $4,400 for men. The cumulative effect across careers is substantial" (Hagan 1990, 845). This study concludes that while there has been a "tremendous growth" in women entering the profession, "areas of law are still highly sex typed and gender cross-cuts other cleavages that stratify legal practice" (Hagan 1990, 849). Women lawyers are still less likely than their male colleagues to be made partners (Graham 1986; Hagan et al. 1991). In fact, a study on the effects of centralization and concentration of law partnerships found that the reduction of female partners was far greater than the corresponding decrease in male partners; this was most acute in small firms (Hagan et al. 1991).

Women lawyers' careers are more governed than men lawyers' careers by decisions to have children (Graham 1986). Women lawyers are also likely to struggle with whether they should appear "feminine" or "masculine" in order to be most effective (Blodgett 1986). This is similar to Martin's finding of women emphasizing the femininity in police*women* roles, and trying to negate femininity in the *police*women roles. Male judges are also known to have reinforced sexist stereotypes of women lawyers. In July 1986, Circuit Court judge Arthur Ceislik said to attorney Susan Tone Pierce in a pretrial conference on a rape case:

> "I am going to hear the young lady's case first. They say I'm a male chauvinist. I don't think that ladies should be lawyers. I believe that you belong at home raising a family. Ladies do not belong down here. Are you married?"
>
> *(quoted in Blodgett 1986, 48)*

Women are not as highly represented in judge positions as they are in the attorney pool as a whole. Predictably, when women are elected or appointed judges, it is frequently to judgeship roles consistent with stereotyped gender roles, especially "family law," divorce courts, juvenile courts, and the lower municipal courts. Women were first appointed to minor judicial positions in 1884, but only a "sprinkling" of women judges were appointed by various states in the following century (Epstein 1983, 239). One study found the higher a woman's income and the lower the birth rate in a state, the more women judges in the state (Cook 1978). Women judges made up only 1 percent of federal judges until President Jimmy Carter made a concerted effort to appoint more women and people of color to the federal bench in the 1970s (Epstein 1983). Sandra Day O'Connor, the first woman on the U.S. Supreme Court, was nominated by President Ronald Reagan in 1981. At that time, women made up about 5 percent of both state and federal court judges (Morello 1986). Moreover, it was not until 1979 that all states had at least one woman serving in some judicial capacity (Morello 1986).

Research comparing female and male judges finds "that women judges tend to be younger, more liberal, less interested in politics, less wealthy..., and that they possess a higher degree of scholarship and academic talent on the average than the men" (Morello 1986, 246). It was also noted that women judges are more likely than male judges to do their own housework, and that Supreme Court Justice O'Connor's pushing her own cart in the grocery store might make her more in touch with the average citizen (Morello 1986).

CLASSIFICATIONS OF WOMEN
EMPLOYEES IN MALE-DOMINATED JOBS

Kanter's (1977b) research on women tokens in corporations found that the men tended to place women coworkers in female roles that were familiar to them, since "female coworker" was not a familiar role. The types of familiar female roles included "mother," "pet," "seductress," and "iron maiden." The *mother* and *seductress* roles are self-explanatory. The *pets* were the resident "cheerleaders" whose priority seemed to be to support male coworkers and build up their egos. The *iron maidens,* on the other hand, were women who did not fit into any of the other categories, possibly resisting them by choice.

Policewomen

Consistent with some of Kanter's roles, a study on policewomen found that one-third of the women did not feel supported by policemen, while the two-thirds who reported feeling close to policemen expressed being viewed as "mothers," "sisters," and "women," but not as police officers (Jacobs 1987). Similarly, another study found that policemen uncomfortable with police-women's presence resolve their own confusion by placing women into such stereotypical categories as "seductress," "mother," or "lesbian" (Hunt 1990).

As noted above, some "macho" male police and prison officers are threat-ened by the idea that a woman can perform "their" job; they believe it is im-possible that a person can be a woman *and* an officer. Thus, it is probably not surprising that the earliest research on policewomen on patrol found a ten-dency for these policewomen to accent either the police *or* the woman aspect of being a police officer (Martin 1979). *Police*women emphasized professional-ism, assertiveness, occupational achievement, and departmental loyalty, while downplaying their female status. On the other hand, police*women* emphasized their female identity, often acquiescing to ascribed female roles (for example, "little girl"), and were isolated from "real" police work. Notably, the police-men didn't appear to value either *police*women or police*women*. *Police*women-were seen as strange women, while police*women* were viewed as incompetent officers. Thus, policemen seemed threatened by evidence that women could do the job, as well as by evidence that they could not.

In a more recent study, working as a researcher in a police department, Jennifer Hunt (1984) found that her male coworkers frequently "tested" her (including showing her pornography and taking her to topless bars). She re-ports a tendency to dichotomize policewomen as "dykes" or "whores." She learned, like many other policewomen and women prison workers, to com-bine elements of both masculinity and femininity in order to gain acceptance:

> I was aggressive, tough, hard and corrupt like a "dyke" or a "whore." I was also sexually aloof, empathetic and vulnerable like a moral woman. As part man, I could be trusted to back up my partner and lie for the police....
> My displays of masculinity, craziness and resistance were also important to the development of trust because they defined my opposition to the elite and identification with the rank and file.
>
> *(Hunt 1984, 293)*

Women Prison Workers

Zimmer (1986) has identified three roles women working in men's prisons are likely to fall into, which she labels "adjustment strategies." The *institutional role* officers are similar to Martin's (1979) *police*women. They are rule and policy followers and tend to downplay their female status. They expect to do the same job as the male officers, and are invested in maintaining professional relation-ships with everyone they work with in the prison. Zimmer's (1986) *modified role* is analogous to Martin's (1979) police*women*. These officers don't view them-selves as being as capable as men of performing the job, and prefer safe assignments where they have no contact with the prisoners. They often rely on male officers to back them up. Unlike Martin's (1979) policewomen roles, Zimmer has a third role for women prison workers: the *inventive role*. Women in this role don't view themselves as equal to or less capable than male officers, like the institutional and modified officers do. Instead, they see women officers as *advantageous* to the prison system. These women see their physical weakness (relative to men's) as *over*compensated for by their communication skills and respect for prisoners. They believe in the importance of seeing the prisoners as individuals and count on backing from the prisoners. These officers receive the most hostility from male coworkers, and are the most openly resentful of this hostility.

Prior research has also been concerned with how women prison workers develop strategies for coping with their often stressful jobs. Jurik (1988), drawing on Kanter's (1977b) categories of pet, mother, seductress, and iron maiden, found that women prison workers deal with negative stereotyping by "striking a balance" between these competing negative stereotypes. "Avoiding the role traps of incompetent *pet* and *seductress* often leaves female officers with a third *iron-maiden*-like stereotypic role. Female officers who work hard to demonstrate competence are alternatively described as 'climbers,' 'dykes,' or 'cold'; they are isolated and distrusted by their colleagues" (Jurik 1988, 295). In fact, some of the strategies women officers developed to combat this oppression included emphasizing humor, professionalism, a team approach, and sponsorship (Jurik 1988).

Women Attorneys

Research examining the experiences of women attorneys classified the women by professional role orientation into two groups (Rosenberg et al. 1993). *Feminists* displayed strong support for feminist positions, were members of women's organizations, and viewed the position of women in the legal system from a feminist base. *Careerists,* on the other hand, while supporting basic economic rights for women, rejected feminist labels. They were also less likely to conduct pro bono work for women's rights, support feminist candidates, or view the subordinate status of women lawyers as political. Instead they believed refining their legal skills was the best avenue for improving the position of women lawyers. Unexpectedly, the careerists were more likely than the feminists to report experiencing sexual harassment and gender-disparaging comments (Rosenberg et al. 1993).

SUMMARY

This chapter traces the history of women in crime-processing jobs, which moved from being nonexistent, to volunteer, to paid work. The paid women workers in most current crime-processing employment, at least in theory, have the same responsibilities as their male coworkers. Nonetheless, this chapter points out how their experiences and opportunities often differ significantly from those of their male colleagues.

The history and experiences of women prison and police officers have been quite similar—generally sexist, hostile, and stressful, probably because of the belief that women aren't "macho" enough to control male offenders. Women's experiences in the field of law have also been stressful, but breaking into legal practice has not been as difficult as breaking into policing and prison work. Significant changes in women's employment in crime processing resulted from the 1972 Title VII amendment to the Civil Rights Act. Additionally, this chapter points out the frequent discrimination that women police officers, prison workers, attorneys, and judges continue to face.

REFERENCES

Balkin, Joseph. 1988. "Why Policemen Don't Like Policewomen." *Journal of Police Science and Administration* 16:29–38.

Bartlett, Harold W., and Arthur Rosenblum. 1977. *Policewoman Effectiveness.* Denver: Civil Service Commission and Denver Police Department.

Baunach, Phyllis J., and Nicole H. Rafter. 1982. "Sex-Role Operations: Strategies for Women Working in the Criminal Justice System." Pp. 341–358 in *Judge, Lawyer, Victim, Thief,* edited by N. H. Rafter and E. A. Stanko. Stoughton, MA: Northeastern University Press.

Becraft, Carolyn. 1993a. "Women in the Military, 1980–1990." *Women and Criminal Justice* 4:137–154.

⸻. 1993b. "Women in the U.S. Armed Services: The War in the Persian Gulf." *Women and Criminal Justice* 4:155–164.

Belknap, Joanne. 1991. "Women in Conflict: An Analysis of Women Correctional Officers." *Women and Criminal Justice* 2:89–115.

Belknap, Joanne, and Jill Kastens Shelley. 1993. "The New Lone Ranger: Policewomen on Patrol." *American Journal of Police* 12:47–75.

Bell, Daniel. 1982. "Policewomen: Myths and Reality." *Journal of Police Science and Administration* 10:112–120.

Berger, Margaret A. 1980, May. *Litigation on Behalf of Women: A Review for the Ford Foundation.* New York: Ford Foundation.

Bernat, Frances P. 1992. "Women in the Legal Profession." Pp. 307–322 in *The Changing Roles of Women in the Criminal Justice System,* 2nd ed., edited by I. L. Moyer. Prospect Heights, IL: Waveland Press.

Bernat, Frances P., and Linda L. Zupan. 1989. "Assessment of Personnel Processes Pertaining to Women in a Traditionally Male Dominated Occupation: Affirmative Action Policies and Practices in Prisons and Jails." *The Prison Journal* 9:64–72.

Bloch, Peter B., and Deborah Anderson. 1974. *Policewomen on Patrol.* Washington, D.C.: The Police Foundation.

Blodgett, Nancy. 1986. "I Don't Think That Ladies Should Be Lawyers." *ABA Journal* December 1:48–53.

Bradwell v. *Illinois*, 83. U.S. (16 Wall.) 130 (1873).

Brown v. *Board of Education,* 347 U.S. 483 (1954).

Chapman, J. R., E. K. Minor, P. Ricker, T. L. Mills, and M. Bottum. 1980. *Women Employed in Corrections.* Washington, DC: Center for Women Policy Studies.

Christopher, W., J. A. Arguelles, R. Anderson, W. R. Barnes, L. F. Estrada, M. Kantor, R. M. Mosk, A. S. Ordin, J. B. Slaughter, and R. E. Tranquada. 1991. "Report of the Independent Commission on the Los Angeles Police Department."

Cook, Beverly B. 1978. "Women Judges: The End of Tokenism." Pp. 84–105 in *Women in the Courts,* edited by W. L. Hepperle and L. L. Crites. Williamsburg, VA: National Center for State Courts.

Deaux, K., and J. Taynor. 1973. "Evaluation of Male and Female Ability: Bias Works Two Ways." *Psychological Reports* 32:261–262.

DeCrow, Karen. 1974. *Sexist Justice.* New York: Random House.

Dothard v. *Rawlinson,* 433 U.S. 321 (1977).

Drachman, Virginia G. 1989. "My 'Partner' in Law and Life: Marriage in the Lives of Women Lawyers in Late 19th and Early 20th Century America." *Law and Social Inquiry* 14:221–250.

Dreifus, Claudia. 1982. "Why Two Women Cops Were Convicted of Cowardice." Pp. 427–436 in *The Criminal Justice System and Women,* edited by B. R. Price and N. J. Sokoloff. New York: Clark Boardman

Epstein, Cynthia F. 1982. "Women's Entry into Corporate Law Firms." Pp. 283–306 in *Women and the Law,* Vol. 2, edited by D. Kelly Weisberg. New York: Schenkman.

——————. 1983. *Women in Law.* Garden City, New York: Anchor Books.

——————. 1988. *Deceptive Distinctions: Sex, Gender, and the Social Order.* New Haven, CT: Yale University Press.

Feinman, Clarice. 1986. *Women in the Criminal Justice System.* New York: Praeger.

Felkenes, George T., Paul Peretz, and Jean Reith Schroedel. 1993. "An Analysis of the Mandatory Hiring of Females: The Los Angeles Police Department Experience." *Women and Criminal Justice* 4:31–64.

Felkenes, George T., and Jean Reith Schroedel. 1993. "A Case Study of Minority Women in Policing." *Women and Criminal Justice* 4:65–90.

Felkenes, George T., and L. Trostle. 1990, July. *The Impact of Fanchon Blake v. City of Los Angeles.* The Claremont Graduate School.

Flynn, Edith E. 1982. "Women as Criminal Justice Professionals: A Challenge to Tradition." Pp. 305–340 in *Judge, Lawyer, Victim, Thief,* edited by N. H. Rafter and E. A. Stanko. Stoughton, MA: Northeastern University Press.

Freedman, Estelle B. 1981. *Their Sisters' Keepers: Women's Prison Reform in America, 1830–1930.* Ann Arbor, MI: University of Michigan Press.

Gates, Margaret J. 1976. "Occupational Segregation and the Law." Pp. 61–74 in *Women and the Workplace,* edited by M. Blaxall and B. Reagan. Chicago: University of Chicago Press.

Graham, Deborah. 1986. "It's Getting Better, Slowly." *ABA Journal* December 1:54–58.

Grennan, Sean A. 1987. "Findings on the Role of Officer Gender in Violent Encounters with Citizens." *Journal of Police Science and Administration* 15:78–85.

Gross, Sally. 1984. "Women Becoming Cops: Developmental Issues and Solutions." *Police Chief* (January): 32–35.

Gruhl, John, Cassia Spohn, and Susan Welch. 1981. "Women as Policymakers: The Case of Trial Judges." *American Journal of Political Science* 25:308–322.

Hagan, John. 1990. "The Gender Stratification of Income Inequality Among Lawyers." *Social Forces* 68:835–855.

Hagan, John., Marjorie Zatz, Bruce Arnold, and Fiona Kay. 1991. "Cultural, Capital, Gender, and the Structural Transformation of Legal Practice." *Law and Society Review* 25:239–262.

Hale, Donna C. 1992. "Women in Policing." Pp. 125–142 in *What Works in Policing? Operations and Administrations Examined,* edited by G. W. Cordner and D. C. Hale, Cincinnati: Anderson.

Homant, Robert J., and Daniel B. Kennedy. 1985. "Police Perceptions of Spouse Abuse: A Comparison of Male and Female Officers." *Journal of Criminal Justice* 13:29–47.

Hughes, Everett C. 1944. "Dilemmas and Contradictions of Status." *American Journal of Sociology* 50:353–359.

Hunt, Jennifer C. 1984. "The Development of Rapport Through the Negotiation of Gender in Field Work Among Police." *Human Organization* 43:283–296.

_____. 1990. "The Logic of Sexism Among Police." *Women and Criminal Justice* 1:3–30.

Jacobs, P. 1987. "How Female Police Officers Cope with a Traditionally Male Position." *Social Science Review* 72:4–6.

Jordan v. Gardner 986 F. 2d. 1521 U.S. App. 1993

Jurik, Nancy C. 1985. "An Officer and a Lady: Organizational Barriers to Women Working as Correctional Officers in Men's Prisons." *Social Problems* 32:375–388.

_____. 1988. "Striking a Balance: Female Correctional Officers, Gender Role Stereotypes, and Male Prisoners." *Sociological Inquiry* 58:291–304.

Kanter, Rosabeth M. 1977a. "Some Effects of Proportions in Group Life: Skewed Sex Ratios and Responses to Token Women." *American Journal of Sociology* 82:965–990.

Kanter, Rosabeth M. 1977b. *Men and Women of the Corporation*. New York: Basic Books.

Kennedy, Daniel B., and Robert J. Homant. 1983. "Attitudes of Abused Women Toward Male and Female Police Officers." *Criminal Justice and Behavior* 10:391–405.

Kissel, Peter J., and Paul L. Katsampes. 1980. "The Impact of Women Corrections Officers on the Functioning of Institutions Housing Male Inmates." *Journal of Offender Counseling, Services and Rehabilitation* 4:213–231.

Koenig, Esther J. 1978. "An Overview of Attitudes Toward Women in Law Enforcement." *Public Administration Review* 38:267–275.

Laws, Judith L. 1975. "The Psychology of Tokenism: An Analysis." *Sex Roles* 1:51–67.

Marshall, Patricia 1973. "Policewomen on Patrol." *Manpower* (October):15–20.

Martin, C. A. 1983. "Women Police and Stress." *Police Chief* 50:106–109.

Martin, Susan E. 1979. "*Police*women and Police*women*: Occupational Role Dilemmas and Choices of Female Officers." *Journal of Police Science and Administration* 7:314–323.

_____. 1980. *Breaking and Entering: Policewomen on Patrol*. Berkeley: University of California Press.

_____. 1989, May. *Women on the Move? A Report on the Status of Women in Policing*. Washington, D.C.: The Police Foundation.

_____. 1992. "The Changing Status of Women Officers." Pp. 281–305 in *The Changing Roles of Women in the Criminal Justice System*, 2nd ed., edited by I. L. Moyer. Prospect Heights, IL: Waveland Press.

Merton, Robert K. 1972. "Insiders and Outsiders: A Chapter in the Sociology of Knowledge." *American Journal of Sociology* 78:9–47.

Moran, Beverly I. 1990–1991. "Quantum Leap: A Black Woman Uses Legal Education to Obtain Her Honorary White Pass." *Berkeley Women's Law Journal* 6:118–121.

Morash, Merry, and Jack R. Greene. 1986. "Evaluating Women on Patrol: A Critique of Contemporary Wisdom." *Evaluation Review* 10:230–255.

Morello, Karen B. 1986. *The Invisible Bar: The Woman Lawyer in America, 1638 to the Present*. Boston: Beacon Press.

Morris, Allison. 1987. *Women, Crime and Criminal Justice*. Oxford, England: Basil Blackwell.

Morton, Joann B. 1981. "Women in Correctional Employment: Where Are They Now and Where Are They Headed?" Pp. 7–16 in *Women in Corrections,* edited by B. H. Olsson. College Park, MD: American Correctional Association.

Nallin, J. A. 1981. "Female Correctional Administrators: Sugar and Spice Are Nice but a Backbone of Steel Is Essential." Pp. 17–26 in *Women in*

Corrections, edited by B. H. Olsson. College Park, MD: American Correctional Association.

Officers for Justice et al. v. Civil Service Commission of the City and County of San Francisco, C-73-0657 RFP (N.D. Cal.) (1975).

Ott, E. M. 1989. "Effects of the Male–Female Ratio at Work: Policewomen and Male Nurses." Psychology of Women Quarterly 13:41–58.

Pollock, Joyce M. 1986. Sex and Supervision: Guarding Male and Female Inmates. New York: Greenwood.

Poole, Eric D., and Mark R. Pogrebin. 1988. "Factors Affecting the Decision to Remain in Policing: A Study of Women Officers." Journal of Police Science and Administration 16:49–55.

Pope, K. E., and D. W. Pope. 1986. "Attitudes of Male Police Officers Toward Their Female Counterparts." The Police Journal 59:242–250.

Price, Barbara R. 1974. "A Study of Leadership Strength of Female Police Executives." Journal of Police Science and Administration 2:219–226.

Rafter, Nicole H., and Elizabeth A. Stanko. 1982. "Introduction." Pp. 1–28 in Judge, Lawyer, Victim, Theif: Women, Gender Roles and Criminal Justice, edited by N. H. Rafter and E. A. Stanko. Stoughton, MA: Northeastern University Press.

Remmington, P. W. 1983. "Women in Police: Integration or Separation?" Qualitative Sociology 6:118–133.

Rhode, Deborah L. 1989. Justice and Gender: Sex Discrimination and the Law. Cambridge, MA: Harvard University Press.

Rivlin, G. 1981. "The Last Bastion of Macho: Policewomen." Update on Law-Related Education 5:22–24,65–67.

Rosenberg, Janet, Harry Perstadt, and William R. Phillips. 1993. "Now That We Are Here: Discrimination, Disparagement, and Harassment of Work and the Experience of Women Lawyers." Gender and Society 7:415–433.

Schulz, Dorothy M. 1989. "The Police Matron Movement: Paving the Way for Policewomen." Police Studies 12:115–124.

_____. 1993. "Policewomen in the 1950s: Paving the Way for Patrol." Women and Criminal Justice 4:5–30.

Sherman, Lewis J. 1973. "A Psychological View of Women in Policing." Journal of Police Science and Administration 1:383–394.

_____. 1975. "An Evaluation of Policewomen on Patrol in a Suburban Police Department." Journal of Police Science and Administration 3:434–438.

Sichel, Joyce, Lucy Friedman, Janet Quint, and Michael Smith. 1978. Women on Patrol: A Pilot Study of Police Performance in New York City. Washington, D.C.: National Institute of Law Enforcement and Criminal Justice.

Simpson, Sally, and Mervin F. White. 1985. "The Female Guard in the All-Male Prison." Pp. 276–300 in The Changing Roles of Women in the Criminal Justice System, edited by I. L. Moyer. Prospect Heights, IL: Waveland Press.

Sokoloff, Natalie J. 1988. "Evaluating Gains and Losses by Black and White Women and Men in the Professions, 1960–1980." Social Problems 35:36–53.

Timmins, William M., and Brad E. Hainsworth. 1989. "Attracting and Retaining Females in Law Enforcement." International Journal of Offender Therapy and Comparative Criminology 33:197–205.

Townsey, Roi D. 1982a. "Female Patrol Officers: A Review of the Physical Capability Issue." Pp. 413–426 in The Criminal Justice System and Women, edited by B. R. Price and N. J. Sokoloff. New York: Clark Boardman.

_____. 1982b. "Black Women in American Policing: An Advancement Display." Journal of Criminal Justice 10:455–468.

U.S. Federal Bureau of Investigation. 1993. Uniform Crime Reports for the U.S. 1992. Washington, D.C.: U.S. Government Printing Office.

U.S. Federal Bureau of Prisons. 1993. *Federal Bureau of Prisons Annual Statistical Report Calendar Year 1992.* Washington, D.C.: U.S.:GPO.

Van Voorhis, Patricia, Francis T. Cullen, Bruce G. Link, Nancy T. Wolfe. 1991. "The Impact of Race and Gender on Correctional Officers' Orientation to the Integrated Environment." *Journal of Research in Crime and Delinquency* 28:472–500.

Warner, Rebecca L., Brent S. Steel, and Nicholas P. Lovrich. 1989. "Conditions Associated with the Advent of Representative Bureaucracy." *Social Science Quarterly* 70:562–578.

Weisberg, D. Kelly. 1982. "Barred from the Bar: Women and Legal Education in the U.S., 1870–1890." Pp. 231–258 in *Women and the Law,* Vol. 2, edited by D. Kelly Weisberg. New York: Schenkman.

Weisheit, Ralph A. 1987. "Women in the State Police: Concerns of Male and Female Officers." *Journal of Police Science and Administration* 15:137–143.

Wexler, Judi G., and D. D. Logan. 1983. "Sources of Stress Among Women Police Officers." *Journal of Police Science and Administration* 11:46–53.

Williams, Christine L. 1992. "The Glass Escalator: Hidden Advantages for Men in the 'Female' Professions." *Social Problems* 39:253–267.

Wright, Kevin N., and W. G. Saylor. 1991. "Male and Female Employees' Perceptions of Prison Work: Is There a Difference?" *Justice Quarterly* 8:505–524.

Yoder, Janice D. 1991. "Rethinking Tokenism: Looking Beyond Numbers." *Gender and Society* 5(2):178–192.

Zimmer, Lynn E. 1986. *Women Guarding Men.* Chicago: University of Chicago Press.

_____. 1987. "How Women Re-Shape the Prison Guard Role." *Gender and Society* 1:415–431.

_____. 1988. "Tokenism and Women in the Workplace: The Limits of Gender-Neutral Theory." *Social Problems* 35:64–73.

_____. 1989. "Solving Women's Employment Problems in Corrections: Shifting the Burden to Administrators." *Women and Criminal Justice* 1:55–80.

Zupan, Linda A. 1992. "The Progress of Women Correctional Officers in All-Male Prisons." Pp. 232–244 in *The Changing Roles of Women in the Criminal Justice System,* 2nd ed., edited by I. L. Moyer. Prospect Heights, IL: Waveland Press.

PART V

Conclusions

11

✵

Effecting Change

This book describes the state of women and girls as victims and offenders in the crime-processing system, and the experiences of women crime-processing professionals. It also discusses how laws have differentially affected women, particularly in terms of employment outside of the home. Chapters 1–10 portray the invisibility and negative state of women and girls in crime processing, whether it is as workers, offenders, or victims. This concluding chapter summarizes and describes recent advances in the visibility of females in criminological theories and the crime-processing system. Additionally, it offers some hope of solutions to the existing problems.

NEW THEORIES

Chapter 2 provides a discussion on various criminological theories and how women and girls were routinely excluded from most studies and theories, or if included, were done so in gender-stereotypical ways. Since the 1980s, feminist researchers have worked to make female offenders and victims visible (Morris and Gelsthorpe 1991). Given that criminological theories are more interested in explaining offending, this section focuses on recent advances in theorizing about female (and male) offending.

Two refreshing changes with regard to female crime and gender differences in crime can be seen in James Messerschmidt's (1993) "masculinities and crime" theorizing, and Kathleen Daly's (1992) hypothesis on women's pathways to lawbreaking.

Messerschmidt's Masculinities and Crime Theories

James Messerschmidt's (1993) rethinking of feminist theory focuses on *structured action* and *gendered crime*. Messerschmidt addresses the impact of gender not only on women's criminality, but also on men's. He defines *social structures* as "regular patterned forms of interaction over time that constrain and channel behavior in specific ways" (1993, 63). Messerschmidt identifies three social structures as important to understanding our gendered society: the gender division of labor, gender relations of power, and sexuality. Moreover, class, race, and gender relations are interconnected to a number of social structures, and thus are related to *social actions.*

To Messerschmidt, *masculinity* is key to explaining criminality. He carefully examines how race, class, and gender interact within various social structures that encourage the preponderance of criminality perpetrated largely by young males. Accounting for differences among males, Messerschmidt describes how middle-class Anglo males can use power structures, such as a good education and respectable careers, to obtain masculinity and provide for themselves and their families. Lower class males and males of color have fewer legitimate options, however, and thus are more likely to use crime and delinquency to prove masculinity. Accounting for gender differences, it is far more important for males than for females to show power, or to need to prove masculinity. Regarding sexuality, more respect is accrued to heterosexuals than to lesbians and gay men, and, as discussed in Chapter 4, consensual (hetero)sexuality is more permissible by society and the crime-processing system when it is by males than when it is by females. Messerschmidt effectively uses these variables of class, race, and sexuality to explain rape causality, the differential treatment of males and females who are sexually active, and participation in various crimes and offenses ranging from sexual harassment to robbery and homicide.

This new approach to studying crime causation is appealing in that it accounts for both males and females, as well as the impact of gender, race, and class. Furthermore, it explains crime and criminal processing within the important social structures that shape society and the individuals in it.

Daly's Pathways to Lawbreaking

Kathleen Daly (1992) examines both male and female offenders, but focuses on women's distinct pathways to lawbreaking. Specifically, she uses felony court presentence investigation reports (PSIs) as biographies of offending women. Daly identifies five categories of women: street women, harmed-and-harming women, battered women, drug-connected women, and "other." Although there is considerable overlap between the women's experiences (for example, battering victim/survivor, alcohol and drug abuse, and abuse or neglect as children), each category identifies a specific feature that brings the woman to felony court.

The *street woman* draws on Eleanor M. Miller's (1986) work and book of the same title. The street woman has typically experienced significant amounts of physical and psychological damage as a child or adult, and she hustles on the street to "eke out a living" (Daly 1992, 37). Street women often support their drug habits by prostitution, selling drugs, and stealing, which is usually what brings them to court. The *harmed-and-harming woman,* on the other hand, is characterized by abuse and neglect as a child, which led to "acting out" and being labeled a "problem child." Alcohol often leads to her becoming violent, and she may be drug-addicted. The harmed-and-harming woman's inability to cope with a certain situation, such as feeling someone "did her wrong," is what brings her to court. Also, unlike the street woman, the harmed-and-harming woman is not living on the streets and hustling, and she harms others because she is angry.

Daly's (1992) third category of women's pathways to lawbreaking is the *battered woman.* This woman is either currently in, or just ended, a relationship with a violent man. Although women in some of Daly's other categories were also battered, being involved with a violent man is what brings the women in the battered woman category to court. The "crime" for which the battered woman goes to court is typically for harming or killing the abusive man during an assault on her. The *drug-connected woman,* on the other hand, uses or sells drugs as a result of her relationships with her male intimate, children, or mother. Her drug experiences are recent, and like the battered women, she does not tend to have much of a criminal record. For example, of the women Daly classified as "drug-connected," one woman allowed her boyfriend to use her apartment to sell drugs, and another stole and pawned her parents' silverware to support her and her husband's drug habit.

Daly's (1992) final category, which she labels *other,* can best be defined as economically motivated. Either greed or a pressing economic circumstance motivated the crimes. *Other* women do not have a history of abuse or problems with drugs or alcohol. For example, Daly describes a woman who embezzled over $125,000 although she and her husband had no major debts. Daly believes that the street woman pathway to crime is probably more common in the misdemeanor than the felony courts, but offers the remaining four categories of pathways as a means to "argue for a more multi-dimensional portrait of why women get caught up in crime" (1992, 45).

CHANGING THE TREATMENT
OF FEMALE OFFENDERS

Edwin Schur (1984, 235) states: "The persisting inclination to label women deviant is, quite simply, a deplorable fact of social life. It must be faced up to, if it is to be eliminated." Schur applies this deviance-labeling of women to numerous aspects of women's lives, but focuses, as this section does, on female offenders. Schur (1984, 237) points out that men have been given the power to control labeling: "it usually has been men who have been in a position to define situations that might occasion the use of deviance labels." Furthermore, the mismatch between data from the experiences of women's lives and data from the legal definitions and assumptions about certain life situations reveals "whose power is being served by the law as it exists, what aspects of women's lives are legally visible, and how women's experience is distorted by the law" (Wishik 1985, 74).

U.S. law has historically grouped women, children, and the mentally feeble as deficient in the qualities necessary to own property and vote (Wikler 1987). The role of legal precedent and the isolation and insulation of judicial decision making serve to "allow" judges in the crime-processing system to maintain gender-role stereotyping in their rulings. As long as women were not part of the judicial "brotherhood," this was extremely difficult to challenge. Many women lawyers in the late 1960s and 1970s were concerned with how male judges' personal sexist biases and stereotypes strongly influenced their behavior and undermined legal reforms (Wikler 1987).

A national judicial education program on gender bias was first conceived by Sylvia Roberts, a Title VII litigator and counsel for the NOW Legal Defense and Education Fund (NOW LDEF) in 1970. Because of a lack of financial support—a result of many people's unwillingness to believe that judges could make biased decisions—the idea for a program to educate judges on sexism was delayed until 1979, when the National Association of Women Judges was formed (Wikler 1987). The role of these women judges as "insiders" helped launch NJEP—the National Judicial Education Program to Promote Equality for Women and Men in the Courts—in 1980. NJEP has been responsible for designing and implementing a number of educational programs on gender bias for judges, but its most significant impact has probably been the outgrowth of the Gender Bias Task Forces implemented in thirty-five states. At least twenty-five of these states have published reports (Van Voorhis et al. 1993). "Today the multiple efforts of NJEP, the state task forces, and the National Gender Bias Task Forces (created in 1985 by the National Association of Women Judges) continue the work of educating the judiciary on gender bias" (Wikler 1987).

Chapter 4 includes a discussion of the "evil woman," "chivalrous," and "equal treatment" hypotheses on the processing of female offenders, as compared to the processing of male offenders. In an ideal world, it would seem that equal treatment should be the goal. Given that women and men have such varied experiences in terms of public, private, and criminal lives, however, "equal treatment" may have some detrimental effects for women offenders (Brodsky 1975; Daly and Chesney-Lind 1988). For example, laws proposed to create equality for women in the areas of divorce and child custody frequently worked to the disadvantage of women. No-fault divorces, supported by feminists to ease women's access to divorce, actually decreased divorcing women's "bargaining chips" and resulted in divorced women being significantly less well-off economically than before these no-fault divorce procedures were implemented in the 1970s (Weitzman 1985). Similarly, sentencing reforms designed to reduce class and race bias in *men's* sentencing may also negatively affect the sentencing of women by increasing their incarceration rates and the lengths of sentences (Daly and Chesney-Lind 1988). Daly and Chesney-Lind (1988, 526) conclude: "Criminologists, especially those involved in the formation of policy, should be aware that equal treatment is only one of several ways of redressing discrimination and of moving toward a more humane justice system."

In the early 1980s, Rafter and Natalizia (1981) made three recommendations regarding feminist research on crime processing: (1) Gather more data on female criminality; (2) provide extensive research on the social contexts of women's crime and the punishment of women; and (3) research the attitudes of crime-processing personnel toward female victims, offenders, and coworkers. This book exemplifies that research on female offending has grown exponentially since the 1960s. Moreover, despite a backlash against women offenders, feminist criminologists have increasingly conducted this research. Nonetheless, research on female offending, particularly the imprisonment of women, must be more rigorously addressed.

Sarri (1987) points out that women's prior victimizations place them at risk for offending, and also that our prisons are highly, disproportionately populated with African American women and other women of color. This may be due to high unemployment rates, federal resistance to affirmative action, and the many ways their "loser status" is reinforced. Society seems quite willing to allow women

> … to drift into crime in order to survive; then they end up in correctional facilities where the cost of their care exceeds any welfare benefit that they might have received by several hundred percent. Moreover, their children will be placed in foster care, which is both damaging and costly for them and for society. This is nearly the ultimate Catch-22.
>
> *(Sarri 1987, 418)*

The numerous problems facing women in prison and jails are discussed at length in Chapter 5. Not only do women experience worse conditions than men, but they also have special concerns, such as pregnancy/medical needs and the ability to maintain contact with and custody of their children. Given that incarcerated women experience worse conditions and have fewer opportunities than men, efforts must be made to improve women's prisons.

A number of solutions to these problems have been offered in the form of recommendations, some of which have been implemented. First, women's prisons need to provide *programs and opportunities to maintain contact between incarcerated women and their children* (American Correctional Association 1990; Baunach 1992; McCarthy 1980; McGowan and Blumenthal 1981; Stanton 1980). Second, appropriate, adequate, and continuous *child-care/temporary custody alternatives* should be made for the children of incarcerated women (Brodsky 1975; McGowan and Blumenthal 1981), including *housing for infants or even small children within the prison structure* (American Correctional Association 1990; Baunach 1992; Haley 1980; Knight 1992; McCarthy 1980; McGowan and Blumenthal 1981; Schupak 1986).

Third, *improved medical services* should be provided, including the needs of special populations such as HIV positive and pregnant women (American Correctional Association 1990; Barry 1991; Clark and Boudin 1990; Knight 1992; McGowan and Blumenthal 1981; McHugh 1980; Ross and Fabiano 1986; Schupak 1986; Wooldredge and Masters 1993). Many of the supporters of pregnant prisoners advocate that they should not be in prison for part or all of their pregnancy and for some period thereafter. (This recommendation is congruent with the following one.)

The fourth recommendation of women prisoner advocates is to *stop the building of maximum security prisons and provide alternative housing,* particularly for the majority of women prisoners who are nonviolent, nonserious offenders with dependent children (American Correctional Association 1990; Baunach 1992; Chesney-Lind 1991; Immarigeon 1987a, 1987b; Immarigeon and Chesney-Lind 1992; Rafter 1985; Von Cleve and Weis 1993). The fifth recommendation is to *improve drug/alcohol treatment programs* (American Correctional Association 1990; McGowan and Blumenthal 1981); the sixth is to *improve legal services* available to incarcerated women (McGowan and Blumenthal 1981; Pendergrass 1975); and the seventh is to *improve vocational and educational programs,* particularly literacy programs and training in traditionally male labor skills (American Correctional Association 1990; Feinman 1984; Knight 1992; McGowan and Blumenthal 1981; Ross and Fabiano 1986; Stanton 1980).

The final three recommendations regarding the incarceration of women are somewhat related. The eighth recommendation is to *improve therapy and counseling* (Haley 1980; McGowan and Blumenthal 1981); the ninth recommendation is to *provide empowerment programs* (for example, participatory management in the prison system and peer counseling) (Baunach 1992; Kendall 1994; Hardesty et al. 1993; Pendergrass 1975; Pollack 1994); and the final recommendation is to *provide postrelease services* to help women incorporate themselves back into nonprison life (American Correctional Association 1990; McGowan and Blumenthal 1981).

Most of these recommendations have been tried in some women's prisons in the United States. Unfortunately, budget constraints and the lack of power of incarcerated women often keep innovative programs from being funded or from being maintained once implemented. Also, there is little in the way of evaluative research and analysis to rate the effectiveness of these programs. The same can be said regarding innovative programs for girl offenders (Chesney-Lind and Shelden 1992).

Notably, many of the preceding recommendations exist in a women's prison in Mexico. Jennifer Pearson (1993) studied *Centro Feminil* and reported positive, supportive conditions: Children can live inside the facilities with their mothers, a sense of respect and caring exists between the prisoners and the guards, visits and communication with family members are facilitated, and human rights are emphasized and based on the needs of the collective unit.

The Mexican prison system I observed appeals to the strengths, rather than the weaknesses, of the inmates and their families. Imprisonment deprives a prisoner of her liberty. However, it seeks to do so as little as possible. Not only is it more humane, its costs—both social and economic—to society as a whole are far less. Deviants who can be reincorporated back into the community through their primary networks are not incarcerated, a much less costly alternative.

(Pearson 1993, 89–90)

Thus far, this chapter has focused on women's offending. The next section is an analysis of changes and recommendations in response to male violence against females.

CHANGING RESPONSES TO MALE VIOLENCE AGAINST WOMEN

Abusive men have been structurally and psychologically accustomed to taking out their anger on women, and both sexism and violence against women are commonplace (Klein 1981). Moreover, inequality between women and men fosters male violence against women (Russell 1984; Sanday 1981; Schwendinger and Schwendinger 1983). Therefore, any discussion of effecting change regarding male violence against women must begin with the notion that abusive men and the societal factors that perpetuate male dominance and violence must change. Women and girls do not cause their sexual and battering victimizations. For abusive men to discontinue their violent and violating behaviors, the socialization of men and boys must change, as well as crime-processing system reactions to these abusers and the victims. Finally, we must also empower women and girls to resist these victimizations.

Sexual Victimization

During the 1970s and 1980s, every state repealed or modified traditional rape laws and enacted evidentiary reforms (Spohn and Horney 1992).

> The most common changes were (1) redefining rape and replacing the single crime of rape with a series of graded offenses defined by the presence or absence of aggravating conditions; (2) changing the consent standard by eliminating the requirement that the victim physically resist her attacker; (3) eliminating the requirement that the victim's testimony be corroborated; and (4) placing restrictions on the introduction of evidence of the victim's prior sexual conduct.
>
> *(Spohn and Horney 1992, 21)*

Many states have enacted rape law reforms to help victims prosecute, to broaden the definition of rape to include forms other than penile–vaginal, and to assert that rapes are actual assaults rather than crimes "of passion" (as they are commonly portrayed in the media and in rape trials). Unfortunately, at present, rape law reform appears to be more symbolic than productive. That is, although rape law reform is *necessary* to address the complex issues surrounding sexual victimizations, the reforms are not *sufficient* to ensure that changes are actually practiced (Berger et al. 1988; Caringella-MacDonald 1988; Horney and Spohn 1991; Spohn and Horney 1991, 1992, 1993). Therefore, although the first step has been taken—to change the rape laws—it is now important that these laws be used to protect all rape victims, regardless of the victim–offender relationship, the victim's prior sexual history, and the form the abuse takes. (It should be noted that there are still major shortcomings to law reforms, including the fact that some states exempt marital rape.)

The chart on the bottom of this page summarizes the changes that need to occur within communities in order to deter sexual victimization (Koss and Harvey 1991). The remainder of this section discusses these issues.

Given that women can't count on rape law reform or individual violent men to stop raping, it is necessary to recognize and foster empowering behaviors and actions in women and girls. The research on sexual victimization points to the importance of instilling in women the confidence to identify and escape potentially threatening situations, as well as to physically fight back, where this is possible. Although sexually threatening situations may and often do develop to the point where it is impossible for the woman to escape, Parrot (1986) claims it is often possible to watch for danger signs in order to avoid sexual victimization. Specifically, women should trust their "gut feelings" when they feel that a situation or person is potentially dangerous. Women need to feel strong enough to say "no" or to leave situations in which they are uncomfortable (see Glavin 1986; Parrot 1986). Some women worry that they are "rude," "ungrateful," or even "prudish" if they don't go along with unwanted attention; however, men's offensive behavior frequently preludes sexual victimizations.

Clearly, both women and men need to be educated that women and girls are to be respected, that women are to be believed when they say "no" or "stop," and that women should be able to leave potentially dangerous situations, however they are perceived, without feeling guilty about hurting someone's feelings. Research on both high school and college students has shown that rape awareness programs in the educational environment are effective in dispelling rape myths (Fonow et al. 1992; Proto et al. 1994). Therefore, such programs need to be implemented in all educational environments.

Community Rape Prevention Strategies

- Challenge societal beliefs and cultural values that promote and condone sexual violence.
- Educate potential victims about risk, risk avoidance, and self-defense.
- Reduce the emotional and physical trauma of rape by early and appropriate attention to the needs of individual rape victims.
- Prevent recurrent instances of rape by offender incarceration and treatment.

SOURCE: Koss, Mary P., and Mary R. Harvey. 1991. *The Rape Victim: Clinical and Community Interventions,* 2nd ed. Newbury Park, CA: Sage, p. 246.

Verbal, physical, and legal resistance to sexual victimization may all prove fruitful in deterrence. It is important to note that confronting sexual harassment has effectively raised awareness about it. Three years before the Anita Hill/Clarence Thomas hearings, it was pointed out that African American women have been "at the forefront of the fight against sexual harassment," which has resulted in the legal definitions of sexual harassment, the identification of sexual harassment as sex discrimination, the Title VII prohibition against sexual harassment, and liability for employers who engage in sexual harassment (Eason 1988, 140).

One study found that women college students base their decision to report sexual harassment on (1) severity of the harassment, (2) fear of being accused of lying, (3) perceived effectiveness of reporting, and (4) fear of the reporting procedure itself (Sullivan and Bybee 1987). This implies the importance of universities and other institutions creating and maintaining policies and an environment that facilitate the reporting of and adequate response to sexual harassment charges.

Research evaluating the best way to resist rape once an actual assault has begun consistently finds that in most cases it is best for victims to fight back. Victims who fight back are much less likely to experience "completed" rapes than those who do not resist (Bart and O'Brien 1985; Kleck and Sayles 1990; Ullman and Knight 1992). Of utmost importance is to act immediately to the assault and to combine resistance strategies. The most effective combination of two strategies is physical force and yelling, the single most effective strategy is fleeing, and pleading and begging appear to have a negative effect, increasing the chance of a completed rape (Bart and O'Brien 1985; Ullman and Knight 1992). There is no evidence that resisting an attacker will lead to further injuries in addition to the rape in most cases—resistance rarely precedes injury (Bart and O'Brien 1985; Kleck and Sayles 1990; Ullman and Knight 1992). Moreover, victims who fight back tend to have fewer psychological injuries after the attack, even if the rape was completed (Bart and O'Brien 1985). It is also important to remember that all rapes are not escapable—some women (and men) are simply overpowered despite active resistance. Furthermore, victims who did not resist should not be blamed for their victimizations. As a whole, however, physical resistance appears to be the most powerful hindrance of sexual attacks.

Finally, the crime-processing system must become more responsive to both victims and offenders in an effort to stop sexual victimization. In Chapter 7, the numerous problems associated with crime-processing responses are discussed. The chart on page 268 summarizes factors that are important to enhance victims' likelihood to report sexual assaults to the police and follow through with the courts. Special care must also be taken in crime processing of child sexual abuse, not only to protect the child from further abuse but also to understand the victims' reluctance to answer police questions (Kirkwood and Mihaila 1979).

**Measures to Increase Sexual Assault Victims'
Willingness to Report to the Police**

- Increased and improved training for police to promote sensitivity and reduce victim blaming
- Greater sensitivity from prosecutors
- Better treatment and better laws to protect victims in court
- Public education to increase awareness that rape is a crime and is not the victim's fault

SOURCE: National Victim Center. 1992, April 23. *Rape in America: A Report to the Nation,* p. 11.

Although most of the criticism of the crime-processing system is focused on the police, it is also important that the courts adequately address victims' needs and offenders' responsibility (see Klein 1981; Smart 1989; Spohn and Horney 1992). Regarding legal reform for the processing of child sexual abuse cases, the following goals have been proposed: (1) Expedite the case; (2) provide advocates and guardians for the victims; (3) reduce unnecessary contact of the child with the crime-processing system; (4) institute "child-friendly" procedures; and (5) enhance case development through exceptions to hearsay rules and use of expert witnesses (Whitcomb 1991).

In conclusion, important advances have been made in legal reforms and the general crime processing of sexual abuse cases. It is necessary, however, that the implementation of legal reforms occur, as well as evaluations and improvements of individual crime-processing professionals' responses to victims and offenders.

Woman Battering

Since the 1970s, the battered women's movement has increased public awareness of woman battering.

> For the first time, battered women have been singled out as a special population that needs a range of services. Funds and other material resources have been obtained by anti-wife beating groups. Government agencies and task forces have been established, new laws have been passed, and community organizations are making explicit efforts to aid battered women.
>
> *(Tierney 1982, 215)*

A lack of shelters or available space in existing shelters, and an often unresponsive crime-processing system, continue to be problems. Nonetheless, progress has been made. For example, despite an effort since the early 1990s to withdraw support from pro-arrest policies for woman batterers (See Sherman 1992), current research offers support for the crime-processing system's proactive responses against these offenders. Some scholars have criticized the current attempt to withdraw pro-arrest policies as a narrowly focused view of effectiveness—solely examining arrest and recidivism (Bowman 1992; Frisch

1992; Gondolf and Fisher 1988; Lerman 1992; Stanko 1989). Such a focus ignores that arrest may provide positive outcomes unrelated to recidivism—such as an escape opportunity for victims and their children—and may communicate to all involved parties (the batterer, the victim, the children, and other witnesses) that battering is unacceptable and illegal behavior.

The focus on the arrest decision regarding the system's response to battering ignores the importance of court action (and inaction) in woman battering cases. For example, one study found that for cases where the prosecutor decided to proceed through the initial hearing, the batterer was less likely to recidivate (Ford and Regoli 1992). In addition, two studies have shown how arrest empowers battered women. In one study batterers perceived arrest as increasing both the visibility and the risks of their behavior—including a greater likelihood of going to jail and having their abused partner leave them. The battered women perceived arrest as an opportunity to speak out to the authorities and others against the abuse and to exercise their power (Dutton et al. 1992). Moreover, results from another study (Ford 1991a) suggest that the dropping of charges by battered women does not necessarily negate the usefulness of filing the charges. Rather, battered women can use the threat of prosecution to influence the batterer to change (Ford 1991a). Perceived this way, dropping charges may be an indication that the system does work for some women.

Critics of pro-arrest policies also raise concerns that arresting batterers may place victims at increased risk of violence by retaliation of the offender. Research examining this issue, however, found the majority of battered women are not at risk of increased violence following the offender's arrest (Ford 1991b; Jaffe et al. 1986). For those few women who are more at risk of violence, the police should expand their protection (Stark 1993). At any rate, it is important to allow individual battered women a voice in the decision making of their own cases through discussions with police and court officials (Ferraro and Pope 1993). It may be necessary to allow the victim to unilaterally veto the arrest or prosecution decision, as she knows her situation and risks better than anyone. It is crucial for prosecution decision making to understand victim reluctance; such understanding increases the likelihood of victim cooperation and a successful disposition in court (Hart 1993).

For effective and meaningful responses to battered women to exist, the many arms of the crime-processing system and other health and helping agencies must work together—from the police and the emergency room personnel to the social workers, prosecutors, and judges (see Belknap and McCall 1994; Cahn 1992; Gamache et al. 1988). Courts, in addition to police departments, must have stated policies and goals that recognize woman battering as a crime and force batterers to take responsibility for their behaviors. "They [courts] can then support police in their efforts, help break the cycle of violence, and control the abuser" (Cahn 1992, 177).

It is not sufficient simply to have laws and policies in place to protect battered women—they must also be enforced (Ferraro 1989; McCann 1985). In fact, although policy reforms resulting from feminist activism finally criminalized woman battering, they also effectively moved control of this problem from feminists and battered women's advocates to crime-processing professionals, the press, mental health professionals, and academics who often fail to account for gender inequality in the family (Bush 1993).

Therefore, programs in which battered women's groups are actively involved with the crime-processing professionals are the best hope for effective crime-processing responses to woman battering (Kurz 1992; Pence and Shepard 1988). Pro-arrest policies and other crime-processing actions against batterers may prove fruitless without a systems approach that includes a feminist perspective from battered women's groups (Kurz 1992). Such interaction between battered women's groups and the crime-processing system has provided productive models for change in the system in Denver, San Francisco, and Minneapolis (Kurz 1992).

Chapter 8 includes a discussion of court problems for battered women who killed their batterers in self-defense. Current self-defense laws are insufficient to account for the resistance battered women must use to protect themselves (and often their children). Moreover, acquittal by reason of insanity has obvious negative repercussions for victims who were likely behaving quite sanely; for example, it may be difficult to find employment and retain custody of children. Therefore, some advocates for battered women who have killed abusive mates suggest that an *entrapment defense* be employed, including a psychological self-defense (Ewing 1987; Stark 1992). Such a defense proposes that women may have to use more force than men in similar situations, and that battered women may be entrapped by a combination of social and psychological factors, making it impossible or seemingly impossible to escape (as discussed in Chapter 8).

Finally, the importance of battered women's shelters cannot be overemphasized. Shelters save the lives of battered women, their children, and even the batterers; an increase in shelters is correlated with a decrease in domestic homicides of both women and men (Browne 1992; Steffensmeier 1993; Walker 1989). In addition to providing a safe haven for women and children and decreasing the likelihood of homicides, shelters advocate for and enable women to escape abusive relationships and to view themselves as worthy of respect (Ferraro and Johnson 1983; Pence and Shepard 1988).

CHANGES FOR WOMEN
CRIME-PROCESSING PROFESSIONALS

The experiences of women working in crime-processing jobs are described in Chapter 10. As a result of the women's movement, Title VII of the Civil Rights Act, and affirmative action, women have been accepted into law schools and employed in men's prisons and on police patrol in unprecedented numbers since the 1970s. For example, the percent of women law students has grown from 4.2 percent in 1965 to 42.5 percent in 1991, and the percent of women in the total lawyer population has grown from 2.5 percent in 1950 to 8.1 percent in 1980, and 22 percent in 1990 (American Bar Association 1992). Women have also been elected and appointed judges in larger numbers than ever before, and have been promoted to sergeants, captains, lieutenants, and (rarely) chiefs and wardens (only in women's prisons) at the highest rates ever.

Nonetheless, there is still considerable room for improvement. Many law school programs provide no training and coursework on feminist issues, such as representing battered women victims, battered women who've killed their batterers, rape victims, and women discriminated against in hirings, firings, and promotions. Women still make up less than 10 percent of officers in most police departments and men's prisons. And the research summarized in Chapter 10 suggests that women in these nontraditional, male-dominated jobs continue to face considerable hostility from some of their male coworkers and supervisors.

Martin (1989) lists factors she believes contribute to the slightly higher turnover rate of policewomen as compared to policemen: an unpleasant working environment for women, problems mixing policing with family responsibilities (especially for single parents on rotating shifts), inadequate pregnancy leave and light-duty pregnancy policies, exaggerated views of policework portrayed on television and by police recruiters, and problems associated with being "tokens." These factors are probably equally applicable to women working in men's prisons. (Chapter 10 presents similar hostility and career blocks that women lawyers face.) Thus, policies must be implemented and followed to address conditions that make females' working environments more difficult than those of their male counterparts.

Furthermore, the influence of tokenism is crucial. As long as women are hired as tokens—whether in policing, prison work, law firms, or as elected or appointed attorneys and judges—they are unlikely to be able to perform their duties as "just another professional" on the job. Research has shown that token status in these positions is likely to limit how much women can bring change to these jobs (see Belknap and Shelley 1993). Additionally, the socialization in the training and on the job is so powerful that positive aspects women may bring to the job—such as empathy for rape victims—may be negated (see Spohn 1990). For example, some women may be interested in becoming police officers or judges or lawyers because they want to change things for battered women or rape victims. However, they may be heavily inundated with victim-blaming messages during their "education" or formal and informal training. Thus, we must ask, can women change the way crime-processing jobs are done, or do these jobs change the women who are hired? The latter is far more likely as long as women continue to be hired in token status.

Crime-processing administrators, therefore, need to actively recruit more women *and* determine methods of keeping existing women employees in the field and promoting them. Regardless of whether women will, in fact, bring positive changes to these jobs, hiring, firing, and promotional decisions should not be made simply on the basis of sex.

SUMMARY

Considerable research is presented in this book, describing the invisibility of and injustices experienced by female victims, offenders, and workers in society and the crime-processing system. Important advances in terms of legal reforms and employment practices and policies have been made since the 1970s. Nonetheless, female victims of male violence, female offenders, and women working as crime-processing professionals continue to face damaging stereotypes and discrimination.

The feminist movement has advanced legal reforms and changes in hiring practices; however, further legal and policy reform is still necessary. Moreover, the implementation of policies and laws to improve the recognition and treatment of women and girls as victims, offenders, and workers must be carefully examined and evaluated to ensure gender equality and justice.

REFERENCES

American Bar Association. 1992. *Legal Education and Professional Development and Education Continuum.* Chicago: Report of the Task Force on Law Schools and the Profession: Narrowing the Gender Gap.

American Correctional Association. 1990. *The Female Offender: What Does the Future Hold?* Arlington, VA: Kirby Lithographic Company.

Barry, Ellen M. 1991. "Jail Litigation Concerning Women Prisoners." *The Prison Journal* 71:44–50.

Bart, Pauline B., and Patricia H. O'Brien. 1985. *Stopping Rape: Successful Survival Strategies.* New York: Pergamon Press.

Baunach, Phyllis Jo. 1992. "Critical Problems of Women in Prison." Pp. 99–112 in *The Changing Roles of Women in the Criminal Justice System,* 2nd ed., edited by I. L. Moyers. Prospect Heights, IL: Waveland Press.

Belknap, Joanne, and Jill K. Shelley. 1993. "The New Lone Ranger: Policewomen on Patrol." *American Journal of Police* 12:47–75.

Belknap, Joanne, and K. Douglas McCall. 1994. "Woman Battering and Police Referrals." *Journal of Criminal Justice* 22:223–236.

Berger, Ronald J., Patricia Searles, and W. Lawrence Neuman. 1988. "The Dimensions of Rape Law Reform Legislation." *Law and Society Review* 22:329–357.

Bowman, Cynthia G. 1992. "The Arrest Experiments: A Feminist Critique." *Journal of Criminal Law and Criminology* 83:201–209.

Brodsky, Annette M. 1975. "Planning for the Female Offender: Directions for the Future." Pp. 100–108 in *The Female Offender,* edited by A. M. Brodsky. Beverly Hills, CA: Sage.

Browne, Angela. 1992. "Violence Against Women: Relevance for Medical Practitioners." *JAMA* 267:3184–3189.

Bush, Diane M. 1993. "Women's Movements and State Policy Reform Aimed at Domestic Violence Against Women." *Gender and Society* 6:587–608.

Cahn, Naomi R. 1992. "Innovative Approaches to the Prosecution of Domestic Crimes." Pp. 161–180 in *Domestic Violence: The Changing Criminal Justice Response,* edited by E. S. Buzawa and C. G. Buzawa. Westport, CT: Auburn House.

Caringella-MacDonald, Susan. 1988. "Marxist and Feminist Interpretations on the Aftermath of Rape Reforms." *Contemporary Crises* 12:125–144.

Chesney-Lind, Meda. 1991. "Patriarchy, Prisons, and Jails: A Critical Look at Trends in Women's Incarceration." *Prison Journal* 71:51–67.

Chesney-Lind, Meda., and Randall G. Shelden. 1992. *Girls, Delinquency and Juvenile Justice.* Pacific Grove, CA: Brooks/Cole.

Clark, Judy, and Kathy Boudin. 1990. "Community of Women Organize Themselves to Cope with the AIDS Crisis: A Case Study from Bedford Hills Correctional Facility." *Social Justice* 17:90–109.

Daly, Kathleen. 1992. "Women's Pathways to Felony Court: Feminist Theories of Lawbreaking and Problems of Representation." *Review of Law and Women's Studies* 2:11–52.

Daly, Kathleen, and Meda Chesney-Lind. 1988. "Feminism and Criminology." *Justice Quarterly* 5: 497–538.

Dutton, Donald G., Stephen D. Hart, Les W. Kennedy, and Kirk R. Williams. 1992. "Arrest and the Reduction of Repeat Wife Assault." Pp. 111–127 in *Domestic Violence: The Changing Criminal Justice Response,* edited by E. S. Buzawa and C. G. Buzawa. Westport, CT: Auburn House.

Eason, Yla. 1988. "When the Boss Wants Sex." Pp. 139–147 in *Racism and Sexism,* edited by P. S. Rothenberg. New York: St. Martin's Press.

Ewing, Charles P. 1987. *Battered Women Who Kill.* Lexington, MA: Lexington Books.

Feinman, Clarice. 1984. "An Historical Overview of the Treatment of Incarcerated Women: Myths and Realities of Rehabilitation." *The Prison Journal* 63:12–26.

Ferraro, Kathleen J. 1989. "Policing Woman Battering." *Social Problems* 36:61–74.

Ferraro, Kathleen J., and John M. Johnson. 1983. "How Women Experience Battering: The Process of Victimization." *Social Problems* 30:325–339.

Ferraro, Kathleen J., and Lucille Pope. 1993. "Irreconcilable Differences: Battered Women, Police, and the Law." Pp. 96–126 in *Legal Responses to Wife Assault,* edited by N. Zoe Hilton. Newbury Park, CA: Sage.

Fonow, Mary M., Laurel Richardson, and Virginia A. Wemmerus.1992. "Feminist Rape Education: Does It Work?" *Gender and Society* 6:108–122.

Ford, David A. 1991a. "Prosecution as a Victim Power Resource: A Note on Empowering Women in Violent Conjugal Relationships." *Law and Society Review* 25:313–334.

——————. 1991b. "Preventing and Provoking Wife Battery Through Criminal Sanctioning: A Look at the Risks." Pp. 191–209 in *Abused and Battered: Social and Legal Responses to Family Violence,* edited by D. D. Knudsen and J. L. Miller. New York: Aldine De Gruyter.

Ford, David A., and Mary Jean Regoli. 1992. "The Preventive Impacts of Policies for Prosecuting Wife Batterers." Pp. 181–207 in *Domestic Violence: The Changing Criminal Justice Response,* edited by E. S. Buzawa and C. G. Buzawa. Westport, CT: Auburn House.

Frisch, Lisa A. 1992. "Research That Succeeds, Policies That Fail." *Journal of Criminal Law and Criminology* 83:209–217.

Gamache, D. J., J. L. Edleson, and M. D. Schock. 1988. "Coordinated Police, Judicial, and Social Service Response to Woman Battering." In *Coping with Family Violence,* edited by G. T. Hotaling, D. Finkelhor, J. T. Kirkpatrick, and M. A. Straus. Beverly Hills, CA: Sage.

Glavin, Anne P. 1986. *Acquaintance Rape: The Silent Epidemic.* Massachusetts Institute of Technology: Campus Police Department.

Gondolf, Edward W., with Ellen R. Fisher. 1988. *Battered Women as Survivors.* New York: Lexington Books.

Haley, Kathleen. 1980. "Mothers Behind Bars." Pp. 339–354 in *Women, Crime and Justice,* edited by S. K. Datesman and F. R. Scarpitti. New York: Oxford Press.

Hardesty, Constance, Paula G. Hardwick, and Ruby J. Thompson. 1993. "Self-Esteem and the Woman Prisoner." Pp. 27–44 in *Women Prisoners: A Forgotten Population,* edited by B. R. Fletcher, L. D. Shaver, and D. G. Moon. Westport, CT: Praeger.

Hart, Barbara. 1993. "Battered Women and the Criminal Justice System." *American Behavioral Scientist* 36:624–638.

Horney, Julie, and Cassia Spohn. 1991. "Rape Law Reform and Instrumental Change in Six Urban Jurisdictions." *Law and Society Review* 25:117–153.

Immarigeon, Russ. 1987a. "Women in Prison." *Journal of the National Prison Project* 11:1–5.

_____. 1987b. "Few Diversion Programs Are Offered Female Offenders." *Journal of the National Prison Project* 12:9–11.

Immarigeon, Russ, and Meda Chesney-Lind. 1992. *Women's Prisons: Overcrowded and Overused.* San Francisco: National Council on Crime and Delinquency.

Jaffe, Peter, D. A. Wolfe, A. Telford, and G. Austin. 1986. "The Impact of Police Charges in Incidents of Wife Abuse." *Journal of Family Violence* 1:37–49.

Kendall, Kathleen. 1994. "Creating Real Choices: A Program Evaluation of Therapeutic Services at the Prison for Women." *Forum on Corrections Research* 6:19–21.

Kirkwood, Laurie J., and Marcelle E. Mihaila. 1979. "Incest and the Legal System." *University of California, Davis Law Review* 12:673–699.

Kleck, Gary, and Susan Sayles. 1990. "Rape and Resistance." *Social Problems* 37:149–162.

Klein, Dorie. 1981. "Violence Against Women: Some Considerations Regarding Its Causes and Elimination." *Crime and Delinquency* (January):64–80.

Knight. Barbara B. 1992. "Women in Prison as Litigants: Prospects for Post Prison Futures." *Women and Criminal Justice* 4:91–116.

Koss, Mary P., and Mary R. Harvey. 1991. *The Rape Victim: Clinical and Community Interventions,* 2nd ed. Newbury Park, CA: Sage.

Kurz, Demie. 1992. "Battering and the Criminal Justice System: A Feminist View." Pp. 21–40 in *Domestic Violence: The Changing Criminal Justice Response,* edited by E. S. Buzawa and C. G. Buzawa. Westport, CT: Auburn House.

Lerman, Lisa G. 1992. "The Decontextualization of Domestic Violence." *Journal of Criminal Law and Criminology* 83:217–240.

Martin, Susan E. 1989. "Women on the Move? A Report on the Status of Women in Policing." *Police Foundation Reports* (May):1–7.

McCann, Kathryn. 1985. "Battered Women and the Law: The Limits of the Legislation." Pp. 71–96 in *Women-in-Law: Explorations in Law, Family and Sexuality,* edited by J. Brophy and C. Smart. London: Routledge & Kegan Paul.

McCarthy, Belinda R. 1980. "Inmate Mothers: The Problems of Separation and Reintegration." *Journal of Offender Counseling, Services and Rehabilitation* 4:199–212.

McGowan, Brenda G., and Karen L. Blumenthal. 1981. "Imprisoned Women and Their Children." Pp. 392–408 in *Women and Crime in America,* edited by L. H. Bowker. New York: Macmillan.

McHugh, Gerald A. 1980. "Protection of the Rights of Pregnant Women in Prisons and Detention Facilities." *New England Journal on Prison and Law* 6:231–263.

Messerschmidt, James W. 1993. *Masculinities and Crime: Critique and Reconceptualization of Theory.* Lanham, MD: Rowman & Littlefield.

Miller, Eleanor M. 1986. *Street Woman.* Philadelphia, PA: Temple University Press.

Morris, Allison, and Loraine Gelsthorpe. 1991. "Feminist Perspectives in Criminology: Transforming and Transgressing." *Women and Criminal Justice* 2:3–26.

National Victim Center. 1992, April 23. *Rape in America: A Report to the Nation.* Arlington, VA.

Parrot, Andrea. 1986. *Acquaintance Rape and Sexual Assault Prevention Training Manual.* Department of Human Services Studies. Ithica, New York: Cornell University.

Pearson, Jennifer M. 1993. "Centro Feminil: A Women's Prison in Mexico." *Social Justice* 20:85–128.

Pence, Ellen, and Melanie Shepard. 1988. "Integrating Feminist Theory and Practice: The Challenge of the Battered Women's Movement." Pp. 282–298 in *Feminist Perspectives on Wife Abuse,* edited by K. Yllo and M. Bograd. Newbury Park, CA: Sage.

Pendergrass, Virginia E. 1975. "Innovative Programs for Women in Jail and Prison: Trick or Treatment." Pp. 67–76 in *The Female Offender,* edited by A. M. Brodsky. Beverly Hills, CA: Sage.

Pollack, Shoshana. 1994. "Opening the Window in a Very Dark Day: A Program Evaluation of the Peer Support Team at the Kingston Prison for Women." *Forum on Corrections Research* 6:7–10.

Proto, Laura, Joanne Belknap, and John Wooldredge. 1994. "The Effectiveness of Rape Awareness Programs in High Schools." A paper presented at the 1994 annual meeting of the American Society of Criminology, Miami, FL.

Rafter, Nicole H. 1985. *Partial Justice: Women in State Prisons, 1800–1935.* Boston: Northeastern University Press.

Rafter, Nicole H., and Elena M. Natalizia. 1981. "Marxist Feminism: Implications for Criminal Justice." *Crime and Delinquency* 27:81–98.

Ross, Robert R., and Elizabeth A. Fabiano. 1986. *Female Offenders: Correctional Afterthoughts.* Jefferson, NC: McFarland.

Russell, Diana E. H. 1984. *Sexual Exploitation: Rape, Child Sexual Abuse, and Workplace Harassment.* Beverly Hills, CA: Sage.

Sanday, Peggy R. 1981. "The Socio-Cultural Context of Rape: A Cross-Cultural Study." *Journal of Social Issues* 37:5–27.

Sarri, Rosemary C. 1987. "Unequal Protection Under the Law: Women and the Criminal Justice System." Pp. 427–453 in *The Trapped Woman: Catch-22 in Deviance and Control.* Newbury Park, CA: Sage.

Schupak, Terri L. 1986. "Comment: Women and Children First: An Examination of the Unique Needs of Women in Prison." *Golden Gate University Law Review* 16:455–474.

Schur, Edwin M. 1984. *Labeling Women Deviant: Gender, Stigma, and Social Control.* New York: McGraw-Hill.

Schwendinger, Julia R., and Herman Schwendinger. 1983. *Rape and Inequality.* Beverly Hills, CA: Sage.

Sherman, Lawrence W. 1992. *Policing Domestic Violence: Experiments and Dilemma.* New York: Free Press.

Smart, Carol. 1989. *Feminism and the Power of Law.* London: Routledge & Kegan Paul.

Spohn, Cassia. 1990. "Decision Making in Sexual Assault Cases: Do Black and Female Judges Make a Difference?" *Women and Criminal Justice* 2: 83–106.

Spohn, Cassia, and Julie Horney. 1991. "The Law's the Law, But Fair Is Fair: Rape Shield Laws and Officials' Assessment of Sexual History Evidence." *Criminology* 29:137–161.

—————. 1992. *Rape Law Reform: A Grassroots Revolution and Its Impact.* New York: Plenum Press.

—————. 1993. "Rape Law Reform and the Effect of Victim Characteristics on Case Processing." *Journal of Quantitative Criminology* 9:383–409.

Stanko, Elizabeth A. 1989. "Missing the Mark? Policing Battering." Pp. 46–69 in *Women, Policing, and Male Violence: International Perspectives,* edited by J. Hanmer, J. Radford, and E. A. Stanko. London: Routledge & Kegan Paul.

Stanton, Ann M. 1980. *When Mothers Go to Jail.* Lexington, MA: Lexington Books.

Stark, Evan. 1992. "Framing and Reframing Battered Women." Pp. 271–292 in *Domestic Violence: The Changing Criminal Justice Response,* edited by E. S. Buzawa and C. G. Buzawa. Westport, CT: Auburn House.

_____. 1993. "Mandatory Arrest of Batterers: A Reply to Its Critics." *American Behavioral Scientist* 36:651–680.

Steffensmeier, Darrell. 1993. "National Trends in Female Arrests, 1960–1990." *Journal of Quantitative Criminology* 9:411–441.

Sullivan, Mary, and Deborah I. Bybee. 1987. "Female Students and Sexual Harassment: What Factors Predict Reporting Behavior?" *Journal of the National Association for Women Deans, Administrators and Counselors* 50:11–16.

Tierney, Kathleen J. 1982. "The Battered Women Movement and the Creation of the Wife Beating Problem." *Social Problems* 29:207–220

Ullman, Sarah E., and Raymond A. Knight. 1992. "Fighting Back: Women's Resistance to Rape." *Journal of Interpersonal Violence* 7:31–43.

Van Voorhis, Patricia, Joanne Belknap, Karen Welch, and Amy Stichman. 1993. "Gender Bias in Courts: The Findings and Recommendations of the Task Forces." A paper presented at the 1993 annual meeting of the American Society of Criminology, Phoenix, AZ.

Von Cleve, Elizabeth, and Joseph G. Weis. 1993. "Sentencing Alternatives for Female Offenders." Pp. 94–100 in *Female Offenders: Meeting Needs of a Neglected Population,* edited by the American Correctional Association, Laurel, MD.

Walker, Lenore E. 1989. *Terrifying Love: Why Battered Women Kill and How Society Responds.* New York: Harper Perennial.

Weitzman, Lenore J. 1985. *The Divorce Revolution: The Unexpected Social and Economic Consequences for Women and Children in America.* New York: Free Press.

Whitcomb, Debra. 1991. "Improving the Investigation and Prosecution of Child Sexual-Abuse Cases." Pp. 181–190 in *Abused and Battered: Social and Legal Responses to Family Violence,* edited by D. D. Knudsen and J. L. Miller. New York: Aldine de Gruyter.

Wikler, Norma J. 1987. "Educating Judges About Gender Bias in the Courts." Pp. 227–246 in *Women, the Courts, and Equality,* edited by L. L. Crites and W. L. Hepperle. Newbury Park, CA: Sage.

Wishik, Heather R. 1985. "To Question Everything: The Inquiries of Feminist Jurisprudence." *Berkeley Women's Law Journal* 1:64–77.

Wooldredge, John D., and Kimberly Masters. 1993. "Confronting Problems Faced by Pregnant Inmates in State Prisons." *Crime and Delinquency* 39:195–203.

Subject Index

Author Index